The
Inequality
Crisis

Edited by
Edward Fullbrook & Jamie Morgan

World Economics Association Books

World Economics Association BOOK SERIES

The Inequality Crisis

Edited by Edward Fullbrook and Jamie Morgan

Previously published as issue 92 of *Real-World Economics Review* in June 2020.

ISBN: 978-1-911156-57-4 (paperback)
         978-1-911156-58-1 (eBook, Kindle)

Cover image: picjumbo.com

Published by World Economics Association, Bristol, UK
www.worldeconomicsassociation.org

The **World Economics Association (WEA)** was launched on May 16, 2011. Already over 13,000 economists and related scholars have joined. This phenomenal success has come about because the WEA fills a huge gap in the international community of economists – the absence of a professional organization which is truly international and pluralist.

The World Economics Association seeks to increase the relevance, breadth and depth of economic thought. Its key qualities are worldwide membership and governance, and inclusiveness with respect to: (a) the variety of theoretical perspectives; (b) the range of human activities and issues which fall within the broad domain of economics; and (c) the study of the world's diverse economies.

The Association's activities centre on the development, promotion and diffusion of economic research and knowledge and on illuminating their social character.

The WEA publishes books, three open-access journals (*Economic Thought, World Social and Economic Review* and *Real-World Economics Review*), a bi-monthly newsletter, blogs, holds global online conferences, runs a textbook commentaries project and an eBook library.

Contents

Chapter 1

The three options: an introduction

Edward Fullbrook

The everyday operations of our economies produce the goods and services that keep us alive and enable us to enjoy life. But that is not the only way that those operations effect our lives; they also effect societies and ecosystems. The Inequality Crisis, which threatens our societies, and the Climate Crisis, which threatens both our societies and our species, are also, no less than **production**, brought about directly by the everyday operations of our economies.[1]

But for two hundred years the economics profession has in the main excluded from its study of economies two of their three categories of primary effects. And given the profession's influence, this exclusion of **societal** and **ecological** effects has promoted the intellectual invisibility of these two categories, thereby helping to bring about the two crises.

---

[1] Edward Fullbrook and Jamie Morgan (editors) (2019) *Economics and the Ecosystem*. World Economics Association BOOKS.

Compared to the Climate Crisis, which, although only recently acknowledged, has been in the making for over a century and a half, the Inequality Crisis is young. The massive redistribution of income and wealth which brought it about began in the 1970s, but until 2014 that redistribution was, except in the *Real World Economics Review* and other journals outside the neoclassical mainstream, almost never mentioned. Although there is still a long way to go, Thomas Piketty's *Capital in the Twenty-First Century* changed that.[2] Many kinds of intellectuals took notice, and literally within months of the book's publication it became socially acceptable, even among economists, to talk about growing inequality – the by then already long-term upward redistribution of income and wealth.

Meanwhile, the effects of that redistribution have become increasingly manifest, so much so that even in time of pandemic they make the daily news. In democracies it seems to be that the more extreme the upward redistribution becomes, the more politically aggressive the ultrarich become. And when they capture political parties and then, as in the United States, rule and reshape their countries' institutions, a moral vacuum emerges wherein victims of the redistribution look for vulnerable groups to scapegoat, and a populism of the pre-fascist variety takes hold.[3]

---

[2] Edward Fullbrook and Jamie Morgan (editors) (2014) *Piketty's Capital in the Twenty-First Century.* World Economics Association BOOKS.
[3] Edward Fullbrook and Jamie Morgan (editors) (2017) *Trumponomics: Causes and Consequence.* World Economics Association BOOKS.

But income and wealth distributions, unlike gravitational forces, result not from the natural order but from human decisions. And the general direction of those decisions now needs to become part of open public discussion. Regarding the distribution of income and wealth, human society now has three basic options:

1. Continue with the upward redistribution,
2. Maintain the current distribution,
3. Reverse the redistribution of recent decades.

If you favour Option 1, you may not want to read *The Inequality Crisis* and you for sure will want to discourage others from reading it. Why? Because all its papers offer insights into how Options 2 and 3 could be realized, and all are ultimately committed to empiricism rather than to axiomatics.

It is hoped that this collection will be only part of the beginning of a new focus in economics. On the topic of economic inequality, many papers and books that are both truth-seeking and sincerely in the spirit of goodwill towards humanity are now urgently needed.

Chapter 2

Rethinking the world economy as a two bloc hierarchy

Robert H. Wade[1]

"Even if economists did not use terms like purchasing power, bargaining power, and monopoly power, it ought to be obvious that the market or price system is a *power system*" (Charles Lindblom, 1966, emphasis added).

I begin with a letter to the *Financial Times*, 2–3 May 2020. The writer, a professor of psychiatry, says:

"The early spread of Covid-19 outside China clearly tracked flight paths, chiefly to rich countries. Despite the substantial problems that the virus presents in these settings, rich countries are still better placed to contain it: better sanitation, better nutrition, better healthcare.

---

[1] Robert H. Wade is professor of global political economy at the London School of Economics. He was awarded the Leontief Prize in Economics, 2008, and his *Governing the Market*, was awarded Best Book or Article in Political Economy by the American Political Science Association.

> "The picture will be very different in poor countries where most people who die of the virus will, in truth, die of a combination of poverty and Covid-19" (Kelly, 2020).

The writer uses our everyday distinction between "rich" countries and "poor" countries, treating them as roughly homogeneous groupings in terms of characteristics relevant to disease. "Rich and poor" maps to everyday language of developed and less developed countries, core and periphery, and North and South.

What is strange is that our main sources of data about the world economy hardly use this breakdown into two big polarized groupings.

1. Statistical and theoretical occlusion of the north-south dualism

In 2010 the president of the World Bank, Robert Zoellick, declared the distinction between developed and developing countries to be obsolete.

> "If 1989 saw the end of the 'Second World' with Communism's demise, then 2009 saw the end of what was known as the 'Third World'. We are now in a new, fast-evolving multipolar world economy – in which some developing countries are emerging as economic powers; others are moving towards becoming additional poles of growth; and some are struggling to attain

their potential within this new system" (Zoellick, 2010).

The World Bank often uses a four-fold classification by average income: high income countries; upper middle income countries; lower middle income countries; and low income countries – with fairly arbitrary US dollar thresholds. It also uses categories like "Poor and Indebted", and "Poor, Struggling, Converging, and Affluent". And various geographical categories like "Middle East and North Africa".

The IMF identifies "Advanced Countries" (a category which includes the ones commonly understood to be developed / the North / the core); and for the rest, categories that blend geographical and development criteria, such as "Emerging Developing Europe" and "Middle East, North Africa, Pakistan, Afghanistan".

What we don't find from these organizations is data which illuminates the internal coherence of North and South and the size and trend in gaps between them. That inattention in turn sustains the core mainstream understanding that less developed countries are in that category because of *their delay in adopting fully capitalist institutions and policies* – Walt Rostow's *The Stages of Economic Growth* (1959) being a famous early example.

The ur-image is development as a marathon race: all runners could conceivably cross the finish line at the same time, and their finishing order reflects differences in conditions internal to each runner; *there is no structure to the race such that some run faster on account of the fact that some run slower.*

Globalization theory, which became "hegemonic" in the 1980s, turbo-charged this understanding, with its implication that less developed countries can (eventually) catch up, each on their own, by adopting fully capitalist institutions and policies in the image of the developed countries. Globalization theory is a sub-set of neoliberal theory, which advances an agenda of low taxes, low public spending, and capital and labour free to be bought and sold in global markets, because this freedom will maximize material prosperity and liberty for all.

Three quotes bring out the core idea. First, a New York Times journalist covering the 2002 World Economic Forum meeting summarized the prevailing wisdom among the Davos elite: "A nation that opens its economy and keeps government's role to a minimum invariably experiences more rapid economic growth and rising incomes" (Uchitelle, 2002).

Second, Martin Wolf, distinguished columnist for the *Financial Times* and author of *Why Globalization Works*, declared:

> "It cannot make sense to fragment the world economy more than it already is but rather to make the world economy work as if it were the United States, or at least the European Union.... The failure of our world is not that there is too much globalization, but that there is too little. The potential for

greater economic integration is barely tapped" (Wolf, 2004: 4).

Third, John Williamson, who coined the phrase and gave the content of the Washington Consensus, asserted: "in the long run, countries' progress is primarily dependent on their own efforts rather than on the [passive] international environment" (Williamson, 2004: 197).

The northern states – and the international organisations they largely control – give financial aid and technical assistance to developing countries in order, they say, to reduce the delay in the latter adopting fully capitalist regimes, with conditionalities in line with the Washington Consensus about "best practice" institutions and policies. For example, the World Bank has long deployed the Country Policy and Institutional Assessment (CPIA) formula to score countries by the "goodness-for-development" of their policies and institutions, and then factors the score into its lending decisions and country dialogues. The scoring criteria for the trade regime imply that a completely free trade regime is best for development. The criteria for labour markets give the highest score to countries with maximum employer flexibility and minimum worker security (Wade, 2010).

And in fact, "globalization" has vastly increased over the past several decades. World trade rose from 39 per cent of world GDP in 1990 to 58 per cent in 2018. International assets and liabilities rocketed from 128 per cent to 401 per cent of GDP. On both measures the world is far more integrated than it was in 1914, the last peak of globalization (*Economist*, 2019). *Yet the promised catching-*

up of the South has barely occurred, except for a short period from around 2002 to 2012, when fast growth in the South was driven mainly by surging Chinese demand for commodities. (For purposes of the statistical comparison of the two blocs, the South excludes China and the transitional economies.)

The Swahili proverb says, "Until the lions have their own historians the history of hunting will always glorify the hunters". The mainstream's explanation for the slowness of catching-up – due to slowness of southern governments and businesses to adopt the institutions and policies of advanced capitalism – illustrates history being written, rules set, by the winners. It is in line with what could be called a "law" of modern-era power hierarchies: elites legitimize their success in terms of universalistic and meritocratic qualities, like initiative, hard work, commitment to the scientific method, and legitimize others' lower rank in terms of their failure to match these qualities, their excessive dedication to identity politics, corruption, leisure (and white populations have long used the non-universalistic criterion of skin colour to claim superiority). In Max Weber's words from 1915:

> "The fortunate man is seldom satisfied with the fact of being fortunate... He needs to know that he has a right to his good fortune. He wants to be convinced that he 'deserves' it... in comparison with others... [G]ood *fortune thus wants to be legitimate fortune"* (emphasis added).

In short, the mainstream view of development does not see the world economy in terms of two encompassing and hierarchically-ordered blocs, with internal coherence and with mechanisms (instrumental and structural) linking them which tend to sustain the hierarchy. And not just the mainstream; many analysts who consider themselves broadly on the left and sympathetic to the idea of "combined and uneven development", originally coined by Trotsky, also consider that the developed/less developed distinction too broad to be meaningful.

This essay aims to bring out the internal coherence of the two blocs and the mechanisms that tend to perpetuate the hierarchy. It suggests that seeing the world order in this way helps us to understand many contemporary trends as - in part - effects of the two bloc structure: such as the persistence of high levels of national (vertical) inequality, immigration from South to North, rise of illiberal democracies in North and South, northern countries' wars in the South, and more. The shift in perspective is akin - if a slight exaggeration be permitted - to the jump Copernicus made in formulating a model that placed Sun rather than Earth at the center of the universe.

2. Indicators of the North-South duality

Here are several indicators of the North-South duality.

2.1 How much catch-up?

First, an impressionistic measure of the Great Divergence : the number of non-western countries that have become "developed" in the past two centuries. The number depends on how broadly we categorize "non-western", "countries", and "developed". *Even stretching them out (to include Russia as non-western, Hong Kong as a country), we get maybe seven:* Japan, Russia, Hong Kong, Taiwan, South Korea, Singapore and Israel. This "fact" should be but is not front and center to the whole discipline of "development studies".

Notice that most of the countries had small populations during their fast-industrialization phase, and also one or more powerful external enemies threatening the state's existence. The common threat produced a "fellowship of the lifeboat", without which state incumbents might have taken a more cavalier approach to defrauding the state and used their power to suppress opponents ("enemies") rather than promote a national development project able to create a unified- enough polity to dissuade an external enemy. And Japan, Taiwan, South Korea and Israel – four of the seven – received very large amounts of American financial, technical and military aid in the post-war decades to keep them firmly within the US geopolitical orbit; while Hong Kong was an outpost of British rule and British business until 1997 (Wade, 2019).

Another pointer to low upward mobility comes from a World Bank study (2013), which finds that *in 1960 there were 101 "middle-income" countries, using the Bank's absolute income thresholds in US dollars. Only 13 had risen to "high-income" by 2008, four on the periphery of western Europe, five in East Asia.* Most of them have populations less than 20 million; they account for an insignificant fraction of the world's population.[2]

2.2 The North-South income gap across time

The size of the income gap across time can be measured by the ratio of the North's average GDP to the South's GDP. GDP is measured at market exchange rates, not at purchasing power parity exchange rates, because the former gives a more accurate measure of the ability of residents of a country to buy goods and services in other countries, and hence is a better measure of *relative structural power* in the inter-state system (Wade, 2017, Box 12.1). Alan Freeman (2020) defines the ratio of the North's GDP per capita in market exchange rates to that of the South as the Monetary Inequality Index (MII). [3]

The MII has risen substantially from 1950 till today, meaning that the North-South gap has widened substantially. *From 1954 to 2000 it rose three times, from 7 to 21, and especially fast during the 1980s (coinciding with the full-force application in the South of the Washington Consensus liberalisation recipe). Then it fell from 21 to around 11 in 2012, when it flatted out and started to rise again.* This fall in MII – or "catch up" for the South in ability to purchase goods and services from the North – was the effect of the commodity price boom for commodity

---

[2] Cherif and Hasanov (2019) take 182 countries and classify them by the percentage of their average income relative to that of the US in 2005, and cut the distribution at 50% of US average income to give the threshold of "high income". They find that between 1970 and 2014 only 13 out of 148 low and middle income countries reached the high income threshold; of which 6 peripheral Europe, 3 tiny oil exporters, and 4 East Asian. (They use PPP 2011, Penn World Tables 9.0).

[3] My account of the income gaps draws heavily on Freeman 2020.

exporters largely to China, which raised southern "price times output" growth rates well above those in the North, but locked the South more firmly into commodity specialization.

Another gap measure is the density distribution of global employment by value-added per worker or per hour. This too shows a pronounced two hump structure. The high labour productivity hump covers the North, with about 15% of world employment, the low labour productivity hump covers the South, with around 60-70 of world employment (here including China) (Gomulka 2006).

Another measure of the North-South gap: *the average income of the wealthiest quartile of the population of the South ($8,700 in 2015) was only about a quarter of that of the poorest quartile of the North ($30,400).*

2.3 Internal income coherence

The two blocs are relatively coherent in terms of their internal income distribution, in the sense that within the blocs, inter-country income inequality is much less than between the blocs. Countries of the North have converged together in GDPPC over 1970-2015, and not converged with the South.

Drawing again on Alan Freeman (2020), we can divide the South into six geographical regions: "East Asia of the South" (excluding Northeast Asia and Singapore), Pacific, South Asia, Middle East and North Africa, Sub-Saharan Africa, and Latin America and Caribbean.

Over almost half a century, *from 1970 to 2016, the average incomes of these southern regions remain within 50% and 250% of the average of the South, with no region "breaking free" towards the North and no trend towards divergence within the South.* The average income rank order in 2016 was: Latin America and Caribbean, Middle East and North Africa, East Asia of the South, Pacific, and Sub-saharan Africa equal with South Asia. Over the half century from 1970, East Asia of the South rose in the rank order, and Sub-saharan Africa fell. The others kept the same rank order in 2016 as in 1970. A remarkable continuity. The gap between the six regions is smaller than the gap between them and the North.

2.4 Income inequality between North and South in relation to global income inequality

Income inequality between North and South (average income of both at market exchange rates) accounts for most of the inequality between all countries. And income inequality between countries accounts for more of global income inequality (between all people regardless of country) than income inequality within countries. Inter-bloc inequality (now four blocs: North, South, China, transitional economies) contributes between 4 and 7 times more to global inequality than intra-bloc inequality, over the whole period from 1970 to 2015 (Freeman 2020).

2.5 Conclusion

The bottom line is that North and South are coherent blocs in important ways. The income gap between the North-South blocs is – persistently – larger than the income gaps within them. If we plot the share of world population living in countries arranged by average income we see a pronounced bimodal distribution, with not much population in between.

Countries of the North enjoy common economic benefits from their superior position in the world hierarchy, making for common interests in protecting their position from challengers. They translate common interests into political treaties, such as free trade agreements (e.g. NAFTA), political federations (eg European Union), and security agreements (eg NATO); and into common agreements linking groups of northern countries with regions of the South (e.g. Lome Convention, a trade and aid agreement between the European Economic Commission and 71 African, Caribbean and Pacific countries, signed in 1975). The seven leading economies of the North have concerted their actions through the G7 summits, claiming to be the top table of governance for the world (though not replacing the UN Security Council on security issues); and supported by tiers of other G7 coordination forums.

Countries of the South have broadly similar income levels and are subject to broadly similar pressures from the world economy. But they are much less organized in collective action organizations than countries of the North – whether regional or cross-regional (e.g. G77, and G24 which coordinates developing countries in the World Bank and IMF, with a tiny budget). For example, the Chiang Mai Initiative was created after the Asian financial crisis of 1997-99 to organize currency swaps within Northeast and Southeast Asia, so as to reduce the reliance on emergency financing from the western-dominated IMF. But it has barely functioned, owing partly to deep suspicion between the two countries with the biggest foreign exchange reserves, China and Japan (Wade 2013).

We can see the North–South difference in the contrast between G7 and G20. *The G7 includes only the major northern economies, which share high rank in GDP and in GDP per capita, with a correlation coefficient of around 0.7 –* suggesting strong common interests and relatively high ability to concert their actions. The G20 (formed at finance minister level after the Asian financial crash of 1997-99 and at summit level after the North Atlantic financial crash of 2008-09) includes 11 developing countries, and *the corresponding correlation coefficient is around 0.3 –* suggesting much less common interest among the member states (Vestergaard and Wade, 2012a; 2012b).

3. Effects of the North–South dualism

The North–South dualism is the starting point for understanding key trends:

1) high and/or rising inequality *in the North*, as cheap labour in the South puts downward pressure on wages in the North;
2) high and/or rising inequality *in the South*, as southern elites aim for northern elite consumption levels. (Milanovic [2019] reports that the average income of the bottom five percent of Chile equals the bottom five percent of Mongolia, one of the poorest countries in the world; the average income of the top two percent

in Chile equals the average of the top two percent in Germany);

3) migration waves from South to North, which roil the politics of the North;

4) shift towards "illiberal democracy", "identitarian politics" in the North as right-wing political leaders build support on the back of voters' "left-behind" grievances by blaming migrants, Jews, Muslims or still Others for shortages of housing, health care and employment;

5) reinforcement of authoritarian rule and repression in the South as elites defend against social unrest fuelled by relative deprivation, amped up by social media images;

6) the main states of the North act semi-concertedly to prevent or selectively channel the rise of countries of the South, which might challenge the market and technological dominance of northern corporations and challenge the ability of northern states to set global agendas. The North-South income hierarchy looks pleasing and "natural" to the North, as Max Weber would expect. Some of the techniques used to split the South and hinder upward income mobility of most of its members include: war (think Iraq, 2003); economic sanctions; anti-communist rhetoric to camouflage actions to block economic/technological challenges from the South; and the economic liberalization plus poverty focus of the Washington Consensus.

4. Mechanisms of structural power of North over South

The techniques just mentioned are techniques of "instrumental" power used by northern states to restrain the rise of the South. I now turn to the mechanisms of "structural" power by which the hierarchy came into existence and is sustained. Structural power is the kind of power that business gets over states when it can exit from a jurisdiction whose government intends to do something business does not want, something that curbs its profits; or when the government actually does it and then faces a capital exit, with a hit to employment, incomes, and tax revenue, inducing the government to back off. Structural power is also the power the IMF has over heavily indebted countries (what we in the North commonly call "the Asian crisis" of 1997-99 is commonly called "the IMF crisis" in South Korea). China gets structural power over many countries which depend heavily on export revenues from China, including Australia and New Zealand. The Chinese government doesn't need to warn them belligerently not to criticise China's revanchism in the South China Sea or repression in Xinjiang, and not to hinder its influence campaigns in Australian and New Zealand politics (Brady 2017). As of the past few years, however, the Australian government has pushed back, leading to frequent flare-ups.

4.1 Origin

Let us start with the origin of the modern core-periphery or North-South system. From before the Industrial (Energy) Revolution the northern countries have typically tried to prevent developing countries from entering or remaining in dynamic sectors or segments of value chains with *increasing* returns to scale, limiting them to sectors with diminishing returns to scale; they recognized, as neoclassical economists did not, that *economic development is activity-specific.* Building the skill- and linkage-intensive activities within the national territory is what being a structurally dominant country is all about.

During colonial times, actors in the European colonial project – governments, militaries, companies – created dependent colonial and slave economies to which they outsourced land-intensive production. This structure delivered an "agricultural windfall", which allowed labour at home to be used for industrialization and provided an export market for manufactures. The British government or its agents ensured that British colonies or dependencies – by the early twentieth century accounting for an area 125 times the area of Britain, about one quarter of the Earth's habited area and almost a quarter of its population, the biggest empire in world history by far – specialized in commodity production for export to the core. For example, soon after the English government conquered Ireland by 1691 it closed down the prosperous Irish woollen industry; and the British East India Company closed down production of cotton textiles in its (effective) colony of Bengal in the early nineteenth century, so that Bengali farmers exported raw cotton to the textile mills of Manchester. Textiles was the technologically leading sector of the day – relatively capital intensive, with economies of scale, learning economies, linkages to other sectors, and demand for organizational innovations (e.g. factories).

No nation of size became developed without a coercive system of this kind and/or a prolonged Listian phase of infant industry protection (after Friedrich List, *The*

National System of Political Economy, 1841). And once a nation was at or near the frontier of development, it switched to articulating a simplified version of Adam Smith and "free trade for all" (Reinert 1994). The English economist-financier-politician David Ricardo (1772–1823) developed the theory of comparative advantage and the derived policy of free trade to legitimize such a switch for all. In his famous example, if England specializes in textiles and Portugal in wine and they trade their surpluses, they can each consume more of both than if they both produce textiles and wine. He forgot to mention that this gave England the sector with skill requirements and growth potential and Portugal the one with stagnation, and that English families owned a good part of Portugal's wine exporting business.

Generations of mainstream economists have subscribed to the theory of comparative advantage and the policy of free trade on grounds not much more sophisticated than this; and especially after the neoliberal turn in the 1980s, have urged developing countries to practice free trade with memes like "Why throw rocks in your own harbour?" Recall the Swahili proverb, and Max Weber on the drive to make good fortune legitimate fortune.

The globalization literature tends to slight the point that the dramatically increased market integration in the past several decades has occurred in the context of a hierarchically structured world economy, in which northern countries have more activity in increasing return, high profit, high wage activities, and able to set the rules to give themselves competitive advantages and generous rewards of profits and rents (Wade, 2003a; 2003b).

Starting from the structure of the 19th century world economy, path dependence and cumulative causation along well-institutionalized power relations have produced "combined and uneven" development between the two blocs over the past several decades, through mechanisms including the following:

First, the tendency for supply to exceed demand in the core (a point emphasized by the classical economists and later by John Maynard Keynes), making the North dependent on the South as a source of demand for its industrial, service and agricultural exports.

Second, the North's dependence on imports of natural resources and cheap-labour manufactured goods from the periphery.

Third, the core's dependence on people of varying skill levels coming to work there.

Fourth, the tendency for the periphery to run trade and current account deficits, financed by credit from the core (and by aid, foreign investment, and US spending on military bases, around 700 in 130 countries in 2003, according to Defence Department reports: Johnson 2004). The deficits reflect the high-income elasticity of demand for industrial and service imports in the periphery and typically lower income elasticity of demand for commodities in the core. The periphery's foreign debt – which must be repaid in reserve currencies, generally US dollars (Africa's foreign debt is 70 per cent denominated in US dollars) – easily rises above its capacity to repay, resulting in debt traps, followed by emergency loans from core-controlled international organizations and core banks freighted with tough neo-liberal – privatizing and market-opening – conditionalities.

Fifth, the tendency to deficits and debt traps is part of a larger tendency to *highly volatile growth in the periphery*, resulting from (a) dependence on commodity exports, (b) dependence on tourism and remittances, and (c) easy entry and exit of capital from the North. *Dependence on commodity exports has been higher since the 1990s than before, because of "premature de-industrialization". Commodity prices and capital inflows to the South are strongly correlated, yielding twin booms and twin busts; and stronger in recent decades because large financial firms have come to dominate commodity markets* (Akuz 2020).

Aiyer at al. (2013) find that *middle-income countries tend to experience more volatile growth than either low- or high-income countries*, with periods of super-fast growth (GDP growth at 6 per cent a year or more) followed by protracted slowdowns. Indeed, using evidence going back several centuries, two economic historians find that: "improved long run economic performance has occurred primarily through a decline in the rate and frequency of shrinking, rather than through an increase in the rate of growing" (Broadberry and Wallis, 2016).

More recently yet another polarizing mechanism has come into play: peripheral states protect themselves from shocks coming from core economies by building up foreign exchange reserves, mainly in low-return assets such as US Treasury bills, while opening the economy to higher-return foreign investment by core country firms, resulting in a large resource transfer from periphery to core (see below).

Through these several mechanisms the core–periphery structure tends to reproduce itself. Of course, this is a highly simplified picture, which omits major real-world complexities – including rivalries within the core, the position of the US as large-scale international debtor, and China as a major source of demand for the South and a challenger to existing great-powers, including through "infrastructure alliances" in place of military ones, like the Belt and Road Initiative. China is now a bigger creditor to developing countries than the IMF and the World Bank.

In what follows I elaborate briefly on some of these structural mechanisms, starting with the most fundamental of all, not so far mentioned.

4.2 The free market in choice of legal systems enables capital owners to be footloose, pocket profits anywhere, and escape social costs

The state needs capital, and capital needs the state. The state needs capital to generate wealth within its territory and enough prosperity for the population to sustain the state and its provision of public goods. Capital needs the state to enforce the legal contracts which enable the holders of capital to create wealth and enjoy exclusive returns on it. (Capital includes land, machinery, and –

especially important today – intangibles that exist only in legal code, like corporate shares and bonds.) Capital can exercise rule behind the state, not through force but through ensuring that the state vindicates the claims of capital holders in law, including claims for protection against the state and claims for state protection against other interests. The latter include protection of shareholders' claims to future profits against workers' expectations to future income, for example (Pistor 2019). This mechanism is a powerful driver of trickle-up in North and South, and from South to North, thanks to the way the law enables capital to privilege its interests ahead of the state's achievement of other social goals.

Note the contrast with the eighteenth century mechanism identified by Adam Smith and his "invisible hand", by which capitalists' pursuit of self-interest invisibly generates social betterment. It depended less on the state and more on local knowledge.

> "Every individual endeavours to employ his capital as near home as he can, and consequently as much as he can in support of domestic industry .... [Why? Because] *he can know better the character and situation of the persons whom he trusts, and if he should happen to be deceived, he knows better the laws of the country from which he must seek redress*" (Smith, 1776, book IV, chapter 2, p.475, quoted in Pistor, 2019, p.7, emphasis to "deceived" added, remainder added by Pistor).

Globalization, including of law, has fundamentally changed Smith's equation. Capital owners can now choose among many legal systems where they incorporate their assets, to find the one that offers them the best benefits in terms of taxes, regulation, shareholder benefits, profit repatriation, entry and exit – without having to move themselves or their business there. They are analytically like "roving bandits" looking for legal backup from suitable states. States which intervene to help the less advantaged in their populations can easily be punished by capital exit.

Katharina Pistor explains the consequences of states competing to attract capital.

> "States have actively torn down legal barriers to entry and offered their laws to willing takers and have thereby made it easier for asset holders to pick and choose the law of their liking. Most states recognize foreign law not only for contracts but also for (financial) collateral, corporations, and the assets they issue; they use their coercive powers to enforce it, and they allow domestic parties to opt into foreign law without losing the protections of local courts. The phenomenal expansion of trade, commerce, and finance globally would have been impossible without legal rules that enable asset holders to carry their local rules with them, or, if they prefer, to opt into foreign law.... *For the global capitalists, this is the best of all worlds, because they get to pick and*

> *choose the laws that are most favourable to them without having to invest heavily in politics to bend the law their way*" (Pistor, 2019, pp.7–9, emphasis added).

It need hardly be added that "global capitalists" are in large part based in the North.

4.3 Global value chains (GVSs), trade agreements, and patents, facilitate large resource transfers from South to North

World trade increased by five times between 1993 and 2013, and the IMF estimates that almost three quarters of the increase was due to the growth of global supply chains. Mainstream eyes see increased southern firms' and economies' participation in GVCs as almost synonymous with industrialization, thanks to gains from specialization in line with comparative advantage and opportunities for knowledge spillovers (as compared to arms-length and full-product trade). The resulting productivity growth generates higher profits and investment, higher wages and tax collections, and more development. The process can continue over the long term in the form of moving up the value-added chain, or "climbing the value-added ladder" (Gupta, 2017). The argument has become especially popular in international organizations and northern aid agencies since the 1990s, as an addition to the core Washington Consensus. It is complemented by the argument for developing countries to enter formal trade treaties with developed countries to mutual benefit.

But this rosy view obscures power. Lead firms in GVCs, generally northern firms, commonly construct the value chains with command mechanisms through which they capture higher profits for themselves through several mechanisms, including: transfer pricing along the chain (Nike based in the US transferring value from producers in Bangladesh, for example); or barriers to entry; or product standards and intellectual property rights. The common denominator is the ability to extract rents from foreign (southern) firms (Milberg and Winkler, 2013; Hopkins and Wallerstein, 1977). A study of 59 countries in 1995 and 2011 found that *of the top ten countries in terms of gains from participation in GVC trade, nine were northern in both years* (Turkey was in the top ten in 1995, China in 2011) (Smichowski et al., 2018). Here the measure of gain is the exports of non-primary products divided by total GVC-related trade (exports plus intermediate imports).

Many developing countries have been stuck in the low value-added parts of global value chains, under intense competitive pressure to "run faster in order to stand still" – to produce more pairs of jeans for the same revenue as before, under threat that if the producer declines the buyer will simply find a more compliant producer elsewhere (Kaplinsky and Morris, 2001; Selwyn, 2019). Lower prices per unit of output can offset increases in quality or quantity, resulting in lower value capture on the part of southern firms. Workers may benefit little without increases in wages or tax-funded public goods. In particular, middle-income countries are prone to get stuck in a "middle-income" or "middle-capability trap", their manufacturing and service firms unable to break into innovation-intensive activities or the market for branded products where the high profits are to be made, and outcompeted by firms based in China and Southeast Asia.

Legitimized by the Washington Consensus, most developing country governments have sought to accelerate their integration with developed economies by signing bilateral or regional trade and investment agreements – yet these agreements restrict their ability to complement improved market access with the macroeconomic and industrial policies needed to intensify input-output linkages within the domestic economy. *The agreements typically contain "rules of origin" and tariff escalation clauses which tend to lock low-cost economies into low-value added segments of value chains as a condition of tariff-free access to the dominant economies.* The agreements even restrict developing countries' access to life-saving medications thanks to the way US, European and Japanese pharmaceutical companies use them to boost their profits (Wade, 2003a; 2003b).

Many of these agreements also require "investor-state dispute settlement" (more accurately, investor-*versus*-state dispute settlement) by which foreign corporations can sue host governments for actions which threaten the corporation's *expected future* profits (even including regulations to curb cigarette smoking or protect rainforests). They sue governments at an international arbitration panel, which operates in secrecy with a pool of lawyers and arbitrators drawn mostly from western countries, who face obvious conflicts of interest (today's prosecutor for a corporation may be tomorrow's arbitrator for a case prosecuted by today's arbitrator).

The panel cannot adjudicate *governments suing corporations* for failure to fulfil their responsibilities. ISDS panels have awarded damages against governments running into billions of US dollars, and even just a corporation's threat to bring a suit has been enough to chill socially responsible regulation. Since the 2008 Crash a sizable industry has arisen of "third party financiers", money firms which agree to finance a company's case at the arbitration panel in return for a share of the winnings. The money firm makes a bet on the decision of a judge. This is not only very profitable (commonly eight to ten times upfront costs), but also the winnings are not closely correlated with fluctuations in returns in other financial markets.

Whatever the specific causes case by case, the global effect is that the price of the South's products have been falling for decades, with the commodity boom of 2002–12 as the main exception. The South's average real rate of output growth has been higher than the North's for most of the time since the 1960s, but the South earns less and less on this rising output as prices of its products trend down – keeping wages and incomes low. The North enjoys the opposite configuration (Freeman 2020).

The North enjoys the opposite configuration not least because firms and organizations from the top 10 northern countries hold more than 90% of patents granted by US Patent and Trademark Office (USPTO) in 1997–2004 (Shadlen, 2009). A chart of countries' internationally registered patents against GDP divided by labour inputs (working hours) shows a single big hump at the countries classed as developed (Gomulka, 2006). Since the 1980s northern states have pushed to harmonize the international governance of intellectual property in line with northern-style IP protection; for example, the Agreement on Trade-Related Aspects of Intellectual Property Rights (TRIPS) in the WTO. The North justifies global application of northern-style IP protection on grounds that strong IP protection is an important cause of economic development, at all income levels.

4.4 Financial integration facilitates huge resource transfers from South to North

The North has operated since the 1990s with a "hyper-globalist" model of progress, in which financial capital is set free from national control and economic growth depends increasingly on rising levels of debt – on asset bubbles at home or, for Germany, Japan and China, asset bubbles and current account deficits elsewhere.

The owners of financial capital seek yield in high-risk, high-return assets globally. This produced, pre-C19, the combination of northern stock markets at record levels, and global debt at record levels relative to GDP.

Northern agents have pressed emerging economies to integrate fully into the global financial system, lifting restrictions on the inflow and outflow of finance and on the establishment of financial corporations (Wade, 2003a; 2003b; 2017).

As emerging economies integrate into the global financial system they become vulnerable to changes in Western (especially US) interest rates, exchange rates, asset prices, to swings in capital inflows and outflows, and to swings in the value of their stocks of international assets and liabilities.

Not only are they vulnerable to external (Western) instabilities, they also transfer huge amounts of resources to the core countries. Some are from equities, in the form of capital (or wealth) losses and yield losses (payments on liabilities minus income from assets). The South's capital losses and yield differentials on equities go mainly to the private sector in the North, boosting income inequality in the North. As for debt, a large part of the transfers goes to international lenders (banks and bond holders) in the North. Another large part goes to northern governments, mainly the US, through purchases of US Treasuries as foreign exchange reserves, which in effect gives a subsidy to the US government.

The upshot is that nine emerging economies in the G20 have transferred around 2.3 per cent of their combined GDP per year through 2000–16, almost all to advanced countries, especially US, Japan, Germany, and the UK; and 2.7 per cent in 2016 (Akyuz 2018). The combination of low-yielding assets in their reserves and high-yielding liabilities generates what looks to be "protection money" paid to the core – the source of the shocks. It is still another mechanism for maintaining the hierarchical core-periphery structure of the world economy, dressed as "win-win".

5. The pinnacle of global corporate power

What is the private corporate power hierarchy behind contemporary globalization? At the pinnacle of global corporate power is a *super-cluster of around 150 densely linked firms accounting for a high share of global corporate revenues. It is itself dominated by finance: all of the top fifty except one are financial firms, headquartered in developed countries* (Coghalan and MacKenzie, 2011). Oligopolistic financial firms, at the intersection of the investment, credit, savings processes of the global economy, are able to reap the bulk of the returns from production. This helps to explain how *the value of international financial transactions to global GDP rose from about 14 in 1997 to almost 70 today, so that the realm of finance now swamps the realm of GDP (the "real economy").*

The hub of global financial transactions is in the North, specifically New York and London,[4] not to forget South

---

[4] The UK has 26 organizations tasked as anti-money laundering regulators. Of them, 14 are tasked with regulating accountants; of these, 12 *also act as accountants' trade bodies in charge of promoting the interests of their members.* Anyone can set up business and call themselves an accountant, unlike "lawyers" or "barristers". One of the 26 regulators regulates "notaries public", who specialize in authenticating documents, a key nodal point in money laundering. This agency is called the Faculty Office of the Archbishop of Canterbury, established in 1533. It is meant to do a lot of other things as well as regulate notaries public, such as issue marriage certificates in the case of unusual weddings. Each notary public gets inspected on average once every 35 years. The UK government says "we are very concerned to stop money laundering, look at all the agencies we have." In fact, the system is designed to "fail". It allows UK to be "... one of the most attractive destinations for laundering the proceeds of grand corruption", said a government report in 2017 on its anti-corruption strategy (Bullough, 2019a).

Dakota, now one of the most profitable places for the global super-rich to hide their billions (Bullough, 2019b).

Profits too are concentrated in the North. Of the biggest 2,000 publicly traded companies compiled by *Forbes Global 2000, US companies had the biggest share of global profits in eighteen out of twenty-five sectors across 2006-2017* (sectors such as electronics, heavy machinery, aerospace, banking, health equipment and services, media) — 72 per cent of the total – including the technologically most sophisticated (Starrs 2019). China is the only developing country with even a toehold in the distribution of global profits.

6. Conclusion

I started with statistical evidence that – contrary to both neoclassical and some dependency theories – the world economy can plausibly be seen as a two bloc income hierarchy, with more equal income distribution within each bloc than between them, remarkably little movement up or down between the blocs even over the past two centuries – despite the existence of a "development" industry in the past seven decades devoted, apparently, to the aim of promoting the catch-up of "developing countries". This division of rich and poor countries is no surprise in terms of everyday speech; but it is a surprise in terms of its lack of salience in the prevailing macro understanding of the world economy, as in the picture from the IMF, the World Bank, OECD and other such (northern-dominated) inter-state organizations.

If I were running the world from the North I would not want my social scientists to highlight the North-South division. I would not want them to bring out that the prosperity of northern populations rests on their ability to buy goods and services made by much poorer people (even as those northern populations would be quite prepared to accept that the prosperity of the "free" two thirds of the population of ancient Rome rested on the labour of the enslaved one third). I would not want my social scientists to highlight that in the *past two centuries only around seven non-western, mostly small-population countries have become developed* like the North. I would not want them to bring out that specialization in commodities, tourism and remittances, plus full financial integration with the North, is a recipe for volatility, and that this volatility, especially long periods of shrinkage, is a big help in maintaining the North-South hierarchy. On the other hand, I would want them to emphasise disaggregations, divisions, especially within the South. I would want them to justify, legitimize, the prosperity of the North by affirming the truth of the law of modern-era power hierarchies and the theory of comparative advantage and policy of free trade (and say no to anything that sanctioned the state imparting "directional thrust" to the economy, especially in industry). I would want them to find that the main reasons for southern countries not catching up are to do with their delays in adopting modern capitalist institutions – not to do with relations with the North. I would want countries of the South to see themselves as having very different interests in their dealings with the North. The model would be the European Union during the North Atlantic Financial Crisis and its eurozone ramifications: crisis states of the

European south each talked first to Brussels and Berlin and Paris, and only later, maybe, to each other, with next to no concerting of actions.

The North was clearly in economic trouble long before C19: sluggish investment and growth, high income inequality, low wage growth (*across 25 developed countries in 2014, two thirds of households had lower or equal real market incomes than in 2005*), low inflation, low interest rates, high debt. The basic causes have been (a) wage suppression (real wage growth less than productivity growth, falling share of wages in national income) and (b) concentration of wealth at the top of the distribution. In addition, (c) cheap and tax deductible debt has encouraged company managers to use leverage to game earnings per share and performance targets – helping the managers to "earn" Croesus-like wealth while they skimp on productivity-raising investment.

In the South, the kindling for another big debt crisis has been building for years, and is now aflame. Thanks to two decades of very low interest rates, governments and businesses loaded up on debt from mostly western sources and China, and are now on the hook for billions of dollars in interest and principal repayments, just when their currencies have steeply devalued. Until recently the IMF was opposed to governments using capital controls to stem inflows and outflows; and even now sanctions them only when a country is already in or on the edge of crisis, not as a legitimate tool of normal macroeconomic management. The South now faces a more extensive stalling of economic development even than Latin

America did in its debt crisis of the 1980s, the period known as Decada Perdida, the Lost Decade.

Meanwhile, eight out of ten common measures of global integration fell or remained constant between 2007 and 2018, including trade to world GDP, long-term cross-border investment (FDI), cross-border bank loans, and gross capital flows. The trend has been dubbed "slobalisation" (*Economist*, 2019). The C19 pandemic is causing another turn in the ratchet of slobalisation.

The central point is that dysfunctional performance in both North and South is intensified by the underlying, long-institutionalized income and wealth inequality between the two blocs. In the face of the financial crises in developed countries in 2007–12 and the "rise" of a few developing countries in the past several decades (China above all), and in the face of the steady aging of their societies, the developed countries have become jealously protective of their present privileged position. Indeed, the two hegemonic states of the past 150 years, the UK and the US, have become intensely *assertive* (not just protective) of their sovereignty since 2016, as in "take back control" – which seems to offer a solution to diminished status and democratic deficit, especially for those who see themselves most hit by automation and foreign workers. Emerging powers, on the other hand, have become jealously assertive of their sovereignty in a multilateral order they have never really felt part of, because designed and dominated by the North, and worried that they will become old before they become wealthy. Global cooperation in most fields is gridlocked just when we need it most. See the G20.

Irrespective of climate change, migration pressure from South to North – from Africa and Asia across a narrow sea to Europe, from Latin America across the long land border with the US – will only intensify in the face of the North-South income gap, amped up by social media, and will push northern politics towards "illiberal democracy" and "identitarian" politics ("rule by law" edging out "rule of law") for many decades ahead.

We have seen an impressive level of international cooperation in the hunt for a C19 vaccine, as earlier for Ebola, whose vaccine was discovered in Canada, developed in the US and manufactured in Germany. But we have also seen a broken inter-state order on full display in the battles between nations over supplies of tests and personal equipment, and in the undermining of the WHO by leading states, notably the US and China.[5] The great question for when a vaccine is discovered is whether the global governance system will treat it as a global public good and make it available to the world's poor as well as to the rich (Pilling 2020).

The C19 crisis is likely to intensify the inequalities within the blocs over the next decade. (For example, northern central bank actions support bond and equity prices, which benefits the rich, since they own these assets.) My

---

[5] Through January 2020 WHO statements about C19 to the world echoed China's official statements, which denied evidence of human-to-human transmission. Even in late January as China began to include caveats like, "the possibility of limited human-to-human transmission cannot be excluded", WHO statements did not include the caveats. In late January WHO director-general Tedros – appointed with strong backing of China – visited China and praised the leadership for "setting a new standard for outbreak response", even as evidence of cover-up in Wuhan was clear (Gilsinan, 2020). The US and Trump were hostile to the WHO long before C19 and more so after.

point is that *to understand trends within countries or within blocs we must understand – contrary to general understanding – that inequalities between the North-South blocs help to drive the internal inequalities on both sides.* Which implies that the study of development be embedded in the study of international relations, and freed from the metaphor of the marathon race.

References

Aiyar, S. et al. (2013) "Growth slowdowns and the middle-income trap." WP 13/71, International Monetary Fund.

Akyuz, Y. (2018) " External balance sheets of emerging economies: low-yielding assets, high-yielding liabilities." WP 476, Political Economy Research Institute, University of Massachusetts Amherst.

Akyuz, Y. (2020) "The commodity-finance nexus: twin boom and double whammy." *Revista de Economia Contemporanea*, 24 (1): 1 -13.

Brady, A. M. (2017) "Magic weapons: CCP political influence activities under Xi Jinping." At https://www.wilsoncenter.org/article/magic-weapons-chinas-political-influence-activities-under-xi-jinping

Broadberry, S. and J. Wallis (2016) "Shrink theory: the nature of long-run and short-run economic performance." www.econweb.umd.edu/~davis/eventpapers/WallisShrinkTheory.pdf

Bullough, O. (2019a) "Wages of sin: The City of London is a key hub in the rampant kleptocracy, financial crime and tax evasion that is afflicting the world." *Prospect* June .

Bullough, O. (2019b) "The great American tax haven." Long Read, *The Guardian*, 14 November.

Cherif, R. and F. Hasanov (2019) "The leap of the tiger: escaping the middle-income trap to the technology frontier." *Global Policy* July at https://onlinelibrary.wiley.com/doi/abs/10.1111/1758-5899.12695.

Coghalan, A. and D. MacKenzie (2011) "Revealed: the capitalist network that runs the world." *New Scientist*, 2835.

Economist (2019) "Briefing: Slobalisation." January 26, 13:16.

Freeman, A. (2020) "The geopolitical economy of international inequality." manuscript, April .

Gilsinan, K. (2020) "Coronavirus: Covid-19, how China deceived the world." *The Atlantic*, April 12, at https://www.theatlantic.com/politics/archive/2020/04/world-health-organization-blame-pandemic-oronavirus/609820/

Gomulka, S. (2006) "Mechanism and sources of world econ growth." http://www.pte.pl/pliki/1/210/SG-econ-growth.pdf.

Gupta, P. (2017) "Global production networks." In K. Reinert (ed) *Handbook of Globalisation and Development*, pp.153-68, Edward Elgar.

Hopkins, T. and I. Wallerstein (1977) "Patterns of development of the modern world-system." *Review* (Fernand Braudel Center), 1.

Johnson, C. (2004) "America's empire of bases." *Global Policy Forum*, January.

Kaplinsky, R. and M. Morris (2001) "A handbook for value chain research." Report prepared for the International Development Research Centre (IDRC), Ottawa.

Kelly, B. (2020) "The spread of disease is always political but then so is the cure." Letters, *Financial Times*, 2/3 May.

Milanovic, B. (2019) "GlobalInequality: Chile: the poster boy of neoliberalism who fell from grace." October 26, http://glineq.blogspot.com/2019/10/chile-poster-boy-of-neoliberalism-who.html.

Milberg, W. and D. Winkler (2013) *Outsourcing Economics: Global Value Chains in Capitalist Development.* Cambridge University Press.

Pilling, D. (2020) "Any Covid-19 vaccine must be treated as a public good." *Financial Times* 14 May.

Pistor, K. (2019) *The Code of Capital: How the Law Creates Wealth and Inequality.* Princeton University Press.

Reinert, E. (1994) "Catching up from way behind. A Third World perspective on First World history." In J. Fagerberg et al (eds), *The Dynamics of Technology, Trade and Growth*, Edward Elgar.

Rostow, W. (2016[1959]) *The Stages of Economic Growth: A Non-Communist Manifesto.* Cambridge University Press.

Selwyn, B. (2019) "Poverty chains and global capitalism." *Competition & Change*, 23 (1): 71-97.

Shadlen, K.C. (2009) "Harmonization, differentiation, and development: the case of intellectual property in the global trading regime." In Silvia Sacchetti and Roger Sugden, eds., *Knowledge in the Development of Economies: Institutional Choices under Globalisation.* Edward Elgar , pp. 44-66.

Smichowski, B., C. Durand, S. Knauss (2018) "Participation in global value chains and varieties of development patterns." At hal-01817426.

Smith, Adam (1776) *The Wealth of Nations.* University of Chicago Press.

Starrs, S.K. (2019) (under review), *American Power Globalized: Rethinking American Power in the Age of Globalization.* Oxford University Press.

Uchitelle, L. (2002) "Challenging the dogmas of free trade." *New York Times*, 9 February.

Vestergaard, J. and R. H. Wade (2012a) "The governance response to the Great Recession: the 'success' of the G20." *Journal of Economic Issues*, XLVI, 2, June.

Vestergaard, J. and R. H. Wade (2012b) "Establishing a new Global Economic Council: governance reform at the G20, the IMF and the World Bank." *Global Policy* 3, 3, September.

Wade, R.H. (2000) "Wheels within wheels: rethinking the Asian crisis and the Asian model." *Annual Review of Political Science*, v.3: 85-115.

Wade, R.H. (2001) "The revenge of capital: the IMF and Ethiopia." *Challenge*, 44 (5): 67-75.

Wade, R.H. (2003a) "What development strategies are viable for developing countries? The World Trade Organisation and the shrinking of 'development space'." *Review of International Political Economy*.

Wade, R.H. (2003b) "The invisible hand of the American empire." *Ethics and International Affairs*, 17, 2: 77-88.

Wade, R.H. (2010) "The state of the World Bank." *Challenge*, July-August: 1-25.

Wade, R.H. (2013) "The art of power maintenance: how western states keep the lead in global organizations." *Challenge*, 56 (1), Jan/Feb, 1-35.

Wade, R.H. (2017) "Global growth, inequality, and poverty: the globalization argument and the 'political' science of economics." Chapter 12 in J. Ravenhill (ed), *Global Political Economy*, 5th ed, Oxford University Press.

Wade, R.H. (2019) "East Asia." In D. Nayyar (ed) *Asian Transformations: An Inquiry into the Development of Nations*, Oxford University Press.

Williamson, J. (2004) "The strange history of the Washington Consensus." *Journal of Post Keynesian Economics*, 27 (2): 195-206.

Wolf, M. (2004) *Why Globalization Works*. Yale University Press.

World Bank (2013) *China 2030: Building a modern, harmonious and creative society*. Washington DC.

Zoellick, R. (2010) "The end of the Third World." Address to Woodrow Wilson Center for International Studies, Washington DC, 14 April.

Chapter 3

Global inequality in a time of pandemic

Jayati Ghosh

A global pandemic is a particularly bad time to be reminded of existing inequalities. But there is no doubt that the Covid-19 pandemic has highlighted the extent of inequalities between and within countries. Whatever may be the fond sentiments expressed by at least some global leaders, we are clearly *not* "all in this together". It is true that in principle, a virus is no respecter of class or other socio-economic distinctions: it enters human hosts without checking for such attributes. And the rapid global spread of this particular virus has shown that it is no respecter of national borders either, which points to the more fundamental truth that as long as anyone anywhere has a contagious disease, everyone everywhere is under threat. This should have made it obvious that ensuring universal access to health care and prevention is not about compassion, but about the survival of all. Unfortunately, that obvious truth is still not adequately recognised, mainly because existing structures of authority and power imbalances ensure that the rich and powerful continue to be more protected from both health risks and material privation.

Diseases tend to strike people differently depending not just on the strength of public health systems, but on existing fissures in society: of class, race and ethnicity, gender, caste and other divisions. There are poverty traps caused by negative feedback loops between the squalor associated with income poverty and infectious diseases. In unequal societies, poor and socially disadvantaged groups are both more likely to be exposed to Covid-19 and more likely to die from it, because the ability to take preventive measures, susceptibility to disease and access to treatment all vary greatly according to income, assets, occupation, location, and the like. That is why, even in rich countries like the United States, it has been found that death rates from coronavirus for blacks are nearly three times greater than those for white people (APM Research, 2020) and in some states, the ratio is as high as 6 or 7. In developing countries, such divisions are often even sharper. Perhaps even worse, the governments' containment policies for Covid-19 within countries have also shown extreme class bias, with possibly the most egregious example coming from India, where migrant workers have been at the receiving end of a particularly brutal yet ineffective lockdown that failed to control the virus yet devastated livelihoods, especially of informal workers (Stranded Workers Action Network 2020).

However, the differences across countries that have been revealed by this pandemic are also very stark. Globally, developing countries have been particularly hard hit by the economic forces that have been unleashed by economic lockdowns, the collapse of international trade and the volatility of cross-border capital flows. These adverse effects just over the months of March and April 2020 were significantly worse than the impact after the Global Financial Crisis in 2008 (UNCTAD, 2020a). These forced many developing and emerging market economies into severe crisis even *before* the health crisis really hit them; and have also reduced their capacity to deal with the likely health impact. There are three features of the nature of the global economy that are driving the dramatic increase in spatial inequalities in the period of the pandemic. These are: the differences in degrees of formalisation of labour market and legal/social protections available to workers; the nature of the external constraints, including volatile trade and capital flows; and the varying willingness and/or ability of governments to respond with fiscal stimuli.

The domination of informal work in the developing world

It is obvious that the worst material impacts of the lockdowns and other restrictions are being felt by informal workers, who face a dismal spectrum of probabilities of loss of livelihood, from declining earnings among the self-employed to job losses among paid workers. These are likely to intensify in the coming months. Even so, barring just a handful of countries, very few governments have declared strong measures to cope with these effects – and therefore they are letting loose forces that could be even more devastating for poor people across the world. In the worst-case scenario, this could even mean that more people could die from hunger and the inability to treat other health problems, than from the Covid-19 virus.

Just how seriously should we take the concerns of informal workers alone? The answer partly depends on how extensive the problem is. The ILO considers a worker to be informal if s/he is a worker whose social security is not paid for by the employer, is not entitled to paid annual leave and paid sick leave; or works in a household; or owns and runs an informal enterprise, typically in the form of self-employment, but also including micro-enterprises. Figure 1 shows that, according to the ILO, 61.2 per cent of all employment was informal, and most of this was also in informal sector enterprises that rarely if ever get the benefit of any government subsidies or protection even in periods of crisis. However, the point is that this is less of a problem in developed countries, where employment is still dominantly formal. In the emerging and developing countries as a group, informal workers account for as much as 70 per cent of all employment, so two out of every three workers are informal.

These are workers who lack most rights at work, decent working conditions and most forms of social protection except whatever minimal amounts may be provided by the state. They and their families are clearly the most vulnerable to any economic downturn. When such a downturn comes in the wake of an unprecedented public health calamity, the concerns are obviously multiplied.

Figure 1 Share of informal in total employment

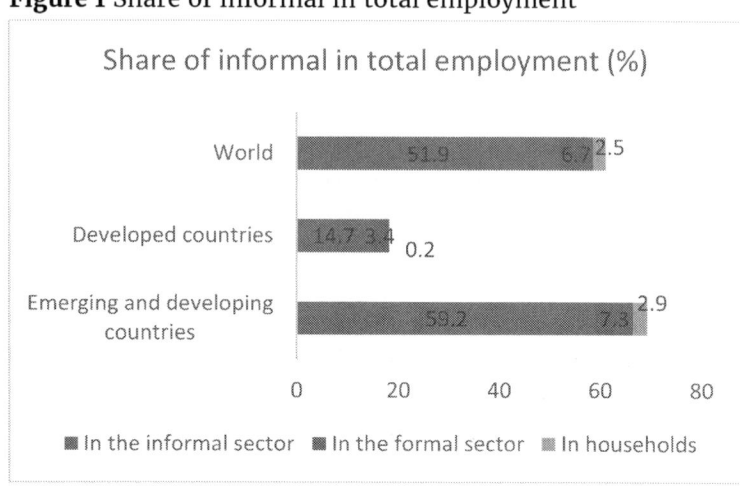

Source: Women and Men in the Informal Economy: A Statistical Picture, Geneva: ILO, 2018.

Figure 2 Informality in non-agricultural activities

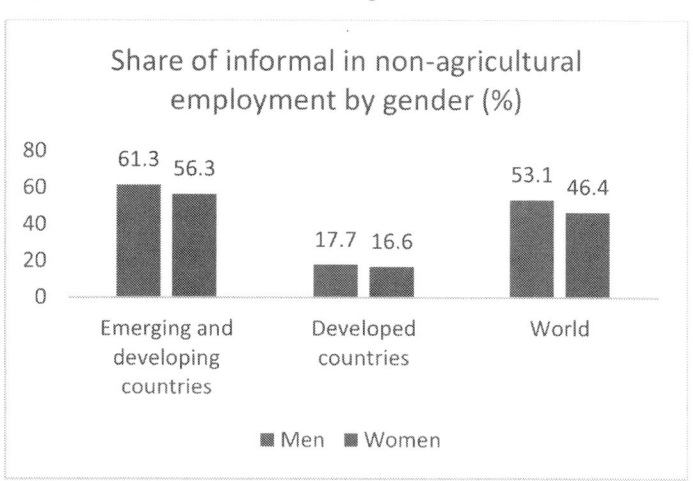

Source: Women and Men in the Informal Economy: A Statistical Picture, Geneva: ILO, 2018.

It is sometimes argued that, among informal workers, farmers do not need the same safety nets as other workers and can survive even in critical economic conditions because of the nature of their activity. This is no longer true given the interconnectedness of economies, and agriculturalists very much also need bailout packages specific to that sector. But the notion that informality is higher in developing countries because of the greater significance of agricultural employment is dispelled by Figure 2. Even in non-agricultural activities, informal workers predominate in the Global South, to the extent of making up 60 per cent of all such workers.

Figure 3 Informality across developing regions

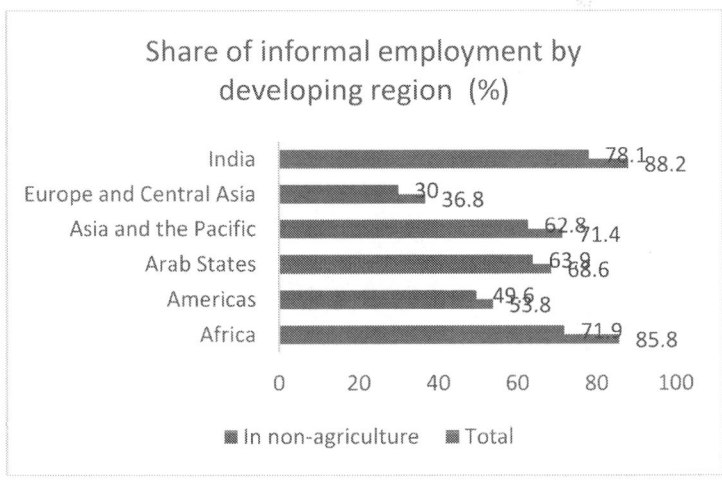

Share of informal employment by developing region (%)

India	78.1	88.2
Europe and Central Asia	30	36.8
Asia and the Pacific	62.8	71.4
Arab States	63.9	68.6
Americas	49.6	53.8
Africa	71.9	85.8

■ In non-agriculture   ■ Total

Source: Women and Men in the Informal Economy: A Statistical Picture, Geneva: ILO, 2018.

Within in the developing world, there are significant variations across regions, as Figure 3 indicates. For example India – which is on the verge of a very substantial spike in Covid-19 cases, has a very large population and is poorly equipped to deal with an epidemic of such proportions – has one of the highest rates of employment informality in the developing world, much higher than the average of Asia and the Pacific or African countries. It is also the country that has implemented the most stringent lockdown, with devastating consequences for employment and livelihoods of informal workers. As Figure 4 indicates, many developing countries with extremely severe or moderately severe Covid-19 containment measures have disproportionately shares of informal workers.

Figure 4 Informal workers under lockdown and other containment measures

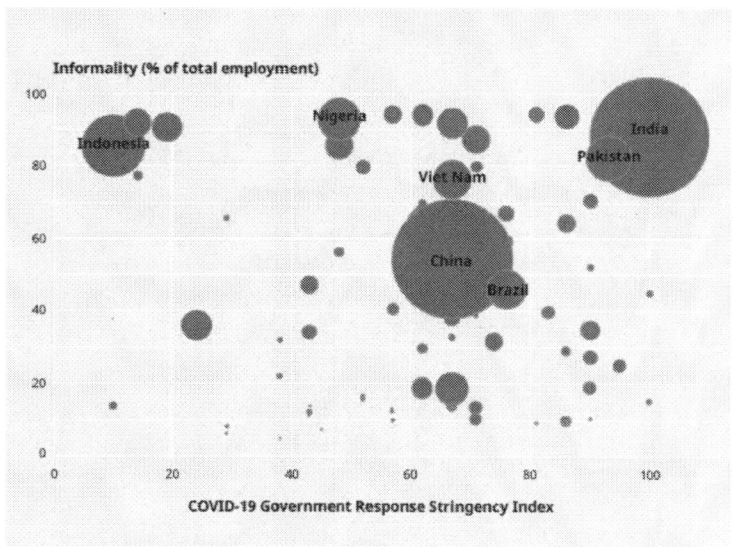

Source: ILO Monitor Covid-19 and the World of Work, 2ⁿᵈ edition 7 April 2020, Figure 3. Geneva: International Labour Organisation.

Note: The x-axis of this chart displays University of Oxford's COVID-19 Government Response Stringency Index. The vertical, y-axis shows informal employment as a share of total employment in the respective country, based on internal ILO calculations. As a third dimension, the respective size of each bubble shows the relative size of total informal employment in each country, which is calculated by multiplying the percentage of informal employment (i.e. the value shown on the y-axis) by total employment as per ILOSTAT's modelled estimates for 2020.

It is obvious that if the human suffering caused by this pandemic is to be minimised or reduced, both public health measures and safety net policies have to recognise this basic reality. Sudden cessation of economic activity through lockdowns can wreak havoc and cause acute distress among workers who lose incomes without any compensation and who do not benefit from any social protection. Further, it is not enough to recommend or even try to enforce the poorly phrased "social distancing" (more properly physical distancing) as a preventive measure, if people's conditions of work and life simply do not allow it. Containment policies have to provide the infrastructure and facilities that would enable people to follow the required rules: at the minimum, the wherewithal for cleanliness (like adequate clean water and soap) and ensuring physical distance. However, in most developing countries, containment strategies have broadly followed the pattern set by China and some developed countries, of strict lockdowns, exhortations to maintain physical distancing and frequent handwashing, with little regard to the practical feasibility or economic impact of such measures.

Also, to enable such workers and their families to follow rules that would minimise contagion, and survive both the possible onslaught of the disease and extreme loss of livelihood over this crisis period, income support and food provision are essential. In many developing countries, free public provision of basic food items (some of which are already supplied by the public distribution system) and time-bound cash transfers to all those who are not formally employed would be important measures for this. However, the institution of such measures has been mostly inadequate, uneven and patchy – for reasons that are not unrelated to the fiscal constraints discussed later. This means that greater proportions of the population in the developing world are both less protected from the virus and more adversely impacted by the containment measures, than in the developed countries.

A major macroeconomic consequence of the greater informality of employment prevalent in the developing world is the proportionate absence of automatic stabilisers, such as unemployment insurance or health insurance, that are typically associated with formal employment or more widely to be found in economies with greater proportions of formal workers. This can be especially significant when the pandemic and lockdowns lead to contracting economic activity, because stabilisers mitigate the reduction of demand that would inevitably result from such closures. By contrast, in developing countries where little or no such protection exists for the greater part of the workforce, restrictions on economic activity have even more adverse implications for aggregate demand. In the absence of adequate countercyclical fiscal policies (which are in fact less likely in developing countries, as argued below) this means that such economies are likely to experience deeper and possibly more prolonged declines in activity.

Trade, balance of payments and external debt concerns

Figure 5 Primary commodity prices by category over past year

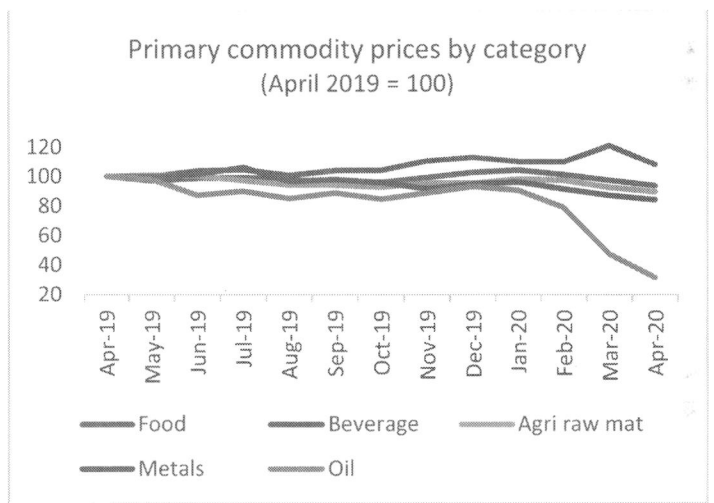

Source: https://www.imf.org/en/Research/commodity-prices, last accessed on 4 June 2020.

World trade in both goods and services is currently in sharp decline: the WTO expects world trade to fall anywhere between 12 and 32 percent over 2020 (WTO 2020a). Even these dismal projections could well be underestimates, because they implicitly rely on relatively rapid containment of the spread of the virus and lifting of lockdown measures by late summer 2020. During the phase of lockdown, cross-border trade in goods – other than those deemed "essential" – have effectively ceased in many countries; travel has declined to a tiny fraction of what it was and tourism has also stopped for the time being; various other cross-border services that cannot be delivered electronically are contracting sharply. While trade volumes are declining across the board, the sharpest price declines in global trade have been in primary commodities, which are of greater export importance for developing countries. Trade prices had already fallen from the recent peaks of 2013 and then 2018, but the most recent declines have been very sharp (Figure 5). Between December 2019 and April 2020, the index of all primary commodity prices fell by more than 40 per cent, while that of energy declined to less than half.

However, even within primary commodity prices, there were differences, with oil prices being the weakest, followed by metals and then agricultural raw materials (Figure 6). Unsurprisingly given the worldwide curbs on travel and transport as well as cutbacks in material production, oil exporting countries have been the worst hit. Oil prices in April 2020 were only one-third of their level in December 2019. The prices of metals and agricultural raw materials also showed around 12 per cent declines over these four months. Food prices, while falling, did not initially seem so badly affected, but this seems to have changed by May when they fell by a further 2 percent (Reuters 2020), as the lockdown impact resulted in lower real incomes and falling demand for food in much of the world. These declines in export prices add to the woes created by falling export volumes, in sharply reducing foreign exchange earnings for most developing countries.

Figure 6 Primary commodity prices since 2010

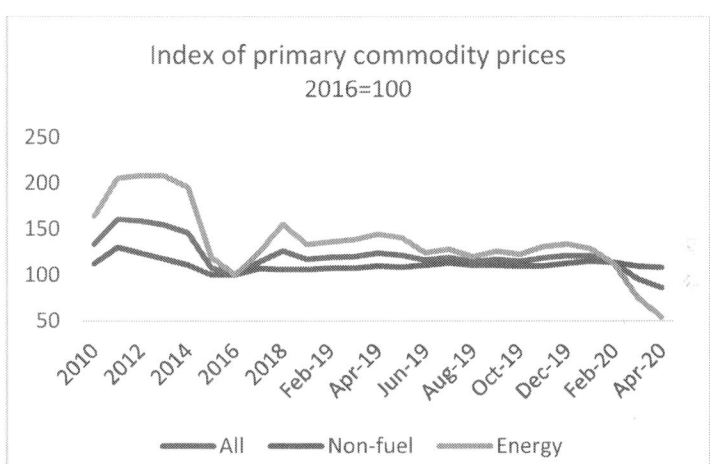

Source: https://www.imf.org/en/Research/commodity-prices, last accessed on 4 June 2020 (IMF 2020a).

Developing countries have also been more impacted by the decline in tourism and travel-related services than developed countries: such travel accounted for nearly one-third of the services exports of developing countries, and half for the least developed countries. (WTO, 2020b) In addition, developing countries are in general much more dependent on remittances from migrant workers in other (typically advanced) countries and such transfers have also been hard hit in the ongoing crisis.

This reduction in foreign exchange earnings on the current account is of greater concern because of the volatility of capital flows as a result of the pandemic, which initially engendered yet another "flight to safety" among global financial investors. Net capital flows to emerging markets as a group effectively stalled in February 2020, amounting to just $0.2 billion, and then turned hugely negative in March, with net outflows of more than $100 billion. There was a slight recovery in April, with net inflows of around $17 billion. However, this did not reflect any real change in the economic prospects of these economies; rather, it was the outcome of the crisis-response policies adopted by central banks in the US and other developed countries, which dramatically increased the flow of liquidity to banks and non-bank institutions, and cut interest rate to near-zero, zero or even negative levels. Such policies create large incentives for the carry trade based on interest rates differentials. And since they enable access to capital at extremely low rates, they encourage investment in various other emerging market assets (such as in equity and bond markets) that are lucrative even when they offer relatively low nominal rates of return.

The outcome for developing countries is hardly to be celebrated, since they are rendered vulnerable and experience large swings in capital flows that do not necessarily reflects changes in their own policies and prospects, but depend much more on policy and other changes in the advanced economies. The selective targeting of particular emerging markets by global investors is problematic, because the country chosen as the favoured destination may change, or new fears generated by the pandemic and the crisis it has induced may trigger another episode of capital flight. As a result, even as developing countries attempt to address the real economy crisis they are engulfed in, they also have to deal with processes generated by the monetary policy response so widely favoured in the advanced economies, of injecting even more cheap money into the system. They therefore need to devise policies that prevent a speculative surge in financial markets riding on that increased liquidity, such as capital controls, without which they are buffeted by these highly speculative movements of capital in a way that most advanced economies are not.

This in turn generates financial fragility that can explode whenever even slight shifts in expectations occur. Today's financial fragility obviously predates the COVID-19 "black swan". Given the massive accumulation of debt (Basu, 2020) in both developed and developing countries since the 2008 financial crisis, it has long been clear that even a minor event – some "known unknown" – could have far-reaching destabilizing effects. Yet, until recently, rising asset prices – owing to a long period of extraordinarily loose monetary policies in advanced economies – disguised mounting debt levels. As the recent scare in global equity markets indicates, asset bubbles cannot last forever. By contrast, in the absence of active public pressure or state intervention to facilitate their resolution, debts do not deflate on their own.

This is what makes the recent debt build up in the developing world of particular concern (UNCTAD, 2020b). In 2018, the total debt (private, public, domestic, and external) across developing countries was equal to almost twice their combined GDP – the highest it has ever been. Particularly concerning is the build-up of private debt by non-financial corporations, which now amounts to nearly three-quarters of total debt in developing countries (a much higher ratio than in advanced economies). According to UNCTAD, inherently volatile "foreign shadow financial institutions" have played a major role in fueling this accumulation, such that around one-third of private non-financial corporate debt in developing countries (with the exception of China) is denominated in foreign currency and held by external creditors. Very large amounts of sovereign-debt repayments on short-maturity international bonds will soon be due. Short-term external debt poses a real problem: as much as $1.62 trillion is due to be repaid by developing countries this year, with another $1.08 trillion due in 2021. This would have been a struggle before; now, the Covid-19 crisis makes it impossible. The tsunami of falling export and tourism revenues and dramatic outflows of capital causes sharp currency depreciation, making it harder to repay foreign currency debts. Without quick and substantial action, many governments will be forced into debt defaults. And in any case this also limits the capacity to undertake the required fiscal responses that appear to have come so easily to the developed world.

Inequalities in fiscal response

Among the many inequalities the pandemic has exposed and accentuated within and between nations, one of the most striking is the dramatic divergence in fiscal responses. Economic activity has collapsed in most parts of the world because of the pandemic and associated lockdowns, and unemployment has gone up sharply. In response, several developed countries have already put in place some of the biggest fiscal stimuli ever. The additional spending of the US government announced since March already amounts to more than 14 per cent of GDP (IMF, 2020b). Japan's Emergency Economic Package is more than 21 per cent of GDP, Australia's increased spending is nearly 10 per cent and Canada's comes to 8.4 per cent. In Europe, the absence of agreement on a strong joint stimulus effort across the eurozone has created more varied responses, from 9 per cent of GDP in Austria to 4.9 per cent in Germany and 5 per cent in France, to only 1.6 per cent in Spain and 1.4 per cent in Italy. Rigid EU rules continue to limit government spending in precisely those countries that need larger fiscal stimuli.

In addition, monetary policy adds to fiscal capacity at sub-national levels of government. From lower interest rates to central bank purchases of provincial and municipal bonds to new facilities for lending to different sectors and enterprises, the US Fed and other major central banks have sought to keep borrowing costs down and sustain liquidity for public agencies.

By contrast, in most developing countries, the fiscal response has been underwhelming. This is not because they face any less of an economic challenge: if anything, the lockdowns and global headwinds have already caused much greater macroeconomic disaster than in the advanced world. In India, it is estimated that 122 million people lost their jobs in April because of the lockdown

(CMIE, 2020), even as the number of Covid-19 cases continued to increase rapidly. In other developing countries, even those with less stringent lockdowns, economies have been battered by sharply falling export and tourism revenues and declining remittance inflows, directly and indirectly causing large job losses. Yet in most countries, there has been relatively little response in terms of increased public spending to counter these dramatic declines in income and employment.

These differences are evident even within the G20. By the end of April 2020, emerging markets in the G20 averaged new public spending of 2 per cent of GDP, compared to 11.7 percent for advanced countries (Segal and Gerstel, 2020). As Table 1 indicates, developing countries that are in the G20 have not only gone for relatively modest fiscal expansion, (other than South Africa, for which the estimate has been questioned), but the current fiscal packages are in general significantly smaller than they were in 2009, in the wake of the Global Financial Crisis. This is surprising, because the impact on real economies is already larger and likely to be more severe than in 2009. Meanwhile, other low-income countries are struggling to put together even relatively tiny packages, which are completely inadequate to combat either the spread of the virus or the economic collapse.

Table 1 G20 Variations in fiscal stimulus packages

	2009	2020	Difference
Argentina	2.5	1.2	-1.3
Brazil	0.5	6.5	6
China	8	3.5	-4.5
India	4.1	0.8	-3.3
Indonesia	2.5	2.8	0.3
Mexico	1	0.7	-0.3
Russian Federation	1.7	3	1.3
Saudi Arabia	11	2.8	-8.2
South Africa	4	10	6
Turkey	6	2	-4
Australia	4.1	9.9	5.8
Canada	2.8	8.4	5.6
France	0.7	5	4.3
Germany	4	4.9	0.9
Italy	5	1.4	-3.6
Japan	2.2	20	17.8
Republic of Korea	9	0.8	-8.2
United Kingdom	1.5	5.1	3.6
USA	5.9	11	5.1

Source: https://www.atlanticcouncil.org/blogs/econographics/how-does-the-g20-covid-19-fiscal-response-compare-to-the-global-financial-crisis/
Note: The stimulus for South Africa may be overstated, as various estimates have suggested it is significantly lower, a small fraction of the stated amount. (https://iej.org.za/wp-content/uploads/2020/04/IEJ-COVID-19-emergency-rescue-package-summary.pdf)

What explains this reticence, this unwillingness or inability to increase public spending in developing countries at a time of unprecedented need? Much of this difference in fiscal response can be explained by the other, more systemic inequalities in the global economy. Developing countries that do not issue internationally accepted reserve currencies and are forced to borrow in those currencies simply do not have the fiscal freedom available to those that do. As noted above, many developing countries were already struggling with a mountain of external debt that was problematic even before the pandemic struck. African countries as a group are still spending more on external debt servicing than on public health, and will need substantial debt relief to combat the pandemic (Okonjo-Iweala and Coulibaly, 2020). In any case, the imminent implosion of global debt will inevitably force major restructuring of developing country debt, even if bondholders and other creditors are refusing to accept this for now. This burden of external debt dramatically alters the possible contours of fiscal policy for many developing countries. This is why a global issue of new SDRs and immediate action on debt reduction are both so important.

For countries that do not face immediate external economic threats, there are concerns about domestic resource mobilisation. Domestically, all countries are faced with massive declines in public revenues, as the cessation of economic activity leads to falls in tax collection. Even if government spending were not to increase at all, this would imply a significant increase in the fiscal deficit. Since more government spending is required if only to deal with the pandemic, the first option is direct borrowing from the central bank during the crisis. Yet most developing country governments, with a few exceptions, have been remarkably hesitant to do this. Even countries that do not have immediate debt repayment concerns are showing little inclination to raise public spending to anything like the levels necessary just to stop the process of economic decline.

Why is this? The short answer is fear of private capital flight. How severe that can be was already evident in March 2020, and the minor recovery of capital flows into emerging markets in April has done little to assuage fears of renewed outflows. Aside from foreign currency debt, more than a quarter of even local currency debt is held by foreigners, making them very vulnerable. Meanwhile, liberalised exchange rules have made it easier for domestic residents to shift their funds abroad. The fear of financial markets thus acts as a major constraint on even the most obvious and urgently required policies. In India, for example, a Finance Ministry official justified the pathetically low government response by explicitly linking the possibility of fiscal stimulus packages with the country's sovereign ratings – even though it condemns the country to a major economic collapse with hundreds of millions facing poverty and hunger (Noronha and Sikarwar, 2020). In South Africa the Deputy Finance Minister was attacked for the perfectly reasonable suggestion that the central bank should buy government bonds directly (Richardson, 2020). In this self-imposed ordo-liberal policy climate, fiscal expansion through increased public expenditure is automatically ruled out because of the possibility that it could result in capital flight. Of course, it would be possible to avoid this by instituting capital controls that would prevent extreme volatility of capital flows, but this is also seen in the same policy-making circles as an unacceptable measure because it is assumed to frighten away foreign investors.

The economic absurdity of such a position is at one level obvious. It is clear that significantly increased public expenditure is absolutely essential for most developing economies to address their public health challenges and even to attempt economic revival. Fiscal austerity at this point would have the inevitable effect of further aggravating the downturn, thereby also causing tax revenues to decline further and ending up with an even higher fiscal-deficit to GDP ratio. In any case, global finance is hardly likely to be attracted to devastated economies, other than for a few forays to buy up existing assets on the cheap. However, despite the counterproductive nature of such a strategy, it is the one that continues to be advocated by global finance, and most developing countries that have succumbed to international financial integration (for the dubious pleasure of being described as "emerging markets") find that straying from this comes with immediate threats and costs imposed by international rating agencies, bond market investors and global creditors.

The expression of this particular global inequality is therefore more complex, but no less lethal for that. It is preventing many, if not most, developing countries from increasing public spending at a time when failure to do so has devastating effects on the health of the people and the level of economic activity and employment. How much more disastrous this will be when the existential threat of climate change becomes even more real, creating yet another tragedy about to unfold.

References

APM Research (2020) "The color of coronavirus: Covid-19 deaths by race and ethnicity in the US." APM Research Lab, May 27th. At: https://www.apmresearchlab.org/covid/deaths-by-race

Basu, K. (2020) "The approaching debt wave." January 31st. *Project Syndicate.*

CMIE (2020) "The jobs bloodbath of April 2020." May 5th. Centre for Monitoring Indian Economy

IMF (2020a) Primary Commodity Prices. June 4th, IMF. Available: https://www.imf.org/en/Research/commodity-prices

IMF (2020b) Policy Responses to Covid-19. IMF. Available: https://www.imf.org/en/Topics/imf-and-covid19/Policy-Responses-to-COVID-19#U

ILO (2018) *Women and Men in the Informal Economy: A Statistical Picture.* Geneva: ILO.

ILO (2020) *Monitor Covid-19 and the World of Work*, 2nd edition, April 7th Geneva: ILO.

Noronha, G. and Sikarwar, D. (2020) "Coronavirus: There's no free lunch says CEA on demand for big-bank stimulus." May 6th. *The Economic Times.*

Okonjo-Iweala, N. and Coulibaly, B. (2020) "Africa needs debt relief to fight Covid-19." April 9th. *Project Syndicate.*

Reuters (2020) "World food price index hits 17-month low in May U.N." June 4th, Reuters.

Richardson, P. (2020) "South Africa's Masondo Backs Central Bank bond purchases." May 3rd. Bloomberg.

Segal, S. and Gerstel, D. (2020) "Breaking down the G-20 Covid-19 fiscal response." April 30th. Centre for Strategic and International Studies.

Stranded Workers Action Network (2020) "32 Days and Counting." May 1st. SWAN.

UNCTAD (2020a) UN calls for $2.5 trillion coronavirus crisis package for developing countries. March 30th Available: https://unctad.org/en/pages/newsdetails.aspx?OriginalVersionID -2315

UNCTAD (2020b) "The coronavirus shock: A story of another global crisis foretold and what policymakers should be doing about it." March 9th.

WTO (2020a) "Trade set to plunge as COVID-19 pandemic upends global economy." April 8th. WTO. Available: https://www.wto.org/english/news_e/pres20_e/pr855_e.htm

WTO (2020b) "Trade in services in the context of Covid-19." May 28th. WTO.

Chapter 4

The United States of inequality

David F. Ruccio

> "People on the streets are starting to say, enough. Enough of the inequality, and enough of not having a story about how this ever gets better" (Paul Mason, "Capital in the 21st Century").

We're not all in this together

I'm almost sick of hearing the refrain, "We're all in this together".

I say almost, because I do think there's a utopian moment in that phrase in the midst of the current pandemic. It speaks of solidarity, of being in common, of paying attention to and honoring healthcare workers and others who are currently laboring in "essential" activities while the rest of us are instructed to stay at home. In that sense, it betokens – or at least aspires to – a thinking about and caring for others.

Otherwise, and this is why I'm getting tired of it, the expression serves to deflect our attention from and to paper over the obscene inequalities that afflict American society. I'm referring not only to the pre-existing unequal condition of the United States – the sharp fissures and enormous chasms that were prevalent before COVID-19, which have been highlighted by its spread – but also to the ways the gap between the haves and have-nots has played an important role in actually causing the spread of the dreaded disease, as well as to the real possibility those inequalities will only get worse as a result of the pandemic and the way the response to it has been devised and implemented in the United States.

It has now become almost commonplace, at least within the liberal mainstream media, to note that the unfolding of the novel coronavirus pandemic and the ensuing economic crisis have focused a spotlight on the grotesque inequalities that preceded their onset. With every day that goes by, it has become clearer that the spread of the virus has been profoundly lopsided and uneven – from access to testing and decent, affordable healthcare through who's been able to shelter in place to the presence of underlying "comorbidities", all of which have made the virus both more prevalent and more lethal among working-class Americans, including black bus drivers and Hispanic meatpackers, who had already been left behind.

The pandemic has also brought with it an escalating economic crisis – and that too has reflected existing inequalities. On one hand, tens of millions of low-wage workers have been especially vulnerable to layoffs, furloughs, shortened hours, and pay cuts, with restaurant and retail workers particularly at risk, increasingly obliged to acquire sustenance for themselves and their families in the country's understocked food pantries. On the other hand, millions of other workers – who change the linens in hospitals, aid the sick and dying in nursing homes, pack and transport commodities, pick strawberries, and deliver food – have been forced to have the freedom to continue to commute to and labor at their jobs in perilous conditions, increasing the risk of contagion to themselves, their families, and the communities in which they live.

Meanwhile, the former or current employers of those same workers have been lining up to receive loans from private banks and through the various government bailouts, with few if any restrictions (e.g., on stock buybacks and dividend payments to shareholders), billionaires like Jeff Bezos and Elon Musk have profited handsomely and have seen their wealth soar, and high-profile chief executives of corporations have announced voluntary salary cuts, which turn out to be nothing more than publicity stunts.

Not only do the consequences of the pandemic appear to reflect existing inequalities. It also seems to be the case that those same inequalities are acting as multipliers on the coronavirus's spread and deadliness. It is no coincidence that the United States, with the most unequal distribution of income and wealth among rich countries, also has the highest number of confirmed cases of and deaths from the coronavirus. One reason is that, as inequality has increased, health disparities themselves have widened – and lower-income Americans are much likelier than those at the top to have one or more chronic health conditions, thus exposing them to more risk from the coronavirus. Moreover, those same people are the ones who have been continuing to work in their "essential" in-person jobs, which require more contact both with other workers and customers. In other words, workers, who have more health problems and less health care, are at greater risk of transmission.

The pandemic under extreme inequality thus involves a devastating feedback loop, for workers and society as a whole. The people who can least afford it, given their health and working conditions, are forced into the position of being more exposed to contagion and becoming agents of transmitting the disease to others – in their workplaces and households and in the wider community.

And there's another feedback loop, or cycle of injustice – from existing inequalities through the uneven effects of the pandemic to even more inequality in the future. As Charlie Cooper has argued,

> "With social distancing here to stay for the foreseeable future, it's becoming increasingly clear that the next stage of the pandemic is going to change many lives for the worse.
>
> Specifically, it's going to exacerbate existing inequalities, as the privileged buffer themselves against its pernicious effects while the world's most vulnerable struggle

not to fall through the rapidly widening economic fissures."

For one thing, even after recovery from the immediate affliction, the coronavirus infection may cause lasting damage throughout the body, thereby worsening both the health and economic activity of some (still unknown) portion of an entire generation.

On top of that, the effects of the economic crisis, with tens of millions of workers furloughed or laid off while banks and corporations are bailed out and the stock market is on the rebound, may be even worse than those of the Second Great Depression. Let's remember that, aside from a brief hiatus (in 2009), the trend of growing inequality that preceded the crash of 2007-08 was quickly restored during and after the so-called recovery.

For example, in 2007, the top 1 percent of Americans captured 19.6 percent of pretax national income (the red line in Figure 1), while the bottom 90 percent had only 55 percent (the blue line). By 2016 (the last year for which data are available), the percentages were 19.3 and 54.3, respectively.

The story of wealth inequality is even more dramatic: while the share of wealth owned by the top 1 percent (the green line in Figure 2) grew from 34 percent in 2007 to 36.6 percent in 2016, the small share owned by the bottom 90 percent (the purple line) actually fell, from 30.9 percent to 28.7 percent. Meanwhile, the share of total wealth owned by the bottom 50 percent of U.S.

households barely changed, rising from a miniscule 0.3 percent to a still–tiny 0.4 percent.

Figure 1

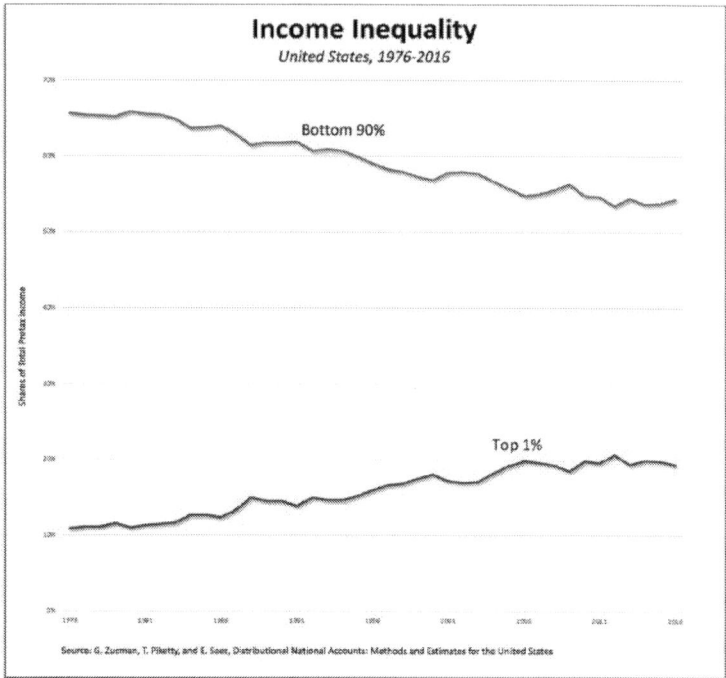

Since we're only two months into the current crisis, we still don't know what the final outcome will be. Even a quick, V–shaped economic recovery (which Trump and his economic advisers are promoting but about which I have serious doubts) would still be accompanied, according to current modeling, with millions of cases of coronavirus and more than 100 thousand deaths, spread unevenly across the U.S. population (especially now that the Trump administration and many governors are focused almost entirely on reopening businesses and forcing workers off unemployment, to compete with one another for the smaller number of existing jobs). While the effects of a longer and more severe downturn – a Third Great Depression, perhaps – will likely be characterized, especially since there have been no major policy shifts compared to a decade ago, by the same kind of unequalizing dynamic.

Figure 2

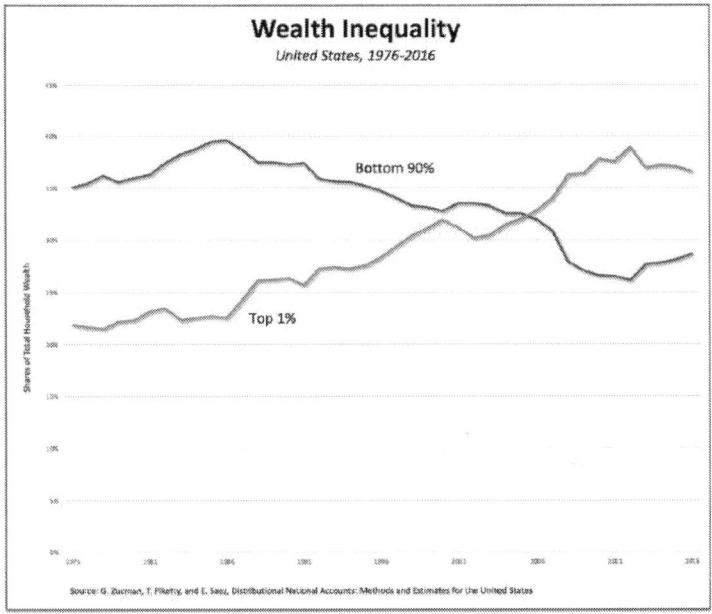

All signs, then, point to the fact that existing inequalities will give rise, on their own and through the consequences of the pandemic, to even more obscene levels of inequality in the immediate future – unless, of course, there is a profound change in the way the American economy and healthcare system are currently organized. Only by eliminating those inequalities can Americans create the real conditions, during the pandemic and after, for being in this together.

What inequality?!

The fact is, even before the novel coronavirus pandemic started to ravage the country, economic inequality in the United States was so obscene, and had convinced more and more people to do something about it, that the business press had initiated a campaign to deny its very existence.

They and the interests they represent were already losing the battle of public opinion. And they decided to do whatever they could to turn things around.

First up was *The Economist*, the "newspaper" of record for liberal capitalism, claiming that new research undermines the pillars of the seemingly universal belief that "inequality has risen in the rich world." Yes, as I have documented from the very beginning on my blog, there are plenty of mainstream economists who have attempted to prove that inequality isn't really a problem – either because it doesn't really exist or, if it does, it's not something we can or should do much about. So, *The Economist* managed to find pieces of research that call into question some of the key pillars of the inequality argument – that the gap between the top 1 percent and everyone else is growing, the middle-class is shrinking, capital is gaining at the expense of labor, and wealth inequality is soaring.

There's no need to waste readers' time repeating the arguments I and many other real-world economists have made on all four of those points over the past decade. Readers can use the search function on this blog to see what I and others have written on these issues – or just read the recent report from the Congressional Budget Office, which I discuss below.

What's more interesting is where *The Economist* wants to take the discussion – away from wealth taxes (of the sort proposed by Democratic presidential candidates Bernie Sanders and Elizabeth Warren) and toward the sorts of policies that, while they won't lessen the degree of inequality, conform to *The Economist's* fantasy of liberal capitalism. Thus, they propose more building (so that young workers can afford housing), antitrust regulation (as if capitalism didn't have an inherent tendency toward monopoly), less regulation of high-income professions (to create more competition for those high-paying jobs), and fewer restrictions on immigration (but only for "high-skilled" workers).

That's *The Economist's* derisory attempt to minimize the existence of inequality (against most of the available evidence and widespread belief) and to devise some tiny tweaks in existing economic arrangements (and thereby avoid more serious efforts to lessen the degree of inequality).

The *Wall Street Journal* also decided to confront the growing campaign against economic inequality by attempting to show that Donald Trump's administration has done more to decrease inequality than Barack

Obama's, by promoting economic growth through deregulation and increased business investment. Now, it's true, Obama oversaw a bailout of Wall Street and a return (after, as I explain above, a brief hiatus in 2009) to the same unequalizing trends that predated the Second Great Depression. So, that's a very low bar to surpass.

And even though the wages of low-income workers had been rising at a faster rate before the pandemic (the supposedly "happy wages of a growing economy"), it is still the case that the wage share of national income (as seen in Figure 3) is still less than what it was in 2008 (when it was 44.9, compared to 43.2 in 2018) and far below its postwar peak in 1970 (at 51.6).

Figure 3

Figure 4

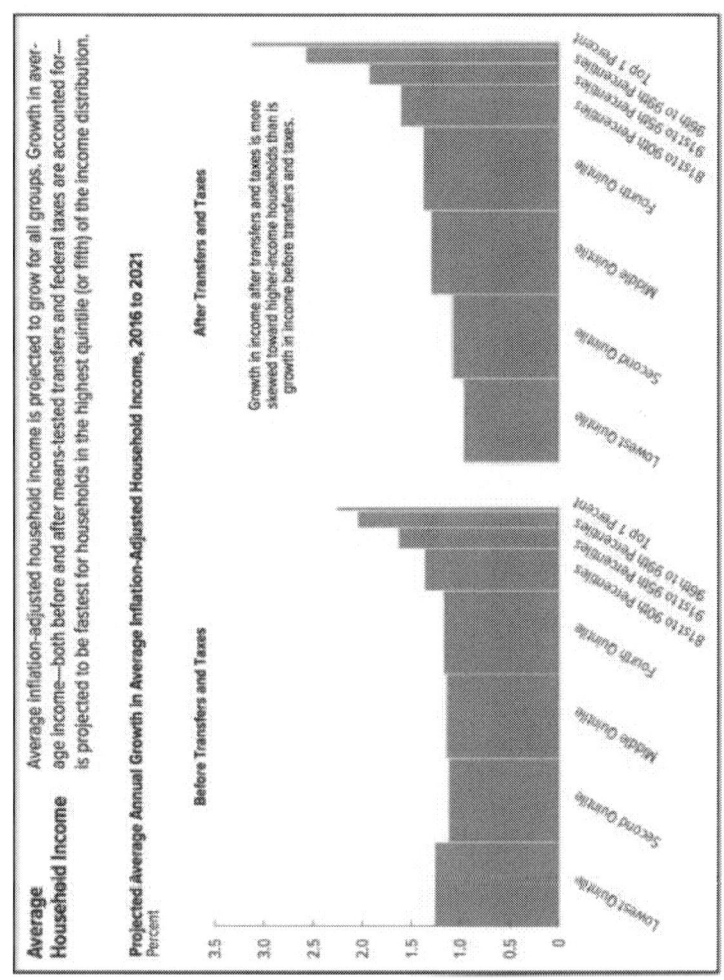

77

To rely on continued growth to solve the problem of inequality is simply a pipe dream, which is even less convincing than the castle in the air invented by the business press on the other side of the pond.

The fact is, the Congressional Budget Office projects that income in the United States – both before and after transfers and taxes – will be more unevenly distributed in 2021 than it was in 2016. That's because, even though average incomes for the bottom four quintiles are expected to grow, incomes for the top quintile (and especially for the top 1 percent) are expected to grow even faster.

Thus, for example, since 1979, while the average incomes of the middle three quintiles are expected to grow (after transfers and taxes) by a total of 57 percent, the incomes of those in the top 1 percent are projected to increase by a whopping 281 percent by 2021.

There's no other way around it: inequality in the United States is obscene, and something – much more than minor regulations and continued growth – needs to be done to overcome it. As it turns out, Americans are fully aware of the problem. For example, according to Gallup, the overall opinion of capitalism held by young adults (both Millennials and Gen Zers) has deteriorated to the point that capitalism and socialism are tied in popularity.

And a recent Reuters/Ipsos poll found that nearly two-thirds of respondents agree that the very rich should pay more.[1]

Among the 4,441 respondents to the poll, 64 percent strongly or somewhat agreed that "the very rich should contribute an extra share of their total wealth each year to support public programs" – the essence of a wealth tax. Results were similar across the lines of gender, race and household income. While support among Democrats was stronger, at 77 percent, even a majority of Republicans, 53 percent, also agreed with the idea.

Moreover, when asked in the poll if "the very rich should be allowed to keep the money they have, even if that means increasing inequality," 54 percent of respondents disagreed.

That's the reason *The Economist* and *The Wall Street Journal* decided to launch their campaign about inequality – to attempt to undermine the widespread belief that inequality is growing and, even more, to challenge any and all efforts to actually do something to create a more just, less unequal economy and society.

Such a campaign may satisfy their readers, at least in the short run, but the problem itself will remain. This

---

[1] Ironically, another recent attempt to undermine the Sanders-Warren proposals of new, higher wealth taxes actually serves to reinforce how extreme wealth inequality is in the United States. While admitting that "only a small segment of the population would be subject to the top rate," the American Action Forum's Douglas Holtz-Eakin and Gordon Gray can only conclude that the taxes would have "broad impacts" only because the wealth holdings of that group "constitute a significant share of the investable wealth in the economy."

election year, especially in the midst of the latest wave of the COVID-19 pandemic, I expect the growing gap between the tiny group at the top and everyone else to overshadow their shabby efforts.

Wages, relative immiseration and surplus

Wages and productivity

Mainstream economists continue to insist that workers benefit from economic growth, because wages rise with productivity.

Here's the argument as explained by Donald J. Boudreaux and Liya Palagashvili:

> Firms cannot afford a misalignment of their workers' pay and productivity increases – the employees will move to other firms eager to hire these now more productive workers. Higher economy-wide productivity, after all, means that workers add more to the bottom lines of employers throughout the economy. To secure the services of these more-productive workers, firms bid up worker pay. This competition for labor services is what links pay to productivity.

Except, of course, the link between wages and productivity has been severed for decades now, going back to the late-1970s. Since then, as the research staff of the Economic Policy Institute have shown, productivity has increased by 70.3 percent but average worker's wages have risen by only 11.1 percent.

Figure 5

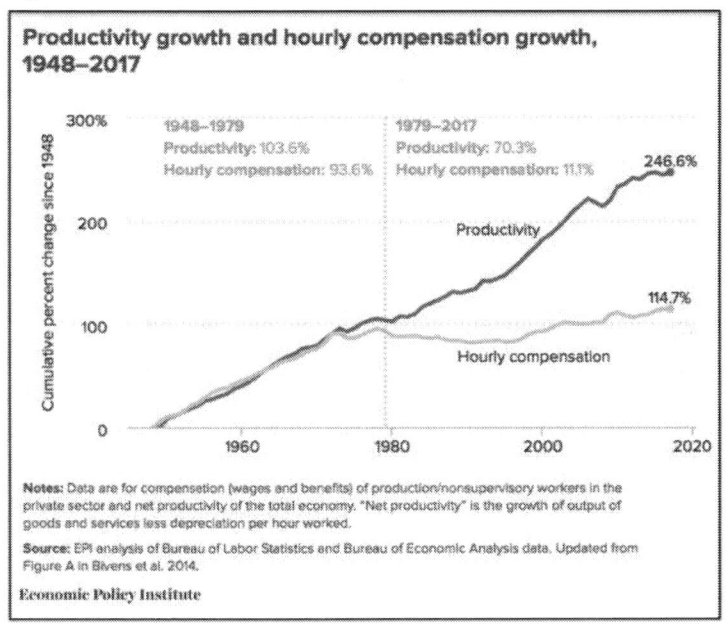

Productivity growth and hourly compensation growth, 1948–2017

Notes: Data are for compensation (wages and benefits) of production/nonsupervisory workers in the private sector and net productivity of the total economy. "Net productivity" is the growth of output of goods and services less depreciation per hour worked.

Source: EPI analysis of Bureau of Labor Statistics and Bureau of Economic Analysis data. Updated from Figure A in Bivens et al. 2014.

Economic Policy Institute

So, no, there is no necessary or automatic link between productivity and wages within the U.S. economy. There may have been such a relationship after World War II, during the so-called Golden Age of American capitalism, but not in recent decades.[2]

---

[2] Even then, as I explained back in 2017: "The fact is, the supposed Golden Age of American capitalism was based on a set of institutions that allowed the boards of directors of large corporations to appropriate a growing surplus and to distribute it as they wished. At first, during the immediate postwar period, that meant growing incomes for those in the bottom 90 percent. But, even then, the mechanisms for distributing income remained in the hands of a very small group at the top. And they had both

A natural question that arises is just where did the excess productivity – the extra surplus U.S. employers appropriated from their workers – go? A significant proportion, as I showed last year, went to higher corporate profits. Another large portion went to those at the very top of the wage distribution.

As is clear in Figure 6, the top 1 percent of earners saw cumulative gains in annual wages of 157.3 percent between 1979 and 2017 – far in excess of economy-wide productivity growth and nearly four times faster than average wage growth (40.1 percent). Over the same period, top 0.1 percent earnings grew 343.2 percent, with the latest spike reflecting the sharp increase in executive compensation.

In other words, corporate executives – on both Main Street and Wall Street – have been able to share in the extra booty captured from American workers, who were forced to have the freedom to sell their ability to work for wages that have barely increased in recent decades.

It's clear then that, for decades now, American workers have been falling further and further behind. And there's simply no justification for this sorry state of affairs – nothing that can rationalize or excuse the growing gap between the majority of people who work for a living and the tiny group at the top.

---

the interest and the means to stop the growth of wages, get even more surplus (from U.S. workers and, increasingly, workers around the globe), and distribute a greater share of that surplus to a tiny group at the very top of the distribution of income."

But that doesn't stop mainstream economists from trying.

Figure 6

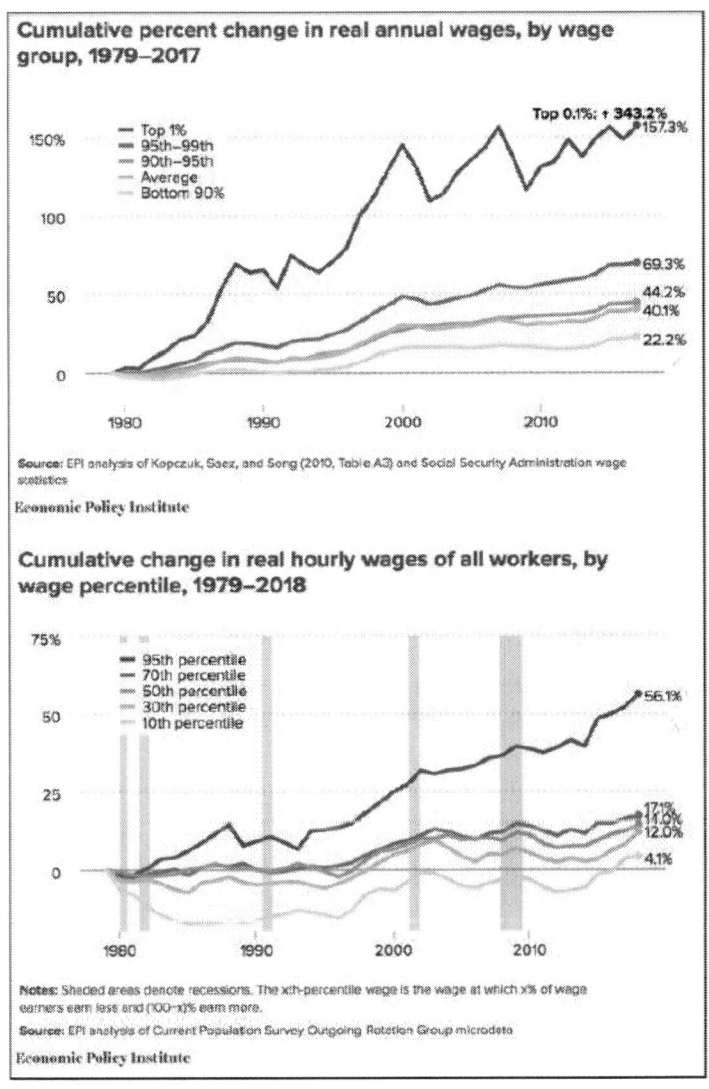

Cumulative percent change in real annual wages, by wage group, 1979–2017

Top 0.1%: ↑ **343.2%**
157.3%

- Top 1%
- 95th–99th
- 90th–95th
- Average
- Bottom 90%

69.3%
44.2%
40.1%
22.2%

Source: EPI analysis of Kopczuk, Saez, and Song (2010, Table A3) and Social Security Administration wage statistics

Economic Policy Institute

Cumulative change in real hourly wages of all workers, by wage percentile, 1979–2018

- 95th percentile
- 70th percentile
- 50th percentile
- 30th percentile
- 10th percentile

56.1%

17%
14.6%
12.0%

4.1%

Notes: Shaded areas denote recessions. The xth-percentile wage is the wage at which x% of wage earners earn less and (100-x)% earn more.

Source: EPI analysis of Current Population Survey Outgoing Rotation Group microdata

Economic Policy Institute

Figure 7

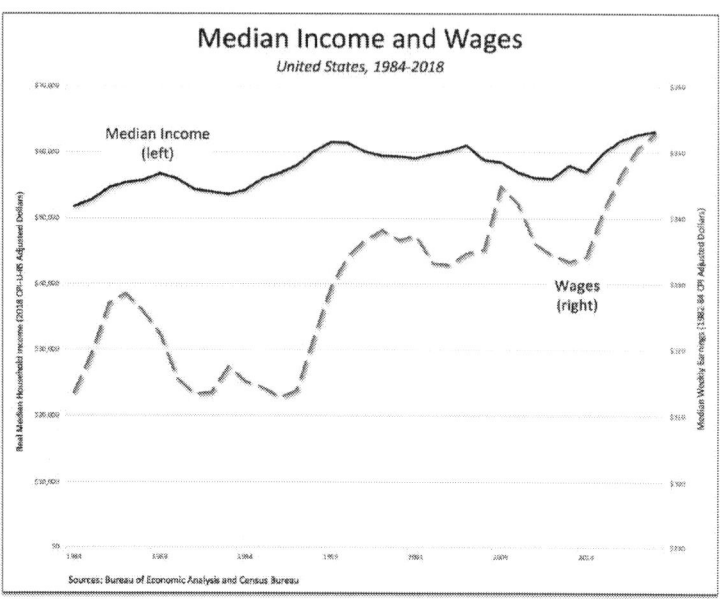

Median Income and Wages
United States, 1984-2018

Look, they say, American workers are clearly better off than they were before. Both real median weekly earnings (the dashed line in Figure 7) and median real household income (the solid line) are higher than they were thirty years ago.

There's no denying that, on average, the absolute levels of worker pay and household income have gone up. That's proof, mainstream economists argue, that workers are enjoying the fruits of their labor.

The problem, though, is that, as I showed above (see Figure 5), the increase in workers' wages pales in comparison to the rise in labor productivity.

In other words, American workers are producing more and more but getting only a tiny share of that increase.

It should come as no surprise, then, that the wage share of national income has fallen precipitously – by 8 percent since 1987 and by 16.5 percent since 1970.[3]

American workers are in fact experiencing a relative immiseration compared to their employers, who are able to capture the additional amount their workers are producing in the form of increased profits. Moreover, American employers have every interest – and more and more means at their disposal – to continue to widen the gap between themselves and their workers.

Not surprisingly, the relative immiseration of American workers shows up in growing inequality – with the share of income captured by the top 1 percent increasing and the share going to the bottom 90 percent falling (as shown in Figure 1 above). Each is a consequence of the other.

---

[3] Let's remember that the wage share is itself not an accurate representation of the share of income going to workers. That's because, as I explained back in 2017, the wage share includes both the labor compensation of proprietors (and thus a portion, minus the capital share, of the income going to proprietors) as well as the multi-million-dollar salaries of corporate executives.

American workers are getting relatively less of what they produce, which means more is available to distribute to those at the top of the distribution of income.

That's what mainstream economists can't or won't understand: that workers may be worse off even as their wages and incomes rise. That problem flies in the face of every attempt to celebrate the existing order by claiming "just deserts."

There's nothing just about the relative immiseration and growing inequality faced by American workers. And nothing that can't be changed by imagining and creating a radically different set of economic institutions.

Surplus

Inequality in the United States is now so obscene that it's impossible, even for mainstream economists, to avoid the issue of surplus.

Consider the two charts at the beginning of this essay. Income inequality is illustrated by the shares of pre-tax national income going to the top 1 percent (the red line) and the bottom 90 percent (the blue line). Between 1976 and 2016 (the last year for which data are available), the share of income at the top soared, from 10.9 percent to 19.3 percent, while for most everyone else the share has dropped precipitously, from 65.6 percent to 54.3 percent.

The distribution of wealth in the United States is even more unequal, as illustrated in Figure 2. From 1976 to 2016, the share of wealth owned by the top 1 percent (the green line) rose dramatically, from 21.9 percent to 36.6 percent, while that of the bottom 90 percent (the purple line) tumbled from an already-low 35.1 percent to an even lower 28.7 percent.

The obvious explanation, at least for some of us, is surplus-value. More surplus has been squeezed out of workers, which has been appropriated by their employers and then distributed to those at the top. They, in turn, have managed to use their ability to capture a share of the growing surplus to purchase more wealth, which has generated returns that lead to even more income and wealth – while the shares of income and wealth of those at the bottom have continued to decline.

But the idea of surplus-value is anathema to mainstream economists. They literally can't see it, because they assume (at least within free markets) workers are paid according to their productivity. Mainstream economic theory excludes any distinction between labor and labor power. Therefore, in their view, the only thing that matters is the price of labor and, in their models, workers are paid the full value of their labor. Mainstream economists assume we live in the land of freedom, equality, and just deserts. Thus, everyone gets what they deserve.

Even if mainstream economists can't see surplus-value, they're still haunted by the idea of surplus. Their cherished models of perfect competition simply can't generate the grotesque levels of inequality in the distribution of income and wealth we are seeing in the United States. That's why in recent years some of them have turned to the idea of rent-seeking behavior, which is associated with exceptions to perfect competition. They may not be able to conceptualize surplus-value but they can see – at least some of them – the existence of surplus income and wealth.

The latest is Mordecai Kurz, who has shown that modern information technology – the "source of most improvements in our living standards" – has also been the "cause of rising income and wealth inequality" since the 1970s.

For Kurz, it's all about monopoly power. High-tech firms, characterized by highly concentrated ownership, have managed to use technical innovations and debt to erect barriers to entry and, once created, to restrain competition.

Figure 8

Company	Monopoly Wealth (2015 billions $)
Apple	435.9
Alphabet (Google)	396.2
Amazon	294.5
AT&T	269.5
Facebook	267.9
Verizon	260.1
Microsoft	258.2
Johnson & Johnson	238.1
Procter & Gamble	209.6
Pfizer	203.6

Thus, in his view, a small group of U.S. corporations has accumulated "surplus wealth" – defined as the difference between wealth created (measured as the market value of the firm's ownership securities) and their capital (measured as the market value of assets employed by the firm in production) – totaling $24 trillion in 2015.

Here's Kurz's explanation:

> "One part of the answer is that rising monopoly power increased corporate profits and sharply boosted stock prices, which produced gains that were enjoyed by a small population of stockholders and corporate management. . .
>
> Since the 1980s, IT innovations have largely been software-based, giving young innovators an advantage. Additionally, "proof of concept" studies are typically inexpensive for software innovations (except in pharmaceuticals); with modest capital, IT innovators can test ideas without surrendering a major share of their stock. As a result, successful IT innovations have concentrated wealth in fewer – and often younger – hands."

In the end, Kurz wants to tell a story about wealth accumulation based on the rapid rise of individual wealth enabled by information based innovations (together with the rapid decline of wealth created in older industries such as railroads, automobiles, and steel), which differs from Thomas Piketty's view of wealth accumulation (presented in his now-famous *Capital in the Twenty-First Century*) as taking place through a lengthy intergenerational process where the rate of return on family assets exceeds the growth rate of the economy.

The problem is, neither Kurz nor Piketty can tell a convincing story about where that surplus comes from in the first place, before it is captured by monopoly firms and transformed into the wealth of the tiny group of households at the top of the distribution.

Kurz and an increasing number of mainstream economists who have latched onto the rent-seeking story (such as Joseph Stiglitz and Paul Krugman) are concerned about obscene and still-growing levels of inequality, and thus remained haunted by the idea of a surplus. But they can't see – or choose not to see – the surplus-value that is created in the process of extracting labor from labor power.

In other words, mainstream economists won't acknowledge the surplus that arises – in the dramatic language of the original critique of political economy – from capitalists' "vampire thirst for the living blood of labor."

Back to the future

The United States can't stay this way forever – with physical distancing (even as some states have decided, precipitously, to allow many businesses to reopen), schools closed (and operating with a semblance of education through online teaching), and economic activity nosediving (even as the stock market soars).

The question that seems to be on everyone's minds is, when are things going to go back to normal?

As I see it, the real question is, who wants to return to normalcy? The novel coronavirus pandemic has revealed, if nothing else, just how dysfunctional the situation was in the United States even before COVID-19 started to cut its deadly path from coast to coast. Tens of millions of workers have been furloughed or laid off and there's still little relief for them in sight.

Instead, they're being forced to have the freedom to drive to food banks to obtain groceries and other household supplies. All the while, their fellow employees, who labor in activities that have been deemed essential, are told to endure dangerous commutes on public transportation and to continue to work under perilous conditions, with little regard for their personal safety. Workers didn't have any say before in the decisions concerning their jobs, let alone in the other policies adopted by their corporate employers – and they certainly don't now.[4]

The pandemic has only served to demonstrate just how unequal life was in the United States before its arrival. According to the Federal Reserve's *Report on the Economic Well-Being of U.S. Households* (updated to include some of

---

[4] Unless, of course, they threaten to withhold their labor or go on strike, which more and more groups of American workers have begun to do, even as the unemployment numbers have soared.

the initial effects of the current crisis), many Americans came into the nationwide lockdown in a precarious financial situation, despite the so-called recovery from the Second Great Depression. At the end of 2019, three in ten adults said they could not cover three months' worth of expenses with savings or borrowing in the case of a job loss, "indicating that they were not prepared for the current financial challenges." Then things got worse: one in five people who were working in February reported that they lost a job or were furloughed in March or the beginning of April 2020, and the effects have been highly concentrated among low-wage workers. Fully 39 percent of former workers living in households earning $40 thousand or less a year lost their jobs, compared with 13 percent in those making more than $100 thousand.

A return to normalcy means going back to those same conditions – in which workers, blacks, Hispanics, and others who make up the bottom of the economic and social pyramid are assaulted by and fundamentally excluded from the major decisions that govern their economic and social lives.

Who would want to return to that?

Chapter 5

Fixing capitalism: stopping inequality at its source

Dean Baker

The basic facts on the growth in inequality in the United States and elsewhere over the last four decades are well-known. There has been a rise in inequality throughout the OECD, but it has been most pronounced in the United States where the share of income going to the top ten percent has risen by 20 percentage points, with the top one percent alone gaining 10 percentage points of national income. If these gains were reversed, it would allow for an increase in the before-tax income of the bottom ninety percent of the population of almost 40 percent.[1]

The usual response from those on the left to these facts are proposals for strengthening labor unions, higher minimum wages, and other labor market protections, as well as more progressive tax and transfer policies to make after-tax income less unequal. While these are sound policy proposals, it is important to recognize that

---

[1] These numbers are drawn from Saez, 2018.

the upward redistribution that we have seen did not just happen as a natural outcome of the market.

The upward redistribution was the result of deliberate policies that were put in place for the purpose of redistributing income upward. These policies could be altered in ways that don't lead to the same degree of inequality, and which are also likely to increase the efficiency of the economy.

The most obvious, and probably most important, of these policies are patents and copyrights. These government-granted monopolies have been strengthened and lengthened over the course of the last four decades. Patents and copyright monopolies do serve a public purpose; they provide incentives for innovation and creative work. However, they are not the only ways to provide incentive. Furthermore, they can always be made stronger or weaker, depending on policy goals and the relative efficiency of these mechanisms compared with alternative incentive mechanisms.

It speaks to the bankruptcy of economics that it is standard for economists to assert that technology is a major or *the* major factor driving inequality, when it should be completely evident that it is our policies on technology, not technology itself, that leads to inequality. In a world without patents and copyrights, Bill Gates would likely still be working for a living instead of being one of the world's wealthiest people.

This paper analyzes some of the ways in which our policies have led to the immense wealth held by those at the top of the income distribution. In addition to patent and copyright monopolies, it also discusses the treatment of the financial sector, rules of corporate governance, and the laws governing Internet intermediaries like Facebook and Google.

The point of this exercise is to show ways in which we can structure the market differently so that it does not lead to extreme inequality. It is fine to try to address inequality with tax and transfer policy, but it is much better to structure the economy in ways that do not generate so much inequality in the first place.

The rich and very rich have long recognized that capitalism in an incredibly malleable system. They have taken advantage of this malleability to structure it in ways that make them the main beneficiaries of economic growth. If progressives fail to recognize this malleability, and instead treat market outcomes as largely given, we will be at an enormous disadvantage in the debate over reducing inequality.

Patent and copyright monopolies

It is truly astounding that the role of patent and copyright monopolies in redistributing income upward is not more widely recognized. These government-granted monopolies are quite explicitly policy interventions, yet they are routinely treated as though they are an inherent feature of the market, with their specific form (e.g. length and scope) rarely figuring in a discussion of income distribution.

At the most basic level, we could envision capitalism without these monopolies existing at all. An economy with all the same property relations we have today, except for patents and copyrights, would have a very different distribution of income. It is standard wisdom among economists and other policy professionals that technology has increased the demand for education, especially for skills in the science, technology, engineering and math (STEM) areas. This is in turn has been a major factor in the growth in wage inequality of the last four decades.

But suppose we were in a world without patents and copyrights, and we had no alternative policies in place to replace the incentives provided by these monopolies. In that case the amount of money going for research into the development of new drugs, medical equipment, chemicals, software and computers would plummet. The demand for workers with skills in these areas would also plunge. In that case, we would not be seeing any technology-induced increase in wage inequality, as there would be no reason to believe that people with college and advanced degrees in the STEM fields would be doing especially well in the labor market.

The price of all these items would be far cheaper, since they would sell in a free market where anyone could produce the latest prescription drug, MRI machine, or computer without regard to who might take credit for their invention. That would mean that real wages for workers with less education would be considerably higher, since the price of much of what they consume would be much lower.

This simplistic thought experiment is important since it should drive home at a very basic level the fact that inequality in market outcomes is entirely the result of how we choose to structure markets, not the exogenous development of technology. This doesn't mean that we have not benefitted enormously from the innovations that have come about as a result of the incentives that were provided by patent and copyright monopolies. But we have to understand that these are policy tools that can be altered and, in some cases replaced by alternative mechanisms that might be equally or more effective in providing incentives, while not producing the same amount of inequality.

The area where the strongest case can be made that patent monopolies have not been a good mechanism for supporting research is prescription drugs. Patent monopolies both create the absurd problem of making life-saving drugs unaffordable and lead to perverse incentives for drug manufacturers.

The first point is straightforward. Drugs are almost invariably cheap to manufacture and distribute. Without patent monopolies, most drugs would be selling for little more than the price of generic aspirin. There would no issue of affordability, except for the very poor.

However, when we give companies patent monopolies, we get into a situation where drug companies can charge enormous prices for drugs that are often essential for people's health and/or their life. Then we have the absurd situation where progressives push for government intervention to impose price controls or negotiate prices, as though the world with a government-granted patent monopoly is somehow a free market.

In addition to the problem that the government has created an artificial monopoly, we can't even tell the standard story of consumer sovereignty, where the consumer knows how much a product is worth to them. In the case of prescription drugs, we almost always have third party payers, in the form of either the government or insurers. The price that is paid is therefore almost entirely the result of political decisions, either directly as a result of a government determined price, or indirectly through government regulation of insurers.

But coping with exorbitant prices is perhaps the less important part of the problem. Patent monopolies not only provide incentives for drug companies to develop new drugs, they also provide incentive for them to market them as widely as possible. This means that they have incentive to promote their drugs in contexts where they may not be the best treatment for a specific condition. They also have incentive to conceal evidence that their drugs may not be as effective as claimed or that they could be harmful.

The most obvious example of companies responding in this way to patent incentives is the pushing of opioids by Purdue Pharma and other manufacturers. These companies have paid billions in settlements based on the allegation that they deliberately misled doctors on the addictiveness of their new generation of opioid drugs in order to maximize sales. Needless to say, these drug companies would have had much less incentive to lie to doctors if their opioids were selling as cheap generics.

The patent system also encourages secrecy in research. Science advances most quickly when it is fully open and findings are widely shared. However, a company hoping to gain a key patent on an important drug is not going to make its latest research available for potential competitors. We see this sort of situation with the coronavirus, where research teams around the world raced to develop an effective vaccine. Progress would almost certainly be far quicker if all their results were shared so researchers could benefit from the successes and failures of their fellow scientists.[2]

It is of course possible to have alternative mechanisms to finance research. The United States spends more than $40 billion a year financing biomedical research through the National Institutes of Health. This funding could be expanded to replace the roughly $75 billion a year in private research supported through patent monopolies.[3]
The additional money could be routed through private drug companies in a manner similar to the way the Defense Department awards long-term contracts to develop weapon systems. The big difference is that, while there are good reasons for keeping military research secret (we don't want ISIS to be able to get information on our latest weapons systems off the web), there is no reason to want to keep biomedical research secret. A

---

[1] To some extent this sort of sharing is happening with research on vaccines and treatments of the coronavirus, but it would be even more pervasive if no one had an interest in gaining a patent monopoly.
[3] The figure for 2018 was $75.1 billion, Bureau of Economic Analysis, National Income and Product Accounts, Table 5.6.5, Line 9.

condition of the funding can be both, that any patents are in the public domain, so new drugs are sold as cheap generics, and that all findings must be posted on the web as soon as practical.

It is not necessary to go into great detail here on the mechanics of a system of publicly funded drug research, the point is that there are plausible alternatives to the system of patent monopoly financing that are arguably far more efficient.[4] And, it is important to realize that there is an enormous amount of money at stake. In the case of prescription drugs alone, the difference between the monopoly protected prices we pay now, and the free market price, would almost certainly come to more than $400 billion annually. This is approximately 1.8 percent of GDP, far more than the current amount raised through the corporate income tax.

And prescription drugs are just part of the story of the impact of patent and copyright monopolies. Medical equipment is expensive almost entirely because there are patents on MRIs and other scanning devices, kidney dialysis machines, and other forms of therapeutic equipment. The difference between current prices and free market prices would almost certainly be more than $100 billion a year. Software could be transferred at zero cost in the absence of patent protection. If we add in video games, books, recorded music, movies, and other video material, we could easily be looking at savings of

---

[4] For more discussion of alternative funding systems see Baker, Jayadev, and Stiglitz 2017, Baker 2016a, and Baker 2020.

more than $1 trillion a year in a patent/copyright free world, roughly half of annual corporate profits.[5]

In short, there is an enormous amount of money at stake with the current patent and copyright system. And, the beneficiaries are of course primarily those at the top end of the income distribution. In addition to Bill Gates, the list of the country's richest people is chock full of those who have made their fortunes from patent and copyright monopolies. An analysis of the 100 richest people on the Forbes 400 found that more than 27 percent of the estimated wealth came from sources that were heavily dependent on patent and/or copyright monopolies. Adding in the marginal cases brought the figure to more than 43 percent of their wealth (Baker, 2020; Dolan and Kroll, 2018).

It is an enormous analytic and political mistake for progressives to treat these vast fortunes as simply market outcomes. The beneficiaries of patent and copyright monopolies have been quite active in structuring them in ways that ensure they get as much money as possible. Progressives should be every bit as active in pushing in the opposite direction.

The financial industry: making vast fortunes and only incidentally serving the real economy

A vibrant economy clearly needs a strong financial sector capable of both quickly and cheaply processing transactions and also providing capital to businesses and

---

[5] These calculations are explained in more detail in Baker, 2020.

households. Unfortunately, this is not a good description of the U.S. financial industry. While it provides the basis for a larger share of top one percent incomes than any other sector of the economy (Bakija et al., 2012), it is certainly not efficient in processing transactions and channeling capital to its best uses.

At the most basic level, the narrow financial sector (securities and commodity trading and investment banking) has exploded as a share of GDP. This sector increased from 0.44 percent of private sector output in 1970 to 2.35 percent of private sector output in 2018.[6] Given the Internet bubble in the 1990s and the housing bubble in the last decade, it would be difficult to maintain that the sector has been directing capital to its best uses.

Other parts of the financial industry also do not seem to be serving the real economy well. Private equity and hedge fund partners disproportionately sit among the list of the very highest paid people in the country, often drawing annual pay checks in the tens of millions and sometimes hundreds of millions. It is difficult to see what these people do to justify such extraordinary incomes. This is not a moral judgement on the behavior of private equity and hedge funds (which is often bad for both the economy and society), it is simply a comment on their failure to produce outsized returns to their investors.

---

[6] The size of the sector was calculated from Bureau of Economic Analysis data by taking the lines for compensation in the securities and commodities trading industry and also investment funds and trusts (Bureau of Economic Analysis, National Income and Product Accounts Tables, Table 6.2D, lines 59 and 61 for 2014 and Table 6.2B, lines 55 and 59 for 1970).

In the 1980s and 90s, private equity funds did consistently outperform the S&P 500 index by substantial margins. Since 2006, however, the median private equity firm's performance just matched the S&P 500 and underperformed broader indexes, like the Russell 3000, that include the smaller companies that PE firms typically buy (Appelbaum and Batt, 2017).

Many hedge funds have done even worse by their investors. A recent study of the ten-year returns of the endowments of the Ivy League schools found that the endowments of all eight schools lagged a simple indexed portfolio that was 60 percent stock and 40 percent bonds (Markov Processes International, 2018). In some cases, the gap was substantial. Harvard set the mark with its annual returns lagging a simple 60/40 portfolio by more than 3 percentage points. This is actually a very low bar, since hedge funds are inherently risky, which means that a more appropriate comparison might be a 70/30 portfolio or even 80/20. Comparisons with these higher-risk portfolios over this period would make the performance of the endowments look even worse. Needless to say, the hedge fund managers, who control the bulk of the money in these endowments were very well compensated for losing these schools large amounts of money.

Another way that the financial industry makes large amounts of money at the expense of society is by writing deceptive contracts that effectively allow it to exploit its customers. For example, many banks charge large fees for late mortgage checks or for even short term overdrafts of a bank account that many of their customers are not aware of until they have to pay them.

There is no social purpose served by providing incentives for deceptive contracts that allow for abusive practices. We should not want to give companies incentives to find creative ways to cheat their customers. Nor should we want to force people to carefully scrutinize contracts to ensure that they are not being ripped off. This is a case where regulations requiring simple standardized contracts can provide clear efficiency gains to the economy and likely much less revenue to the financial industry.

Another area where the financial industry makes large profits at the expense of the economy and society is by designing tax avoidance schemes. There is insufficient appreciation of tax avoidance as a source of inequality. If a company can save $1 billion on its taxes, in principle it would be willing to pay lawyers or accountants up to $999 million to do it. The tax avoidance industry can be quite lucrative for effective practitioners. (This can blur into outright tax evasion, but we can be generous and focus on legal activity.)

There are simple policies that can radically reduce the amount of resources drained off by the financial sector and the extraordinary incomes going to its top earners. At the top of the list would be a modest financial transactions tax. This would drastically reduce the volume of trading in the sector, while raising a substantial amount of revenue. For example, a tax set at 0.2 percent on stock trades, and scaled for other assets, could raise in the neighborhood of $120 billion annually, more than 0.5 percent of GDP (Baker, 2016b).

Most estimates put the elasticity of trading volume with respect to price near -1.0, which means that the reduction in expenditures on trading would be roughly equal to the amount of revenue raised from the tax. This would mean that ordinary investors would effectively see the burden of the tax fully offset by a reduction in other trading costs, leaving them unharmed by the tax. The burden of the tax is then borne fully by the financial industry in the form of less trading revenue. (This assumes that the cost of the tax is passed on fully in higher costs per trade.)

This sort of tax can be seen as equivalent to a sales tax on the financial industry. There is no reason that the financial sector should be exempted from the sort of sales taxes, or value-added taxes, that are imposed on other industries, a point that has even been noted by the International Money Fund (2010).

Also, it is important to remember that the financial markets depend in very fundamental ways on the backstop of the Federal Reserve Board and other central banks. We saw this in the financial crisis in 2008 and 2009, where the major banks were directly bailed out by central banks and governments. There were also numerous interventions to keep markets operating smoothly.

This happened again with the coronavirus, where the Federal Reserve Board engaged in trillions of dollars of asset purchases to sustain an orderly market. These interventions are arguably desirable from the standpoint of the economy as a whole, but they undeniable help to prop up the financial industry. The sector would face enormously higher risks if it did not have central banks and treasuries explicitly providing insurance against extreme events.

The private equity industry also relies very directly on the government since it makes much of its money through the public sector. More than a quarter of its funding comes from public sector pension funds. Public sector funds have an incentive to place money with private equity funds because they can impute higher returns to these investments than their investments in equities or other assets. As a result, the pensions appear better funded, even though returns on private equity have not been exceeding returns on market indexes.

Private equity funds are also benefited by the secrecy around their fees. It is a standard practice for private equity funds to prohibit their investors from disclosing their fees. It is likely that fees would be considerably lower, along with the paychecks to private equity partners, if public pension funds were required to clearly disclose all terms of their contract.

There is a similar story with hedge funds. They routinely require their clients not to disclose the terms of their contracts. This means that students, professors, and other employees at major universities will never know how much money they paid hedge fund partners to lose their schools money. In the case of hedge funds, their income is probably also helped by the fact that many hedge fund partners are friendly with the university administrations that employ them. While it may not be appropriate for the government to require private universities to disclose hedge fund fees, that is the sort of demand that progressive students, faculty, and workers can reasonably demand of a university administration.

Getting rich through deceptive contracts is exactly the sort of abuse that the Consumer Financial Protection Bureau was intended to stop. Obviously, the Trump administration supports deceptive contracts as a way to get rich, but that is not intrinsic to capitalism.

In the case of the tax shelter industry, the best way to limit its size is to limit opportunities and incentives for avoidance. This means thinking carefully about the structure and the size of a tax. A more progressive tax is not always better, if it proves not to be enforceable. As a simple and obvious point, if we impose a 90 percent marginal tax rate, we are paying the rich 90 cents to hide $1.00 of income. When we are talking about incomes in the millions and tens of millions of dollars, many rich people will find ways to take advantage of this implicit payoff.

Much tax avoidance is in the corporate sector. We can design a simple and virtually unavoidable corporate income tax. We can simply require companies to give the government non-voting shares in an amount equal to the legislated tax rate (e.g. a 25 percent tax rate means the government's shares are equal to 25 percent of the total shares outstanding). These shares get the same dividend or buyback treatment as any other shares. This means that the only way that companies can cheat the government out of its tax take is by cheating its shareholders as well (Klein, 2017).[7]

While the policies outlined here just scratch the surface, they show that there are effective ways to limit the vast fortunes that are being made in the financial sector. None of these or other proposals in any way imply the end of capitalism as a system. A capitalist economy with a financial transactions tax and a requirement that corporate income taxes be made through government-owned non-voting stock shares, is still very much a capitalist economy. However, it would be a capitalist economy with far fewer vast fortunes being made in the financial sector

Out of control CEO pay

In the last four decades, CEO pay at large corporations has increased from 20 to 30 times the pay of the typical worker, to more than 200 times the pay of a typical worker. It is not uncommon to see CEOs of major corporations earn more than $20 million in a single year, and paychecks of $30 or $40 million are no longer rare.

---

[7] There have been efforts in recent years to limit one aspect of corporate income tax gaming by making the share of a multinational corporation's income that is taxable in a country, proportional to its sales in that country (Morgan 2016, Morgan 2017). This limits a common form of tax avoidance where companies claim the bulk of their income accrued in countries with low tax rates. The system of basing taxes on returns to shareholders described above would require this sort of mechanism, but it has the advantage of getting around other forms of gaming that result in the understatement of profits.

No one can question the explosion of CEO pay over the last four decades, but there is a dispute over whether it can be justified. The argument in support of soaring CEO paychecks is that their pay reflects returns to shareholders. In this story, if shareholders skimped on CEO pay, say by giving them \$2–\$3 million instead of \$15 to \$20 million, they would get less talented people as CEOs, or alternatively they would get CEOs who did not work as hard. The result would be lower stock returns. So, in a world where stockholders are assumed to be the ultimate controllers of the corporation, the extraordinary CEO pay that we have seen is justified by the returns they produce for shareholders.

The big problem with this argument is that returns to shareholders do not appear to be closely related to CEO pay. In their book, *Pay Without Performance*, Lucien Bebchuck and Jesse Fried (2006), reviewed a large body of evidence suggesting that CEO pay had little relationship to the returns they produced for shareholders. There is much evidence in this book to support that view, but just to give the most egregious failing in the structure of CEO pay, the incentive component of CEO pay rarely compares returns to a reference group. This means that if the stock price of the company rises due to a general rise in the stock market, the CEO will be richly rewarded. Or when events outside the CEO's control leads to industry specific gains, such as the impact of a rise in world oil prices on the shares of an oil company's stock price, the CEO is again richly rewarded. It is possible to write contracts that base CEO pay on stock returns relative to a set of comparable companies, but pay packages are rarely designed this way.

Since Bebchek and Fried wrote their book there have been several other noteworthy studies on this topic. For example, Shue and Townsend (2016) did an analysis of awards of stock options in the 1990s as the stock market soared. The huge run up in the market meant that the value of an option increased enormously over the course of the decade, yet almost no boards reduced the number of options granted to their CEOs. They suggest a form of "money illusion" in the awarding of stock options. Boards did not want to be seen as cutting CEO pay.

Schieder and Baker (2017) looked at patterns in CEO pay in the health insurance industry following the implementation of the Affordable Care Act (ACA) in 2013. One of the provisions in the ACA ended the tax deduction for CEO pay in excess of $1 million. With the 35 percent corporate tax rate in effect at the time, this implied an increase of more than 50 percent in the after-tax cost of CEO pay to employers. If insurers were equating the returns provided by the CEO with their pay, this change in the tax treatment should have unambiguously led to a reduction of CEO pay in health insurance relative to other industries.

The paper reviewed a wide variety of specifications, controlling for revenue growth, profit growth, stock price appreciation and other factors. In none of them did it find any evidence of a fall in CEO pay in the health insurance industry relative to other sectors.

Another study (Marshall and Lee, 2016) examined patterns in CEO pay for 429 large firms over the years 2006-2015. It found that CEO pay was actually negatively correlated with returns to shareholders. Again, this is hard to reconcile with a story where high CEO pay is explained by the returns they provide to shareholders.

Perhaps the most damning piece of evidence in this respect is the simplest. If we take returns to shareholders over the last two decades, they have actually have been relatively low by historical standards. From 2000 to 2020, real annual returns have averaged less than 4.0 percent. That compares to a longer-term average real return in prior decades of 7.0 percent. This story is changed little if we move our reference point back a couple of years to 1998 to avoid the peak of the bubble or move back to January of 2020, to skip the recent fall related to coronavirus pandemic. Returns have still been low by historic standards.

It is hard to tell a story of companies being run to maximize shareholder returns, in contrast to a prior period where companies were ostensibly pursuing a broader range of goals, if shareholders have not actually been getting especially good returns. What corporate management has most obviously succeeded in doing is maximizing the pay of corporate management. Since CEOs have been more successful at getting high pay for CEOs than getting high returns for shareholders, it reasonable to assume that this is what in fact they have been trying to do.

It is easy to tell a story whereby CEOs and top management are effectively able to rip off the companies for which they work. Corporate boards typically owe their allegiance to top management, who usually play a large role in their selection. Once a person gets on a board, it is almost impossible for them to be removed by shareholders. Well over 99 percent of the board members nominated for re-election by the board win re-election.

Since being a board member of a large corporation is extraordinarily lucrative – the pay is typically well over $100,000 a year for roughly 150 hours of work – most board members will want to remain on the boards where they serve (Clifford, 2017). The route to keeping a seat is by not offending other board members. This presumably means not asking questions like "could we get a CEO who is just as good for half the pay?" In this world, board members are sitting on huge piles of corporate money and have no reason not to want to keep their CEO and other top management happy. This means that CEO pay essentially can rise without check.

It is also important to understand that this is not just an issue with the CEO; after all, there are not that many CEOs. If the CEO is getting paid $15 to $20 million, it is likely that the chief financial officer and other top executives are getting paid close to $10 million. And the third tier in the corporate hierarchy can be getting pay in the range of $2 to $3 million. It would be a very different world if the CEO was getting a paycheck in the range of $2 to $3 million, as would be the case if we still saw the pay ratios of the 1960s and 1970s. And of course, more pay going to the top means less pay for everyone else.

The excessive pay for CEOs also affects pay in other sectors of the economy. It is common for top executives for charities and major universities to earn more than $1 million a year. This is justified by the valid claim that they would be earning far more money if they were running a corporation of comparable size.

There is nothing intrinsic to capitalism that requires a corporate governance structure that effectively gives control to top management. There are many ways that governance can be reformed to give more effective control to shareholders and/or workers.[8]

One very simple reform would be to take advantage of the "Say on Pay" provision that was put in place in 2010 Dodd-Frank financial reform bill. This provision requires that the CEO's pay package be put up for a non-binding vote of shareholders every three years. As it stands, the vote is non-binding and less than 3.0 percent are voted down.

However, it would be possible to have some real consequence for a negative vote. Suppose corporate boards would forfeit their pay if a pay package was voted down. It probably would not take too many negative votes to get boards to start asking whether they could get away with paying their CEOs less money.

There are undoubtedly other changes to corporate governance that could be effective in putting downward

---

[8] Under Germany's "co-determination" policy, workers hold 50 percent of the board seats of major corporations. CEO pay is considerably lower on average in Germany.

pressure on CEO pay, but the point is that there is nothing intrinsic to capitalism that requires CEOs get paid $15 to $20 million a year. We have in place a structure that promotes these sorts of pay packages. We could have a different structure, that is every bit as capitalistic (perhaps even more so if it gives more control to shareholders), but has much lower pay at the top.

The United States would still be capitalist if Facebook was subject to the same libel law as CNN

Two of the great sources of personal fortunes in the last decade are Facebook and Google. Both companies have near monopolies in their respective areas, which raises serious anti-trust concerns. Their near monopoly status is undoubtedly due in part to network effects which give a dominant actor a large advantage over smaller competitors, but both companies have acted aggressively to buy up potential competitors. If we are concerned about equality, and efficiency, then we need an effective anti-trust regime, which does not appear to have been the case in recent decades.

However, beyond the issues of anti-trust, there is also a question of how these huge companies are regulated. Most immediately, it is difficult to understand the rationale for Section 230 of the 1996 Communications Decency Act. This is a provision that exempts Internet intermediaries from being subject to the same rules on libel as traditional media.

This provision, which was passed into law in the early days of the Internet, arguably makes sense insofar as intermediaries can be seen as common carriers, like a phone company, which has no involvement with content. But a company like Facebook, that sells ads, sells promoted material on people's pages, and sells personal information about its users, does not fit the conventional definition of a common carrier.

Since Facebook is heavily involved with the content on its system, there is no reason it should not be subject to the same liability laws as media outlets like CNN or the New York Times. This means not only that it would be responsible for any items that it sponsored, but also for circulating libelous material through its system.

This point is important and often missed in the discussion. If the *New York Times* were to run an op-ed column or an ad with material that was false and damaging to an individual or corporation, it could face substantial legal liability, even though it was not the originator of the content. By contrast, Section 230 exempts Facebook from the same responsibility for spreading false and damaging claims through its system.

It would be impossible for Facebook to effectively screen the hundreds of millions of items posted daily by its billions of users. However, it could review items that are called to its attention and remove them if it determines them to be libelous. Since Facebook also has a record of all the people who viewed a specific item, it could also be required to send a correction to all of these people.

If Facebook faced such requirements, it would require a large amount of additional staffing, which would substantially reduce its profits. However, this is a requirement that Facebook's competitors in the traditional media have long been subject to since their inception. There is no obvious rationale for holding Facebook, or other Internet intermediaries to a more lenient standard, simply because it is on the Internet.

Setting up such a system would be very expensive for Facebook. And, Mark Zuckerberg has said that he doesn't want to be responsible for determining what is true and what isn't. But this is a call that his competitors in traditional media outlets have to make all the time. If Zuckerberg decides that he and his corporation lack the same capabilities as a traditional media company, then he can turn to operating Facebook like a common carrier, which means no charging for ads or tracking users' behavior. Facebook, can just be a bulletin board where people pay a fee for the service.

This would likely be a huge hit to Facebook's profits. The company would likely have to hire tens of thousands of people to review complaints. It would undoubtedly also occasionally lose libel suits as a result of failing to promptly remove libelous material. A less profitable Facebook would make Mark Zuckerberg and other Facebook millionaires and billionaires considerably less rich.

Ending the Section 230 exemption would have an impact on other Internet companies as well. The impact would almost certainly not be as large as with Facebook, but this would amount to a leveling of the playing field between Internet media outlets and traditional ones. This is a reform that would in no way jeopardize the status of the U.S. as a capitalist system, but it would limit one of the main routes to great fortunes in recent years and also make a far more level playing field in the media industry.

Conclusion: capitalism does not have to be structured to give all the money to the rich

Capitalism is an incredibly malleable system. This is a fundamental point that anyone with an interest in politics or economic policy should recognize. It is important for two reasons.

First, we don't have a spare system in the trunk. For better or worse, we are going to have a capitalist economy long into the future. This is in part because of the inherent difficulties in constructing a fundamentally new system. We can't just get out our blueprints and then put them into practice. But part of the difficulty also stems from the malleability of the capitalist system. If the system were ever threatened in some fundamental way, there is enormous room to make changes to head off the challenge: in effect buying off the opposition.

The other reason it is essential to recognize the malleability of capitalism is because we must realize that the massive increase in inequality over the last four decades was by design. There was nothing intrinsic to the dynamics of capitalism that led to this inequality. The rich used their power in ways to redesign the structure of the economy so that a much larger share of income flowed upward. To a large extent they were able to get away with this restructuring because they altered important rules, like those on patent and copyright monopolies, when no one else was paying attention.

The time has come for progressives to start paying attention. We have to look at how the rules are structured. And, we have to be every bit as aggressive in restructuring them in ways that lead to more equality as the rich have been in rigging them to make themselves richer.

References

Appelbaum, Eileen and Rosemary Batt (2017) "Update: Are Lower Private Equity Returns the New Normal?," Center for Economic and Policy Research, February.

Association for Accessible Medicines (2017) "Generic Drug Access & Savings in the U.S.." Washington, DC: Association for Accessible Medicines (AAM). https://accessiblemeds.org/resources/blog/2017-generic-drug-access-and-savings-us-report.

Baker, Dean (2016a) "Rents and Inefficiency in the Patent and Copyright System: Is There a Better Route?" Washington, DC: Center for Economic and Policy Research. http://cepr.net/images/stories/reports/rents-inefficiency-patents-2016-08.pdf?v=2

Baker, Dean (2016b) "Reining in Wall Street to Benefit All Americans," New York, NY: Century Foundation https://www.cepr.net/images/stories/reports/reining-in-wall-street-to-benefit-all-americans.pdf?v=2.

Baker, Dean (2020) "Is Intellectual Property the Root of all Evil." In Stiglitz, J.E. and R. von Arnim eds, *The Great Polarization: Economics, Institutions and Policies in the Age of Inequality.* Cambridge University Press Initiative for Policy Dialogue, NY, NY.

Baker, Dean, Arjun Jayadev and Joseph Stiglitz (2017) "Innovation, Intellectual Property, and Development: A Better Set of Approaches for the 21st Century." AccessIBSA: Innovation & Access to Medicines in India, Brazil & South Africa.

Bakija, J., A. Cole, and B. Heim (2012) "Jobs and Income Growth of Top Earners and the Causes of Changing Income Inequality: Evidence from U.S. Tax Return Data." Manuscript, Williams College.

Bebchuck, Lucian Arye and Jesse Fried (2006) *Pay Without Performance: The Unfulfilled Promise of Executive Compensation.* Cambridge, Mass.: Harvard University Press

Bureau of Economic Analysis (2020) "NIPA Tables." Suitland, MD: Bureau of Economic Analysis. https://apps.bea.gov/iTable/iTable.cfm?ReqID=19&isuri=1&step= 4&0=flatfiles#reqid=19&step=4&isuri=1&1921=flatfiles.

Clifford, Steven (2017) *The CEO Pay Machine: How It Trashes America and How to Stop It.* New York: Penguin Random House.

Collins, Simon (2016) "1,000-Fold Mark-Up for Drug Prices in High Income Countries Blocks Access to HIV, HCV and Cancer Drugs." HIV i-Base, October 24. http://www.thebodypro.com/content/78658/1000-fold-mark-up-for-drug-prices-in-high-income-c.html.

Dolan, Kerry A. and Luisa Kroll. 2018. "The World's Billionaires List." *Forbes*, March 6. https://www.forbes.com/billionaires/list/.

International Monetary Fund (2010) "A Fair and Substantial Contribution by the Financial Sector: Final Report to the G-20." Washington, DC: International Monetary Fund.

Klein, Matthew (2017) "The Most Elegant Corporate Tax Reform." *Financial Times*, October 31.

Markov Processes International (2018) "Measuring the Ivy 2018: A Good Year for Returns, but Is Efficiency Becoming an Issue?" November 29.

Marshall, Ric and Linda-Eling Lee (2016) "Are CEOs Paid For Performance? Evaluating the Effectiveness of Equity Incentives." New York, N.Y.: MSCI.

Morgan, Jamie (2016) "Corporation Taxation as a Problem of MNC Organizational Circuits: The Case for Unitary Taxation." *The British Journal of Politics and International Relations*, 2016, Vol. 18(2) 463–481.

Morgan, Jamie (2017) "Taxing the powerful, the rise of populism and the crisis in Europe: the case for the EU Common Consolidated Corporate Tax Base." *International Politics*, V54, pp. 533–551.

Saez, Emmanuel (2018) "Income Inequality in the United States, 1913-1998" with Thomas Piketty, *Quarterly Journal of Economics*, 118(1), 2003, 1-39" Updated to 2018.

Schieder, Jessica, and Dean Baker (2018) *Does Tax Deductibility Affect CEO Pay? The Case of the Health Insurance Industry.* Economic Policy Institute, March 2018.

Shue, Kelly and Richard Townsend (2016) "Growth Through Rigidity: An Explanation for the Rise in CEO Pay." Cambridge, Mass.: National Bureau of Economic Research. Working Paper 21975. http://www.nber.org/papers/w21975.

Chapter 6

Inequality challenge in pursued economies[1]

Richard C. Koo

Income inequality has become one of the hottest and most controversial issues in economics not only in the developed world but also in China and elsewhere as well. Many are growing increasingly uncomfortable with the divide between the haves and the have-nots, especially after Thomas Piketty's *Capital in the 21st Century*[2] sparked a fresh debate on the optimal distribution of wealth, an issue that had been largely overlooked by the economics profession.

This paper argues that the determinants of income inequality changes depending on the stage of economic development. The three stages of industrialization identified for this purpose are: urbanizing era, when the economy has yet to reach the Lewis Turning Point (LTP), post-LTP maturing or golden era when the economy moves along an upward sloping labor supply curve, and

---

[1] This paper draws heavily from Chapters 3, 4 and 5 of the author's *The Other Half of Macroeconomics and the Fate of Globalization* published in 2018 by John Wiley but is reorganized with a focus on inequality.
[2] Piketty, Thomas. (2014) *Capital in the Twenty-First Century*. Belknap Press

pursued era, when the return on capital is higher abroad in emerging economies than at home. The LTP refers to the point at which urban factories have finally absorbed all the surplus rural labor. (In this essay, the term LTP is used only because it is a well-known expression for a specific point in a nation's economic development; the use of this term does not refer to the model of economic growth proposed by Sir Arthur Lewis.)

At the advent of industrialization, most people are living in rural areas. Only the educated elite, who are very few in number, have the technical knowledge needed to produce and market goods. Families whose ancestors have lived on depressed farms for centuries have no such knowledge. Most of the gains during the initial stage of industrialization therefore go to the educated few, while the rest of the population simply provides labor for the industrialists. And with so many surplus workers in the countryside, worker wages remain depressed for decades until the LTP is reached.

Exhibit 1 illustrates this from the perspective of labor supply and demand. The labor supply curve is almost horizontal (DHK) until the Lewis turning point (K) is reached because there is an essentially unlimited supply of rural laborers seeking to work in the cities. A business owner can attract any number of such laborers simply by paying the going wage (DE).

Exhibit 1 Three phases of industrialization/globalization

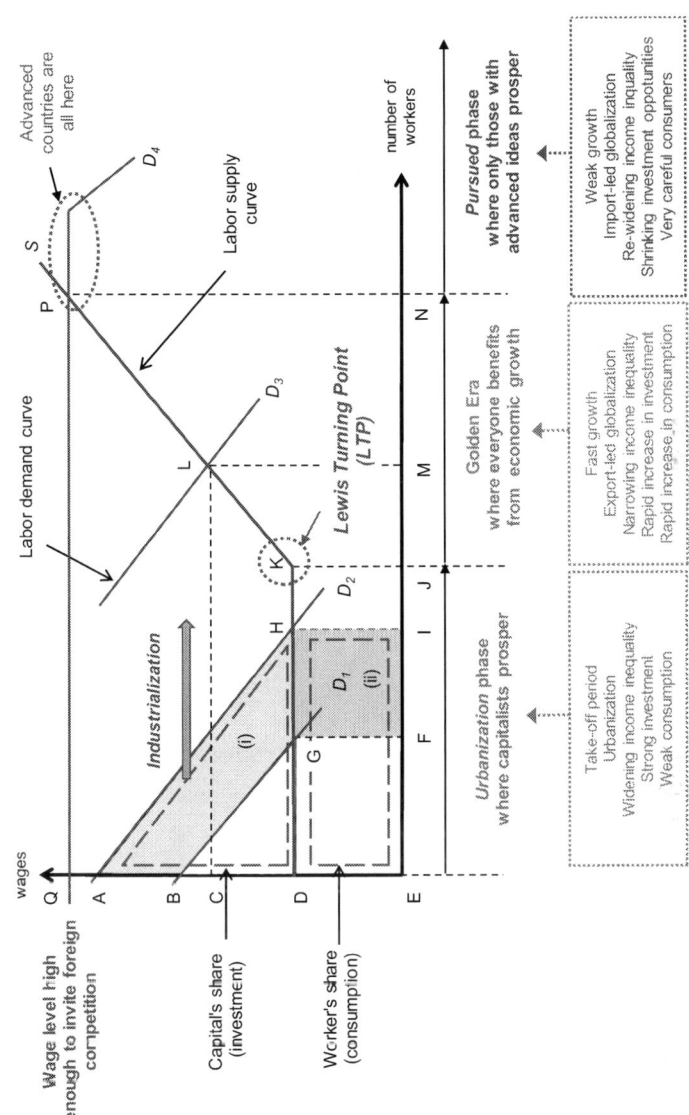

In this graph, capital's share is represented by the area of the triangle formed by the vertical axis on the left, the labor demand curve, and the labor supply curve, while labor's share is represented by the rectangle below the labor supply curve. At labor demand curve D_1, capital's share is the triangle BDG and labor's share is the rectangle DEFG. During this phase of industrialization, the capital share BDG may be shared by only a few persons or families, whereas the labor share DEFG may be shared by millions of workers.

Successful businesses continue investing in an attempt to make even more money. That raises the demand for labor, causing the labor demand curve to shift steadily to the right (from D_1 to D_2) even as the labor supply curve remains flat. As the labor demand curve shifts to the right, total wages received by labor increase from the area of the rectangle DEFG at time D_1 to the area of the rectangle DEIH at time D_2 as the length of the rectangle below the labor supply curve grows. However, the growth is linear. The share of capital, meanwhile, is likely to increase at more than a linear rate as the labor demand curve shifts to the right, expanding from the area of the triangle BDG at D_1 to the area of the triangle ADH at D_2.

Growth exacerbates income inequality in pre-LTP stage

Accordingly, the portion of GDP that accrues to the capitalists is likely to increase with GDP growth until the LTP is reached, exacerbating income inequalities. A key reason why a handful of families and business groups in Europe a century ago and the zaibatsu in Japan prior to World War II were able to accumulate such massive wealth is that they faced an essentially flat labor supply curve (wealth accumulation in North America and Oceania was not quite as extreme because these economies were characterized by a shortage of labor). Some in post-1978 China became extremely rich for the same reason.

During this phase, income inequality, symbolized by the gap between rich and poor, widens sharply as capitalists' share of income (the triangle) often increases faster than labor's share (the rectangle). Because capitalists are profiting handsomely, they continue to re-invest profits in a bid to make even more money. Sustained high investment rates mean domestic capital accumulation and urbanization also proceed rapidly. This is the takeoff period for a nation's economic growth.

Until the economy reaches the Lewis Turning Point, however, low wages mean most people still lead hard lives, even though the move from the countryside to the cities may improve their situations modestly. For typical workers this was no easy transition, with 14-hour factory workdays not at all uncommon until the end of the 19th century. According to the OECD, the annual working time in Western countries averaged around 2,950 hours in 1870 or double the current level of 1,450 hours[3]. Business owners, however, were able to accumulate tremendous wealth during this period.

---

[3] Maddison, Angus, (2006), *The World Economy: A Millennial Perspective (Vol. 1), Historical Statistics (Vol. 2)*. OECD, Paris, p. 347.

Stage II of industrialization: the post-LTP maturing economy

As business owners continue to generate profits and expand investment, the economy eventually reaches the LTP. Once that happens, urbanization is largely finished and the total wages of labor – which had grown only linearly until then – start to increase much faster because any additional demand for labor pushes wages higher. In other words, the post-LTP labor supply curve takes on a significant positive slope.

Even if labor demand increases only modestly in Exhibit 1, from D_2 to D_3, total wages accruing to labor will rise dramatically, from the area of rectangle DEJK to the area of rectangle CEML. This means labor's share of output is likely to be expanding relative to capital's share. It is at this point that the income inequality problem begins to correct itself.

Once the LTP is reached, labor also gains the bargaining power to demand higher wages for the first time in history, which reduces the share of output accruing to business owners. But businesses will continue to invest as long as they are achieving good returns, leading to further tightness in the labor market.

A significant portion of the US and European populations still lived in rural areas until World War I, as shown in Exhibit 2. Even in the US, where – unlike in Europe – workers were always in short supply, nearly half the population was living on farms as late as the 1930s. Continued industrialization as well as the mobilizations for two world wars then pushed these economies beyond the LTP, and the standard of living for the average worker began to improve dramatically.

Exhibit 2 Western urbanization* continued until 1960s

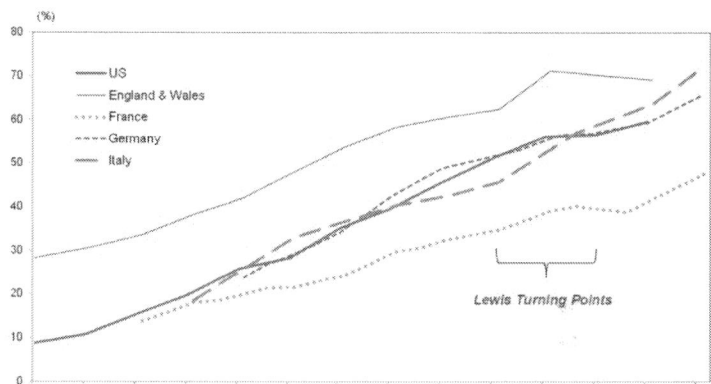

*Percentage of population living in urban areas with 20,000 people or more in England and Wales, 10,000 or more in Italy and France, 5,000 or more in Germany and 2,500 in the US.
Sources: US Census Bureau (2012), *2010 Census*, Peter Flora, Franz Kraus and Winfried Pfenning eds (1987) *State, Economy and Society in Western Europe 1815-1975*

As labor's share increases, consumption's share of GDP will increase at the expense of investment. At the same time, the explosive increase in the purchasing power of ordinary citizens means most businesses can increase profits simply by expanding existing productive capacity. Consequently, both consumption and investment will increase rapidly.

From that point onward the economy begins to "normalize" in the sense in which the term is used today. Inequality also diminishes as workers' share of output increases relative to that of capital. In the US, that led to the so-called Golden Sixties where everyone benefitted from economic growth. With incomes rising and inequality falling, this post-LTP maturing phase may be called the *golden era* of economic growth.

Once the economy reaches the LTP and wages start growing rapidly, workers begin to utilize their newfound bargaining power. The numerous strikes experienced by many Western countries from the 1950s to the 1970s reflects this development.

Capitalists initially respond to labor movements with union busters and strike busters. But as workers grow increasingly scarce and expensive, the capitalists must back down and begin accepting some of labor's demands if they want to keep their factories running. After 20 years or so of such struggles, a new political order is established as both employers and employees begin to understand what can be reasonably expected from the other side. The political order in the West and Japan until recently, which was dominated by center-left and center-right political parties, reflected this learning process.

Higher wages force businesses to look harder for profitable investment opportunities. On the other hand, the explosive increase in the purchasing power of ordinary workers who are paid ever-higher wages creates major investment opportunities. This prompts businesses to invest for two reasons.

First, they seek to increase worker productivity so that they can pay ever-higher wages. Second, they want to expand capacity to address workers' increasing purchasing power. Both productivity- and capacity-enhancing investments increase demand for labor and capital that add to economic growth. In this phase, business investment increases workers' productivity even if their skill level remains unchanged.

With rapid improvements in the living standards of most workers, the post-LTP golden era is characterized by broadly distributed benefits from economic growth. Even those with limited skills are able to make a good living, especially if they belong to a strong union. Government tax receipts also increase rapidly during this period, allowing the government to offer an ever-expanding range of public services. That, in turn, further reduces the sense of inequality among the population. This golden era lasted into the 1970s in the West.

Stage III of industrialization: the pursued era

This golden era does not last forever. At some point, wages reach a level where foreign competition can gain a foothold. The first signs of a serious threat to Western economic growth appeared when businesses in the US and Europe encountered Japanese competition in the 1970s.

Many in the West were shocked to find that Japanese cars required so little maintenance and so few repairs. The Germans may have invented the automobile, and the Americans may have established the process by which it could be manufactured cheaply, but it was the Japanese who developed cars that did not break down. The arrival of Nikon F camera also came as a huge shock to the German camera industry in the 1960s because it was so much more rugged, adaptable, easy to use and serviceable than German Leicas and Exaktas, and professional photographers around the world quickly switched to the Japanese brand. For the first time since the industrial revolution, the West found itself being pursued by a formidable competitor from the East.

Once a country is being chased by a technologically savvy competitor, often with a younger and less expensive labor force, it has entered the third or "pursued" phase of economic development. In this phase, it becomes far more challenging for businesses to find attractive investment opportunities at home because it often makes more sense for them to buy directly from the "chaser" or to invest in that country themselves.

Businesses in the pursued country no longer have the same incentive to invest in productivity- or capacity-enhancing equipment at home because there is now a viable alternative – investing in or buying directly from lower-cost production facilities abroad. In this phase, capital invested abroad, especially in manufacturing, earns a higher return than capital invested at home. With constant pressure from shareholders to improve the return on capital, firms are forced to shift investments to locations with a higher return on capital.

Once this stage is reached, productivity gains at home from investment in productivity-enhancing equipment slow significantly. According to US Bureau of Labor

Statistics data compiled by Stanley Fischer at the Fed[4], productivity growth in the non-farm business sector averaged 3.0 percent from 1952 to 1973, before falling to 2.1 percent for the 1974 to 2007 period and 1.2 percent for 2008–2015. These numbers not only confirm the trend mentioned above, but also suggest that worker productivity in the future will depend increasingly on the efforts of individual workers to improve their skills instead of on corporate investment in productivity-enhancing equipment.

In a pursued economy, labor demand curve (D_4 in Exhibit 1) becomes largely horizontal at wage level EQ, where outsourcing to foreign production sites becomes a viable alternative. This means real wage growth will be minimal from this point onward, except for those workers with abilities that are not easily replicated abroad. It should be noted that the level of EQ depends not just on domestic wage inflation, but also on foreign productivity gains. For example, if the Japanese products in the 1970s were not so competitive, EQ for the West would have been much higher.

With domestic investment opportunities shrinking, economic growth also slows in the pursued countries. This is very much the reality facing most advanced countries today, while a steadily increasing number of emerging countries are joining the rank of chasers.

---

[4] Fischer, Stanley (2016) "Reflections on Macroeconomics Then and Now," remarks at "Policy Challenges in an Interconnected World" 32nd Annual National Association for Business Economics Economic Policy Conference, Washington D.C., March 7, 2016.

Some of the pain workers in advanced countries felt was naturally offset by the fact that, as consumers, they benefited from cheaper imports from emerging economies. Businesses with advanced technology continued to do well, but it was no longer the case that everyone in society was benefiting from economic growth. Those whose jobs could be transferred to lower-cost locations abroad saw their living standards stagnate or even fall.

Inequality worsens in pursued stage

Exhibit 3-4 shows the real income of the lowest quintile of US families from 1947 to 2015. Even in this group, incomes grew rapidly in the post-LTP golden era that lasted until around 1970. But income growth subsequently stagnated as the country entered the pursued phase. Exhibit 5, which illustrates the income growth of other quintiles relative to the lowest 20 percent, demonstrates that the ratios remain remarkably stable until 1970 but diverge thereafter.

Exhibit 3-6 shows annualized income growth by income quintile in the post-LTP golden era from 1947 to 1970 and the pursued phase from 1970 to 2015. It shows that the lowest 60 percent actually enjoyed slightly faster income growth than those at the top before 1970, indicating a reduction in income inequality. This was indeed a golden era for the US economy in which everyone was becoming richer and enjoying the fruits of economic growth.

Exhibit 3 Western urbanization slowed in 1970s

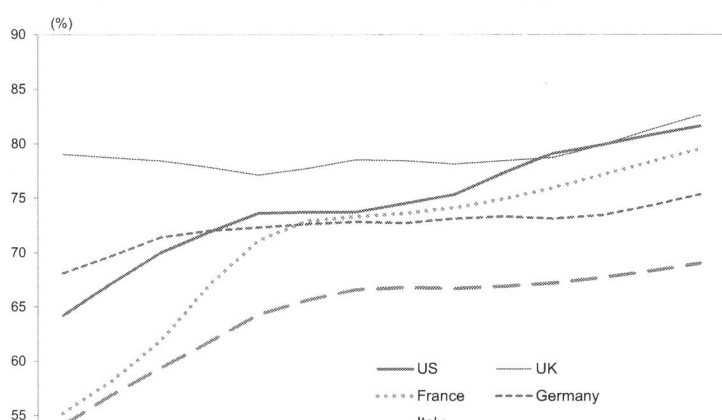

Source: United Nations, Department of Economic and Social Affairs, Population Division (2014). World Urbanization Prospects: The 2014 Revision, custom data acquired via website.

The situation changed drastically, however, once Japan started chasing the US. Exhibit 4 shows that income growth for the lowest quintile has been stagnant ever since. Exhibits 5 and 6 show that income growth for other groups was only slightly better – except for the top 5 percent, which continued to experience significant income gains even after 1970. This group probably includes those who were at the forefront of innovation along with those who were able to take advantage of Japan's emergence.

Exhibit 4 Incomes of lowest 20% of US families shot up until 1970 but stagnated thereafter

Income Upper Limits for Lowest Fifth of Families: 2015 US dollars

Source: US Census Bureau, Current Population Survey, 2016 Annual Social and Economic (ASEC) Supplement

Exhibit 5 US income inequality began to worsen after 1970

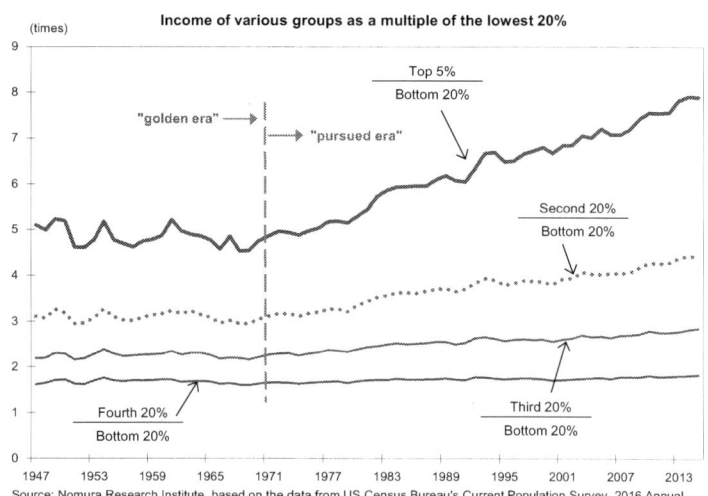

Income of various groups as a multiple of the lowest 20%

Source: Nomura Research Institute, based on the data from US Census Bureau's Current Population Survey, 2016 Annual Social and Economic (ASEC) Supplement

Exhibit 6 Annualized growth rates of US family income by income quintile

					(annualized, %)
	lowest 20%	second 20%	third 20%	fourth 20%	top 5%
Post-LTP maturing phase 1947-1970	2.805	2.854	2.861	2.719	2.496
Post-LTP pursued phase 1970-2015	0.189	0.436	0.737	0.996	1.298

Source: Nomura Research Institute, based on the data from US Census Bureau's Current Population Survey, 2016 Annual Social and Economic (ASEC) Supplement

Exhibit 7 Real wages in six European countries after WWII

Source: Nomura Research Institute, based on the data from IMF, *International Financial Statistics*
Office for National Statistics, UK, *Analysis of Real Earnings*, and Swiss Federal Statistical Office, *Swiss Wage Index*

Exhibit 6 demonstrates that income growth for different income quintiles was quite similar during the golden era but began to diverge significantly once the US became a pursued economy. Income growth for the top five percent dropped from 2.50 percent per year during the golden age to just 1.30 percent during the pursued phase, but that is still seven times the rate for the lowest 20 percent.

Similar developments were observed in Europe. Exhibit 7 shows real wages in six European countries. With the possible exception of the UK, all of these countries experienced rapid wage growth until the 1970s followed by significantly slower growth thereafter.

The three stages of industrialization in pursued countries

Japan reached the LTP in the mid-1960s, when the mass migration of rural graduates to urban factories and offices, known in Japanese as *shudan shushoku*, finally came to an end. Once Japan reached that point, the number of labor disputes skyrocketed, as shown in Exhibit 8, and Japanese wages started to increase sharply as shown in Exhibit 9. In other words, Japan was entering the post-LTP golden era that the West had experienced 40 years earlier.

Japan was fortunate in that it was not being pursued at the time, enabling it to focus on catching up with the West. Wages were rising rapidly, but Japanese companies invested heavily at home to boost workforce productivity. Japan's golden era of strong growth and prosperity could continue as long as productivity rose faster than wages.

Exhibit 8 Demand from labor surges once Lewis Turning Point is passed (1): Japan

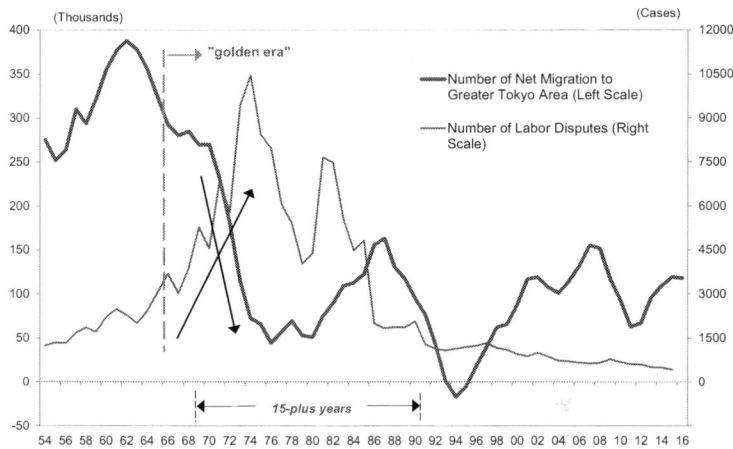

Note: Greater Tokyo Area consists of Tokyo Metropolis, Kanagawa prefecture, Saitama prefecture and Chiba prefecture.
Sources: Ministry of Internal Affairs and Communications, *Report on Internal Migration in Japan*, and Ministry of Health, Labour and Welfare, *Survey on Labour Disputes*

Exhibit 9 Japanese wages peaked in 1997 when country entered pursued phase

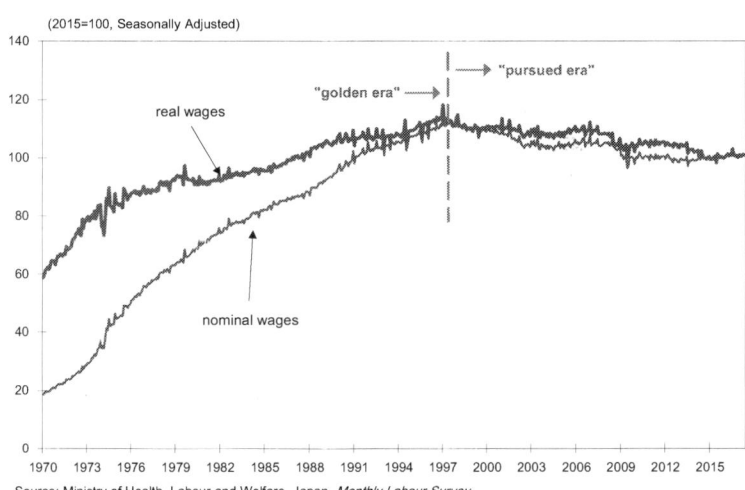

Source: Ministry of Health, Labour and Welfare, Japan, *Monthly Labour Survey*

137

Labor's share of profits rose along with wages, and Japan came to be known as the country of the middle class, with more than 90 percent of the population identifying itself as such. The Japanese were proud of the fact that their country had virtually no inequality. Some even quipped in those days that Japan was how Communism was *supposed* to work.

The happy days for Japan lasted until the mid-1990s, when Taiwan, South Korea and China emerged as serious competitors. By then, Japanese wages were high enough to attract pursuers, and the country entered its pursued phase. As shown in Exhibit 9, Japanese wages stopped growing in 1997 and then stagnated or fell.

Today the Japanese are worried about income inequality as highly paid manufacturing jobs have migrated to lower-cost countries. They are also concerned about the emergence of the so-called working poor who were once employed in manufacturing but have now been forced to take low-end service jobs. Some estimate that as many as 20 million out of a total population of 130 million are now living in poverty[5]. Their suffering, however, has been eased somewhat by a flood of inexpensive imports that has substantially reduced the cost of living. This means Japan is reliving the West's experience when it was being chased by Japan.

Similar concerns are being voiced in Taiwan and South Korea as they experience the same migration of factories

---

[5] *Nikkei Business* (2015) Tokushu: Nisen Mannin-no Hinkon ("20 million Japanese in poverty"), in Japanese, Nikkei BP, Tokyo, March 23, 2015, pp. 24-43.

to China and other even lower-cost locations in Southeast Asia. These two countries passed their LTPs around 1985 and entered a golden age that lasted perhaps until 2005. The frequency of Korean labor disputes also shot up during this period (Exhibit 10) as workers gained bargaining power for the first time and won large wage concessions. In Taiwan, wages climbed sharply during the post-LTP golden era but peaked around 2005 and stagnated thereafter (Exhibit 11). Both countries are now feeling the pinch as China steadily takes over the industries that were responsible for so much of their past growth.

Exhibit 10 Demand from labor surges once Lewis Turning Point is passed (2): South Korea

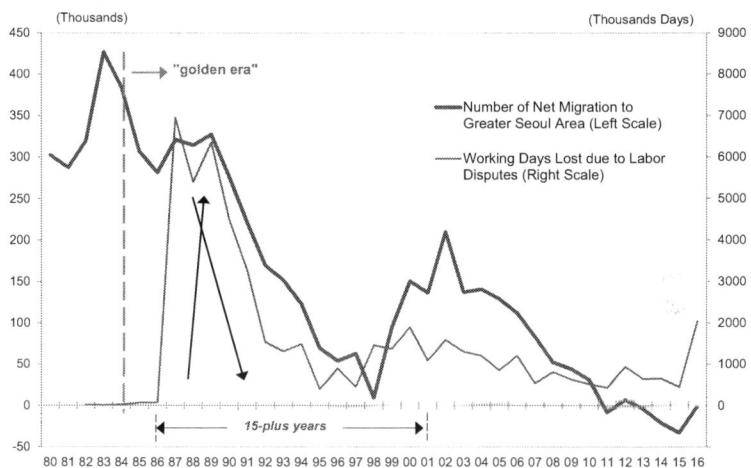

Note: Greater Seoul Area consists of Seoul city, Incheon city and Gyeonggi-do.
Sources: Ministry of Employment and Labor, *Strikes Statistics*, Statistics Korea, *Internal Migration Statistics* and *Korea Statistical Year Book*

Exhibit 11 Taiwanese wages peaked around 2005 when country entered pursued phase

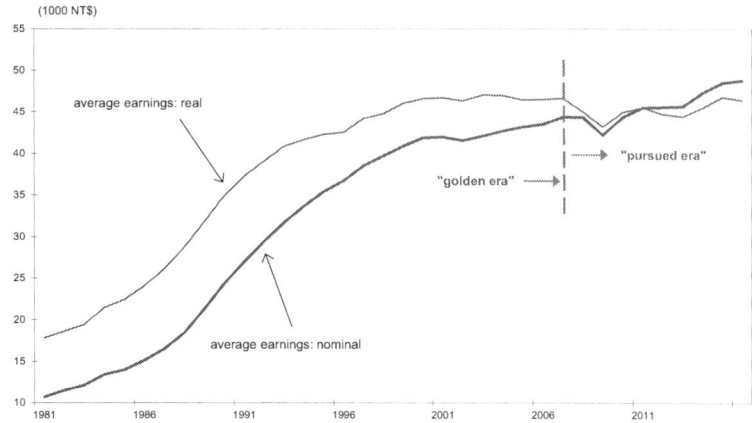

Source: Nomura Research Institute, based on the data from Directorate General of Budget, Accounting and Statistics (DGBAS), the Executive Yuan, Taiwan, *Consumer Price Indices* and *Average Monthly Earnings*

China is not immune from this process of globalization either. Even though China's per capita GDP has grown 30 times since 1978 when the country opened its economy to the outside world, higher wages in China are now prompting both Chinese and foreign businesses to move factories to lower-wage countries such as Vietnam and Bangladesh. This is increasing fears in China that the country will get stuck in the middle-income trap.

This trap arises from the fact that once a country loses its distinction as the lowest-cost producer, many factories may leave for lower-cost destinations, resulting in less investment and less growth. In effect, the laws of globalization and free trade that benefitted China when it was the lowest-cost producer are now posing real challenges for the country.

If China hopes to maintain economic growth in the face of rising wages (and a shrinking workforce), it needs to increase incentives for the businesses to continue investing at home. This means supply-side reforms such as deregulation and tax cuts to increase return on capital at home are needed. But these policies are likely to worsen income inequality as experienced in other countries. These are precisely the challenge advanced countries faced when they were pursued by China and other emerging economies in earlier decades.

Manufacturing and happiness of nations

If a nation's happiness can be measured by (1) how quickly inequality is disappearing and (2) how fast the economy is growing, then the post-LTP golden era would qualify as the period when a nation is at its happiest. During this period, strong demand for workers from a rapidly expanding manufacturing sector forces all other sectors to offer comparable wages to retain workers. Since manufacturing jobs do not require advanced education, the whole of society benefits when the economic growth is propelled by manufacturing as wages rise for everybody. People are hopeful for the future, and inequality shrinks rapidly.

In this sense manufacturing is a great social equalizer: when manufacturing industries are prospering, those without advanced (and expensive) education can still earn a decent living. When manufacturing is driving job creation, it raises the wages of even the least skilled. That, in turn, raises wages in all other sectors.

US manufacturing employment peaked in 1979 at 19.6 million, with the bulk of the increase taking place from 1946 (12.7 million) to 1969 (18.8 million). This timeframe coincides with the period of shrinking income inequality in the US as noted above. Manufacturing employment has now fallen to 12.4 million, or just 8.5 percent of total nonfarm employment. The corresponding figure in 1946 was 32 percent[6]. A similar loss of manufacturing jobs has been observed in all advanced countries.

Exhibit 12 Growth, happiness and maturity of nations

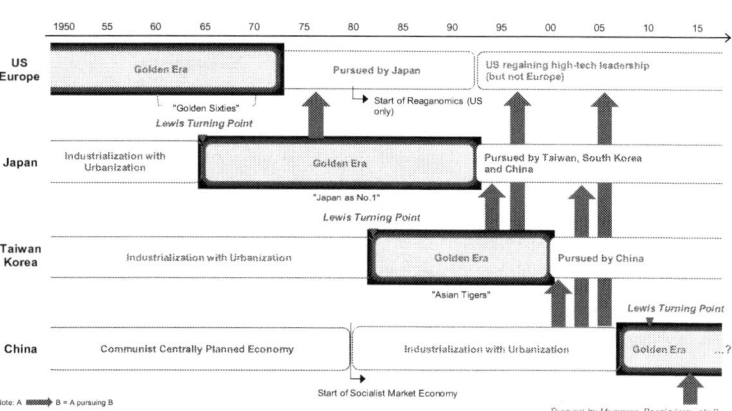

Manufacturing is also where the greatest productivity gains can be expected. The above rise and fall of manufacturing employment in the US are consistent with the productivity growth numbers for the US from Stanly Fisher as noted earlier. Income inequality begins to worsen once manufacturers start migrating to lower-cost

---

[6] These figures are calculated with the data from U.S. Bureau of Labor Statistics.

countries, and only those with advanced education and skills can keep up with the changes and continue to do well.

Disappointment with post-industrial society

The concept of "post-industrial society" popularized by authors such as Daniel Bell and the present concept of pursued era are both referring to the same period in history. When the former concept was first introduced in the 1970s, people were excited about the prospect of societies becoming cleaner and more humane as knowledge-based businesses become more dominant in the economy. This contrasts with the age of industrialization where pollution problems were pervasive, and people had to work long hours in dirty and oily factory floors.

Today, most advanced countries are indeed enjoying cleaner air with fewer factories operating inside their borders. But for a large part of the population, the rosy and humane scenario promised by the proponents of post-industrial society never materialized. Instead, many are feeling more insecure and less hopeful now than they felt in the manufacturing-dominated golden era.

The rosy and humane scenarios of post-industrialization never came true because for that scenario to come true, highly paid knowledge-based jobs must be increasing so rapidly that they are taking workers away from the manufacturing industries. If that were the case, manufacturers would be forced to leave the country because they cannot compete for workers when knowledge-based businesses are paying such high wages.

What actually happened, however, was that advanced countries were *forced* to de-industrialize because the wages were lower and the return on capital was higher abroad than at home. In this case, the society will suffer from a slower growth in productivity and wages as well as widening income inequality because only those with advanced degrees needed for knowledge-based jobs will do well.

Although knowledge-based businesses are expanding in most societies, their expansions are far from enough to offset the loss of jobs in manufacturing industries. The result is the slow growth and increased inequality advanced countries face today. Since these developments are not positive for a large part of the society, the author coined the term "pursued era" instead of using the term "post-industrial society" to convey the sense of urgency that is needed to address the difficulty posed by the inferior return on capital at home.

Labor's progression during three stages of economic development

In formulating the policy response to this predicament, it is important to know where the problem unique to the pursued economy originates. It was already noted that when the economy is in the pre-LTP urbanizing phase, capitalists can take advantage of workers because there are so many of them in rural areas who are willing to work for the going wage in urban factories. Workers also have no bargaining power prior to reaching the LTP. During this phase, the limited opportunities for education and vocational training in rural areas mean most workers are neither well-educated nor highly skilled when they migrate to the cities. And with so many of them competing for a limited number of urban jobs, there is little job security.

Once the economy passes the LTP, however, the tables are turned completely in favor of the workers. The supply of surplus workers in rural areas is exhausted and the labor supply curve takes on a significant positive slope. As long as some businesses seek to increase their workforce, all businesses will be forced to pay ever-higher wages. At this stage, businesses also have plenty of reasons to expand because workers' purchasing power is growing rapidly. Expansion here means *domestic* expansion: firms have little of the experience or know-how needed for overseas production, and as long as domestic wages are below EQ, they are likely to be competitive.

To satisfy increasing demand while paying ever-higher wages, businesses invest in both productivity- and capacity-enhancing equipment. Investments in additional equipment effectively raise the productivity of employees even if the workers themselves are no more skilled or educated than before the country reached its LTP.

With wages rising rapidly, job security for workers also improves significantly as businesses try to hold on to their employees. Lifetime employment and seniority-based remuneration systems become more common. Working conditions improve as businesses offer safer, cleaner working environments to attract and retain workers. The emerging power of unions also forces employers to enhance job security. In contrast to the pre-LTP period, when businesses were effectively exploiting workers because there were so many of them, businesses in the post-LTP golden era "pamper" their employees with productivity-enhancing equipment so they can afford to pay them more.

Workers are on their own in pursued phase

At some point, however, wages reach point EQ in Exhibit 1, and businesses are forced to look for alternative production sites abroad because domestic manufacturing is no longer competitive. It is at this point that firms realize that capital invested abroad earns higher returns than capital invested at home.

In the new pursued era, the way businesses perceive workers changes once again because they now have the option of tapping overseas labor resources. With capital going much further abroad than when invested at home in labor-saving equipment, businesses have fewer incentives to undertake domestic investment. As investment slows, growth in labor productivity, which shot up during the golden era, also starts to decelerate, a trend that has been observed for some time now in most advanced countries.

It is at this point that the ability of *individual* workers begins to matter for the first time because only those able to do things that overseas workers cannot will continue to prosper. This stands in sharp contrast to the previous two stages, where wages were determined largely by macro factors such as labor supply/demand and institutional factors such as union membership, both of which had little to do with individual skills. Once the supply constraint is removed by the option of producing abroad or engaging in outright outsourcing, the only reason a company will pay a higher wage at home is because a particular employee can do something that cannot be easily replicated by a cheaper foreign worker.

If workers were "exploited" during the pre-LTP urbanization era and "pampered" during the post-LTP golden era, they are entirely "on their own" in the pursued era because businesses are much less willing to invest in labor-saving equipment to increase the productivity of the domestic workforce. Workers must invest in *themselves* to enhance their productivity and marketability.

In this pursued phase, job security and seniority-based wages become increasingly rare in industries that must become more agile and flexible to fend off pursuers. It is no accident that lifetime employment and seniority-based wages, which were common in the US until the 1970s, disappeared once Japanese competition appeared. The same thing happened to the Japanese labor market with an increased use of "non-regular" workers after China emerged as a competitor in the mid-1990s. Achieving a more flexible labor market has also been a major social and political issue in Europe.

Workers who take the time and effort to acquire skills that are in demand will continue to do well, while those without such skills will end up earning close to minimum wage. Those who benefited from union membership during the post-LTP golden era will find the benefits of membership in the new pursued era are not what they used to be. Income inequality will increase again, even though *when adjusted for skill levels* it may not change all that much.

Workers who want to maintain or improve their living standards in a pursued economy must therefore think hard about their individual prospects and the skills they should acquire in the new environment. To the extent that the answer to this question differs for each individual, workers are truly on their own. The "good old days," when businesses invested to increase worker productivity so they could pay employees more, are gone for good. In some sense this is only fair, since it means workers who put in the time and effort to improve their productivity will be rewarded more generously than those who do not.

Increased importance of education in pursued era

The fact that workers are on their own and most good jobs in de-industrializing pursued economies are in "knowledge-based sectors" means that the importance of education is far greater in the pursued era than in the golden era. This means any attempt to reduce inequality in the pursued era must start with the provision of equal access to quality education. If it is difficult to ensure equality of income in a pursued era, the least the policy makers can do is to ensure equality of access to quality education.

President Ronald Reagan, in the face of Japanese onslaught, pushed hard to increase return on capital at home by cutting taxes and deregulating the economy. Although such supply-side reforms are necessary in pursued economies, he did the opposite with expenditure on education. As Peter Temin pointed out, this is one of the key reasons why the inequality and social divide have grown so large in the US three decades later[7]. Although President Donald Trump's effort to help manufacturers in the country is laudable, he is also making exactly the same mistake Reagan made in cutting budget on education.

The government in a pursued economy should be increasing resources for education so that everyone who wants to study has access to quality education. As workers are entirely "on their own" in the pursued era, access to quality education is where the battle to contain inequality should be fought.

Inequality and social choice

The above also suggested that there is an economic reason for inequality to increase in a pursued era. But even within the pursued economies, the degree of inequality differs greatly which suggests that policy choices can have an influence on the degree of inequality even if the direction toward a greater inequality cannot

---

[7] Temin, Peter, (2017), *The Vanishing Middle Class: Prejudice and Power in a Dual Society,* Cambridge, MA: MIT Press, p.22 and Chapter 10.

be changed. Those policy choices, in turn, have a lot to do with societal choices.

The US is considered one of the most un-equal countries in the developed world, where the top few percent owns a large share of the assets in the country. But when one looks at who is at the very top, they are mostly founders of new companies (Exhibit 13) that literally transformed the way people live and work all around the world. In other words, except for Warren Buffet who made money investing in the stock market, all others became rich because they took the risk and brought something completely new and useful to the world.

Exhibit 13 Richest persons in the United States

Rank	Name	Industry	Net wealth
1	Jeff Bezos	founder Amazon	$114 B
2	Bill Gates	founder Microsoft	$106 B
3	Warren Buffett	Berkshire Hathaway	$80.8 B
4	Mark Zuckerberg	founder Facebook	$69.6 B
5	Larry Ellison	founder Oracle	$65 B
6	Larry Page	founder Google	$55.5 B
7	Sergey Brin	co-founder Google	$53.5 B
8	Michael Bloomberg	founder Bloomberg LP	$53.4 B

Source: Forbes, "The Forbes 400: The Definitive Ranking Of The Wealthiest Americans," October 2, 2019, Edited by Luisa Kroll and Kerry A. Dolan,

https://www.forbes.com/forbes-400/#45b49a177e2f

There are those further down the list who made money in largely zero-sum finance/real estate investments or through established companies and inheritance. But no other country in the world has the top ranks of the wealthiest people dominated by those with transformative technology. The fact that seven out of eight at the very top are self-made individuals with transformative ideas suggests that the implication of US inequality is different from those of the other countries where the top ranks are mostly filled with more traditional and established types.

This may have a lot to do with the transparency of the US economy where the people (and products) are valued for what they can do, not where they come from. That, in turn, may have a lot to do with the fact that the US is an immigrant society in comparison to traditional societies of Japan and Europe with their attendant baggage. In those traditional societies, someone like Steve Jobs, a college drop out with a humble background, would have faced a far greater resistance to realizing his ideas than in the US.

Another frequently raised inequality issue in the US is the high cost of medical care. This is important because most Americans, who are brought up in the pioneering spirit of self-reliance, really do *not* want to talk about inequality as long as they are earning a living wage and have a dignified life.

Their rugged sense of self-reliance, however, could be shattered overnight with a catastrophic medical bill. Indeed, a huge share of personal bankruptcies filed in the

US is due to this cause. Even for those who are lucky enough to be healthy and have good health insurance, the fear that they might lose one or both at any time is undermining their faith in the system.

There is a huge room for improvement in the US medical industry, especially in comparison to those available in Japan and some other countries. For example, an appendicitis operation in the US can easily cost 20,000 dollars when the same operation in Japan can be done with only 3,000 dollars[8]. Although Japanese doctors frequently complain that they are not paid enough, this one-to-seven difference in cost is adding to the sense of inequality and insecurity among many people in the US. In other words, if an average American faced Japanese medical bills, his or her sense of inequality would be far less.

At the same time, it is said that almost all new drugs that are brought to the market in the world today are developed in the US. This is because the US does not impose a cap on drug prices the way it is imposed in very many other countries including Japan. As a result, drug companies can recoup the enormous cost of developing a new drug *only* in the US. This is indeed one of the reasons why the medical cost in the US is so high.

If the US imposed a cap just like the one in Japan, chances are high that the research and development on new drugs will come to a standstill which it almost did

---

[8] Wakakura, Masato, (2006), "Kokusai Hikaku: Nihon-no Iryo-hi ha Yasusugiru (International Comparison: Japan's Medical Costs are too Inexpensive.)," *Voice*, June 2006, Tokyo, PHP Institute, p.159

when Hillary Clinton tried to devise a national health insurance with a cap on drug prices when her husband was the President of the US. Some would argue that such a stoppage in medical research would be against the interest of humanity.

This American preference on growth and progress instead of on redistribution served the country well during its golden era because its strong manufacturing-led growth improved the life of everybody and reduced inequality, as noted earlier. The question is whether the same trade-off is appropriate in a pursued economy where inequality is destined to rise with highly undesirable social consequences.

It has been reported, for example, that among the young people in the US today, the word socialism does not have the same bad connotation which it had with the earlier generations who fought the cold war. Wall Street Journal for January 17, 2020, for example, wrote "Fifty percent of adults under 38 told the Harris Poll last year that they would 'prefer living in a socialist country'. That outlook recurs in many more surveys and far surpasses figures from even the radical hey days of the 60s and 70s." [9] This fifty percent is probably feeling that with a huge student loan burden, high housing costs and prohibitive medical bills, the present system is working only for the old and the rich, that the deck is stacked against them.

The continued popularity of leftist politicians such as Bernie Sanders and Elizabeth Warren also reflect this

---

[9] Ukueberuwa, Mene, (2020), "Boomer Socialism Led to Bernie Sanders," *Wall Street Journal*, January 17, 2020.

dissatisfaction. This means some re-balancing of priorities in the US is imminent not only because the economy is in a pursued phase but also because the weight of those younger voters will only grow in the future.

Although some shifts in priorities are imminent, those shifts must be in correct direction to be beneficial to the public. This is because the pursued era imposes its own constraints and dynamics on the economy that did not exist during the golden era. In particular, the return on capital must be raised so that more investment and jobs are created at home. That means *lower*, not higher taxes on those who are making investment decisions. This is the opposite of the traditional leftist agenda pursued by the above two politicians.

For example, the US was able to win back the high-tech leadership from Japan in the late 80s thanks to the Reaganomics which drastically reduced taxes and deregulated the economy. Those policy changes encouraged those with ideas to try harder, and all those with transformative technology in Exhibit 13 realized their ideas during this period. But the same policy also increased income inequality.

In contrast, the Japanese and Europeans, who shied away from such drastic supply-side reforms, fell behind on the high-tech race and experienced slower job growth and investments. It is indeed ironic that all those young people who are complaining about inequality and espousing socialism are also the most avid users of devises and services pioneered by those who are at the top of the list of richest persons in America.

Right kind of supply side reform needed

Moreover, overzealous effort to correct inequality can have big negative consequence on growth. Japan's inheritance tax, for example, kicks in with a very low deductible and its marginal rate increases to 55 percent very quickly. As a result, there is a huge industry in Japan on how to reduce this tax liability, and many successful business people are wasting their time on such tax-reduction activities instead of using their time on what they do best, i.e., pursue their dreams by expanding their businesses. Some have moved out of Japan altogether.

Forcing people with a track record of success to waste their time renting apartment houses, which anybody can do, or leave the country altogether constitute a huge misallocation of entrepreneurial resources in the country. After all it is these people who create new jobs and industries, not academics or bureaucrats. For Japan, which has one of the lowest rates of new business formation among advanced countries, such a loss of talent is nothing short of suicidal.

The key question, therefore, is that of balance. The policy makers must constantly fine-tune the tax structure so that it will result in most investments at home while securing sufficient tax revenue to maintain necessary government services including education.

In 2008, the Taiwanese government drastically reduced its tax rate on inheritance and gifts to 10 percent so that Taiwan's pool of entrepreneurial resources will not be wasted on efforts to reduce this tax liability. In doing so the government fully expected the revenue from these taxes to fall and that was reflected in their budget for the following year (Exhibit 14).

The actual tax receipts, however, did not fall at all. This is because many people simply decided to pay the tax so that they don't have to waste time crafting elaborate schemes to minimize the tax liability.

This is an example of supply side reform implemented correctly. It encouraged talented people to concentrate their effort on what they do best while maintaining the tax revenue for those who need help. Although such reforms will increase relative inequality, it will help the economy to grow which should help those who are not so talented.

The policy makers who are concerned about the slowdown in growth and an increase in inequality in pursued economies should be concentrating their efforts in devising such tax structures. They should also explain to the public why the golden era tax regime, which looked fair and worked well when there was a surfeit of attractive domestic investment opportunities, is not necessarily the best for the economies in the pursued era, when a conscious effort is needed to encourage businesses to increase investment at home.

Exhibit 14 Taiwan's inheritance and gift tax cuts enhanced efficiency of resource allocation, and tax revenues did not fall

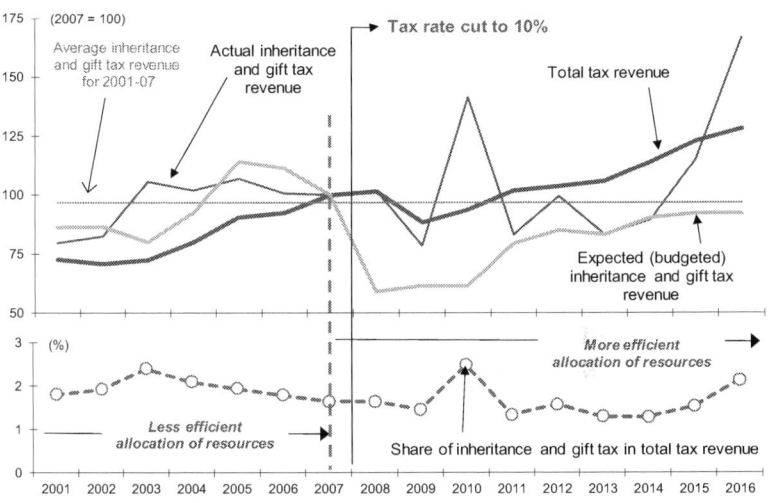

Source: Nomura research Institute, based on the data from Ministry of Finance R. O. C.

Real source of Thomas Piketty's inequality

The analysis presented here contradicts one of the key historical points Piketty makes. Namely, he claims that the extreme inequality that existed prior to World War I was corrected by the wealth destruction of two world wars and the Great Depression. He then goes on to argue that the retreat of progressive taxation in the developed world starting in the late 1970s ended up creating a level of inequality that approaches that seen prior to World War I.

Although he has ample data to back his assertions, his pre-World War I results may also be due to the fact that those industrializing countries were all in the pre-LTP urbanization era, which is characterized by a rapid increase in inequality. His post-World War I findings may also be attributable to the West's entering the post-LTP golden era where a rapidly expanding manufacturing sector allowed everyone to enjoy the fruits of economic growth accompanied by shrinking inequality. Piketty attributes this to the destruction of wealth brought about by two world wars and the introduction of progressive income taxes, but this period was also characterized by an end to rapid urbanization in most of these countries. For Western economies, the four decades through 1970 was their golden era as their manufacturers were ahead of everyone else and were being chased by no one.

Finally, Piketty's post-1970 results may be due to the fact that Western economies entered their pursued era as Japan and other countries began chasing them. For Western capitalists able to utilize Asian manufacturing resources, this was a golden money-making opportunity. But it was not a welcome development for a large number of Western factory workers who had to compete with competitively priced imports.

This also suggests that the favorable income distributions observed by Piketty in the West before 1970 and in Japan until 1990 were *transitory* phenomena. These countries enjoyed growing incomes and shrinking inequality not because they had the right kind of tax regime but because they were in a golden era when manufacturing prospered. And manufacturing prospered because the global economic environment was one in which these countries were either ahead of everyone else or chasing others but were not being pursued, i.e., the return on capital was the highest at home.

Just because such a desirable state of affairs was observed once does not mean it can be maintained or replicated. Any attempt to preserve that equality in the face of fierce international competition would have required massive and continuous investment in both human and physical capital combined with trade protectionism, something that most countries are not ready to implement.

It is not even certain whether such investments constitute the best use of resources, since businesses may still find that the return on capital is higher elsewhere. To the extent that businesses are under pressure from shareholders to invest in countries offering the highest returns, forcing them to invest at home is no easy task.

Conclusion

In a pursued economy which is characterized by a paucity of domestic investment opportunities, the government must implement a two-pronged approach to address the challenges of slow growth and increased inequality. First, the government must push for supply-side reforms to increase return on capital at home in order to encourage businesses to invest more at home. Even though such business-friendly measures may increase the sense of inequality among some groups, they are needed in the pursued era to accelerate growth and create jobs.

Second, because workers in a pursued era are largely on their own, the government should help them improve their skills by providing affordable access to quality education. Furthermore, because good jobs in a de-industrializing pursued era are likely to be in knowledge-intensive sectors where the level of educational attainment matters a lot, the government should push for improved access to education at all levels. This is where the battle to contain inequality should be fought in a pursued economy. And for the US, a more affordable healthcare system would be of great help in reducing the sense of vulnerability and inequality felt by a large part of the society. Perhaps the recent disaster with the COVID-19 pandemic will finally push the country to address this long-overdue issue.

Unfortunately, there has been virtually no macroeconomic theories or models that address the policy implications of capital earning higher returns abroad than at home, and very little of the policy debate in advanced countries is couched in these terms. On the contrary, economist's continued emphasis on the efficacy of monetary policy and disdain for fiscal policy are all based on the assumption that the economy is still in a golden era where the private sector is faced with a surfeit of attractive domestic investment opportunities.

In the golden era, the choice between supply side reforms such as tax cut and increased expenditures on social programs such as education was a matter of preference. In the present pursued era, when businesses are hard pressed to find attractive domestic investment opportunities and inequality is increasing amid slow growth, both supply-side reforms *and* increased expenditure on education are needed to hold the country together.

Since the former requires a lower tax rates while the latter requires higher tax revenue, a carefully calibrated tax structure is needed to achieve both. All of this suggests that economic management in the pursued era is far more demanding than in the golden era. Although many people are still longing for the return of the golden era while others are espousing socialism, none of them will be able to improve people's lives until they recognize the reality of the pursued economies in a global context.

References and bibliography

Directorate General of Budget, Accounting and Statistics (DGBAS), the Executive Yuan, Taiwan. Consumer Price Indices.

Directorate General of Budget, Accounting and Statistics (DGBAS), the Executive Yuan, Taiwan. Monthly Average Earnings.

Fischer, Stanley (2016), "Reflections on Macroeconomics Then and Now," remarks at "Policy Challenges in an Interconnected World" 32nd Annual National Association for Business Economics Economic Policy Conference, Washington D.C., March 7, 2016.

Flora, Peter, Franz Kraus and Winfried Pfenning ed. (1987) *State, Economy and Society in Western Europe 1815-1975. Volume II. The Growth of Industrial Societies and Capitalist Economies.* Campus Verlag: Frankfurt am Main.

Forbes (2019) "The Forbes 400: The Definitive Ranking of The Wealthiest Americans." Edited by Luisa Kroll and Kerry A. Dolan, October 2 https://www.forbes.com/forbes-400/#6ad234a57e2f

Koo, Richard C. (2018) *The Other Half of Macroeconomics and the Fate of Globalization.* John Wiley & Sons Ltd.

Maddison, Angus (2006) *The World Economy: A Millennial Perspective (Vol. 1), Historical Statistics (Vol. 2).* OECD, Paris.

Ministry of Employment and Labor, Korea. Strikes Statistics.

Ministry of Finance, Republic of China. Finance Statistics, in traditional Chinese.

Ministry of Health, Labour and Welfare, Japan. Monthly Labour Survey.

Ministry of Health, Labour and Welfare, Japan. Survey on Labour Disputes.

Ministry of Internal Affairs and Communications, Japan. Report on Internal Migration in Japan

Nikkei Business (2015) "Tokushu: Nisen Mannin-no Hinkon" ("20 million Japanese in poverty"), in Japanese, Nikkei BP, Tokyo, March 23.

Office for National Statistics, UK. Analysis of Real Earnings.

Piketty, Thomas (2014) *Capital in the Twenty-First Century.* Belknap Press.

Statistics Korea. Internal Migration Statistics.

Statistics Korea. Korea Statistical Year Book.

Swiss Federal Statistical Office. Consumer Prices Index.

Swiss Federal Statistical Office. Swiss Wage Index.

Temin, Peter (2017) *The Vanishing Middle Class: Prejudice and Power in a Dual Society.* Cambridge, MA: MIT Press.

Ukueberuwa, Mene (2020) "Boomer Socialism Led to Bernie Sanders," *Wall Street Journal*, January 17.

United Nations, Department of Economic and Social Affairs, Population Division. (2014) World Urbanization Prospects: The 2014 Revision.

United Nations, Department of Economic and Social Affairs, Population Division. International Financial Statistics.

US Department of Commerce, Census Bureau (2012), 2010 Census.

US Department of Commerce, Census Bureau. Current Population Survey.

Wakakura, Masato (2006) "Kokusai Hikaku: Nihon-no Iryo-hi ha Yasusugiru (International Comparison: Japan's Medical Costs are too Inexpensive.)" *Voice*, June 2006, Tokyo, PHP Institute.

Chapter 7

Inequality under globalization: state of knowledge and implications for economics[*]

James Galbraith and Jaehee Choi[°]

1. A brief history of inequality in modern economics

In the years following World War II the division of labor between neoclassical micro-economics and pseudo-Keynesian macroeconomics was pioneered at MIT and disseminated worldwide from there. Macro held a narrow strip of economic territory: unemployment, inflation, interest rates and money supply, the business cycle, the rate of growth and their interrelations through the quantity theory, the Phillips Curve and Okun's Law. The personal distribution of income fell squarely into the microeconomics of labor markets, governed by supply and demand for various levels of skill, alongside such ad

[*] Adapted from James Galbraith and Jaehee Choi, "Inequality Under Globalization: State of Knowledge and Implications for Economics," in Edward Webster, Imraan Valodia and David Francis, eds., Inequality Studies from the Global South. Routledge, 2020. Used with permission.
[°] James Galbraith is Lloyd M. Bentsen Jr. Chair in Government/Business Relations, Lyndon B. Johnson School of Public Affairs, and Professor of Government, The University of Texas at Austin. Jaehee Choi is Post-doctoral Research Fellow, University of Texas Inequality Project.

hoc matters as firm-size effects, industry-specific labor rents, imperfect competition and efficiency wages. A theory of changing inequality was offered for developing countries by Simon Kuznets in 1955, positing a rise in inequalities in the early stages of development but a decline later on. For the rich, the Kuznets evolution was supposedly complete, the Cobb-Douglas distribution theory with Hicks Neutral Technical change predicted stable functional shares, and national income accounts appeared to bear this out. So the functional distribution – the division between wages, profits and rent – was hardly spoken of.

Beginning in the late 1970s and early 1980s, circumstances began to force a change. An early hearing on rising inequalities at the Joint Economic Committee (1982)[1] pointed an accusing finger at right-wing policies, and this message was restated by Bluestone and Harrison (1988), who laid the blame on de-industrialization and the war on unions, conspicuous features of the Reagan and Thatcher years. The point seemed obvious enough, but there was a subtle difficulty. The severing of micro from macro made it conceptually difficult for many economists to tie the Reagan Recession of 1981-82 and its UK counterpart – major drivers of deindustrialization – to a distributional outcome. Instead the emphasis fell on specific anti-worker political actions – in the US these included the firing of air traffic controllers, deregulation of trucking, a radical-right National Labor Relations

---

[1] The hearing was organized by the senior author here at the direction of the committee chair, Rep. Henry S. Reuss (D-Wis.) It was difficult to find academic witnesses as the subject was out of fashion and obscure.

Board. Still this was a minor muddle compared with what was to come.

It was only in the early 1990s that mainstream economics began a concerted search for a less-contentious explanation of rising inequality, rooted in the labor market analysis to which distribution issues had been consigned. Given the evolving preference of applied micro-economists for data based on surveys of household characteristics – however limited these may be by survey-takers' fixation on race, gender, age, education and a handful of similarly simple categories – the evidentiary basis for a labor market analysis of inequality was remarkably thin. It consisted of little more than widely-separated surveys of earnings, stratified by worker characteristics, and largely confined to a small handful of wealthy countries.

Bound and Johnson (1992) set the template for neoclassical investigation. Rising in- equality was a matter of changing relative demand for skills, a characteristic unobservable in practice but usually approximated by the number of years spent in school. Demand being driven by technology, the underlying cause had to be a "bias" in the character of technological change. The remedy to the resultant inequality could only be an increased supply of skill – more years in school. This remedy had the peculiar feature that if enough people pursued it, the advantage accruing to each would diminish until it disappeared. Education was economically worthwhile, but only if it is restricted – a truism that is nevertheless in its way subversive. The labor economists Goldin and Katz (2008) eventually produced a thick book on this theme, from which the ugly class politics of the 1980s had disappeared.

The discipline of economics is such that to have purchase with the profession, any argument counter to "skill biased technological change" had to adapt the same broad framework of labor market supply-and-demand. Such an alternative was presented by Wood (1994), who argued that North-South trade in manufactures would expand the effective supply of unskilled workers in the Global North, driving down their wages in rich countries but raising them among the poor (where Wood argued factory workers form an intermediate skill class) thus moving inequality in opposite directions in the two hemispheres. Wood's argument gained an audience briefly but was ultimately dismissed by the mainstream; among other things the encouragement it would have given to skeptics of free trade made it politically incorrect.

In the mid 1990s an analysis based loosely on the Kuznets hypothesis revived, thanks in part to efforts at the World Bank to begin to compile a comprehensive global data set of inequality measures, along with income measures prepared by the Penn World Tables and Purchasing Power Parity (PPP) estimates of the relative purchasing power of different national currencies. Fairly soon after the publication of the landmark Deininger and Squire (1996) data set there were multiple efforts to trace the growth (or decline) of inequality on the world scale, resolving roughly into three conceptual measures as described by Milanovic (2005): inequality between countries pure and simple (Concept I), inequality between countries weighted by population (Concept II), and inequality across individuals or households irrespective of nationality (Concept III). The diversity of concepts brought with it new sources of uncertainty in the result and indeed inconsistent – on more precisely, divergent – conclusions depending on the concept deployed. Thus, while inequality between countries (Concept I) tended to rise, inequality between countries (Concept II) fell. The difference was largely due to the rise in average Chinese incomes. Meanwhile Concept III inequality could be calculated only by merging data sets from different countries, a task of heroic proportions; the extensive data requirements meant that only few years (initially just three) could be brought to fruition. Changes in Concept III inequality from one period to the next generated the famous "elephant curve" showing sharp gains for those at the very top of the global income scale, substantial gains for the lower middle (mostly Chinese and Indian) masses, and stagnation for the incomes of the middle classes in the already-wealthy countries. These numbers too were driven largely by national-average movements (mainly the rise of average incomes in China) rather than by measures of inequality per se.

At the other end of the measurement-method scale, the Luxembourg Income Study set out to blend and homogenize household and personal income surveys so as to permit detailed and accurate welfare comparisons – but with the limitation that such surveys are sparse, restricted mainly to the wealthy countries and for the most part to recent years. What one gains in fine detail on household characteristics one loses on the capacity for extensive international and historical comparison. In these matters, there are different ways to process a finite body of data but, methodologically speaking, there is no free lunch.

In this cacophony of facts and semi facts, Kuznets' straightforward and intuitive hypothesis did not fare well. Indeed, most researchers citing Kuznets were not much interested in his narrative of intersectoral shifts; rather they sought inverted–U curves anywhere they might find them and made that the test of Kuznets' thesis, irrespective of whether there existed an underlying framework of early-to-late transition from agriculture to industry and from rural to urban life.

For many researchers by then, the relation of inequality to income level was no longer of prime interest. Debates over development, education, industrial policy (the East Asian Miracle) and economic growth directed attention toward the link between initial levels of inequality and later growth rates. Two competing strands emerged. One held that low levels of inequality were good for growth (Birdsall et al., 1995) – citing Korea, Taiwan, Post-Mao China but largely ignoring East Germany and the USSR – while the other advanced the opposite thought, that income and savings must first be concentrated before investment and growth will follow (Forbes 2000). A fair summary of these debates is that by choosing periods, countries, data sources and econometric techniques with sufficient care, either argument can be made. But whatever the result, this literature bore only a slight resemblance or relation to Kuznets. An exception is the work of Deaton (2015), who argues that improvements in human welfare must start by increasing inequalities along the relevant dimension, whether life expectancy, infant mortality, years of education or any other index. Only after an improvement has taken root somewhere first, will it be adopted broadly and so eventually inequalities along that dimension will decline.

2. Some policy-relevant themes

Against this counterpoint of alarm and apology, a few lines of reasoning stand out as having a pragmatic bent and drive toward policy relevance. Of these, perhaps the most significant is the Meidner/Rehn (see Martin, 1981) model of wage compression as a path toward productivity gain in an open economy. Their insight was that the composition and technological level of industry in a small economy such as Sweden is endogenous. Floors on wages drive out weak players and place pressure on stronger ones to modernize. The result over time is a superior industrial mix and a higher standard of life both in absolute and relative terms. Moreover, an advanced industrial base can support a large and well-paid service sector; the downside is that high tax rates may encourage the expatriation of high-income persons, but this is a minor price. The Meidner/Rehn approach is highly validated by the Sweden experience over 70 years, but of less relevance to large economies that cannot export the full spectrum of backward technologies and cheap services.

A second framing of the issue of inequality in policy term builds on the model of Harris and Todaro (1970), who studied urbanization, minimum wages and unemployment in East Africa in the 1960s. Their insight was that an unequal wage structure (say, across an urban/rural divide) generates migration and competition for the better jobs. If these are few and the pay gap is large, then job-seekers must necessarily outnumber jobs and unemployment results. This hypothesis can be extended to migrations in Europe, North America and China, among other cases, and provides a testable hypothesis in contrast to the skill bias model. The latter predicts that more flexible-meaning unequal-labor markets will have less unemployment, since employers will be able to match pay to skills and requirements; they will choose to hire more unskilled workers if the latter are cheaper. The Harris-Todaro model predicts the opposite, namely that societies with compressed and regulated wage structures will (within-limits) tend to enjoy lower unemployment, and also, per Meidner/Rehn, higher rates of productivity growth and larger manufacturing sectors than those who maintain their allegiance to "free and flexible" labor markets. This proves to be one of the rare points on which evidence is spectacularly clear, as reflection on the centralized wage bargains of Scandinavia, Austria and Ireland will attest (Galbraith and Garcilazo, 2004). The preference of employers for flexibility has everything to do with power, and nothing at all to do with combating unemployment.

A third pro-equality argument was offered a few years back by Galbraith et al. (2007, reprised in Galbraith 2016); it is that when countries fight wars, the more equal of two combatants generally wins. This generalization appears to hold going back to classical times. Republics fight their way to independence, become Empires by conquest, fall into decay and disunion, and recede. Communist countries, particularly, did not lose wars unless they fought with each other, at least not until the very last stages of the USSR. And when theocracies collide, the advantage lies not with the richer but with the more compact and coherent, which is to say, usually, with the Islamic.

3. The Piketty phenomenon

None of these arguments are referenced in the 700-page tome of Thomas Piketty (2014) which set out to provide an empirical account of the evolution of inequality worldwide. Piketty's book also sought to embed that record in a theoretical framework capable of bearing the weight of comprehensive explanation. For this, a "new" theory is evidently required, and while Piketty is at pains not to disparage the mainstream labor market education / technology theory, he is not prepared to accept it either. His grand scheme requires a framework capable of operating over a long span of history and pre-history – thousands of years – and for this the concept of skill-biased technology is too specifically modern, too tightly linked to the digital age.

Piketty's proposed solution is superficially macro-economic; it is to base a theory of inequality on the relationship between r and g where r is the rate of profit and g is the rate of economic growth. Where the former exceeds the latter inequality must rise, since capital (and land) are owned by the upper classes. So, it remains for Piketty to establish that $r > g$ is both normal historically and plausible as a matter of theory.

For theory, Piketty however reverts to the neoclassical standard, the marginal productivity of capital,[2] and so muddles the question of whether the key forces are macro- or microeconomic. Piketty argues that a profit/interest rate drive by the marginal productivity of capital typically exceeds overall growth rates, without recourse to the culpable (but correct) proposition that short-term interest rates are set by and for the benefit of the state. Instead, for reasons not entirely clear, technology must keep raising the real rate of return on capital, through the traditional neoclassical mechanics of supply-and-demand.

For Piketty, episodes of income leveling are therefore restricted to short periods of capital destruction in wartime, which actually did not happen in Germany in World War I or in the US or UK in either war, nor to any dramatic degree in World War II in France. Piketty also implicitly assumes that fortunes largely pass unbroken from one generation to the next. Thus he builds his hypothesis that the inequalities of the 19th century were natural and the mitigations of the 20th an aberration, now (however regrettably) receding.

Piketty's celebrated empirical work rests partly on archival research on patrimony in the Paris archives – a narrow foundation – but more on a compilation of income tax records, now presented as the World Inequality Database. There is no doubt value in this collection, but recognizing that value and its limitations

---

[2] This choice requires him to attack the Cambridge Capital Theory, which since the 1960s established that smaller "quantities" of capital do not produce higher rates of return.

requires acknowledging that (a) not every country has income tax and those that do not may not resemble those that do; (b) among countries that do have income tax, tax laws defining taxable income vary, as does the effectiveness of enforcement and degree of evasion, and (c) even in countries with good reporting and enforcement, tax law changes can alter the reported distribution without effect on the underlying reality. Galbraith (2019) provides a thorough survey of this database.

To illustrate point (c), in 1986 in the US tax reform was designed to alter the reported distribution without altering the distribution of the tax burden. The reform required high-income individuals to report more of their income while taxing the whole at a lower rate. The resulting bulge in Piketty's top income share for the US in 1987 et seq. provides a substantial part of his case that rising inequality in America outstrips that in Europe. But it is fictitious. Thus statements attributing US inequality to (for example) allegedly exceptional inequalities in American education lack foundation in fact; compared to Canada or the UK, even by Piketty's own data (with this one correction) the US experience is not exceptional.[3] And as Noah Wright (2015) has shown, even those parts which have an arguable basis in fact do not support his central claim that the rate of profit is again coming to exceed the rate of growth.

---

[3] Further, some of Piketty's longer run data are simply imaginary; there are figures in his book that report values for 2100 and 2200 AD, not even labeled as "projections."

4. The data on inequalities so far

In order to be able to make reliable comparisons, the research community needs a reliable fact-base of information on the evolution of inequality over time and across countries, using a single consistent concept of inequality measured across the full spectrum of nation states and with sufficient density over time to establish trends and turning points reliably. To summarize the state-of-play:

- The World Institute of Development Economics Research (WIDER) has produced a comprehensive bibliographic compilation of inequality surveys. For researchers seeking global coverage from survey data, this remains probably the most thorough source. But any conceptually consistent panel will necessarily be a relatively sparse subset of the full data-base.
- The Luxembourg Income Study has produced a fully-consistent micro data collection but for only a relatively few, mostly high-income, countries and years. The LIS data are of highest quality and the source data have many uses beyond the computation of inequality indices. But limitations of underlying source material restrict the coverage.
- The World Bank has reverted to a data set of inequality numbers, published as the World Development Indicators (WDI), provided by member states with no attempt to assure consistency of concept. Consumption inequality numbers for (say) India are intermingled with income-based numbers for Western countries. The WDI inequality measures are only weakly consistent with the larger literature

and are not a respectable source for comparative inequality measures.

- Piketty and his collaborators, through the World Inequality Database, rely on tax rather than survey data, with advantages in covering top incomes but weak comparability across countries, sparse overall coverage biased toward the rich countries and former UK colonies, and with problems of continuity within countries as tax laws change. Of the major datasets, the WID is the least consistent with all the others (Galbraith, Choi, Halbach, Malinowska and Zhang 2016)

- Milanovic (2005, 2016) has built a unified world inequality measure, condensing all households to a common metric. But this work is based on a melding of within-country inequality measures and between-country comparisons based on PPP estimates. It is largely driven by the latter and subject to their weaknesses; that is, the major forces shaping the "elephant curve" are estimated differences of country-average household income, not the inequalities measured within countries.

- Solt has produced a synthetic data set (the SWIID) covering a very wide range of countries and years, but with a great deal of interpolation and imputation across countries and years. The approach is largely benign where survey data are dense, but unreliable in many cases where they are sparse. (See the comparisons in Galbraith, Halbach, Malinowska, Shams and Zhang 2016.) Solt's data are based in part on the EHII data, discussed below.

These approaches appear to exhaust what can profitably be done from a record of survey and tax data assembled from diverse, incomplete, independent and conceptually autonomous sources. Further progress requires extracting, if possible, reliable information from alternative records. But to undertake this task requires a different method, indeed a different measure of inequality, altogether. As the work of the University of Texas Inequality Project has shown, suitable inequality measures exist – and have existed for decades – and suitable source data are ubiquitous and easy to handle.

5. Measuring inequality from grouped data

The insight behind the UTIP measures touches on several distinct issues, especially the nature of category structures – of taxonomies – and the fractal character of economic distributions, which bears on the relationship between an observable portion of a distribution and the whole thing.

Categories are groups of individuals. The characteristics of a category are the statistical summary of the characteristics of the individuals covered by the category. Changes in the income (say) of individuals within a group change the average income of the group. One can therefore use a change in group average income as a proxy measure of changes affecting the underlying individuals. As group structures become more detailed and refined, the correspondence between group and individual necessarily becomes closer, until the two ways of looking at the data converge with each individual her own group.

This is true irrespective of the overlying character of the group – whether individuals are classed by location, industry, age, gender, body weight, religion, language or any combination of these or other characteristics so long as the groups are "MECE" – mutually exclusive, collectively exhaustive – that is to say, non-overlapping and covering the entirety of that part of the population being observed. At all points, dividing groups into subgroups increases between group inequality. And after a certain point, the movement of a distribution consistently measured across groups must reflect the movement of the same distribution measured across individuals. There is no need for a "random sample" to establish what the ebb and flow of the distribution is. Moreover, if the prime forces driving change in a distribution of incomes or earnings are differences across substantial geographic regions or between different industrial or economic sectors, then a fairly rough group structure will capture the important movements over time – so long as the structure is measured consistently. Administrative data sets, collecting income and population by region and employment and payrolls by sector and industry in hierarchical structures that remain reasonably stable over time, therefore turn out to be highly useful to a project of filling in the historical record of inequality statistics.

A limitation of categorical data in practice is that the group and underlying individuals covered may be a systematic (and therefore biased) subset of the population of interest. Thus, in a survey of manufacturing establishments, workers in units below a certain size may be excluded, while those in agriculture, services and the informal economy are not covered at all. But the fractal character of distributions implies that so long as the broad social relations of a society endure – so long as bankers make more than factory workers who make more than peasants – an increase in the inequality within a given observational frame – say, the manufacturing sector – is far more likely than not to mirror a change in the distribution writ large. By the same token, one can tell the weather – usually though not always – through a window at a glance.

The specific methodological contribution of the UTIP effort was to marry the above insights about categorical data sources – which are cheap and abundant in the real world – to Henri Theil's proposed general entropy measures of between-group inequality, specifically the between-groups component of Theil's T statistic, a simple and flexible formula that requires just two morsels of information on any group structure, namely the total population (or employment) and total income (or payroll) of each group. From this an inequality measure can be computed which is unaffected by sampling error, nor by inflation or by differences / changes in the currency unit over time. Moreover, the measure can be added-up at will across sectors or regions, or divided between them. The statistic is thus well-suited to the construction of dense and consistent time series, on an annual or even monthly basis where sources permit. The production *en masse* of such series from diverse national and regional data sources was an early UTIP contribution (Galbraith, Conceição and Bradford, 2001).

The formula for the between-groups component of Theil's T-statistic across G groups is:

$$T = \sum_{i=1}^{G} p_i R_i ln(R_i) \text{ for } 1 \leq i \leq G$$

where p_i is the population (or employment) share of group i, and R_i is the ratio of average income (or pay) in group i to the average income of the population (or pay of the employed population) as a whole. Thus groups with an above (below) average income (or pay) make a positive (negative) contribution to total inequality, and each group's contribution is weighted by its population (employment) share. The expression to the right of the summation is referred to as the "Theil element" for each of G groups. T is the sum of the "Theil elements" and is always a positive number. Replicating this calculation across adjacent time periods using a stable group structure generates a very sensitive measure of the evolution of inequality, from widely-available source data.

But there was more. For reasons that remain mathematically obscure, in data sets that measure employment and payrolls across consistently-categorized industries or economic sectors – examples include the Industrial Statistics of the United Nations Industrial Development Organization (UNIDO) and Eurostat's REGIO – the between- groups component of Theil's T statistic is effectively normalized, so that measures compared between countries – and not merely through time within a country – tend to correspond closely to the available survey-based measures (especially from harmonized data sets such as LIS) and to evolve smoothly across international frontiers (rising from North to South in Europe, for instance) in ways that strongly suggest that international comparisons with these measures correspond to underlying economic realities. The same cannot be said for at least some of the survey-based data sets, which in some cases show sharp inconsistencies in inequality between neighboring countries (such as France and Germany, for example) with similar average income levels and open borders. But if France were radically more unequal than Germany as some data sets appear to show, then low wage workers would migrate to Germany from France. This does not appear to be a common case.

The discovery that between-groups Theil statistics could accurately depict both the evolution of inequalities over time and comparative levels of inequality between countries (or other geographic entities, such as sub-national regions in Europe, or US states) opened up the prospect of a search for international, inter-continental and global patterns in the evolution of inequality through time, hence the possibility of identifying forces driving a continental or even global macroeconomics of inequality, as well as decompositions of each inequality measure into the specific contributions of each region or sector, enabling a descriptive history of inequality going far beyond, in detail and accuracy the limited information reported on households or persons in surveys. It also became possible to seek the institutional and political correlates of changing inequality within countries, as the measures prove to be sensitive reflections of revolutions, *coups d'état* and regime change. Sometimes even the mundane consequences of ordinary elections can be detected.

6. Quality of the UTIP measures

How do measures of inequality computed in this way – from a limited and systematically–biased underlying data set, such as UNIDO's Industrial Statistics – correspond to measures taken by other researchers over time in the customary ways? To assess this question, UTIP conducted two research exercises.

The first was a comparison by linear regression of the UTIP Theil measures to an early collection of Gini measures from diverse surveys – the Deininger / Squire data set of the World Bank, first published in the mid 1990s, was chosen for this purpose because it has a manageable number of distinct conceptual categories (six) and also because it was the dominant international comparative data set on inequality at the time. The comparison showed that after controlling for concept – whether an inequality measure was gross or net of tax, of income or of expenditure, whether the observational unit was the person or the household – considerable variance in the DS set could be accounted for by just two variables, the share of manufacturing employment in total population and pay inequality measured across industries within the manufacturing sector. Coefficients on both variables were stable and precisely estimated. This permitted the construction of extensive estimated measures of gross household income inequality in Gini format, and so the construction of an dense and consistent inequality data set, covering almost 150 countries from 1963 forward, more than available from any other source not using interpolation across countries or years (Galbraith and Kum 2005).

The second verification exercise compared the UTIP estimates to inequality measures in the published record, a painstaking exercise carried over a period of years (Galbraith, Halbach et al., 2016). There is no easy way to summarize this evidence; it has to be examined and evaluated visually. However, a fair summary is that for wealthy and transition economies, the Estimated Household Income Inequality (EHII) series track available survey evidence on the same concept well, and generally fall – as predicted – between measures of "market inequality" and measures of "disposable" (or net) income inequality – the former high and the latter low. Further, the EHII data set corresponds well to narrower data sets that use consistent concepts, such as those from the OECD, ECLAC and the European Union (Galbraith, Choi et al., 2016).

For developing countries, a similar story holds, except that in some larger countries such as Mexico, Brazil, South Africa, the EHII estimates tend to fall below those found by surveys. The relatively small weight of manufacturing in these economies may be partly responsible, but there is also the fact that in some large, poor countries a significant share of households reports no income at all – about a third, in South African data. This calls into question whether the meanings of "income" and "house- hold" are comparable as between wealthy countries and those with a substantial share of deeply impoverished people.

In South Africa, the EHII estimates run continuously from the 1960s into the early 2000s, thus spanning the liberation in 1994, which is not the case for any survey evidence on inequalities in South Africa. The inequality estimates are tolerably close to survey-based Gini coefficients in the apartheid period, but far below those of more recent years. We suggest two reasons, based on discussions at the Southern Center for Inequality Studies in 2018. First, that in the earlier period, a significant share of the South African population was simply uncounted, because it was officially considered not-South African, but rather citizens of the various apartheid-era homelands. Second, that in the post-liberation years, a great many households have formed that subsist on casual labor and the basic grant, but consider that they have no regular "job'" and report zero income to surveys. If this number indeed approaches thirty percent of all households in South Africa, that would by itself add 30 points to the Gini even if all reported incomes were equal, which is of course not the case. Thirty Gini points is about the difference between the EHII estimate and measures from modern South African surveys.

With respect to the United States, as well, after the early 1990s the EHII estimates fall below survey and tax estimates of inequality, because the wealthiest US households have in these years substantial and rapidly growing income from capital, which they report. This adds an almost unique dimension to measured income inequalities in the US, closely tracking capital asset prices. It is not clear that this indicates actually- greater inequality in the United States as compared to other wealthy countries, but may instead be a consequence of the relative thoroughness and effectiveness of US income tax reporting. So far as it applies to those with high incomes, the US tax system is considerably more rigorous than, say, the Italian.

There are multiple ways in which measurement and recording issues work to show higher inequalities in the United States as opposed to European and other countries. In tax records, a culture of compliance with tax laws – in part because these tend to be lenient toward capital incomes – is one such way. In the survey record, a large jump in the reported inequality in household incomes in the early 1990s was due partly to improved survey methods – use of computers by survey-takers – and in part to an increase in the threshold for top-coding of income responses. A greater proportion of capital assets in publicly-registered and traded companies means greater transparency in capital gains. Less access to and use of tax havens by the broad population of capital asset owners is another factor. And there is the mathematical fact that when distributions have "fat tails," more intensive surveys in the top brackets will reveal more high-income households and therefore yield higher inequality measures. And finally, adding-in the commonly-ignored between-countries component of inequality across Europe reverses the usual notion that pay scales in Europe are more egalitarian than in the United States (Galbraith, Conceição and Ferreira, 1999).

Even after noting the exceptions, the simple UTIP EHII model produces sensible estimates of gross household income inequalities over time, and the EHII data set is the largest available consisting solely of independently measured, consistent inequality concepts.[4]

The creation of conceptually consistent, dense panel data sets on inter-industry pay inequality and its derivative data set on estimated household gross income inequality, each with about 150 countries and about 4000 independent country – year observations beginning in 1963, opens the door to a new kind of global economics. Such an economics integrates distribution – the central preoccupation of microeconomics in mainstream classical and neo-classical theory – with the presence of macroeconomic forces and influences on an international and even planetary basis. It is an economics without *a priori* national or regional boundaries, an economics *sans frontières*, an empirical economics for an age of globalization, an economics which treats interdependence as a foundational fact whose properties are to be analyzed, rather than as an add-on to a prefabricated national model – as in Keynesian macro-economics – or as a mere incantation in a world of insular, supply-and-demand driven labor markets, each with its boundaries fixed, in practice, by the happenstance and whim of national or regional statistical agencies. The work also transcends the conventional distinction between advanced and developing countries,

---

[4] Solt's SWIID is larger, but it is reliant on interpolations across countries and through time to fill in many gaps. And SWIID draws on EHII as one of its source data sets.

blending the two into a portrait of the world economy as a unified whole.

7. What the EHII data reveal

We turn finally to what the analysis shows. Research possibilities are boundless, since inequality measures can be compared not only to each other but also to other socioeconomic variables: income, life, health, violence, happiness, and more.[5]

Basic facts are among the most useful. A glance at a map tells that there is a gradient of inequality measures that runs roughly from North to South, from wealthier countries to poorer ones, and also (to a degree) from East to West, in the sense that socialist or formerly socialist economies (until they collapsed) had egalitarian qualities which their capitalist adversaries did not. This gradient plainly reflects the strength of an industrial and urban middle class in the wealthy countries; without such a class, a country is necessarily both poor and unequal, an amalgam of landlords (and resource barons) and peasants, peons, serfs. Especially high inequality readings turn up – no surprise – in the oil kingdoms and in the mining fiefs of the Third World. Table 1 presents the country fixed-effects from a two-way fixed-effects regression on the measures of inter-industrial pay inequalities, 1963 to 2014. While the coefficients have no intuitive interpretation, they provide a rank-ordering and relative size-effect of the inequalities. The table is a

---

[5] The UTIP team has largely steered clear of these comparisons, in part because the limited span of other data sets means that many comparisons entail many lost observations.

rough cut, and we have not edited out some implausible values, but it represents so far as we know the only effort to achieve this result consistently, so far available.

The two-way fixed-effects model is designed to yield a summary description of the patterns in the data – not to test hypotheses per se but to motivate informed explanation of suitable causal factors. The model equation is:

$$T_{it} = \beta_i X_i + \gamma_t Y_t + \epsilon_{it}$$

where the X and Y are vectors of dummy variables representing countries and years respectively, and T_{it} are the elements of a matrix of inequality measures indexed by country and year. Thus the β_i yield coefficients of country fixed-effects and the γ_t yield a time trend common to the inequality measures in the data set, but relatively insulated from the presence or absence of particular measures for any particular country in any particular year.

Table 1 Country Effects on a Two-Way Fixed-effects Regression Using UTIP-UNIDO Measures of Industrial Pay Inequality

Qatar	0.374	Zambia	0.032	Bulgaria	0.001
Kuwait	0.290	Mauritius	0.031	Nicaragua	0.001
Kyrgyzstan	0.227	Ethiopia	0.030	Hungary	0.000
Peru	0.207	South Africa	0.030	Republic of Korea	−0.001
Trinidad & Tobago	0.114	El Salvador	0.030	Yugoslavia	−0.001
Cameroon	0.087	Pakistan	0.029	Belgium	−0.002
Swaziland	0.085	Macedonia	0.028	Russian Federation	−0.003
Lesotho	0.083	Philippines	0.027	Cyprus	−0.003
Malawi	0.080	Suriname	0.026	Croatia	−0.004
Burundi	0.076	Argentina	0.026	Seychelles	−0.004
Togo	0.074	Egypt	0.025	Germany, Fed.Rep	−0.005
Mozambique	0.074	Sudan	0.024	Romania	−0.005
Papua New Guinea	0.073	Singapore	0.024	Algeria	−0.006
Puerto Rico	0.071	Turkey	0.024	Occpd Palestinian Territory	−0.006
Azerbaijan	0.069	Somalia	0.024	Afghanistan	−0.006
Oman	0.067	Israel	0.023	Canada	−0.007
Yemen	0.066	Burkina Faso	0.021	Iceland	−0.007
Rwanda	0.065	Tonga	0.019	New Zealand	−0.008
Jamaica	0.062	Sri Lanka	0.019	Cuba	−0.009
Morocco	0.061	Georgia	0.018	Germany	−0.009
Kenya	0.060	Fiji	0.017	Czechoslovakia	−0.009
Tunisia	0.060	Panama	0.017	Italy	−0.009
Mongolia	0.060	Kazakhstan	0.017	Austria	−0.009
India	0.052	Libyan Arab Jamahiriya	0.016	Australia	−0.010
Brazil	0.050	Madagascar	0.016	Ireland	−0.010
Indonesia	0.050	Ecuador	0.016	Malta	−0.010
Dominican Republic	0.049	Taiwan	0.015	Poland	−0.010
Ghana	0.048	Japan	0.015	Republic of Moldova	−0.011
Tanzania	0.048	Senegal	0.014	Germany, Dem. Rep	−0.011
Congo	0.045	Nigeria	0.014	United Kingdom	−0.011

Guatemala	0.045	Portugal	0.014	Latvia	-0.013
Honduras	0.042	Myanmar (Burma)	0.013	Slovenia	-0.013
Nepal	0.041	Iran	0.012	China	-0.013
Syria	0.039	Venezuela	0.012	Macao	-0.014
Uganda	0.037	Albania	0.012	Finland	-0.014
Jordan	0.037	Bangladesh	0.011	Luxembourg	-0.014
Thailand	0.037	Mexico	0.011	France	-0.014
Barbados	0.037	Uruguay	0.010	Slovakia	-0.015
Central African Republic	0.036	Colombia	0.007	Netherlands	-0.015
Ivory Coast	0.035	Estonia	0.006	Norway	-0.016
Eritrea	0.035	Iraq	0.006	Hong Kong	-0.017
Chile	0.035	Costa Rica	0.005	Denmark	-0.018
Botswana	0.034	Malaysia	0.004	Sweden	-0.020
Bolivia	0.034	Ukraine	0.004	Vietnam	-0.021
Zimbabwe	0.033	Greece	0.003	Switzerland	-0.024
Zambia	0.032	Spain	0.003	Czech Republic	-0.026
Mauritius	0.031	Lithuania	0.002		

Note: Countries ranked by size of effect. The United States serves as the baseline and thus these values capture the average distance from the baseline after controlling for year effects. These rankings do not reflect any particular moment in time, and in certain cases the inequality measures have changed dramatically over the life of the panel, 1963-2014. The 15 countries with less than 10 observations were removed. Fixed-effects may also be influenced by the years for which data are available.

The table suggests that Kuznets was right – up to a point. There is an organic relation between income and inequality. In general, for most countries in a cross section, inequality declines as income rises. The intuition behind this regularity is plain: in order to be a high-income country on average, a nation must have a strong and prosperous middle class, and therefore relatively low inequalities. As Adam Smith observed, it is not possible for a nation to be prosperous while the large mass of its people remain poor. The main exceptions are a handful of very-high-income resource fiefs – notably the oil kingdoms of the Persian Gulf – whose inequality is an artefact of having imported their manual labor force from other countries, most notably Pakistan, India, Sri Lanka.

Kuznets' view of an initial period of egalitarian peasant agriculture applies only to a handful of cases – such as North America north of the Mason Dixon Line in the 18th and 19th centuries – and in the wider world only if one excludes – as he did – landlords and rental income. In the modern world, the cases of post-revolutionary China and of post-1992 India fit under the rising pattern of Kuznets' inverted U. But a large number of developing countries, notably in Latin America, are squarely on the downward-sloping part of the Kuznets curve; when growth is strong inequalities decline and when it is weak, they rise. In the industrial and semi-industrial world, a relatively egalitarian society with a prosperous middle class is the constructed artifact of industrialization, urbanization and social policies. Countries which have a small urban-rural divide generally achieve this by supporting agriculture from the surplus of the cities.

Meanwhile close examination of a handful of the richest countries – the US, UK, Japan – exposes that in these cases, inequality rises as the economy grows. This is the evident consequence of a structural concentration on technology and finance in a global setting (for an early discussion, see Galbraith, 1989). Countries that export financial services and advanced capital equipment to the world experience rising inequality in investment booms, and falling inequality in a slump. The "Augmented Kuznets Curve" (Conceição and Galbraith, 2001) captures these stylized facts. In short, Kuznets correctly captured the critical role played by intersectoral structural change in inequality. However his historical experience precluded him having applied that correct insight to the peculiar facts of globalization.

A second observation emerges from a glance at maps: that countries of the core   of the world economy – call them the OECD – resemble each other, and resemble their close neighbors more closely than their distant ones. Thus, the Scandinavian countries form a low-inequality unit, so do Germany and its neighbors, while the Mediterranean countries are more unequal. These are signs of economic integration; large differences occur only across substantial boundaries and distances. Further, large continental regions – the United States – are necessarily more unequal than small European states taken individually – although, as noted above, the picture changes if one takes Europe as a single integrated continental economy, adding the between-countries element of pay inequality to the within-country components. (A further difficulty of exact comparison of upper-income inequality lies in the superior tax reporting of the United States compared to the tax-haven-rich European Union.) Examining national patterns over time, it is clear that measures of inequality – particularly those of pay inequality in manufacturing, but also many geographic and intersectoral measures drawn from national data sources, are sensitive mirrors of underlying political events. Thus, the coup in Chile in 1973; in Argentina in 1976, the 1992 liberalizations in India, the reforms after 1993 in China, and above all the collapse of the USSR and of socialism in Eastern Europe show as moments of rising inequality. In some cases, these are dramatic. Meanwhile the Iranian revolution, the Iran-Iraq war and the period of post neo-liberal recovery (and higher commodity prices) in South America and Russia in the 2000s are among the limited instances of declining inequalities. The social implications of declining inequality are not always unambiguous. For example, data for the German Democratic Republic show declining inequality on a steady path until the country disappeared. As a general rule, though, low and stable inequality is associated with strong institutions and wealth; high and fluctuating inequality is the lot of poorer open economies adrift on a sea of debts, unstable commodity prices and fluctuating interest rates, as well as military conflict and political upheaval.

Patterns of geographic contiguity establish the existence of interdependence and of global hierarchies. They validate the center-periphery view of economic relations under global capitalism and put paid to the practice of national economic modeling except for the largest, most autonomous economies of the global center; most countries are not autonomous and their conditions are dominated by global forces and trends. They also establish the transnational scale of distributive relations, calling into question the notion of "microfoundations." Instead of building a consolidated picture from individual or household data, a practice that assumes the autonomy of those units, the world appears to be structured from the top down. And so the question becomes, by what major force or forces?

An answer can be sought in a search in the data for global patterns – trends and turning points through time. The existence of a *common pattern of movement* is evidence *prima facie* of a common underlying force, with broad global effect on national distributions of pay or income. It is also per contra proof that purely national or local analyses of 'market forces' – the stuff and substance of neoclassical microeconomic and labor market analysis – cannot be sufficient to explain the phenomenon under review.

8. Global macroeconomics and inequality

Inspection of trends and changes in inequality gives a strong clue to the sweep of events. There are four trends and three distinct turning points. From 1963–1971, no trend appears, and changes in individual countries are for the most part small. After 1971, while inequality increases in some of the wealthy countries, in much of the world it is declining. After 1980, there is a radical change, and the world enters on a period of large inequality increases, sweeping across regions beginning in Latin America and Africa, hitting Eastern Europe and the (former) USSR after 1989, and moving on to Asia in the 1990s. In 2000 there is a further turning point, after which stabilization and even modest declines in inequality are found in Russia, China, Latin America, parts of Africa and elsewhere. Figure 1 provides this time trend as estimated above, over the entire global data set. The key turning points in the early 1970s, in 1981, and 2000 emerge very clearly.

Figure 1 The Time Trend of Global Inequality

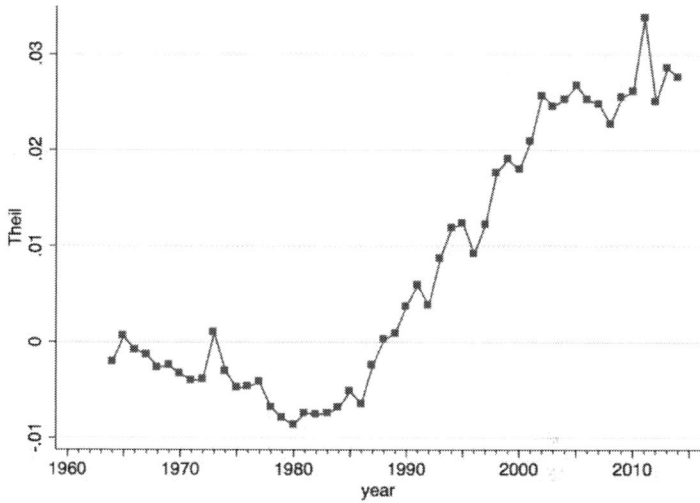

Note: *The trend measured from pay across industrial sectors, and calculated as the time coefficient of a two-way fixed-effects model using the UTIP-UNIDO data set. The reference year is 1963, and thus each coefficient refers to the differences from that year.*

The meaning of these patterns seems accessible from elementary knowledge of key economic developments at global scale. In 1971 the stabilizing exchange rate framework of the Bretton Woods institutions collapsed – or more precisely was torpedoed by the anchor country, the United States. There followed a nine-year boom in commodity prices, led by oil and fueled by the recycling of petrodollars into commercial bank loans to the Third World. Inequality fell in the (numerous, relatively poor) commodity-producing and debt-increasing countries, which grew rapidly: it rose in the fewer (relatively rich) industrialized consumers, especially in the crisis year, 1973. Two simple parameters, debt flow and oil prices, dominated the global pattern, while national institutions and politics affected the timing of effect in particular cases, such as the coups in Chile (1973) or Argentina (1976) on the side of rising inequality as compared with (say) the revolution in Iran (1979).

These patterns are consistent with the central thesis of the original Kuznets hypothesis, in a world where most countries are to be found on the downward-sloping surface of the inverted-U. In most such cases, stronger growth – whether fueled by commodity exports or debt – absorbs surplus labor into formal and informal activities, raising wages more rapidly at the bottom of the pay scale than toward the top. The two great exceptions in those years were China and India, clearly still on the upward-sloping Kuznets surface, but which had not then begun to enjoy their long growth-and-development phases.

In 1981 the global crisis ended the commodities-debt-and-development boom. The crisis hit first in the most exposed indebted countries, provoking a collapse of investment, de-industrialization, a collapse of public revenues and public services, and in certain cases – Chile 1982 – a banking crisis. Inequalities rose as the middle classes were destroyed. Ultimately better-protected countries – the East bloc – also fell before the pressure, along with the internal political strains it had generated and their own structural weaknesses. Financial liberalization and its discontents then spread to the most successful of the developing nations, the East Asian Tigers, who entered crisis in 1997. China experienced rising inequality as reforms and urbanization accelerated in the early 1990s, but having maintained capital controls throughout – and resisted the temptation to lift them[6] – China remained untouched by this final act. That China was therefore poised to reap the spoils in the following decade is therefore not perhaps a surprise.

In the 2000s, following the NASDAQ collapse of April 2000 and the 2001 9-11 attacks, global interest rates fell and with China's growth, commodity prices recovered, giving space for left-wing governments to come to power in South America and in parts of Africa, enabling broad-based growth and poverty reductions. Meanwhile growth in China spread past its initial geographic concentration on Guangdong, Shanghai and Beijing, so that China too moved toward a downward-sloping Kuznets surface (Zhang 2016). In Russia a new government took partial control of the national resource base, stabilized living conditions and arrested the free-fall of life expectancy, fertility, emigration, and violence that had followed the dissolution of the USSR in the early 1990s. So, in Russia too inequality declined after the late 1990s. In the US a saw tooth pattern emerged, of underlying stagnation capped by income gains to property speculators and mortgage fraud, the signature elements of the ages of Bush and Obama. In Europe, the consolidation of the Eurozone replayed the global boom of the 1970s on a regional scale, as capital flowing to Portugal, Ireland, Greece and Spain set the stage for the subsequent collapse.

---

[6] The senior author served as Chief Technical Adviser for macroeconomic reform to the State Planning Commission at this time, and in 1995 organized discussions of capital control for the Chinese economic policy leadership. Robert Eisner and Jane D'Arista spoke at these meetings on the wisdom of maintaining controls.

Curiously the Great Financial Crisis was in the first instance a debacle of the rich countries, reducing measured inequalities for the very richest countries along the augmented, or secondary, upward-sloping surface of the Kuznets Curve. One can see this in national data for the United States, and in Europe-wide data showing the relative losses in London and Paris, the great financial centers. The effects on the wider world ran through other channels: declining commodity prices, the return of reactionary governments (throughout Latin America, also in India) and especially above all, the ironical flight to the US dollar, capital markets and Treasury bonds. A final discovery underscores the point: the relationship of pay inequality to exchange rates, measured against the dollar.

To see the effect of exchange rates on inequality, consider that a manufacturer has only two possible markets – those inside the country and those outside. Typically a country exports its best products, and the pay scales of the exporting sectors exceed those who sell only or largely at home. From this it follows that a depreciation of the national currency raises inequality: the peso or real or rupee income of the exporter rises, while that of the non-exporter stays the same. Inequality rises as a matter of accounting-and all the more so, if the increased local currency flows are concentrated *within* the exporting sector, flowing to upper-income echelons in the sector. No behavioral response or effect on trade flows is required. Devaluations raise inequality. *Overvaluations* therefore create the conditions under which vulnerability to increased inequality grows. These findings thus reinforce the arguments of Bresser Pereira's (2010) new developmentalism. Since we know that variations in pay inequality drive household income inequality, the line of causality is unambiguous; it must run from the exchange rate to the inequality measure.

Table 2 Correlations of Exchange Rates and Theil Index for Selected Countries

Mexico	0.98	India	0.48
Egypt	0.97	South Africa	0.46
Hungary	0.92	Zimbabwe	0.44
Poland	0.91	Malaysia	0.39
Pakistan	0.84	Algeria	0.36
Canada	0.82	Sweden	0.36
Guatemala	0.81	United Republic of Tanzania	0.26
Bangladesh	0.81	Philippines	0.21
Nigeria	0.80	Costa Rica	0.05
Israel	0.77	Norway	-0.08
Cameroon	0.75	Greece	-0.22
Uruguay	0.74	Ireland	-0.27
Jordan	0.71	Denmark	-0.36
Bolivia	0.66	Ethiopia	-0.50
Singapore	0.65	Republic of Korea	-0.52
Senegal	0.63	Austria	-0.63
Czech Republic	0.59	Japan	-0.67
New Zealand	0.58	Iraq	-0.73
Brazil	0.58	Cyprus	-0.77
United Kingdom	0.56	Germany	-0.79
Turkey	0.50		

Systematic comparison of inequality and exchange rates is complicated by – among other things – changes in the currency unit in certain countries. However Table 2 gives correlation coefficients for selected countries. In an examination of data from over 30 countries, Rossi found that while the slope of the relationship varies, depending on proximity to the United States, the relationship is often both strong and inverse (Galbraith and Rossi, 2016). More extensive work on the data is underway, and it suggests broadly that the effect is present in up to two-thirds of countries, strong in a third of them, with the strongest effects found in countries with open capital markets and supplier relationships with the Global North. Large industrial economies and those insulated from global capital are less affected, or not affected at all.

The statistical chase comes to an end: that global financial capital has been driving the movement of inequality, measured within countries, around the world for the years since 1971 seems established. And this, in a nutshell, is what we know about the relationship between globalization and inequality.

References

Atkinson, Anthony B., Lee Rainwater, and Timothy M. Smeeding (1995) "Income Distribution in OECD Countries: The Evidence from the Luxembourg Income Study (LIS)." Organization for Economic Cooperation and Development, Paris.

Birdsall, Nancy, David Ross, and Richard Sabot (1995) "Inequality and Growth Reconsidered: Lessons from East Asia."*The World Bank Economic Review* 9(3):477- 508.

Bluestone, Barry and Bennett Harrison (1990) *The Great U-turn: Corporate Restructuring and the Polarizing Of America.* New York: Basic Books.

Bound, John and George Johnson (1992) "Changes in the Structure of Wages in the 1980s: An Evaluation of Alternative Explanations." *American Economic Review* 82(3):371-392.

Bresser-Pereira, Luiz Carlos (2010) *Globalization and Competition: Why Some Emergent Countries Succeed While Others Fall Behind.* Cambridge: Cambridge University Press.

Deaton, Angus (2015) *The Great Escape: Health, Wealth and the Origins of Inequality.* Princeton: Princeton University Press.

Deininger, Klaus and Lyn Squire (1996) "A New Data Set Measuring Income Inequality." *World Bank Economic Review* 10(3):565-591.

Deininger, Klaus and Lyn Squire (1998) "New Ways of Looking at Old Issues: Inequality and Growth." *Journal of Development Economics* 57(2):259-287.

Forbes, Kristin J. (2000) "A Reassessment of the Relationship between Inequality and Growth." *American Economic Review* 90(4):869-887.

Galbraith, James K. (2019) "Sparse, Inconsistent and Unreliable: Tax Records and the World Inequality Report 2018." *Focus, Development and Change,* March 2019, 329-346. https://onlinelibrary.wiley.com/doi/full/10.1111/dech.12475.

Galbraith, James K. (2017) "The Politics and Pedagogy of Economic Inequality: A short contribution" *Symposium on the Pedagogy of Inequality,* PS, October, 1074-1076. DOI:

10.1017/S1049096517001330 2016. *Inequality: What Everyone Needs to Know.* New York: Oxford University Press.

Galbraith, James K. (2012) *Inequality and Instability: A Study of the World Economy Just Before the Great Crisis.* New York, Oxford University Press.

Galbraith, James K. (1998) *Created Unequal: The Crisis in American Pay.* New York: Free Press.

Galbraith, James K. (1989) *Balancing Acts: Technology, Finance and the American Future.* New York: Basic.

Galbraith, James K., Jaehee Choi, Béatrice Halbach, Aleksandra Malinowska, and Wenjie Zhang (2016) "A comparison of major world inequality data sets: LIS, OECD, EU-SILC, WDI and EHII." In Lorenzo Cappellari, Solomon W. Polachek, and Konstantinos Tatsiramos (eds), "Income Inequality Around the World", *Research in Labor Economics*, Vol. 44, pp 1-48.

Galbraith, James K., Béatrice Halbach, Aleksandra Malinowska, Amin Shams and Wenjie Zhang (2016). "The UTIP Global Inequality Data Sets 1963-2008: Updates, Revisions and Quality Checks." In Kaushik Basu, Vivian Hon and Joseph Stiglitz, (eds,) *Inequality and Growth.* Basingstoke: Palgrave MacMillan. Also appearing as: "The UTIP Global Inequality Data Sets, 1963–2008: Updates, Revisions and Quality Checks." In Joseph E. Stiglitz and Martin Guzman (eds), *Contemporary Issues in Microeconomics*, Basingstoke: Palgrave Macmillan, 2016, pp. 7–39.

Galbraith, James K. and Delfina Rossi (2016) "Exchange Rates and Industrial Wage Inequality in Open Economies." UTIP Working Paper No. 71, April 26.

Galbraith, James K., Corwin Priest and George Purcell (2007) "Economic Equality and Victory in War: An Empirical Investigation," *Defense and Peace Economics*, Vol 18(5), October, 431-449.2005.

Galbraith, James K., Enrique Garcilazo (2004) "Unemployment, Inequality and the Policy of Europe, 1984- 2000." *Banca Nazionale del Lavoro Quarterly Review*, Vol LVII, No. 228, March, 3-28.

Galbraith, James K. and Hyunsub Kum (2005) "Estimating the Inequality of Household Incomes: A Statistical Approach to the Creation of a Dense and Consistent Global Data Set." *Review of Income and Wealth* (1):115-143. 2005.

Galbraith, James K. and Hyunsub Kum (2003) "Inequality and Economic Growth: A Global View Based on Measures of Pay." *CESifo Economic Studies* 49(4):527-556.

Galbraith, James K., Maureen Berner (eds) (2001) *Inequality and Industrial Change: A Global View*, New York: Cambridge University Press. Spanish edition, Disigualdad y Cambio Industrial: Una Perspec AKAL, *Economia Actual*, 2004. Translated by Sergio Cámara Izquierdo.

Galbraith, James K., Pedro Conceição and Peter Bradford (2001) "The Theil Index in Sequences of Nested and Hierarchical Grouping Structures: Implications for the Measurement of Inequality Through Time, With Data Aggregated at Different Levels of Industrial Classification." *Eastern Economic Journal*, 27(4), Fall, 491-514.

Galbraith, James K., Pedro Conceição and Pedro Ferreira (1999) "Inequality and Unemployment in Europe: The American Cure." *New Left Review*, No. 237, September-October, 28-51.

Goldin, Claudia and Lawrence F. Katz (2008) *The Race Between Technology and Education*. Cambridge: Harvard University Press.

Harris, John R. and Michael P. Todaro (1970) "Migration, Unemployment and Development: A Two-Sector Analysis." *The American Economic Review* 60(1):126- 142.

Joint Economic Committee (1982) *Hearings on the Economic Report of the President*. Washington: Government Printing Office.

Kuznets, Simon (1955) "Economic Growth and Income Inequality." *The American Economic Review* 45(1):1–28.

Martin, Andrew (1981) "Economic Stagnation and Social Stalemate in Sweden." In *Monetary Policy, Selective Credit Policy and Industrial Policy in France, Britain West Germany and Sweden*. Washington: Joint Economic Committee.

Meidner, Rudolf and Gosta Rehn (1951) *Fackföreningrsrörelsen och den Fulla Sysselsättningen*, Stockholm: LO.

Milanovic, Branko (2016) *Global Inequality*. Cambridge: Belknap Press of Harvard University Press.

Milanovic, Branko (2005) *Worlds Apart: Measuring International and Global Inequality*. Princeton: Princeton University Press.

Piketty, Thomas (2014) *Capital in the 21s Century.* Cambridge: Harvard University Press.

Piketty, Thomas, et al. (2014) *The World Top Incomes Database*: http://topincomes.parisschoolofeconomics.eu/ Accessed Dec. 19.

Solt, Frederick. The SWIID. http://fsolt.org/swiid/.

University of Texas Inequality Project, working papers, maps and data sets at http://utip.lbj.utexas.edu.

Wood, Adrian J. B. (1994) *North-South Trade, Employment and Inequality.* Oxford: Clarendon Press of Oxford University Press.

World Bank (2007) et seq., "World Development Indicators Online (WDI)" Available at http://www.worldbank.org/.

World Institute of Development Economics Research, accessible at https://www.wider.unu.edu/.

Wright, Noah (2015) "Data Visualization in Capital in the 21st Century." *World Social and Economic Review* No 5, July.

Zhang, Wenjie (2016) "The Evolution of China's Pay Inequality from 1987 to 2012." *Journal of Contemporary Chinese Affairs*, Vol.45, No. 2 (2016).

Chapter 8

Thomas Piketty's changing views on inequality

Steven Pressman

1. Introduction

Thomas Piketty established his professional reputation by using income tax returns to measure income distribution over long time periods in several nations. Long before *Capital in the Twenty-First Century* (hereafter *C21*) appeared, Piketty (2001; 2003; & Saez, 2003) showed that, in many capitalist countries, income flowed to the top 1% (really the top .1%). *C21* made two new contributions – a theory to explain this phenomenon, r>g, and a policy solution, taxing wealth.

Surprisingly, *C21* became an international best seller. Nonetheless, it was criticized by a broad array of economists. Heterodox economists objected to the economic theory Piketty used to explain rising inequality. Neoclassical economists disliked his policy proposal and understood that neoclassical economics didn't support Piketty's explanation of rising inequality. And many economists criticized Piketty's data and his interpretation of the distributional facts (see Pressman, 2016).

Piketty's follow up, *Capital and Ideology*, was published in France last fall; an English version appeared in March of 2020. There are many similarities between the two books. Both are massive tomes,[1] well-written and packed with economic data. Both use the term "capital" when really talking about wealth. Finally, literary references abound to support key points.

Despite these similarities, there are many changes. Gone are r>g and any analysis of inequality that rests on neoclassical economic theory. *Capital and Ideology* contains a different perspective on the causes of inequality. As its title proclaims, it is our beliefs that are crucial. Piketty undertakes a broad sweep of history to argue that the degree of inequality we get depends on how people see inequality and that this varies from time to time and from place to place. A progressive ideology, leading to greater equality during the 20th century, ran out of steam by the end of the century. It was replaced by the view that markets increase human well-being. There is also a new policy proposal – broader representation on corporate boards.

This paper examines Piketty's changing views on the causes of inequality and the policy solutions needed to remedy the problem. Section 2 provides a brief overview of some general perspectives on understanding income

---

[1] *Capital and Ideology* is over 1000 pages. The English version of C21 was cut by 200 pages from the original French version. Something similar should have been done for *Capital and Ideology*.

inequality. Section 3 focuses on how *C21* views the causes of inequality. Section 4 then discusses the causes of inequality according to *Capital and Ideology*. Section 5 looks at key policy proposals to reduce inequality in both books. Section 6 concludes.

2. Understanding inequality

There are three broad viewpoints regarding the determinants of income and the causes of income inequality. The standard economic approach focuses on worker productivity, and how this determines worker wages and income distribution. An institutional or political economy approach sees wages determined by economic power and the willingness of government to counter the power of large firms and reduce inequalities created in the market economy. Finally, a nihilist approach focuses on dumb luck – the luck of being born to rich parents, having a good genetic endowment (Barth, Papageorge and Thom, 2020), and being in the right place at the right time.[2]

According to the standard economic approach, income depends on one's productivity. *Capital and Ideology* calls this the "meritocracy explanation" of inequality; wages depend on individual effort, especially the education or human capital that people accumulate (Becker, 1964; Schultz, 1961). We invest in ourselves through schooling. This yields returns in the form of higher wages, just as investments in machinery yield returns in the form of profits. Other factors, such as globalization (Wood, 1994)

---

[2] US public opinion is moving away from the economic approach and towards the dumb luck approach (Pew Research Center, 2020).

and technology (Bound and Johnson, 1992; Brynjolfsson and McAfee, 2014) also come into play; but these economic forces work in tandem with education to determine incomes and income distribution.

Greater inequality follows from unequal investments in education. The work of Kuznets (1955) can help explain this. Kuznets analyzed what happens when labor moves from rural areas paying low wages to urban centers paying high wages. He noted that as people move to cities, inequality will increase, and it will increase until around half the population lives in urban areas. At this time, migration reduces inequality. This analysis can be extended to education. When few people have college degrees, those with degree will make more money due to their educational credentials, pushing up income inequality. Once a large fraction of the population has graduated from college, the premium for a college degree starts to fall. At the same time, as uneducated workers become scarce, their wages will rise.

Adding globalization, or the greater movement of capital and labor around the world, complements the education story. When firms outsource production, domestic workers must compete with (less educated) foreign workers willing to accept lower pay; if they refuse, firms will relocate production to low-wage countries. Similarly, unskilled workers coming from abroad, will exert downward pressure on domestic wages for those lacking adequate education. Technological change also reinforces the economic story. Technology favors workers able to use new technology; wages fall for those unable to do so. Real world examples of this abound. Automated assembly lines have replaced manufacturing workers. Self-driving cars and trucks threaten the jobs and incomes of cabbies and truck drivers.

There are several problems with this story. It doesn't explain why income has been flowing to the top .1%, who are not the educated elite. It is also not clear why inequality in the US was flat between 1959 and 1989 when the fraction of the population over 25 with a college degree doubled from 10% to 20%, but then soared between 1989 and 2019 when the fraction rose to 36%. Furthermore, the 1.7 million Americans who work as long-haul truck drivers earn around $43,600 a year, down sharply (in real terms) since the 1980s (Gabriel, 2017), well before anyone began talking about robot truckers; and Mishel et al. (2007) note that unskilled workers did better in the 1990s than in the 1980s, although the percentage of foreign-born workers increased twice as much in the 1990s.

The institutional or political economy approach focuses on the ability of large companies to squeeze workers. It also focuses the ability of governments to reduce inequality through fiscal policy, and by passing laws that aid and protect workers (e.g., high minimum wages and laws facilitating unionization).

Disposable income depends on earnings plus government transfer payments less taxes, so fiscal policy plays a large role in distribution. Generous income supports for low-income and middle class workers (such as unemployment insurance, child allowances and old age pensions) raise disposable income for these families.

Progressive taxes reduce the disposable income of the rich and also provide the money to fund spending programs. Hungerford (2011: 11) estimates that tax policy, particularly lower taxes on capital gains and dividends, was "the largest contributor to the increase in ... income inequality" between 1996 and 2006.

Piketty ignores much of this in *C21* by focusing on taxable income (adjusted gross income in the US) rather than disposable income. His approach was to develop an extensive dataset for countries that began in the early 20th century, when income taxes were first introduced. His figures are for the share of taxable income received by the wealthy. This made data collection easier; but it ignored the impact of fiscal policy on distribution, as well as changes in what counts as taxable income over time (see Pressman, 2016: Ch. 2).

Further, as Joan Robinson (1933) noted, when there are few employers, we have a monopoly-like situation that she called "monopsony". In this case, firms hire fewer workers, pay them less, and have unfilled jobs because they are unwilling to raise wages. Monopsony power also keeps workers from earning more money by changing jobs. Non-compete clauses in hiring contracts prevent workers from looking for jobs with better pay or starting up another firm in a specific geographic area or for a specific time, usually 6-24 months (Gilson, 1999). No-poach agreements prevent firms from stealing workers from another firm that is part of the same franchise chain. Nearly 60% of major US franchises require store owners to sign such agreements, up from 36% in 1996 (Starr, 2019).

A final approach to income distribution focuses on randomness or luck. Luck determines whom one meets and marries, whether one is healthy, our genetic capabilities, and the character and quality of one's family (financial and otherwise). All play a large role in determining future income. Robert Frank (2016) remarks that it was a matter of luck that he went to college, which then made a huge difference in his life. After completing his Ph.D., luck landed him a job offer from Cornell the day before he was going to accept an academic position at a mid-west school that would have given him more teaching and less income. At Cornell he had the time and institutional support to be able to write many highly successful books.

Beyond Frank's personal experiences, luck seems important for individual success. What we call "natural ability" is the luck of one's genetic makeup. Top athletes, such as Michael Jordan, and professional musicians, such as Yo-Yo Ma, were blessed with good genes. A good education is also essential for success. This too depends on luck to a large extent. Someone had to teach Michael to shoot and dribble a basketball, and he had to "practice, practice, practice". Yo-Yo needed a first-rate cello and lessons from outstanding cellists. All this requires money. More generally, wealth enables parents to hire private tutors for their children, have their children attend the best possible schools, graduate from top colleges, and earn more money as adults.

C21 favored the dumb luck approach. Parents matter most of all.[3] Contrary to the life-cycle theory of consumption (Modigliani and Brumberg, 1954), those with wealth pass it to their children, who then pass it on to their children. For most of human history, wealth in the form of land went to the eldest living son (the luck of the draw and the luck of survival); more recently, financial assets enabled wealth to be split among children (possibly equally and possibly not). *Capital and Ideology* rejects the dumb luck approach of *C21*. Instead, it provides an institutional or political economy explanation for inequality. What matters is the power of ideas and (indirectly) the economic power of those with wealth.

3. *Capital in the Twenty-First Century* and its shortcomings

The great strength of *C21* was its presentation of economic data, shedding enormous light on the history of income and wealth distribution during the 20th century. The book cleverly linked income inequality and wealth inequality. Average incomes grew by g, the rate of growth of the economy. Wealth inequality led to income inequality via its high rate of return, r, which then contributed to greater wealth inequality because some of these returns get saved, become part of wealth, and provide even more future income (for a numerical example, see Pressman, 2016: 66).

Piketty still needed a theory to explain his empirical results. Because, *unluckily*, he was taught neoclassical

---

[3] Frank (2016) tells us that he was an orphan, but good luck came his way later in life.

economic theory – that is what he knew and what he relied on in *C21*. Post Keynesian theory, where spending by the rich lead to profits for the rich, would have avoided many problems (see Zorn & Pressman, 2020).

Perhaps the biggest problem is that it is unclear why r>g. Piketty (2014: Fig 10.9) presents data estimating that r has averaged 5% over several centuries, while g has averaged only 2% to 3%. *C21* discusses the determinants of g; however, it says nothing about r. Here lies a big problem. If the supply of wealth or capital increases over time, according to standard economic theory its returns, r, should *fall*. *C21* struggled, *unsuccessfully*, to explain why this didn't happen.

Second, the r>g explanation assumes little income or wealth mobility from one generation to the next. This is not true now nor in the past. Some children of the rich splurge and quickly consume their inheritance, while others make unlucky or bad decisions and become poor (as Thomas Mann depicts in *Buddenbrooks*). On the other hand, each generation has its nouveau riche. People on the Forbes 400 list of the richest people in the world change regularly (McBride, 2014). Jeff Bezos, Warren Buffet, Bill Gates, and Oprah Winfrey didn't inherit great wealth from their parents; they are self-made billionaires.

Third, some empirical facts in *C21* contradict the main argument of the book. Barring unforeseen circumstances like war, revolution, or a natural disaster like the coronavirus pandemic, r>g implies that inequality should increase continuously over time and should be increasing everywhere under capitalism. Piketty himself (2014: 25–7, 242–6) emphasizes this point. Yet his data shows that inequality was low and remained low in western nations during the relatively peaceful decades following World War II. Further, inequality rose more in the US than other developed nations in the late 20th century. In other countries (e.g., France) it remained stable throughout the latter half of the century. Different cross-national experiences, and different results in one nation over time, suggest institutional factors are at play in determining inequality.

Recognizing this, *Capital and Ideology* moves away from a luck-centered view of inequality and towards the institutional or political economy approach – what is important are our beliefs about inequality, and the power of corporations to increase profits, and reduce wages and the wage share. These changes are possible because Piketty abandons neoclassical economic theory and uses history to understand income inequality.

4. Capital and ideology

Piketty has commented that his childhood heroes were left-of-center economic historians Fernand Braudel and Lucien Febrvre (Cassidy, 2014). In *Capital and Ideology* Piketty returns to his main interests when growing up.

He abandons his neoclassical education and the theory he absorbed at the London School of Economics. There is no mention of r>g, and no discussion of how this can be reconciled with neoclassical theory. Instead, as the title of the book indicates, the focus is on ideology. What

Piketty means by this, in brief, is that when it comes to inequality, nations get what they believe. The book is also about historical justifications for inequality, and their importance, starting from ancient times and continuing to the present.

More specifically, ideology for Piketty is a set of ideas, or public discourses, that describe how society should be structured and the limits to property rights. Ideology gives answers to questions such as how much should people be taxed (tax regimes), how values and knowledge get transmitted from one generation to another (education regimes), what people can own, and how property can be transferred across generations (property regimes). These ideologies exist in all societies and justify the existing income distribution income (Piketty, 2020: 29). They reduce political opposition to inequality, which may take the form of revolution or the confiscation of private property. By placating people, ideologies reduce the chance of revolution at the ballot box – electing people whose goal is a radical change in the national income and wealth distribution.

The link between ideology and inequality is straightforward. Nations that glorify the competitive spirit and the market are the nations that allow capitalism to run amuck, with little government regulation or oversight. This leads to lower taxes and meager spending programs that might mitigate inequality. Conversely, those nations where people believe that the power of capital needs to be counterbalanced with the power of government (because there is consensus regarding national interests other than profit maximization) do more to reduce inequality through progressive taxation and generous social insurance programs, as well as legal restraints on corporate power.

The Introduction to *Capital and Ideology* notes two shortcomings with *C21* that it seeks to correct – it focuses mainly on developed capitalist nations and it pays insufficient attention to the impact of ideas regarding inequality. I would add two more shortcomings that also get remedied to some extent. *Capital and Ideology* discusses other types of inequality, such as inequality in life expectancy and inequality of education; and it goes beyond economics to examine the political consequences of rising inequality – in particular, how and why low-income and less-educated workers are now supporting right-of-center parties.

Inequality in life expectancy has become a concern of late because life expectancy in the US has fallen, mainly for those with low incomes (Case and Deaton, 2020). As noted above, *C21* ignored the human capital approach that led most economists to focus on education as a cause of inequality in favor of dumb luck as an explanation for the existence of inequality. *Capital and Ideology* accepts a role for education but subsumes this under the more important factor that increases inequality. It notes that a burgeoning conservative ideology resulted in tax cuts for the rich and reduced government expenditures. As a result, substantial spending cutbacks hit the educational sector. Lower quality secondary education led the rich to send their children to private schools, which then opened the door for the children of the rich to attend elite colleges and universities. It also led to sharply rising college costs and enormous college debt, which is crushing many individuals who had to borrow money in order to obtain human capital.

Politics takes up the last part of *Capital and Ideology*. The book presents data on national voting behavior in an attempt to explain Brexit, and the election of leaders like Donald Trump in the US and Viktor Oban in Hungary. This part of the book throws much light on the current political situation throughout the world and its relationship to rising inequality. Many have been left behind in the new competitive global economy, and their political leanings have changed. In the US, over the course of several decades, less-educated and low-income voters moved from supporting the Democratic Party to supporting the Republican Party; at the same time, more educated and higher income voters have moved from supporting Republicans to supporting Democrats. Similar changes have taken place in France, the UK (the other two countries having good data) and elsewhere. According to Piketty this change is due, in part, to changing ideology; it stems from the failure of egalitarians to advance their cause. In addition, low-income voters lacking higher education saw their incomes fall and their lives become more precarious, and felt abandoned by the more liberal national parties. This is why they decided, Piketty contends, to give Trump and Brexit a chance.

The big difference in the two books is that Piketty now recognizes that inequality is *not* the result of broad economic forces (r>g, technology, globalization). No economic or technological imperative drives inequality; and once r>g is dropped, the luck of one's birth is no longer a main factor driving inequality. Rather, as critics of *C21* (e.g., Beker, 2014; Colander, 2014) pointed out, inequality is context dependent. In *Capital and Ideology* inequality varies from time to time and from place to place; it depends on the existing political institutions and ideologies regarding inequality. It depends on the equality of opportunity, especially educational opportunity. Thus, for *Capital and Ideology* history matters.

History matters because it shows us that different nations do different things at different points in time, and that one nation will do different things at different times. Understanding this history shows us that inequality is not inevitable. We can do different things; and doing different things will lead to different distributional outcomes. "The inequalities and institutions that exist today are not the only ones possible, whatever conservatives may say to the contrary" (Piketty, 2020: 7). *Capital and Inequality* sees inequality as stemming from the social institutions within each country – its laws regarding property rights, education and fiscal policy. Property rights concern who can own what and the limits to what property owners can do with their property. Education concerns who has access to education, the quality of education that everyone receives, and its cost. Fiscal policy concerns how taxes and government spending programs reduce inequality and provide different or similar opportunities to all of its citizens.

Piketty starts by taking the reader on a long historical journey. He examines how power arose and how it was justified in ancient times when the population was divided into the three main groups or classes – warriors, priests, and laborers. Land was owned by a small warrior class that became the nobility in Europe. Ideas were the province of the clergy, an equally small group. Everyone else was a worker, with few rights but in great need of protection by the warrior-nobles. As such, power is immediately placed at the heart of wealth or property ownership. So too is ideology. For those without property, salvation was promised by the clergy in an afterlife. This placated workers and helped maintain order in a world of poverty and great inequality. Things changed a bit as a result of the industrial revolution, but it is mainly names that changed; power relations remained the same. The rise of "ownership societies" and a business class reduced the power of the nobility. The business class still needed warriors (now the state) to protect them, priests (now educated intellectuals) to justify their great wealth, and workers to produce it.

According to Piketty (2020: 57), the old order disappeared as the state began to protect average citizens and make the services of the nobility obsolete. Similarly, over time, the state took on responsibility for developing knowledge. As a result, the clergy were no longer needed to perform this function; highly educated individuals naturally assumed this role. These changes took place at different times and with different speeds in different locations. Again, this points to the importance of national policies and ideologies rather than some general economic explanation (such as r>g) that impacts developed nations to the same extent over time.

A focus on colonial and slave societies further broadens Piketty's history of inequality. Colonialism involved the exercise of power by one nation over another; slavery was about some people exercising power over others. The negative economic and social consequences of being conquered explain why inequality in former colonies is among the largest in the world today. The power of property owners was also on full display when slavery ended in the US. Slave owners were compensated for their losses, but not those forced to live as slaves and deprived of property rights over their own body. Former slaves did not even receive the "40 acres and a mule" they were promised. For Piketty, this shows how beliefs in the sanctity of property have long-term distributional consequences, including the ability of accumulated wealth to perpetuate itself over time.

Like *C21*, *Capital and Ideology* does have some limitations. One shortcoming is that it doesn't address the big question of how people come to accept beliefs. If the level of inequality depends on beliefs, then we need to know how people actually view inequality and how these views change. Some research along these lines is beginning (Norton and Ariely, 2011), but this remains a gap in the argument of the book.

C21 ignored critiques of neoclassical distributional theory (e.g., the Cambridge Controversy). Likewise, *Capital and Ideology* pays insufficient attention to an extensive literature justifying the existence of property and acquisitiveness, or *The Political Theory of Possessive Individualism* to invoke the title of a famous book (Macpherson, 1962). From John Locke (1953[1690]) to Robert Nozick (1974) the philosophical justification of private property ownership has buttressed the case for unlimited private accumulation. Not addressing this literature is a huge oversight in a book that emphasizes the importance of ideology. In addition, the rise of dark money (to invoke the title of Mayer, 2016) and right-wing think tanks that promulgate the idea of free markets, low taxes, little government spending and minimal regulation is not addressed. Greater inequality makes it easier for the rich to contribute to political campaigns. This is why the votes of elected representatives in the US Congress tend to follow the preferences of their wealthy donors rather than the preferences of their constituents (Bartels, 2008). And when running for elective office is increasingly expensive, and elected officials need financial support to keep their jobs, they increasingly favor the ideas of those with lots of money (Hacker and Pierson, 2010).

Granted, Piketty is an economic historian and empiricist, rather than a political philosopher. Still, this literature is too important to be ignored. Instead of dealing with it and pinpointing its flaws (as Pressman 2013 does), Piketty (2020: 123) sets up a straw man. He contends that the current ideology takes property rights as sacrosanct, something that can never be abrogated; doing so, even a little, would open a Pandora's Box and lead to ever greater restrictions on property rights.

5.   Policy implications

Although viewing luck as a main cause of inequality, *C21* became institutionalist when it came to policy. This is only to be expected as policy proposals are about changing institutional structures. *Capital and Ideology* consistently focuses on institutions – how they generate inequality and possible solutions to the problem of inequality. In the policy arena ideas are key. Yet power, particularly the power of legislators to approve policy changes, is also important.

The key policy idea in *C21* was a wealth tax. Piketty (2014: Ch. 15) promulgated an annual 1% tax on net worth exceeding $1.35 million, rising to 2% tax on wealth greater than $6.75 million. He emphasized that the tax had to be global to prevent wealth from escaping the tax by moving to countries without a wealth tax and with no requirement to report wealth holdings to other nations.

Pressman (2016: Ch. 7) identified a number of practical problems with this policy, including a lack of liquidity, an inability to value assets, and likely tax avoidance. Two colleagues of Piketty, Saez and Zucman (2019), devised some clever solutions to these problems. They suggest using insurance assessments to value assets that are not traded regularly, and they suggest letting people give the government a fraction of their assets when owners are liquidity constrained. While ingenious, these solutions are still problematic. With so much money at stake, insurance fraud to escape the wealth tax is likely, with one asset value stipulated for the Federal government and a different one for insurance purposes. There is also a problem with assets that cannot be divided easily when someone lacks cash. I can give the government 1% of my stock shares, and probably even 2% ownership in my multi-millionaire dollar homes (effectively having a mortgage held by the government). But what about my collection of classic paintings and fine wines? Even after 20 years I will still own a majority share of these paintings, giving me control over them. And, would I need to send the government a small glass of wine whenever I drink an expensive bottle?

There are also political issues surrounding whether a wealth tax is constitutional. This is important because Piketty is clear that a wealth tax could not work without the US participating, as wealth would flow to the US in order to escape taxation. But getting the US on board is highly doubtful. A little historical background provides some insight. The US introduced an income tax in 1894, which the Supreme Court ruled unconstitutional the following year. It took another 18 years until the 16th Amendment to the US Constitution was passed and an income tax was enacted. Cohen (2020) argues that since the 1970s the Supreme Court has become even more conservative, favoring the rich over everyone else. Rulings have upheld strict voter ID laws and voter purges designed to keep the poor from voting, as well as limitations on class action lawsuits. It is highly likely that the Court would declare a wealth tax unconstitutional.

An amendment to the US Constitution requires support from two-thirds of the Senate and the House, followed by approval by three fourths (38) of US states. It could be stopped by 34 Senators or 13 states that won't pass an amendment because Republicans control either the Governor's mansion or one house of the state legislature. Currently, 26 states have Republican governors, and 31 have Republicans in control of at least one branch of the state legislature (including some states with a Democratic Governor). Furthermore, 20 states are virtually certain to vote to re-elect President Trump in 2020 and have voted Republican in nearly every Presidential election since the 1964 Democratic landslide victory. In this environment, it is hard to believe the US could have a wealth tax in the foreseeable future. Such problems are not unique to the US. A wealth tax in Germany was declared unconstitutional because it lacked clarity in how wealth would be valued (Glennerster, 2011).

Nonetheless, *Capital and Ideology* doubles down on taxing wealth. In fact, Piketty (2020: 976) goes even further, claiming that a wealth tax is *the only way* to reduce income and wealth inequality. Reminiscent of some problems with *C21*, his own data shows this is *not* the case. US inequality was low and stable from the 1940s until around 1980, even though there was no wealth tax during this time. Piketty cannot have it both ways. Either a wealth tax is necessary for keeping inequality under control, in which case there must be problems with Piketty's data, or his data on income distribution in the US during the middle of the 20th century is by and large correct and we don't need a wealth tax to achieve low levels of inequality. I side with the empirical Piketty on this.

The US can return to post-war levels of inequality without a fight over the constitutionality of a wealth tax.

Besides raising estate taxes, top individual income tax rates and corporate income tax rates can be increased, and there could be a significant financial transactions tax.[4] The US could also return to the post-war situation where capital income was taxed at the same rate as labor income, rather than at half that rate. All these changes would fall mainly on the shoulders of the very rich, who own most corporate stock, and would require only Presidential support and a majority of both houses of Congress.

From the perspective of *Capital and Ideology*, we might view *C21* as providing an ideology or justification for taxing wealth. As such, the political impact of the wealth tax proposal must be acknowledged – both Bernie Sanders and Elizabeth Warren advocated rather steep wealth taxes in their 2020 campaigns for the Democratic nomination to be President. However, this positive experience still runs counter to the experience in Europe, where almost every OECD country that had a wealth tax abandoned it, including Piketty's France (beginning in 2018). Reviving wealth taxes in a world of capital mobility where every nation must be on board seems impractical compared to raising existing taxes so that the rich bear a larger share of the national tax burden.

Piketty also undermines his case for the necessity of taxing wealth with a new policy proposal in *Capital and Ideology*, one involving changes in corporate governance and ownership. Chapter 17 pushes for a participatory socialism; among other things, it wants labor and the

---

[4] There is currently a small financial transactions tax that funds the Securities and Exchange Commission.

government to have representation on company boards. This practice has existed in Nordic Europe since the late 1940s and 1950s. Piketty (2020: 494) notes that West Germany passed a law on co-management in 1976 that is still in place, and gives workers some power over corporations. The law requires firms with more than 2000 workers to allocate half the seats on the Board of Directors to labor; and firms with 500 to 2000 workers to allocate one-third of Board seats to labor. Labor can obtain additional seats by owning shares of the firm. Further, Piketty (2020: 974) suggests limiting the percentage of voting shares one person can have in any company. This proposal, also, would reduce the power of business interests in determining corporation policies.

Piketty does recognize that the success of this policy has been limited because in case of a tie on the Board, shareholders rule. Also, much of the decision-making power in German firms adheres in the Directorate of the firm, which has no labor representation. Still, giving labor seats at the table has had a significant impact on CEO pay in Denmark, German and Sweden, which has not increased to anywhere near the level prevailing in the US and other nations where labor has no seat at the table and no voice (Piketty, 2020: 499). And according to Wolff and Zacharias (2009), rising CEO pay has been a major contributor to rising inequality in the US since the 1980s.

There is an even stronger justification for these changes than what Piketty provides. The corporation, unlike individually owned firms, is an entity created by the state in order to protect owners from any liability beyond their financial investment. Without such limited liability there would be no large corporations. This is part of the protective function that governments have played in ownership societies over long periods of time.

Furthermore, as we have seen recently in the US (the 9/11 attack, the Great Recession, and the current Covid-19 depression), large corporations tend to get bailed out by governments rather than being allowed to fail when "the market" says they should go under. As institutions that are, in practice, insured by the government because they are regarded as essential, workers and government officials should have seats on corporate boards to ensure that they act in the public interest rather than doing as they please and taking unacceptable risks with the knowledge that there is no downside because they will be bailed out by the government if anything goes wrong. Effectively, many large companies are public firms and should be seen as such. If firms are unwilling to accept this control, they should not be bailed out by the government; and if they are truly essential for contemporary economies (e.g., banks and airlines), governments may have to take these firms over in the national interest because they are essential for the health of the nation and cannot be allowed to fail. Given a choice between failure during the next crisis and stricter government regulation, shareholders and management may see the virtues of the regulation route.

6. Summary and conclusion

Two broad perspectives prevail regarding how history progresses.

Marx saw history as a power struggle between groups with diametrically opposed economic interests. The famous opening line of *The Communist Manifesto* proclaims: "The history of all hitherto existing society is the history of class struggles" (Marx and Engels, 1948[1848]: 9). In feudal times landowners and serfs struggled over the division of agricultural output. Under capitalism, workers and business owners battle over the division of revenue from selling services and manufactured goods. To the winner of this struggle go the spoils. Winners also write the (economic) history and promulgate the accepted ideas regarding income distribution.

Others have seen history as a struggle of ideas rather than a power struggle. At the end of *The General Theory of Employment, Interest and Money*, Keynes (1936: 383) contends that:

> "the ideas of economists and political philosophers, both when they are right and when they are wrong, are more powerful than is commonly understood. Indeed the world is ruled by little else. Practical men, who believe themselves to be quite exempt from any intellectual influences, are usually the slaves of some defunct economist. Madmen in authority, who hear voices in the air, are distilling their frenzy from some academic scribbler of a few years back. I am sure that the power of vested interests is vastly exaggerated compared with the gradual encroachment of ideas."

C21 sought a middle ground in this debate, a space between the real world of economic power and the academic world of ideas. Using data to show changes in income and wealth distribution over time, it focused on empirics and avoided mentioning either ideas or power. However, in a few places Piketty did see inequality as a struggle over the distribution of the output that gets produced. When discussing a miner's strike in Johannesburg, South Africa, Piketty (2014: 40) notes that the miners lost the strike because mine owners had greater economic power due to their great wealth, which would let them survive during a long strike.

Nonetheless, *C21* explained rising inequality by resorting to r>g, an empirical regularity, and generally ignored real-world power dynamics and the ideology of business interests that opposed taxing the rich. *C21* shined when it focused on these numbers; it dimmed when using economic ideas to explain r>g and thus distributional changes. Its main message was that inequality was all about luck – largely, the luck of the draw in terms of one's parents.

Capital and Ideology likewise seeks a space between power and ideas as the driving force in history. By focusing on ideas and power it overcomes several problems in *C21* and also leads to a deeper and richer understanding of the causes of inequality. As its title proclaims, ideology sustains the current regime of inequality. Piketty does a workmanlike job laying out the history of how ideology sustains inequality. He is also right that we can do better when it comes to reducing inequality. However, his wealth tax remains unworkable and unnecessary; there are plenty of other options for taxing the rich and reducing inequality. Piketty is on stronger ground pushing some sort of participatory socialism to help reduce inequality and other workplace problems (including how workers are treated, something that became a grave issue due to covid-19). The big lesson of the book, and its main advance over *C21*, is that institutions do matter and can be changed. This can be done *both* in the world of ideas and at the ballot box.[5]

References

Bartels, L. (2008) *Unequal Democracy: The Political Economy of the New Gilded Age.* Princeton: Princeton University Press.

Barth, D. Papageorge, N. & Kevin Thom, K. (2010) "Genetic Endowments and Wealth Inequality." *Journal of Political Economy* 128: 1474-1522.

Becker, G. (1964) *Human Capital.* Chicago: University of Chicago Press.

Beker, V. (2014) "Piketty: Inequality, Poverty and Managerial Capitalism." *Real World Economics Review* #69: 167-174.

Bound, J. & Johnson, G. (1992) "Changes in the Structure of Wages in the 1980s: An Evaluation of Alternative Explanations." *American Economic Review* 82: 371-392.

Brynjolfsson, E. & McAfee, A. (2014) *The Second Machine Age: Work, Progress, and Prosperity in a Time of Brilliant Technologies.* New York: W.W. Norton.

Case, A. and Deaton, A. (2020) *Deaths of Despair and the Future of Capitalism.* Princeton: Princeton University Press.

Cassidy, J. (2014) "Forces of Divergence." *The New Yorker*, March 31.

---

[5] The author thanks Annie Tubadji for comments on an earlier version of this paper. The usual disclaimer applies.

Cohen, A. (2020) *Supreme Inequality: The Supreme Court's Fifty-Year Battle for a More Unjust America.* New York: Penguin Press.

Colander, D. (2014) "Piketty's Policy Proposals: How to Effectively Redistribute Income." *Real-World Economics Review,* 69: 161-166.

Frank, R. (2016) *Success and Luck: Good Fortune and the Myth of Meritocracy.* Princeton: Princeton University Press.

Gabriel, T. (2017) "Alone on the Open Road: Truckers Feel Like 'Throwaway People'." *New York Times,* May 22.

Gilson, R. (1999) "The Legal Infrastructure of High Technology Industrial Districts: Silicon Valley, Route 128, and Covenants Not to Compete." *New York University Law Review* 74: 575-629.

Glennerster, H. (2011) *A Wealth Tax Abandoned: The Role of the UK Treasury 1974-6.* Centre for Analysis of Social Exclusion, London School of Economics.

Hacker, J. and Pierson, P. (2010) *Winner-Take-All Politics.* New York: Simon & Schuster.

Hungerford, T. (2011) *Changes in the Distribution of Income Among Tax Files between 1996 and 2006: The Role of Labor Income, Capital Income and Tax Policy.* Washington, DC: Congressional Research Service.

Kuznets, S. (1955) "Economic Growth and Income Inequality." *American Economic Review* 45: 1-28.

Locke, J. (1953[1690]) *Two Treatises of Government,* 2nd ed. New York: Cambridge University Press.

Macpherson, C. (1962) *The Political Theory of Possessive Individualism: Hobbes to Locke.* mOxford: Clarendon Press.

Marx, K. and Engels, F. (1948[1848]) *The Communist Manifesto.* New York: International Publishers.

Mayer, J. (2016) *Dark Money.* New York: Doubleday.

McBride, W. (2014) "Thomas Piketty's False Depiction of Wealth in America." Tax Foundation Report #223.

Mishel, L. et al. (2007) *The State of Working America 2006/2007.* Armonk, NY: M.E. Sharpe.

Modigliani, F. and Brumberg, R. (1954) "Utility Analysis and the Consumption Function: An Interpretation of Cross-Section Data." In *Post-Keynesian Economics*, ed. K. Kurihara. New Brunswick, NJ: Rutgers University Press: 388-436.

Norton, M. and Ariely, D. (2011) "Building a Better America – One Wealth Quintile at a Time." *Perspectives on Psychological Science* 6: 9-12.

Okun, Arthur (1975) *Equality and Efficiency: The Big Tradeoff.* Washington.

Nozick, R. (1974) *Anarchy, State and Utopia.* New York: Basic Books.

Pew Research Center (2020) *Most Americans Point to Circumstances, Not Work Ethic, for Why People are Rich or Poor.* Washington, DC: Pew Research Center.

Piketty, T. (2001) *Les Hauts Revenues en France au 20e Siècle: Inegalités et Redistributions 1901–1998.* Paris: Grasset.

Piketty, T. (2003) "Income Inequality in France, 1901–1998." *Journal of Political Economy* 111: 1004–1043.

Piketty, T. (2014) *Capital in the Twenty-First Century.* Cambridge, MA: Harvard University Press.

Piketty, T. (2020) *Capital and Ideology.* Cambridge, MA: Harvard University Press.

Piketty, T. and Saez, E. (2003) "Income Inequality in the United States, 1913–1998." *Quarterly Journal of Economics* 118: 1–39.

Pressman, S. (2013) "Justice and History: The Big Problem of Wilt Chamberlain." *Economic Issues* 18: 1-16.

Pressman, S. (2016) *Understanding Piketty's Capital in the Twenty-First Century.* London & New York: Routledge.

Robinson, J. (1933) *Economics of Imperfect Competition.* London: Macmillan.

Schultz, T. (1961) "Investment in Human Capital." *American Economic Review* 51: 1-17.

Saez, E. and Zucman, G. (2019) *The Triumph of Injustice: How the Rich Dodge Taxes and How to Make Them Pay.* New York: W.W. Norton.

Starr, E. (2019) *The Use, Abuse, and Enforceability of Non-Compete and No-Poach Agreements* (Washington, DC: Economic Innovation Group). [https://eig.org/wp-content/uploads/2019/02/Non-Competes-Brief.pdf]

Wolff, E. and Zacharias, A. (2009) "Household Wealth and the Measurement of Economic Well-Being in the United States." *Journal of Economic Inequality* 7: 83-115.

Wood, A. (1994) *North-South Trade, Employment and Inequality: Changing Fortunes in a Skill Driven World.* Oxford: Clarendon Press.

Zorn, N. and Pressman, S. (2020) "A Consensus on Taxing the Rich? Comparing Mainstream Economics, Piketty and Post-Keynesian Economics." *International Journal of Political Economy* 49: 43-61.

Chapter 9

Inequality: what we think, what we don't think and why we acquiesce

Jamie Morgan[1]

Introduction

An interest in great inequality and rising inequality have become prominent features of our times. According to Oxfam in 2019 the 26 richest people on the planet had equivalent wealth to the 3.8 billion who comprise the lower 50% of the world population. The previous year it required the top 43 to create this equivalence. The 2020 Oxfam report adds a series of statistical claims: the world's richest 1% have more than twice the wealth of 6.9 billion of the world's population, the 22 richest men have more wealth than all the women in Africa (and the estimated value of the unpaid work of women in the world is $10.8 trillion); a report from the Institute for Policy Studies, meanwhile, highlights that US billionaire's tax obligations as a % of wealth reduced by

[1] Professor Jamie Morgan, School of Economics, Analytics and International Business, Room-520 The Rose Bowl, Leeds Beckett University Business School, j.a.morgan@leedsbeckett.ac.uk.

79% between 1980 and 2018 (Collins et al., 2020).
According to the UK High Pay Centre, the median pay of
CEOs in the UK FTSE 100 was £3.9 million in 2017 (11%
higher than 2016) and it would take a worker on median
pay 125 years to earn this (and the equivalent figures for
the Dow in the US are far greater). According to the
Equality Trust, FTSE 100 CEO "compensation" as a ratio
to their own employees' pay averaged 145:1 in 2017
(rising from 30:1 in 1970 and 50:1 in 1990).

Great wealth and income both fascinates and outrages us
and this is not new. Susan George's *How the Other Half
Dies* was an early reminder that we live in a world of
consequence, whilst Thorstein Veblen's *The Theory of the
Leisure Class* reveals how display and conspicuous
consumption have always been part of social hierarchies.
Public evidence that feeds our modern interest,
meanwhile, can be dated back to the annual Forbes 400
rich list, first published in 1982. There are now many
equivalents or derivatives (such as the UK *Sunday Times*
Rich List) and a variety of databases and sources. Equally
there are problems over how to adequately calculate
wealth and income, since the wealthy are not necessarily
keen to have their full wealth and all their income
sources disclosed (even if there is some competition
involved in being the "richest"). There are, however,
fundamental issues at stake, and the various other essays
in this collection highlight many of them. What I am
interested in is how our capacity to think through the
problems and issues of inequality, and by extension
poverty, globally and locally, have been shaped both by
what we are encouraged to "think" and what we are
discouraged to think about. This is not because I am of

the opinion inequality, poverty etc. are merely epiphenomena, rather the opposite, much of modern thought on the problem is muddied because dominant ways of theorizing the world "pre-persuade" us to accept inequality, even as we think of it as problematic. And clearly, the use of "we" in "we think" may seem presumptuous as a device (who are "we"?), but it seems an appropriate way to make the contrast between different threads of public discourse informed by different academic resources. You may interpolate as this "we" or not. In any case, I begin from noting the role of Thomas Piketty's work in bringing inequality to public prominence in the aftermath of the global financial crisis, and then move on to discuss various features of the measurements that are made, the questions that are asked, and the issues that are foregrounded or absented by the concepts we apply. The material is intended to be wide-ranging and indicative rather than comprehensive.

What we "think" about inequality

When exploring what we think about inequality today a convenient place to start is with Thomas Piketty's *Capital in the Twenty-first Century* (2014). *Capital* appeared at an opportune time because the lived experience of inequality in the wake of the global financial crisis 2008+ had intensified and the media were looking for something to hang stories about discontent on in that wake. It is odd now to think that the global financial crisis was over a decade in the past. To new university students its causes, form and consequences are "adult history" that they originally have a child's recollection of. However, it's legacy lives on and greater interest in inequality is a constituent of that legacy, not least because events in the following decade exhibited a distinct change in policy and public mood. For example, by the time *Capital* was published in 2014:

- "Affluent" states had explicitly turned to "austerity" politics. e.g. the UK (formally by coalition government in 2010 to address a "structural deficit"). Wage freezes, welfare cuts and an increase (since these already existed in flexible labour market systems) in the prevalence of precarious and insecure work forms was occurring and household debt, after a brief collapse, had started to rise again (use of debt had already embedded in many societies during the previous decade as a necessary facet of growing personal consumption in an era of loose lending conditions, but had now turned more towards hard necessity and increasing debt distress, epitomised at the extreme by the rapid expansion of alternative credit providers such as "payday lending" organizations).
- Various tensions between the members of the European Union had begun to manifest based on fiscal and monetary differences, some of them exacerbated by membership of the Eurozone (which very clearly had not conformed to the idea of an "optimal currency area" and which increasingly invoked issues over "sovereign currency issuer" status).
- Beginning in 2010 Greece, via the "Troika", had become a high profile target of structural adjustment policies that the IMF had previously only applied outside the centres of power.

- The "Occupy movement" began in mid-2011. This followed high profile bank bailouts and a wave of house foreclosures in the USA and elsewhere and, by contrast, few prosecutions in the finance sector, despite widespread gross exploitation, mis-selling, fraud and malpractice; by mid-decade the reputation of bankers (as former "Masters of the universe") and the discipline of economics were both low. In the case of economics this was because it was the discipline that had not only abjectly failed to anticipate the crisis, it had provided support for the role of bankers ("efficient monitors") and of structured securities ("risk dispersal") and had asserted that a severe financial crisis was, as a "sigma event", diminishingly unlikely to the point of practically impossible. Moreover, subsequent economic orthodoxy essentially amounted to an endorsement (as a "there is no alternative") of "privatising gains and socialising losses" from the crisis, which returns us to the shift to the incremental effects of austerity policy on populations, of which "Occupy" is one prominent consequence, Occupy made the connection to inequality, trust and a broken system. Occupy's organizing slogan was thus "we are the 99%"...

In any case, the cumulative experience of the subsequent decade after the events of 2008-9, created scope for the issue of inequality to come to the fore. As such, Piketty's work in 2014 was timely. The previous lack of public prominence of inequality as an issue had begun to look suspect. The simple assumption that "all boats rise together" and so inequality is either not an important issue or not a long term concern seemed to contrast sharply with the times. *Capital* provided an attractive way to make sense of discontent through a focus on not just the immediate aftermath of the crisis but the *long term* development of inequality in a world lurching from one problem to another.

Capital's key features were an easily absorbed core graphical presentation (its long term u-curve of falling then rising inequality with a pivot in the late 1970s) and conjoint focus on both asset wealth and income trends. For example:

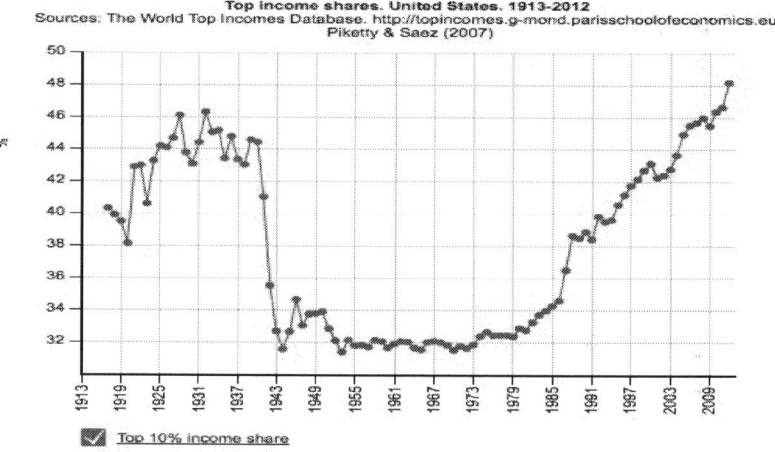

Top income shares. United States. 1913-2012
Sources: The World Top Incomes Database. http://topincomes.g-mond.parisschoolofeconomics.eu/
Piketty & Saez (2007)

Capital makes use of an extensive and still evolving database and this was (is) a collective work: the World Inequality Database (WID).[2] Both *Capital* and the database

---

[2] See: https://wid.world The "World Inequality Lab" (hosted from Paris School of Economics) now publishes an annual "World Inequality Report". WID absorbed the prior World Top Incomes Database in 2015. WTID launched publicly in 2011 and was built as part of projects leading to

draw on an innovative use of tax records to provide new long term data for an initial selection of countries, which is then extended to others (see Pressman, 2016: 19-27).[3] However, just as important as the "evidence" were Piketty's three laws of which the third "tendency" for r>g grabbed the headlines, in so far as r>g suggests that inequality is built into capitalist systems.

As most readers will know, "r" is the rate of return earned by "capital" and "g" is the growth of national income. According to Piketty, if the average % of r is greater than g then by a simple process of compounding (expressed via the previous two "laws") more of national income will flow to capital in general as time passes and if "capital" is initially held unequally then the proportion going to some will rise faster than others, causing inequality to also rise. For Piketty, in the absence of war or institutional restraints (which are difficult to maintain), r>g is a "fundamental force" reflecting the power of the wealthy to promote their interests and this promotion of their interests is a "deep" "structural" feature of capitalism. Concomitantly, Piketty notes that r tends to be higher for the very wealthy (with access to legal and financial advice and opportunity that others do not have) and that inherited wealth is more of a phenomenon than contemporary narratives of new wealth might lead one to expect (though he

---

Top Incomes over the XXth Century (2007) and Top Incomes: A global perspective (2010).

[3] Piketty's oldest and most continuous sources are Britain and France beginning from around 1700, followed by Germany, the USA, and Sweden from around 1800, the rest of Europe, and Japan from the early 20th century, and extending to other nations of the world through the second half of the twentieth century; within a broader database that tracks and estimates other metrics over two millennia (see Morgan, 2015).

acknowledges the systemic scope for super managers to become wealthy based on opportunity).[4]

So, the initial point I am making here is simply that Piketty's *Capital* formed part of a renewed interest and focus on inequality and thus had some influence on its prominence and how we think about it. This is by no means to suggest Piketty was first or was unique in highlighting inequality. The prominence of his work did however influence the subsequent discourse in at least two ways. First, *Capital* became a media phenomenon and bestseller and so mainstream economists and business school academics in general began to take note. The American Economic Association, via its influential journals, solicited essays on *Capital* in particular and inequality-relevant argumentation became a notable aspect of journal articles across business and management studies. Second, non-mainstream scholars with a longstanding interest in inequality or related issues started to incorporate critique of Piketty into their own work. It is important not to be reductive about this, I am not suggesting *Capital* became the sole gravitational centre of a new discourse of inequality, but I am suggesting that it became something one could not ignore if claiming some degree of informed interest in inequality (for something more sophisticated see Rieder and Theine, 2019; Grisold and Silke, 2019). As was also widely reported, however, *Capital* was widely bought, but not often finished.

---

[4] For other evidence corroborating family wealth transmission see Korom et al. (2017).

So, if we look to the subsequent mainstream of economics and of academic business literature, these responded by embracing the newly discovered prominence of inequality whilst drawing its sting. This has had several facets. One facet of the response has been to focus counter evidence on the *rate* of change in inequality in rich countries, drawing attention to data that suggests inequality is little changed in recent years across most of the distribution and may in some cases and some periods have reduced. So, inequality is not the "problem" that Piketty and others might suggest. Another facet has been claims about global trends, specifically that there is a bigger picture of the global poor "catching up", whilst also acknowledging a growth in the number of very wealthy outside the USA. China features prominently in both the "catching up" and the "new wealth outside the USA" claims and both have been deployed to undermine the focus on structural preservation of generational wealth. The latter "new wealth" claim in particular implies there is systemic dynamism – a churn of the wealthy through "creative destruction". This theme of creative destruction has also re-emerged as a way to recontextualise entrepreneurial claims on income and wealth in all countries including the USA. "Disruption" and "disruptors" have become common concepts conjoining great income and new wealth with themes of wealth creation.

The point I want to emphasise here is that there has been a mainstream pushback regarding inequality and this has been ideational, repositioning or de-emphasising inequality by reasserting or modifying other themes in which it might play a part. There are many other strands of argumentation one might draw attention to here. For example, the continued rise of stakeholder theory as a companion to shareholder value theory in business literature; or the headlines that accompanied Jonathan Ostry and others acknowledgment at the IMF that "neoliberalism" *might* have gone too far and *may* have some negative consequences. This you may recall occurred within the context of the institution reasserting – via Christine Lagarde – a standard claim that markets and education remain fundamentals of a mutually beneficial process of growth. In any case, what these examples illustrate is a series of modifications and acknowledgments in academia and influential organizations that have bled through into public discourse in multiple ways. So, one might say that how we think about inequality has some complexity of context based on mainstream modifications, and I will return to this theme later and in the next section.

This brings us to the second strand of influence of *Capital*, non-mainstream scholars with a longstanding interest in inequality or related issues started to incorporate critique of Piketty's *Capital* into their own work (see Fullbrook and Morgan, 2014). This critique ranges from:

1. Arguments regarding the merits of different data sources and data bases (notably tax versus survey data, especially for issues of wealth).
2. Debate over the technical construction of different measurement systems for inequality, notably the

relative merits of Gini coefficients and various alternatives.[5]

3. Argument regarding the merits of different measurement and representation systems of data ("what" to contrast with "what" and how to measure that "what").

4. Criticism that despite Piketty's initial critique of mainstream economics methodology and attitudes (its formalism etc.) and his claim on "political economy", *Capital* is not as radical as it first appears, in so far as its background theory makes use of Cobb-Douglas production functions and has various "neoclassical" commitments (fixed elasticities of substitution etc.).

5. Criticism that its first law is simply an accounting identity, its second requires a lack of genuine interdependency between savings, investment and growth (a non-Keynesian position), and that its third law is incoherent if one approaches r and g more

---

[5] The Gini coefficient is based on a calculation of the area between a Lorenz curve and a perfect equality line and the entire right angle below the perfect equality line. The perfect equality line shows the distribution if everyone received exactly the same income (the first 1% receive 1% of total income, the first 2% receive 2%, so cumulatively this grows to 99% receiving 99% and then 100%). The Lorenz curve shows the actual income distribution (to the first 5%, 10% etc.). If the two curves coincide then the area is zero and income inequality is 0. The more they diverge as Lorenz bends away then the greater the measured inequality up to a coefficient of 1 (all income goes to the top household). As Pressman notes (2016), since the coefficient is a single number to represent a distribution its abstract expression is a barrier to explanation and understanding. It is not clear what it decomposes to and it lacks intuitive or observable meaning: a graph or table of which decile etc received what % of income, wages or wealth is more immediate and makes more sense, as well as immediately makes clear how wealth assets become income, which increases income inequality compared to wages – something Gini simply disguises. Moreover, mathematically the coefficient is more sensitive to changes in the densest (typically middle) part of the distribution. See also Hickel later on the relative measurement problem.

realistically based on differences in each rather than aggregates of both.

6. Criticism that Piketty's concept of "capital" is misleading – no more or less than an adjusted market measure of asset value, rather than, as traditionally conceived, as "produced means of production"; and that Piketty misunderstands the concept and meaning of capital and relevant theory of its constitution (notably via a misrepresentation of the Cambridge Capital Controversies).

7. Criticism that, following 6 (and invoking critique from Marxists, post-Keynesians, Regulation theorists and sociologists with an interest in Polanyi etc.), despite Piketty's claims to have uncovered the "deep structures" of capitalism his main point is not an explanation of real mechanisms of economies but rather a simplistic truism (the powerful seek to reproduce and exploit their power), as such *Capital* reduces to a superficial (if exhaustive) data exercise.

8. Criticism that his preferred solution to long term inequality (a global wealth tax) is a consequence of measurement scale (if it is by aggregation of "capital" that the problem seems uniform and universal then it is at scale the problem is solved, but the solution follows from the aggregation rather than necessarily the different causes) and is, in any case, infeasible (if "capital" has "power" to influence institutions then tax reform is liable to be undermined or captured by Piketty's own "deep structure", so something more fundamental seems to be required by internal coherence of claim).

9. Criticism (mainly in ecological economics) that his projected trends for the future of inequality (continual growth of it) depend on impossible assumptions about institutional inertia and also technological production frontiers and continued exploitation of carbon resources (constituting measured future wealth assets, even as he positions himself as a champion of ecological issues and emphasises that carbon exploitation must change).[6]

Piketty's work has evolved since (see Piketty, 2020) and in drawing attention to this list I by no means wish to denigrate the important *role* played by Piketty's work and that of his fellow travellers at WID (perhaps most prominently the now deceased Anthony Atkinson and more latterly Emmanuel Saez and Gabriel Zucman).[7] Amongst other things, the prominence of Piketty's work placed pressure (as we have already begun to note) on mainstream economics to reconsider inequality; it challenged the basic claim that development and market liberalism (and, especially democracies) were necessarily meritocratic in a sense related somehow to a "Kuznet effect" (typically understood as "inequality reduces as a socio-economy evolves" – though this is reductive in terms of Kuznet's own work). Moreover, by decomposing income and wealth into groupings (the top 10%, 5% 1% etc.) and highlighting the compounding effect of

---

[6] Summarized in Morgan (2017). For context see Gills and Morgan (2019).

[7] Atkinson was a research assistant to Robert Solow at MIT, taught public economics with Joseph Stiglitz at Cambridge and started work on tax and the income distribution in the UK at the LSE in the 1980s; he thus pioneered the modern study of inequality at the margins of the mainstream and his *Inequality: What can be done* (2015) was published just after *Capital.*

proportion of national income in his second law and the role of returns on capital (wealth assets etc.) in his third law, he created a renewed focus on economic "rent" and the potential difference between wealth creation and wealth capture. This created scope for broader public discussion of the "return of the rentier".

The point I want to make, however, is that in becoming an important thread in how we think about inequality, Piketty's work has also provided a perceived need and opportunity for others to respond. So, the sociological significance of *Capital* extends to responses from others on inequality, creating both space for their work but also challenges from their work. Approaches to Piketty's work have been more and less critical in many fields. Where it has been critical this has not been mere carping from detractors, who are simply irritated that he has become famous in a field they have spent years working in (broadly interpreted; see, for example, James Galbraith, Thomas Palley, Dean Baker, Ozlem Onaran, Engelbert Stockhammer, Malcolm Sawyer, Yanis Varoufakis, Ben Fine etc. etc.). Critique, as the list 1–9 indicates, has raised important issues. Equally, where his work has been embraced, and this has mainly been appropriation of data drawn from the WID database, important work has also been done (e.g. Sayer, 2015). Responses, of course, reaffirm, draw attention to and elaborate different ways to think about inequality and this too is important for our purposes, since from an analytical point of view it suggests that perception of inequality is related to how and what is conveyed. *Capital* may have helped to bring the issue of inequality to the fore, but different themes and issues can be revealed or emphasised.

So, amongst other things, it matters that inequality *is* measured, but equally it matters *how* inequality is measured. James Galbraith, for example, distinguishes between WID and other data sets on inequality: the World Institute of Development Economics Research (WIDER) using survey data, the World Bank World Development Indicators (WDI) dataset (provided by member states) and the University of Texas Inequality Project (UTIP), using category data. Galbraith, of course, is closely associated with UTIP and his work on income inequality is longstanding and multi-faceted (e.g. Galbraith, 1998; 2012; 2016).[8] As Galbraith notes, WID's use of tax data solves some problems but creates others; income tax data is only available where income tax is applied, evasion may occur and changes to law change the dataset, but not the underlying reality. According to Galbraith, one of Piketty's key findings, the mid-1980s acceleration of rising inequality in the USA, is a product of change to reporting and not of changes to income. So, whilst the USA may have *high* inequality, its difference to other wealthy states is likely overstated (at this point at least). Collaborators at UTIP by no means condone or downplay inequality, but they have quite a different perspective than Piketty on global mechanisms and relations that underpin inequality.

Jason Hickel is another who makes much of how differences in measurement affect how inequality

---

[8] For UTIP go to: https://utip.lbj.utexas.edu/about.html.

appears to us (Hickel, 2017). Previously I noted that there has been a mainstream pushback regarding inequality and this has been ideational, repositioning or de-emphasising inequality by reasserting or modifying other themes in which it might play a part. I also noted that a significant aspect of this has been a claim on a bigger picture of the global poor "catching up", whilst also acknowledging a growth in the number of high earners and the very wealthy outside the USA. This is essentially an appropriation of Branko Milanovic's work, best known from his book *Global Inequality: A New Approach for the Age of Globalization* (2016), but also widely publicised by the World Bank, beginning with its *Taking on Inequality: Poverty and Shared Prosperity* (World Bank, 2016) report. The key finding of both is that the period of accelerated globalization (increasing capital mobility, out-sourcing, extension of supply chains and increasing trade as a proportion of global GDP) from the late 1980s has coincided with a *fall* not rise in the *global* Gini index. Perhaps the most prominent aspect of Milanovic's work has been the "elephant curve", one version of which is:

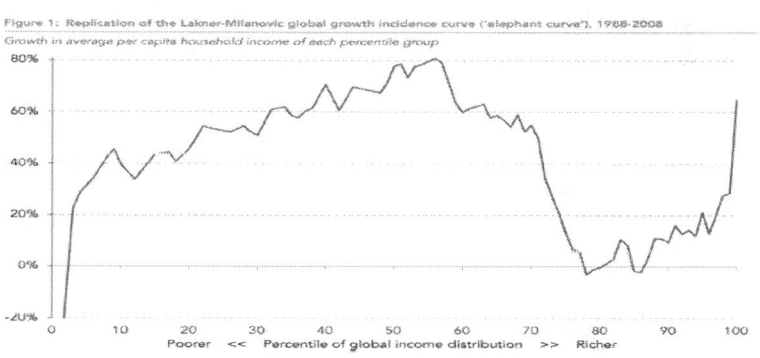

Figure 1: Replication of the Lakner-Milanovic global growth incidence curve ('elephant curve'), 1988-2008

The elephant curve suggests that the *relative* growth in income of households has mainly occurred in the mid-to-lower part of the *global* income distribution and at the very top, but not the upper part of the distribution below the very top. Given that the ordinary middle classes of wealthy capitalist countries are the upper echelons (but not top of the distribution) of a global distribution, the implication is that the curve mirrors the problem of deindustrialization, outsourcing, automation and global labour competition that have hit the incomes of the upper or skilled working class and lower and middle management of wealthy countries. In a sense, it implies a partial success story from "globalization" for great swathes of the world other than these. This general proposition ought to be familiar to any informed reader and has clearly created an important context or consideration for how we think about inequality. Hickel, however, argues that this "counternarrative" is misleading for various reasons:

1. The main data representation treats the world as a single country (and in related representations as anonymous units) which then conceals the difference between real countries.

2. Aggregation to a single global distribution thus disguises that much of the positive change is China (and some of East Asia). However, though the main data representation de-emphasizes China's exceptionalism, the approach also implies China is in general a success story *for* globalization.

3. If one removes China from the Gini calculation then global inequality increases not decreases on the main World Bank measure.

For Hickel, several points follow. First, the use of a relative measure, like the Gini index, obscures absolute changes. Absolute gaps can grow even if a Gini coefficient shows a decline (as he states, a 10% increase in the income of the poor from $5,000 to $5,500 compared to a 9% increase for the wealthy from $50,000 to $54,500 will register as declining relative inequality, but the gap has grown by $4,000). Second, China's intrinsic significant influence on the figures disguises the continued existence of a Global North and Global South distinction for inequality *whilst* also, by anonymizing the role of China in the main metrics, downplaying the significance of both state development strategy and state-specific characteristics (neither of which fit a standard universal globalization narrative). Fundamentally, the global representation both disguises and depoliticizes the causes and consequences of inequality as geo-political economic issues. One consequence of this is that it makes us comfortable with a world of great difference on the basis of global progress that is not actually happening, if by this we mean "catch-up". Different metrics, contrasting specific countries and regions using absolute figures and ratios reveal a quite different picture:

> "In 1960 the per-capita income in the richest country was 31.8 times higher than in the poorest country; by 2010, it was 118 times higher, and the absolute gap between the two had more than doubled. We see a similar divergence if we look at the gap between developed and developing regions... since 1960 the gap between the per-capita

GDP of the US and that of Latin America has grown by 206%; the gap between the US and SSA has grown by 207%; the gap between the US and the Middle East and North Africa has grown by 155% and the gap between the US and South Asia has grown by 196%. From this perspective, global inequality has roughly tripled during the period [1960–2014]" (Hickel, 2017: 2217).

Within this period some ratios did shrink for a subset of the whole in the 21st century, but this was based on Chinese production and infrastructure expansion, which inflated commodity prices (a transfer to commodity producing countries) and this not only appears to have been temporary, it is decisively *not* rooted in a structural change to the dynamics of global economies. In any case, the key point here is that what we think about inequality prevents us asking *why* is inequality not narrowing between rich and poor countries? It tacitly supports globalization whilst discouraging us from thinking about geo-political structures.

January 2005 to July 2018
Figure 9: Great Britain average weekly earnings at constant 2015 prices, seasonally adjusted

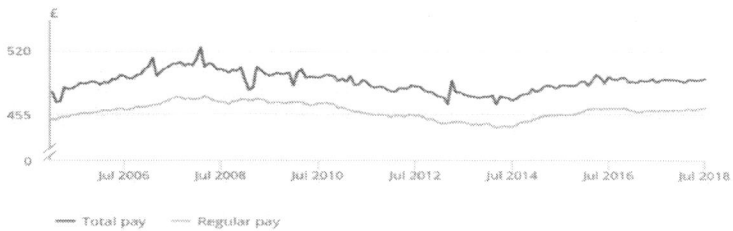

The point, of course, is not unequivocal; dissent over globalization is now widespread and populist reactions in wealthy countries are a well-recognized issue. And to be clear, I am not suggesting inequality and its problems reduce to mere perception. Nor am I dismissing problems of inequality within otherwise wealthy countries. When, for example, the UK Social Metrics Commission (including members from the IFS, Royal Statistics Society and Rowntree) introduced a new more broad-based set of poverty and inequality indicators in 2018 (partly in response to the UK government ceasing to officially use the standard relative and absolute poverty measures for policy in 2015) this was targeted to more adequately "express the reality" of poverty and inequality in the UK.[9] According to the SMC, 14.2 million people were in poverty in 2018 (22% of the population) and 7.7 million in persistent poverty. These included 5.5 million in some kind of work and this is indicative of the rise in working poverty in a country where flexible working practices have proliferated and social welfare systems have been eroded. These are associative indicators rather than inequality itself and inequality and poverty are not necessarily the same thing, but the latter is more likely in societies of low pay, wage stagnation, poor social security and enduring debt dependence issues, all of which subsist in unequal societies (see SMC, 2018).[10] According

---

[9] This paragraph is taken with minor adaption from Morgan (2019a).

[10] A Resolution Foundation report highlights that after taking into account housing costs 40% of low to middle income households (40% of 8.1 million households and 19.1 million people, about a third of the population) were living in relative poverty at the end of 2017, an increase of 10 percentage points since 1994-5 – and this, amongst other things, tracks a fall in home ownership for the group by 25% and a 15 percentage point increase in private renting from 12% to 27% (Corlett et al., 2018: 21

to both the UK Office for National Statistics (ONS) and the Resolution Foundation, average weekly earnings in the UK at the end of 2017 were 3% lower than in 2008 (£12 less at £489), and this decade of austerity was the worst period for change in real pay since the mid-1800s (Gregg and Clarke, 2018; see also Blyth, 2013).

I am not suggesting this work is mere fiction. On the contrary, I am suggesting it is extremely important because what we focus on and how matters. The Covid-19 pandemic is a stark reminder of this. Amongst other things, Covid-19 has exposed the fragilities of our societies based on the structural inequalities that developed within them. Inequality is not just stocks and flows of wealth and income, it vests in work conditions, life chances, insecurity, restricted choices, forced choices, reduced social and economic mobility, poorer quality of life and lower life expectancy (and this too is an important range of issues, as Angus Deaton's work or Wilkinson and Pickett, 2010, indicates). In the case of Covid-19, we count and report deaths and this can be differently measured and more or less accurate, but death is not a discursive event. It is not a text, but it is a rebuke and indictment. And then there is George Floyd...

So, what I *am* suggesting here is that reality becomes more or less visible to those the problem is being conveyed to and this in turn influences how we think about inequality. This, in turn, surely affects reality based on our understanding of the world, the reasons we hold,

---

& 23). Relative poverty is defined in the UK as 60% of the median household income. Figure 9 is from: ONS, 2018: 17.

what makes us passive, what makes us angry, and thus how we act and how we vote. And as this indicates, we live *in* the world, it is not just conveyed *to* us. So, there can be a dissonance between what we experience (our phenomenology) and what we are told. None of which means evidence ceases to matter or ceases to refer to something. The appropriate inferences here are that evidence is corrigible, and that questioning evidence and maintaining an open mind are necessary aspects of contingently improving our accounts of the world, of accepting one explanation, one justification or another for how the world currently is and how it might be in the future. A key feature of this is an awareness of how we are persuaded. This is not just about what we are encouraged to "think", but what we are discouraged from thinking and how we are socialized to acquiesce.

What we don't think about inequality and why we acquiesce

Jason Hickel's work is an important reminder that what we "think", what we are encouraged to think, about inequality is a problem field that can be reversed, in so far as how the world is presented to us can discourage us from thinking about inequality, at least in so far as we have a clear idea of its problematic features. Inequality is not a thing per se, it is a measured consequence of processes, a facet of systems, it is caused and its existence is consequential. But its existence, its causes and its consequences can all be more or less difficult to focus on. This can be confusing and disempowering. And this is not just about how the world is measured and cut up, it is also more fundamentally a matter of theory that shifts emphasis through the way concepts are included or excluded, and ultimately it is a matter of degrees of ignorance created by what we otherwise think of as knowledge. So, it can be important to remind ourselves of the many different resources we have to draw on in thinking about inequality.

Hickel's work, for example, draws some of its inspiration from Robert Wade. Over the years Wade has drawn attention to the way economics tends to render invisible the power relations that reproduce global order, including its trade dynamics, which work to the benefit of some but not others (e.g. Wade, 2017). He has a clear sense of the continued significance of developmental or interventionist states (those with a strategy) and of the problems of integration of these into a world order whose organizations and institutions maintain and exploit the vast majority of the world's countries and people (Wade, 1990). The ideational form behind this, the Washington and Post-Washington consensus, stands at odds to the realities the ideational form produces and reproduces. From this perspective, it is significant that there are basic questions that we are discouraged from thinking about.

Why is it not more obvious to us that the world is comprised of around 200 countries, and yet less than 10 have made any meaningful transition in the last 40 years and more into the upper echelons of wealth and income, and if one looks past Japan and South Korea, none of the other possible candidates are unequivocal? Yet globalization is portrayed as mainly a success, a progressive and *convergent* roadmap for all.[11] Is it? Or is it a hierarchical system that seeks to maintain difference, even if it allows for "development"? One does not need to disparage the Millennium Development Goals or the subsequent Sustainable Development Goals to note that the goals that have been achieved and the ambition that is built into them are extraordinarily low thresholds or targets if placed in the context of how the wealthy world lives. Dragging large numbers (mainly in China) out of extreme poverty is not insignificant, but nor is it a consequence of anything the collective of countries in the world planned and nor is it (in global context) a signal of an *equalising* world.[12]

Behind Wade's work then, there is a whole tradition of work that encourages us to look at the problem differently. International Political Economy and Global Political Economy have a long tradition of exploring and explaining the dynamics of geo-political and economic power hierarchies; from the work of Immanuel Wallerstein, Giovanni Arrighi, and Andre Gunder Frank and Barry Gills on world systems theory (with core-

---

[11] Noting that ultimately globalization is not a theory, it is a term for theories and one which tends to distract form the operation of systems (capitalism etc.).

[12] Goal 1 target 1 of the MDGs (reducing extreme poverty by 50%) was achieved five years ahead of schedule in 2010. As one report put it early in the last decade: "in 2011, 17 percent of people in the developing world lived at or below $1.25 a day. That's down from 43 percent in 1990 and 52 percent in 1981.This means that, in 2011, just over one billion people lived on less than $1.25 a day, compared with 1.91 billion in 1990, and 1.93 billion in 1981. Even if the current rate of progress is to be maintained, some 1 billion people will still live in extreme poverty in 2015 – and progress has been slower at higher poverty lines. In all, 2.2 billion people lived on less than US $2 a day in 2011, the average poverty line in developing countries and another common measurement of deep deprivation. That is only a slight decline from 2.59 billion in 1981."

periphery and transitional relations in a long history of capitalism) to the work on "historic blocs" and "wars of movement and position" of "neo-Gramscians" such as Robert Cox, Stephen Gill, Adam Morton and Andreas Bieler, to the "global Keynesianism" of Heikki Patomäki. And, there is work on Global Value Chains and Global Wealth Chains that explores institutionally embedded exploitation and wealth capture, as well as work in critical development studies, on issues like structural causes and perpetuation of modern forms of slavery and unfree labour (from people like Wendy Olsen, Isabelle Guérin and Genevieve LeBaron).[13] All of these invite us to be skeptical regarding the simple equation between development, globalization, progress and convergence.

By contrast, development economics tends to conform to the more problematic features of mainstream economic inquiry, even as it positions itself as an important "pragmatic" step forwards. Perhaps the highest profile instance of this recently is the project work using Randomized Control Trials (RCTs) by Abhijit Banerjee, Esther Duflo and Michael Kremer. The three were awarded the "Sveriges Riksbank Prize in Economic Sciences in Memory of Alfred Nobel" in 2019. Banerjee and Duflo founded the *Abdul Latif Jameel Poverty Action Lab* (J-PAL) in 2003 with the aim of using RCTs to "answer critical questions in the fight against poverty". Critique of the application of RCTs use in development economics are widespread (Morgan 2019b). RCTs reduce

---

[13] One might also mention Amartya Sen too, who has done a great deal to contest concepts of utility and welfare and their influence on development thinking; and perhaps also Hardt and Negri's work in Neo-Marxism which was influential on the World Social Forum early in the Millennium.

development to a measurable contrastive outcome for some specific small scale intervention at local level, which in principle seems extremely attractive. However, this attraction is also its major defect; donors, funders and policymakers are seduced by the "data" and so development studies and development projects have narrowed down to what can be measured through an RCT. The field has thus been captured and this has had various consequences, not least a tendency for (paralleling Hickel and Wade) development choices to be depoliticised (as though that were possible) and for poverty alleviation projects to lose broader critical focus on structural transformation (a point made across the board and including figures as prominent as Martin Ravallion and Angus Deaton and Nancy Cartwright). Moreover, the method itself is considerably less successful than it first appears – an RCT requires conditions for adequacy that cannot be created in most cases.

Methodologically, the tendency to apply RCTs represents a typical instance of mainstream economic preference for quantitative and model based tests that distort the social reality they address. Again, poverty is not inequality per se, but the two can be associated in one country and in a hierarchical system of difference with some "development", contrastive poverty in one place can be a result of actions elsewhere. So poverty (and relative lack of ambition in resolving it) can be maintained in multiple ways in a globally *unequal* system. It is not irrelevant, therefore, from a sociology of knowledge point of view that development economics is an instance of the way mainstream economics has become a problem rather than a genuine solution to problems. It is "horizon-shortening" rather than merely pragmatic. Where, for example, is the *structural* macro and global critique of the financing systems that extract billions a year from poor countries or the exploitative ownership patterns of commodity extraction or the abusive conditions of "adverse incorporation" along supply chains or the asymmetries in property and land ownership? One does not need to assert Duflo, Bannerjee etc. lack good intentions in order to suggest "Nobel" Prizes convey the *public* impression that state of the art in economics is "best practice" and thus best achievable outcomes, and this is very clearly a dubious set of inferences that we are encouraged *not* to contest (and so appropriate critical questions of context, scope and progress are discouraged). RCTs represent themselves as "value free" science and Duflo and others in the field are disparaging of "political economy".

Reference to political economy and the issue of problems dressed as solutions brings us to perhaps the most fundamental and enduring way we are discouraged from thinking about inequality, and that is mainstream economic form. Mainstream economics renders invisible key features of inequality and of the socio-economic system within which it is produced. Piketty is not wrong about this, even if it is questionable that he has an adequate concept or explanation of both the process and the socio-economic system. That the system and inequality are related, is, of course, the first casualty of the shift from classical political economy (CPE) to what Marx referred to as "vulgar political economy" and to the marginalism that then followed. Though the point is not unequivocal, two main enduring features of the mainstream illustrate what I mean.

First, mainstream economics provides the ideological projection for the layperson of the fundamental framework of capitalist economy: subjective preference tied to effective demand and marginal productivity tied to factor cost of supply, jointly determine price and output in one market and all markets and when "unimpeded" these provide an equilibrating *harmonious* engine of growth through dynamic efficiency. This is interrupted by shocks, confounded (only) in the short term and subverted by crowding, distortion, inefficiency, irrationality, asymmetries and failures – which amounts to the insight that everything works fine and to the interest of all except when things deviate from a calculative, rational, well-informed, self-interested core. Second, in so far as a market system operates harmoniously and efficiently, all factors are paid their appropriate marginally determined price, and labour, by definition is paid what it is worth on the basis of its individual productivity in relation to the overall competitive system of equilibration of prices. As such, market prices are "just" prices and market wages are "fair" wages (representing each individual's contribution to the whole, where the whole is axiomatically a "just distribution"). This argument is typically attributed to John Bates Clarke (though it is debatable what he originally meant).

The point, however is that the deep background ideational framing of capitalist market economy combines the fundamentals of a harmonious capitalist growth engine with a basic claim that the system is fair (and thus in modern theory if you want to be paid more, you should improve your productivity via skills and education and this in itself is sufficient to both facilitate growth for all and achieve higher incomes, through performance review, for each individual). The problem with this, of course, is that it is a pale imitation of reality. Education is not irrelevant, skills matter, but not reductively so, since this lacks any grounding in real societies. The framework renders every facet of real human social conduct exterior to its axiomatic focus (making real people in real societies problems that must be conformed to an impossible ideal), whilst also shunting study and research into real people and real conduct into other disciplines: politics, sociology, history and culture etc.

From the point of view of inequality, it is social stratification and social conflict over the economic product and its surplus that is eliminated. The systemic problem of both power and its expression in economic processes disappears from "distribution" and so the link between opportunity, mechanisms and the differentials in rent, profit and wages likewise cease to be a central concern. As many commentators have pointed out, it is ironic that in placing a claim on the legacy of Adam Smith via the "invisible hand" (something he only mentions three times and never as a positive central element of his thought), and his basic arguments for *contingent* mutually beneficial market exchange, the modern mainstream has eliminated almost every key aspect of Smith's *critical* thinking and that of other originators of CPE, such as David Ricardo.[14] The residue is a system where the claim that all "boats rise together" has a ready discursive scaffold. There is, as such, a long history behind Piketty's observation that the powerful seek to reproduce and exploit their power, but this is *not* what the mainstream encourages us to think about; it replaces this with an impossible model world, with an implicit moral and ethical claim on fairness, rooted in this model world, and with a basic ingrained blind spot regarding power and distribution. This in itself facilitates exploitation in the name of a distributively just system, where those able to leverage power to increase their wealth and income can claim to be "worth it" (the conceptual system favours this language and channels argument towards the role of wealth creators, rather than wealth capture, despite that this so obviously contradicts our experience of the world).

There is, of course, a long history of alternatives that *do* encourage us to think about how inequality can root in systems via distribution. Most prominently in economics, the Sraffians have reoriented economics on a struggle over the surplus. If we expand our horizon to encompass the theme of investment dynamics (another theme that emerges out of CPE) then Michal Kalecki's work highlights the different consequences for production, employment growth and pay that can inhere and this is a

---

[14] This is by no means to suggest CPE constitutes *the* high point of economics to which economics should simply return, it merely suggests the mainstream has taken a wrong turn (CPE is a retrospective construct drawn from multiple works and has numerous debates regarding the status of Say's law, comparative advantage, the Sraffian claim on CPE, the relative status of Petty, Ricardo, Smith etc. and both Mills, and then the marginalists and so on).

theme that returns us to the post-Keynesians. Post-Keynesians in general take an interest in endogenous path dependency in the context of a money economy and fundamental uncertainty. This is a world that cannot be conceived in terms of ideal states where everyone gets what they deserve. Money, meanwhile, invokes the role the financial sector plays in any contemporary economy and this opens up a whole array of different issues regarding the creation of inequality and the role of economic rent (as well as Nicholas Kaldor's important distinction between speculation and productive investment). Piketty may have played a role in returning the issue of rent to prominence, but Marx and the radical political economy tradition never neglected this thread and it is worth noting that modern "financialisation" theory predates Piketty's *Capital* by at least a decade (for range, see Epstein, 2005; Hudson, 2015; Soederberg, 2014; Montgomerie, 2019). Finally, old institutionalists and more recent social and cultural economists have worked to rehabilitate the role of rules, law and habit as expressions of power – a subject that feminist economics has also done much to elaborate in terms of the issue of social reproduction and (lack of) equality through the unpaid exploitation of care.

There are, then, a plurality of resources that bring different perspectives to the problem of inequality and what all of these share is a common focus on social context, power and outcomes. This is precisely what the mainstream *does not* encourage us to think about and this brings us to a final issue for inequality. I suggested at the end of the last section that a key feature of well-informed understanding of inequality is an awareness of how we are persuaded and that this is not just about what we are encouraged to "think", but what we are discouraged from thinking and how we are socialized to acquiesce. Socialization is simply another term for both what we are encouraged and discouraged to "think", but it is one with a broader canvas, since it shifts our focus towards the confluence of consequences that follow for how we act in the world, based on what we are encouraged and discouraged to think. One reason to be a pluralist is the realization that there are so many different attempts to persuade us and that often it is power rather than plausibility that dictates which dominate. As all of what I have written so far indicates economics has played a significant role in "pre-persuading" us that inequality will occur. This is not because we find extreme inequality or poverty necessarily acceptable. It is because our focus on what is in front of our faces is fractured. Globalization and convergence and harmonious economic theory without distributional struggle illustrate this. Michael Hudson, for example, refers to the role of mainstream economics as a kind of "learned helplessness" or functional knowledgeable ignorance and there is another feature one might draw attention to here. In addition to failing to articulate the realities of distributional struggle, theory can also predispose us to unequal *redistributive* consequences. Whilst both distribution and redistribution can be instances where socialization means we do not realize what we are acquiescing *to*, the latter (redistribution) is more obviously of this type.

Tax is not just a tedious domain of regulatory pedantry and accounting precision, it is a field of conflict over fundamental rights to wealth and income and those rights in turn are nested within a whole set of ideas regarding the role of and legitimacy of the state. How we think about tax is indicative of how we think about the role of the individual, the collective, society and government. Few members of the public today could name and explain the Laffer theorem, but we live in societies profoundly influenced by its logic (Berman and Milanes-Reyes, 2013; Morgan, 2020). Laffer argues that there is a trade-off between the tax rate and the tax yield and an optimal tax rate produces a maximum yield. Behind this sits the claim that there is a substitution effect created by the tax rate and that in general lower rates induce higher levels of effort or activity (corporate and personal). Whilst the theorem does not dictate that lower tax rates increase yields, in the hands of the neoliberal right the logic provides a resource for general argument that we should *prefer* lower to higher taxes. The rationale for this is that everyone gains if lower taxes lead to greater economic activity.

However, the general direction of travel towards lower taxes is also typically towards less progressive taxation (with flatter tax bands). These relative changes can have significant absolute effects: high earners and the wealthy retain more income from work and capital and so inequality of both rises (Piketty's compounding effects kick in). This can occur even as the actual % of the total tax take in a country skews towards greater takes from high income earners and the wealthy. So, incrementally we end up with a system of greater wealth and income inequality through both unequal distribution and lack of redistribution. And yet the original argument used to create this situation is that we all gain. In acquiescing to "we all gain" (something that may also be false), we inadvertently acquiesce to an increase in inequality and this consequence has observably been the case in both the USA and UK (and the argument is a constant pressure on traditionally more social democratic states in Europe). Moreover, the cumulative outcomes lead to additional forms of argument that can be deployed to prevent the re-imposition of more progressive tax systems, since there can be a greater tax take from the rich, despite that they are keeping more of their income and wealth, and this can lead to a "dependency" argument. From the point of view of exacerbated inequality, systemic dependency is actually a signal of the *failure* of the system, rather than of the success of "wealth creators". And yet it creates scope for the political right to defend tax issues via an argumentation strategy that suggests tax changes risk "killing the golden goose".

Moreover, the ideological framework behind the argument suggests income is earned, earned income is individually deserved, wealth is deserved and the state is an expropriator. From this perspective, the relation between the individual, the corporation and the state is implicitly one of antagonism. Not only does this sit awkwardly with positive argument for the role of the state, it tends to corrode any sense of obligation to pay taxes and this in turn leads to a framing of tax evasion and avoidance, which exacerbates inequality. Again, mainstream economic theory does not help here. Economic theory treats all economic behaviour as subset cases of rationality. Treating tax evasion and avoidance as rational is treating opportunistic, unethical, anti-social and in some cases criminal behaviour as simply cost-benefit calculations (and it is arguable whether new behavioural approaches to "Tax Morale" alter this).

Calculative mindsets have socialising effects: in one of the Presidential candidate debates with Hilary Clinton in the 2016 campaign, Donald Trump responded to questions regarding his tax affairs by suggesting that paying little was the intelligent thing to do, and he was, in any case, only doing what anyone with sense would (for Trump on breaking convention see Gills et al, 2019). Whilst his comments were clearly egregious, he was also placing a claim on convention – a cultural "common sense". CEOs use this same logic when they respond to public inquiry regarding tax avoidance by suggesting "we pay all legally required taxes" (omitting to note that they employ armies of tax advisers to devise strategies of avoidance and pay millions of dollars to lobbyists to maintain a structural privilege in a global system of reporting, see Seabrooke and Wigan 2020; Christensen et al., 2016; Saez and Zucman, 2019; Zucman, 2016; Morgan, 2017b; 2016). None of this sits well with corporate social responsibility... But it does indicate how the failure of redistribution has multiple channels. In the end, this is not just about a failure to redistribute *downwards* it is a situation of redistribution *upwards*, if and when inequality rises. In the US case, for example, Trump's tax cuts of 2017 led to extensive share buybacks and dividend effects, leading in turn to capital gains windfalls for CEOs (paid in share options over the years) and to the wealthy who own the vast majority of equity.

Socialization then, matters and again, there are those who allow us to look at this differently. For example, post-Keynesians generally, MMT advocates specifically, Tax Justice activists, and new state theorists, such as June Sekera, Neva Goodwin and Mariana Mazzucato. And tax is a particularly productive domain in which to expose themes of implicit hostility to the state. Language itself is part of socialization, affecting what we will acquiesce to. Consider the power of metaphor. The phrase "the tax burden" maps a metaphor of onerous weight onto the payment of tax. The associative meaning of "burden" frames how taxation is conceived. It is subliminally shaped based on an adverse physical experience re-expressed as an emotive monetary relation. The very connotations of the language invite hostile triggers. Tax as a "burden" translates easily into an implicit sense that tax is an appropriation, a weight to be resented. As with all such argument regarding meaning frames, of course, the issue is contextual and conditional. It might, for example, seem odd to reverse the metaphorical intent and refer to paying tax in any and all circumstances as a "privilege". And yet it *could be* if the system were to makes it so. Tax looks different in a pro-social, just and fair system (see Murphy, 2015). The problem is we do not live in that system. The way we have been encouraged to think about and discouraged to think about inequality have scaffolded a very different system, globally and locally in rich and poor countries.

Conclusion

In this essay I have ranged across a number of issues relevant to the problem of inequality. A great deal has been written on this subject over the years and the subject itself has become both academically higher in profile and publicly more prominent in recent years. There is still today a branch of opinion which is not only comfortable with great inequality, but that valorises it. And yet we live in a world where this is increasingly difficult to justify. In this context, Andrew Sayer asks an important question, "can we afford the rich?" His answer is no. His reasoning for this is not just that great and growing inequality are morally objectionable. They are economically and socially harmful through distributional dynamics. Moreover, as degrowth and steady state ecological economists note, great inequality is incompatible with a viable future for humanity. We need to be aware of this and *rethink* what we are encouraged and discouraged to think.

References

Atkinson, T. (2015) *Inequality: What Can Be Done.* Harvard: Harvard University Press.

Berman, E. & Milanes-Reyes, L. (2013) "The politicization of knowledge claims: The "Laffer Curve" in the US Congress." *Qualitative Sociology* 36: 53–79.

Blyth, M. (2013) *Austerity: The History of a Dangerous Idea.* Oxford: Oxford University Press

Christensen, J., Shaxson, N. and Wigan, D. (2016) "The finance curse: Britain and the world economy." *British Journal of Politics and International Relations* 18(1): 255–269.

Collins, C., Ocampo, O. and Paslaski, S. (2020) *Billionaire Bonanza 2020: Wealth, Windfalls, Tumbling Taxes, and Pandemic Profiteers.* Washington DC: Institute for Policy Studies.

Corlett, A., Clarke, S., D'Arcy, C. and Wood, J. (2018) *The Living Standards Audit 2018.* Resolution Foundation, July.

Epstein G. (ed) (2005) *Financialization and the World Economy.* Cheltenham: Edward Elgar.

Fullbrook, E. and Morgan J. (eds) (2014) *Piketty's Capital in the Twenty-First Century.* London: College Books.

Galbraith, J. K. (2016) *Inequality: What everyone needs to know.* Oxford: Oxford University Press.

Galbraith, J. K. (2012) *Inequality and Instability: A Study of the World Economy Just Before the Great Crisis.* Oxford: Oxford University Press.

Galbraith, J.K. (1998) *Created Unequal: The Crisis in American Pay.* New York: Free Press.

Gills, B. and Morgan, J. (2019) "Global Climate Emergency: After COP24, climate science, urgency and the threat to humanity." *Globalizations* https://www.tandfonline.com/doi/full/10.1080/14747731.2019.16 69915

Gills, B., Morgan, J. and Patomäki, H. (2019) "*President* Trump as status dysfunction." *Organization* 26(2): 291-301.

Gregg, P. and Clarke, S. (2018) *Count the Pennies: Explaining a decade of lost pay growth.* Resolution Foundation, October.

Grisold, A. and Silke, H. (2019) "Denying, downplaying, debating: Defensive discourse of inequality in the debate on Piketty." *Critical Discourse Studies* 16(3): 264-281.

Hickel, J. (2017) "Is global inequality getting better or worse? A critique of the World Bank's convergence narrative." *Third World Quarterly* 38(10): 2208-2222.

Hudson, M. (2015) *Killing the Host.* Dresden: ISLET-Verleg.

Korom, P. Lutter, M. and Beckert, J. (2017) "The enduring importance of family wealth: Evidence from the Forbes 400 1982-2013." *Social Science Research* 65: 75-95.

Milanovic, B. (2016) *Global Inequality: A New Approach for the Age of Globalization*. London: Belknap Press.

Montgomerie, J. (2019) *Should we abolish household debt?* London: Wiley.

Morgan, J. (2020) "A critique of the Laffer theorem's macro-narrative consequences for corporate tax avoidance from a Global Wealth Chain perspective." *Globalizations* https://www.tandfonline.com/doi/full/10.1080/14747731.2020.17 60420

Morgan, J. (2019a) "The Left and an economy for the many not the few." pp. 94-137 in D. Scott (ed) *Manifestos, policies and practices: An equalities agenda*. London: Trentham Press/UCL IOE Press.

Morgan, J. (2019b) "A Realist Alternative to Randomised Control Trials: A Bridge Not a Barrier." *European Journal of Development Research* 31(2): 180-188.

Morgan, J. (2017a) "Piketty and the growth dilemma revisited in the context of ecological economics." *Ecological Economics* 136: 169-177.

Morgan, J. (2017b) "Taxing the powerful, the rise of populism and the crisis in Europe: The case for the EU Common Consolidated Corporate Tax Base." *International Politics* 54(5): 533-551.

Morgan, J. (2016) "Corporation tax as a problem of MNC organizational circuits: The case for unitary taxation." *British Journal of Politics and International Relations* 18(2): 463-481.

Morgan, J. (2015) "Piketty's calibration economics: Inequality and the dissolution of solutions." *Globalizations* 12(5): 803-823.

Murphy, R. (2015) *The Joy of Tax*. London: Bantam Press.

ONS (2018) "Statistical Bulletin, UK labour market: September 2018." Office for National Statistics, 11th September.

Oxfam (2020) *Time to Care*. Oxford: Oxfam, January.

Oxfam (2019) *Public Good or Private Wealth*. Oxford: Oxfam, January.

Piketty, T. (2020) *Capital and Ideology.* London: Belknap Press.

Piketty, T. (2014) *Capital in the Twenty-First Century.* London: Belknap Press.

Pressman, S. (2016) *Understanding Piketty's Capital in the Twenty-First Century.* London: Routledge.

Reider, M. and Theine, H. (2019) "Piketty is a genius but...: an analysis of journalistic delegitimation of Thomas Piketty's economic policy proposals." *Critical Discourse Studies* 16(3): 248–263.

Seaz, E. and Zucman, G. (2019) *The Triumph of Injustice.* New York: W. W. Norton.

Sayer, A. (2015) *Why we can't afford the rich.* Bristol: Policy Press.

Seabrooke, L. and Wigan, D. (2020) *Global tax battles: The fight to govern corporate and elite wealth.* Oxford: Oxford University Press.

Soederberg, S. (2014) *Debtfare States and the Poverty Industry.* London: Routledge.

SMC (2018) *A New Measure of Poverty for the UK* London: Social Metrics Commission

Wade, R. (2017) "Global growth, inequality and poverty: The globalization argument and the political science of economics." pp 319–355 in Ravenhill, J. (ed.) *Global Political Economy.* Oxford: Oxford University Press.

Wade, R. (1990) *Economic Theory and the Role of Government in East Asian Industrialization.* Princeton: Princeton University Press.

Wilkinson, R. and Pickett, K. (2010) *The Spirit Level: Why Equality is Better for Everyone.* London: Penguin [with new postscript].

World Bank (2016) *Taking on Inequality: Poverty and Shared Prosperity.* Washington DC: World Bank.

Zucman, G. (2016). *The Hidden Wealth of Nations: The Scourge of Tax Havens.* Chicago: University of Chicago Press.

Chapter 10

The art of balance: the search for equaliberty and solidarity

Peter Radford

The challenge of contemporary inequality is not just to the cohesion of modern society it is also a challenge to economics, because it is economics and its values that sit squarely within the social framework that has allowed inequality to become so pervasive and debilitating. We have built a society resting on only one view of liberty and equality, that of the economic sphere, rather than on a more holistic view that allows the inclusion of other spheres. We persist in believing ourselves as free, but it is a harsh and hollow freedom built upon individuality and isolated action, rather than on solidarity and communal action.

There are economists of a certain type who question whether there is any distortion produced by inequality. They often repeat the claim that inequality is a benign consequence, a side effect of little interest, to the march of economic progress and the accumulation of modern prosperity. It is a profound error to think this. Then again these same people are often oblivious to the existence and importance of society, so they regard themselves as bereft of such an error.

This is a denial of the history of the very ideas that they have used as the foundation of their perspective. Economics did not begin so willful in its exclusivity, but as it became more and more inwardly focused, formal, and narrow it was forced to shed any of its origins that foreclosed on the avenue it chose to follow.

So, to understand the role of economics in fostering our current inequality we need to understand the history of the idea of inequality, and how it became belittled beside the stature of other parts of the project economics has become. This history, of course, began back in the moments when the revolt against centuries of aristocratic, monarchic, and religious oppression were being thrown off. In that early part of our modern world equality was a multifaceted concept. It was relational. Rosanvallon expresses it this way:

> "This relational idea of equality was articulated in connection with three other notions: similarity, independence, and citizenship. Similarity comes under the head of *equality as equivalence*: to be 'alike' is to have the same essential properties, such that remaining differences do not affect the character of the relationship. Independence is *equality of autonomy*; it is defined negatively as the absence of subordination and positively as equilibrium in exchange. Citizenship involves *equality as participation*,

which is constituted by community membership and civic activity... Economic inequalities were seen as acceptable in this framework only if they did not threaten the other modes of relational equality that defined the society of equals" (emphasis in original).

This was a web of interlocking and mutually dependent relationships. It was not simply the equality of equivalence only. Economics appears to have forgotten this. How? Why?

One weapon in the political battles to break free of ancient tyrannies was the notion that there was an alternative arena to the central power base of those forces. There were relationships in society beyond those imposed by the rights and privileges of timeless rank and tradition. Of most interest to the emerging commercial class was the relationship described as the decentralized workings of ordinary people trading between themselves. The strength of this idea was that if those trades were unfettered, if they were allowed to go their own way, and if the benefits of the trading accrued to the people rather than simply to the central authority, then everyone would be better off. It was by making this argument that the newly rising commercial class wanted to create a broader political space for itself. Markets, in other words, were conceived of politically. Equality in one implied equality in the other, and commerce was an alternative domain through which a different kind of power distributed income and wealth. It was a compelling idea. It attracted the best minds of that era. It captivated them. They began the project known as economics in order to reinforce and justify it. That project continues today.

To accomplish their goal, however, early advocates of the market-as-politics had to break asunder the relationship between "liberty" and "equality". They had to narrow and limit liberty to a very specific form. They had to create their own version of liberty so that it appeared benignly apolitical and thus avoid the inevitable push back by the central authority. After all, the elite of the day could hardly be expected to surrender their privileges and power without the expectation of a greater reward. Incentives were needed. There had to be a profit in the accommodation of this alternative power base.

So, through time, economics carefully reduced itself to discovering and promoting the benefits of the relationship encompassed within impersonal markets, cleansed of any explicit notion of power. The journey to a power-free concept of a market took a long time. Its original intent was to create political space for the commercial class, but later on it became necessary to inoculate it against the political claims of the industrial working class. So it was doubly necessary for economics and its primary focus, the marketplace, to appear apolitical. Arguably it was not until after Robbins had delivered the iconic definition of economics as being 'the science which studies human behavior as a relationship between ends and scarce means which have alternative uses' that this cleansing was finally accomplished. Eventually, economists were busy telling everyone that markets were based on liberty, and that there were "scientific laws" which, if free people allowed to play out, would enrich everyone. The key to getting all this greater wealth was to separate economic liberty from social or political liberty, which were still highly contentious and dangerously democratic, and to institutionalize it safely ensconced in what we now call the economy, which became a world unto itself. A world, that in theory, was even abstracted from itself to remove the clutter of reality, and a world where the power struggles inherent in politics were sanitized away by a powerful veneer of science. It was a very modern idea.

This separation in the concept of liberty in order to create a domain for the economy has had profound social consequences. It has been systematized and made more concrete over the decades. Problems as they emerged were ignored if they threatened the autonomy of the market. This was especially true of the breaking apart of the relationships that formed the common culture underlying modern society. Economics needed to isolate itself from society in order to provide a detailed framework for commercial activity and trading, but in order to do so it had to push power relationships outside itself. Power and its distributive consequences remain, perhaps, the primary force gluing society together, but it distorts the magic of the marketplace and thus disrupts the supposedly apolitical and scientific model economics was trying to present, so it had to be re-located away from economic relationships. Since real world economies are riddled through with power relationships, most obviously expressed in the ancient struggle between those who own property and those who provide labor, this left the social elite with a problem: how do they support both the scientific illusion of the market, and yet still exploit it more fully. The solution was to co-opt institutions outside the economy. Which meant that economic liberty had to become pre-eminent and economic relations were forced to become the only ones that mattered. Ultimately this led us to where we are today, where the definition of liberty is the calculus of trading, where only economic liberty truly matters, and the apparatus of the state is deployed to protect it. The result is a level of inequality tolerated and abetted by the elite because the freedoms we enjoy are most enjoyed by them.

Wolfgang Streeck gives us his own image of this separation, which has become significantly hardened in the years since World War II:

> "Two competing principles of distribution were institutionalized in the political economy of postwar democratic capitalism: what I shall call *market justice* on the one hand and *social justice* on the other. By *market justice*, I mean distribution of the output of production according to the market evaluation of individual performance, expressed in relative prices; the yardstick for remuneration according to market justice is marginal productivity, the market value of the last unit of output under competitive conditions. *Social justice*, on the other hand, is determined by cultural norms and is based on status rather than contract. It follows collective ideas of fairness, correctness and reciprocity, concedes demands for minimum livelihood irrespective of economic

performance or productivity, and recognizes civil and human rights to such things as health, social security, participation in the life of the community, employment protection and trade union organization" (emphasis in the original).

The problem, as our current level of inequality suggests, is that economic justice or liberty can become a license for the elite to capture more than a fair share. The elimination of power from the machinery of economics is not a reflection of reality but of need – the need to appear scientific. In contrast, a real unfettered marketplace, with its liberty to trade, is simply another arena in which power can be accumulated, expressed, and exploited. Unlike that pesky social justice arena where efforts have been made to even out power by giving people equal votes, at least in principle, a market is a place where voting rights can be highly asymmetrical. There are all sorts of ways to cheat. Elites are typically good at cheating.

That this is true is surely commonplace knowledge. History, as both Thomas Piketty and Walter Scheidel have taught us recently in their separate ways, is replete with evidence that elites have a knack for ensuring their economic advantage. The hope that the definition and introduction of new ideas of economic liberty would somehow expunge this trend from history was, it turns out, both naïve and foolish. What was missing in economic analysis of was to make room for the exercise of power within the system and not to shunt it off to one side as a subject to be discussed outside of the main debate. Every time progress was made in bringing power and social relations into economics – the many heresies of economics all appear to display this feature, there was a strong and successful counter movement to purify it again. Inequality today reflects the victory of the last such counter movement. The grand idea of economic liberty is nowadays simply a defense of the aggrandizement of the elite.

It is trite to say that ideas matter, I am going to say it anyway: they matter more than anything else. I believe the evolution of a number of ideas beginning sometime in the 17th century that produced the surge towards our current prosperity. We can all quibble over the starting date, but it is only a quibble that ought not distract us. Ultimately these ideas reproduced, morphed, and propagated into the intellectual fabric of modern society. Our circumstances, the great cause for concern for many of us, is that in the mid-twentieth century one set of ideas prevailed. Economic justice became to stand for all justice and to maximize that well of justice we were told to pursue efficiency at all costs. Amongst the ideas giving impetus to this pursuit was that inequality as it deepens, is a minor or inconsequential issue. Efficiency trumps equality. Indeed, the acceptance of an imbalance between efficiency and equality is core to the ideas proselytized by the followers of Hayek. Justice becomes a quantity in their hands. More justice is produced by more efficiency because it is produced by economic processes built upon scientific discovery. The only liberty to be tolerated is that of "free" production and consumption. All else is the road to serfdom.

That this is an error dependent upon a twisted definition of "liberty" ought to be manifest. Freedom, in the hands of Hayek and his followers, became a contorted and diminished shell of its former self. It was reduced to support a redefined individual determined to resist the predations of the state, and along the way all pretense or hope of communal action was deliberately expunged. Now, of course, this reduction of liberty into a fragment of freedom had begun almost as soon as our modern conceptions of freedom were launched, but it was in the context of the social pressures of the Great Depression, and the perceived challenge to the West represented by the Soviet Union, that Hayek and those like him re-introduced the slimmed down notion of liberty with a born-again fervor. Such was the terror with which the advocates of this new definition viewed the community, that even a scintilla of co-operation was regarded as a first step on a slippery slope into a socialist hell. These were the years of the Cold war, and Hayek's message was carefully crafted to take advantage of that climate, especially in the United States. He succeeded, and this chopped down liberty garnered enormous visceral appeal, which explains its popularity even today. It became known as economic liberty or economic liberalism and was converted energetically into a complex and elegant logic, a system so wondrous that it wormed its way into economics, politics, and law and ended up, termite-like, in destroying the social fabric and cohesion necessary for us to deal with inequality.

The key to it all was the absence of government, or at least the absence of centralized control. This gave it an ethical appeal to those caught up in the suspicion of socialism and its emphasis on the community. Its elegance rests on its abstraction, and on the anonymity of the market mechanism central to its operation. Not only was this highly limited notion of liberty key to market transacting, but it made the marketplace a politically potent entity as well. Milton Friedman, one of its main proponents, expressed it as follows:

> "Adam Smith's flash of genius was that prices that emerged from voluntary transactions between buyers and sellers – for short a free market – could coordinate the activity of millions of people, each seeking his own interest, in such a way as to make everyone better off... The price system is the mechanism that fulfills this task without central direction, *without requiring people to speak to one another...* Economic order can emerge as the *unintended* consequence of the actions of many people seeking his own interest. The price system works so well, so efficiently, that we are *not aware of it* most of the time" (emphasis in the original).

Notice the emphasis. Notice what mattered to Friedman. Anonymity. Lack of awareness. Lack of intention. Efficiency. Oh yes, and it is voluntary. That's the liberty bit. Stuff just happens, and it's all good. How can we complain if a little inequality slips in? It's voluntary. And, more to the point, this laudatory system is so good for us all that it obviates the need for political interference in whatever the price system produces. After all, don't consumers "vote" when they go to buy? Why would they want another vote, outside of the market, to intercede in the results of all this anonymity and efficiency?

Economics had worked so diligently to eliminate politics to fend off the unwanted predation of the old landed and the modern working classes, and yet was being highly political in juxtaposition with the central planning of Eastern Europe.

It is hard to say whether the believers of these ideas actually wanted to destroy society. They would probably deny such an intent. Society had little meaning to them. It was, Hayek said, "not a person. It is the organized structure of activities that arises when its members observe certain abstract rules". Which sounds like a market too. Yet it is equally hard to deny the ultimate result of the avid and earnest application of those ideas. The world is rife with unrest, unhappiness, insecurity, and ill-will. If the goal of the scrunched down vision of the liberated individual was to set us all free to pursue our own course to happiness, then it must be marked as a spectacular failure. This set of ideas, centered on the atomistic individual, and which I nowadays loosely call libertarianism, like all utopias is falling under the weight of its own contradictions. And the measure of that failure is the level of inequality that bedevils most modern societies, but which is most prominent in the United States where the ideas have most deeply rooted themselves. The defense of economic liberty was transformed into a defense of *all* liberty. Economics thus became a theory of everything. As long as everything excludes the social.

My rather simple attempts at explaining the problem to my more skeptical friends start with an analogy: temperature is not a quality of an individual atom it is a property of a system of atoms. Likewise, inequality is not a quality that an individual person experiences, they experience issues that stem from the systemic existence of inequality, but it is the system itself that expresses inequality. For those of us concerned with the effects of inequality, therefore, the extent of inequality is a measure of the extent of the imbalances that have accumulated in the system. We have become very good at taking the temperature of our social systems, but because, we are told, the sources of imbalance are the result of perfectly natural forces we are much less well able to confront and diminish inequality. Besides, since it is a property of society, and since society is of little interest, why would we care about inequality?

In its very original state, the idea that if free people are left to their own devices to trade, good things then happen is, indeed, powerful as long as it is regarded as only one of many freedoms. Problems start to arise when the idea is pressed into service too far – when it is fused with political freedom to protect the individual from the state, and when it is used as the font of the efficiency responsible for our modern cornucopia. Succinctly, a paradox creeps in. The power to truck and barter sets us free, which is an inversion of the original argument that we needed to be set free to truck and barter, gets tangled up with why we need to be set free in the first place: to become more prosperous, or to pursue efficiency.

Nowhere is this paradox more evident than in the effort to explain the rise in prosperity unleashed by modernity, or the Great Enrichment as Diedre McCloskey calls it. The fusion of politics back into economics on the one hand, and the need to keep economics steadfastly apolitical on the other leads to contradictions and doubles down on the need to preserve atomistic individuals. This means, inevitably, that democracy, being a social phenomenon, is a problem for economics.

It is easy to see why. So petrified were the originators of this kind of economic thought of the predations, or even the presence of the state, that they were totally incapable of distinguishing between different forms of state. They carried forward into their analysis only one notion of "state": the pre-democratic aristocratic, monarchic, and religious one that economics had been invented to help undermine. The subsequent evolution of democracy was ignored.

In this form the objective of the study of the Great Enrichment became to prove beyond any doubt that our contemporary prosperity was caused by the operations of the free market. Nothing else. Particularly not politics

But underneath all this effort lurked the ongoing oddity that the individual and her liberty was a very perverse being. Increasingly so as the discipline applied itself to explaining the surge in prosperity. It must be, became the centerpiece of thinking, that markets were *necessarily* efficient. And if let alone by the evil state, they would always be efficient. Suddenly as mentioned earlier, efficiency was the goal. The entirety of the project shifted to understanding efficiency. That there might be side-effects of efficiency was irrelevant. The metrics of success were the metrics of efficiency. The distribution of the results of ever greater efficiency was not an issue. The objective was to acquire more efficiency because efficiency was the route to prosperity. Those who criticized the apparent single-mindedness of this thought process were dismissed as confused. Or soft headed. Or misguided souls who did not understand the tough or rigorous nature of what needed to be done.

Advocates of efficiency and the ideas that undergird its expression as economic technology in our markets took on the mantle of being the sensible hard-headed ones. They derided, as they had to in order defend their anti-social stance, anyone interested in outcomes that appeared socially unpleasant. The confrontation between liberty in the marketplace and liberty elsewhere was expunged from discussion. The only liberty that mattered was that identified as driving efficiency.

That, as the Great Enrichment gathered momentum, all sorts of social upheaval took place was dismissed as a side matter. That lives were turned upside down was considered inconsequential. Disruption and "creative destruction" were elevated as scientific causes of enrichment. That the entire history of the Great Enrichment is littered with contest often rising to the level of war is left out of the narrative. Efficiency is what counts.

If, sometimes, efficiency creates huge inequality, so be it. Only the muddle headed would consider that a problem.

Besides anyone who dared think about notions of society or non-economic forms of distribution of prosperity were to be seen as potentially subversive opponents of liberty.

Sometimes this dismissal of the uncomfortable side effects of the rush to efficiency can sound weirdly paternalistic. For instance, the philosopher Harry Frankfurt suggested that calculating inequality was relatively easy compared to what really mattered which was calculating what a person "needs" in order to have enough. Presumably it was only because it was easy to calculate that the muddle-headed worried about inequality. What they should have been vexed over is wondering what a person needs in order to function. The paternalism inherent in that suggestion is off-putting, but Frankfurt is not done. He goes on to argue that "economic equality is not, as such, of particular moral importance". Not at all. The true moral urgency is to preserve economic liberty. Economic *equality* can take a back seat.

It is easy to get the feeling that society outside of the market, that scary dark place so distant from the purity of economics, causes nightmares in the minds of efficiency-first advocates. They can only rest by conflating things like dignity with liberty, but not democracy.

It is, in their telling, liberty that bestows "dignity", not citizenship or sharing in self-governance on an equal footing with all our fellow citizens. Our goal has become to create this dignity by bestowing upon our poor a lifestyle so full of bounty that even our most privileged ancestors would have been jealous of their lifestyle. Our goal, in other words, is to have lots of stuff. It is not to concern ourselves with how much stuff anyone else has. Such a concern is called envy. Greed is good. Envy is not.

This single-minded pursuit of the individual as liberated actor in the marketplace is the primary difficulty we face in getting inequality resolved. Thinkers in this tradition often avoid engaging with democracy in the manner Frankfurt did. Elevating the poor into participation in democratic society was, for example, the very last thing on Hayek's mind. Hayek had, he said, "no intention … of making a fetish out of democracy". He goes on:

> "It may well be that our generation talks and thinks too much of democracy and too little of the values which it serves … Democracy is essentially a means, a utilitarian device for safeguarding internal peace and individual freedom. As such it is by no means infallible or certain."

There you have it.

Democracy is a device to safeguard individual freedom, by which we mean economic freedom. It can be tolerated as long as it serves the market. But, it is a fallible device. In the wrong hands it might intrude onto the territory Hayek reserves jealously for his precious liberty to be free from state intrusion or interference in the marketplace.

And here we arrive on the battlefield: we have the inversion of economics serving politics. Now it is the other way around. Democratic capitalism, as it became known in the post-war years, serves two masters not one. The phrase is a contradiction. It poses two forces and two concepts of liberty against each other. It is constantly tugged back and forth between them. Hence the lack of resolution to the problem of inequality. Hence the need to double down and push back against those who simply deny the existence of the problem. Or, worse, those who see inequality as something virtuous and in no need of fixing at all.

By becoming the study of efficiency in a world of scarcity, economics has played its part in developing the intellectual defense of inequality. Especially by stressing its virtues, and even more especially by embracing a perverse and idiosyncratic definition of liberty. It is no accident that Margaret Thatcher could channel her hero, Hayek, and dismiss the notion of society with such ease. Hayek himself referred to society as being a slippery concept of vague definition. Apparently, such vagueness, which was a primary cause for criticism by Hayek of anything social, was not an issue in the definition of a market. That both markets and society are comprised of the same people and overlap so much that we argue over the extent to which one is embedded in the other, is a fact allowed to slide from view by the defenders of Hayek's version of liberty. It is our job to pull that fact back into view and to go further: we have to dispute the notion of liberty that economists have deployed as they constructed their elegant theories of economics.

As we attempt to re-engineer the concept of liberty and tame it such that it doesn't do the damage it has in the hands of Hayek and his ilk, we need to go back to the beginning. There was a time, as Etienne Balibar reminds us that the concept that became the liberty that subsequently produced the idea of marketplaces in our modern sense, was conflated with a notion of equality. The literature and correspondence of the early history of the United States is littered with references to both liberty and equality. At times the two ideas can be interchanged as if they are aspects of the same concept. Balibar gives this conflated concept a name: "equaliberty" which would, in his words,

> "be essentially constructed as a double unity of opposites: a unity ... of *man* and *citizen*, which from then on would appear as correlative despite all the practical restrictions on the distribution of rights and powers; and a unity ... of the concepts of *freedom* and *equality*, perceived as two faces of a single 'constituent power' despite the constant tendency of bourgeois political ideologies (what we could generically call 'liberalism') to give the former an epistemological and even ontological priority by making it a "natural right" par excellence..." (emphasis in the original).

This fusion of two conflicting aspects of liberty, one expressed through economic freedom and the other expressed through political action, is essential to our modern world. By splitting them apart and giving priority to the first our opponents have played a trick on us. They have co-opted the word liberty and given it such emphasis that our ability to muster the second as a balancing idea to mitigate the potential excesses of the first has been severely limited. Indeed, in the hands of economic purists the second is denigrated as misguided or fanciful. We are told that there is only one liberty: that of agents in the marketplace. Although, perhaps, not in the marketplace of ideas where the second lingers on as an antidote to its twin.

Once this perverse and singular definition of individual liberty was let loose it was a short step to a similar attempt to separate the domain of economics from society itself. We suddenly began to talk of the market as if it was suspended in its own neutral substrate in a scientific laboratory. It was cleansed of social or political pollution. It was purified and lifted onto a pedestal. It became regarded as the causal power of our modern prosperity. It was given magical properties.

Later thinkers who extolled the virtues of this singular liberty, in their zeal to make it impregnable to attack, doubled down on this extraction of the market from society. They took Adam Smith's nuanced expression of wonder that private greed, or perhaps we should say self-interest, could accumulate magically into social benefit, and they hammered it into an ever more constrained straitjacket. They began to twist his observation that some semblance of social order appeared to emerge from the various individual uncoordinated acts, and eventually enshrined it in a definition so tight that it was no longer a reflection of the real world. It was isolated from interaction. This became more necessary as the project morphed from description of the world as it is, to theorizing about the world as it *ought* to be. Or as it might be if only those who carried a preference for equality would stop interfering.

Balibar is right to note the tendency of those who prioritize economic liberty over any other form of freedom to root it in nature. This makes them indifferent to criticism that they harbor ideological intent. Perhaps, in our context, nowhere is this more apparent than in the technology they devised to explain the "natural" distribution of our prosperity. The arrival of marginal analysis on the scene marked a pivotal moment in the steady adoption of this natural stance. Here is John Bates Clark making the case:

> "It is the purpose of this work to show that the distribution of the income of society is controlled by a natural law, and that this law, if it worked without friction, would give to every agent of production the amount of wealth which that agent creates."

How can we, who want to combat inequality, dare intrude on nature? Clark swats us away. Worse still is the unstated, but clear message that mucking about with nature will upend the wondrous machinery of the economy.

It is important for those who wish to defend this natural law position, which some call market justice, to ensure that the economy is fenced off from society in general. On the other side of that fence are all sorts of subversive thoughts that must not be allowed to infect the purity of the market. Streeck makes us aware of this danger: "from the point of view of market justice there is a constant danger that ideas of social justice will usurp the public power through a democratic majority and then regularly distort the operation of the market". Persisting in this cramped definition of market justice requires the adoption of an ethical stance that justifies whatever outcome pops out of the market machine. The result is ethical because it is natural. Any amount of inequality is justified because it is natural.

Within the walls of the hermetically sealed off market unequal outputs are to be explained by unequal inputs. It is all wonderfully self-supporting and elegantly described. Marginal productivity, as this neat trick is called, is not empirically based but sure looks scientific. Goodness knows how busy the Queen of England must be. Her productivity is monstrous compared with the maid who cleans her floors. Clark says so. And, as well, do far too many economists. Just look at the relative earnings. The Queen's income must represent astonishing productivity. It's natural.

I wonder what Balibar would say.

I know what Thompson would say. He said it. "The market cannot be isolated and abstracted from the network of political, social, and legal relations in which it is situate". But if you are going to persist in theorizing about the market in terms of natural laws it cannot be embedded in something as human as all that. It must sit outside. Especially if you want, as Hayek wants, to maintain a healthy distance from democracy.

PETER RADFORD

This leads to contradictions and oddities that are worth pondering. Those economists who pursued the logic of their theories into the very farthest of dead ends described their liberty laden agents as supremely rational. That this robbed them of true agency, because they were reduced to automatons slavishly obeying the diktats of economic laws, was an irony unnoticed by the more zealous. Nonetheless these rational agents behaved dutifully like mice on a treadmill to keep the operation of the models running smoothly. Presumably it was rational to accept any amount of rising inequality as they did so. Not that they would notice, only a representative sample were ever allowed in to perform their duties. Now comes the oddity. When those agents stepped outside of the model market, they suddenly displayed all sorts of irrational behavior. They started, amongst other things, voting in support of redistributive policies. How could this be? Were they schizophrenic? Or were they upset at the allotment of prosperity determined by Clark's nature?

Could it be that our agents, when released from the strictures of the economist's rational straight jacket, realized that there is a second, and equally legitimate, arena for the distribution of prosperity? Could it be that they discovered democracy? Could they, in other words, be reclaiming a second form of liberty, one that asserts equality as an ethical component? Could it be that they see, as Polanyi asserted, that "to allow the market mechanism to be sole director of the fate of human beings and their natural environment, indeed, even of the amount of purchasing power, would result in the demolition of society"?

And here, I think, is the fertile territory on which we carry the fight forward. We simply deny that liberty is a single thing. We assert that it is multi-faceted, and that the pursuit of efficiency must bow, periodically, to correction if we can show that it produces a reduction in liberty more broadly defined. In this stance we echo Arthur Okun who wrote:

> "If both equality and efficiency are valued, and neither takes absolute priority over the other, then, in places where they conflict, compromises ought to be struck ... In particular, social decisions that permit economic inequality must be justified as promoting economic efficiency. That proposition is not original, but it is important and apparently remains controversial."

It is shocking to recall that when Okun was writing this about the tradeoff between equality and efficiency, inequality was benign by our current standards. It was also almost the same time that the Hayek and Freidman inspired distortion was about to get underway. Okun, in other words was warning us about something about to explode onto the scene.

By refusing to accept the perversity of the asymmetrical tilt towards efficiency at the expense of equality we assert that there has to be a balance. And the art of balance must, necessarily, open up the discussion of the generation of prosperity to issues and ideas long removed from the limited version of economics derived from the

Hayekian tradition. This produces an economics of a different kind and recognizes and embraces the variety of thought that the expanded definition of liberty requires.

One of the fatal flaws of the restricted economics promulgated by the heirs to Freidman is that it is built upon a seriously deficient vision of what actually goes on in the marketplace. This is odd because much of its heritage flows from the Smithian observation of the division of labor at work. It is a contradiction to restrict liberty to the economic actions of an atomistic individual in an arms-length marketplace and also to ignore the consequences of the division of labor. As economic activity was ever further sliced into smaller and more specialized slices market participants became more dependent upon one another. They had to move from either producing or consuming as single individuals to becoming part of an increasingly complex production, distribution, and consumption process. The vaunted coordination of all this amassing complexity is, to listen to Freidman and his heirs, the price mechanism.

Perhaps, but it is the price mechanism with an enormous assist from something we have difficulty finding in their literature: the modern corporation. Indeed, the entire history of the Great Enrichment could as easily be told as a triumph of the development of the corporation, as of the freedom to trade. This is hardly a novel observation. Shonfield said that a private firm "sees itself as a permanent institution, entrusted with functions that transcend the search for maximum profits and are at times compatible with it" with a structure and intent "more and more reminiscent of certain public institutions". Along the same lines Kenneth Galbraith wrote:

> "The modern industrial system is no longer essentially a market system. It is planned by large firms and in part by the modern state. It must be planned, because modern technology and organization can flourish only in a stable environment, a condition that the market cannot satisfy."

We are a long way from the Friedman world at this point. The key being that the rise of an economy dependent upon increasing division of labor introduces issues only solvable by taking swathes of it out of the market and into the firm. This is not at all what Friedman envisages. It is an inversion of his thoughts quoted earlier, what goes on inside a corporation is all about intention, familiarity, and awareness. The modern business firm is the living denial of free market thinking. It is centralized and heavily managed. The organization is not an unintended consequence of people going about their singular ways, it is the result of the careful coordination of a series of roles and routines that accumulate into single whole. The difference could not be more stark. Not just this, but the role of the individual inside this aggregation of roles and routines is hardly one of economic liberty. It is one of relentless oversight.

Some economists are all too well aware of this contradiction. The existence of the business firm as a coordinator of activity beyond the boundaries of the marketplace is a paradox first articulated by Ronald Coase as long ago as 1937. Coase asked a rather important question:

> "In view of the fact that, while economists treat the price mechanism as a coordinating instrument, they also admit the coordinating function of the 'entrepreneur'. It is surely important to enquire why coordination is the work of the price mechanism in one case and of the entrepreneur in another."

I would answer the increasingly complex content of products requires administration rather than simple coordination. The price mechanism is not up to the job. But Coase looked elsewhere.

A whole sub-literature called transaction cost economics has been developed to try to tame the firm and steer it back into conformity with free market orthodoxy. Unsuccessfully. The paradox is beyond resolution. The reality is that the corporation is the dominant mediator of economic activity in modern societies precisely because the division of labor demands complex coordination. It demands cooperation. No one individual can claim to play an indivisible role. Marginal productivity disappears under a cloud in a such an interconnected world: how can any task be truly separated? Not only this but any ethics built upon atomistic individuals also disappears. A new ethics built upon *cooperation* is required. And if this is true, how can economic inequality based upon Clark's natural law be tolerable? It cannot. Okun's request that we demand a justification for economic equality from those who pursue economic efficiency takes on a new light, because efficiency is derived not from economic liberty, but from economic solidarity.

Elizabeth Anderson suggests we need a new definition of this solidarity. She calls it "democratic equality". It is the beginning of our discovery of a new balance and a way to highlight the inequity of using an antiquated definition of liberty simply in order to defend the marketplace from a criticism of its poor distribution of our jointly produced prosperity. Anderson discusses "equality of fortune" in contrast with her democratic equality, with the former being more what many of us have in mind when we restrict ourselves to talking about inequality in purely economic terms. In her words:

> "democratic equality is what I shall call a relational theory of equality: it views equality as a social relationship. Equality of fortune is a distributive theory of equality: it conceives of equality as a pattern of distribution. Thus, equality of fortune regards two people as equal so long as they enjoy equal amounts of some distributable good – income, resources, opportunities for welfare and so forth. Social relations are seen largely as instrumental to generating such patterns of distribution. By contrast, democratic equality regards two people as equals when each accepts the obligation to justify their actions by principles acceptable to the other, and in which they take mutual

consultation, reciprocation, and recognition for granted."

There are hints of equaliberty in this expression of equality. The error of the extreme individualists can be overcome by the adoption of a conception of this sort.

We are not yet done with the corporation. It is important to note the date of the Shonfield and Galbraith comments, they came just as Hayek's victory became absolute. It is no accident that our current egregious levels of inequality followed upon that victory. The misconception of liberty and its separation from its democratic counterpart was about to do its worst.

Despite the corporation's contradiction of Friedman's core ideas, he felt free to opine on its purpose. More exactly, he felt free to opine on the objective of the management of a corporation. This objective was to maximize shareholder value. There are two contestable components that comprise this thought. The first is expressed in this statement by Friedman:

> "In a **free-enterprise**, **private-property** system, a **corporate executive** is an employee of the owners of the business. He has direct responsibility to his employers. That responsibility is to conduct the business in accordance with their desires... the key point is that, in his capacity as a corporate exccutive, the manager is the agent of the individuals who own the corporation... and his primary responsibility is to them."

The second, from the same source is this: "There is one and only one social responsibility of business – to use it resources and engage in activities designed to increase its profits."

These two concepts: the ownership of the corporation by shareholders, and the need for management to work exclusively for them, set in motion a great suppression of wages and the privilege of profit that lie at the root of inequality. At least at the root of the inequality of fortune, to channel Anderson. The mismanagement of the modern corporation that came subsequent to Freidman's call to arms, is one of the great consequences of the perversion of the notion of liberty embedded in his thought. It is also an object lesson in how ideas matter in very material ways.

It was not long after Friedman launched the profit-maximizing ship that theories of shareholder value and the role of management with respect to profit became the feature of the business school curriculum. Generations of managers have been brought up to believe in the essential truth that they operate purely to maximize shareholder wealth. That this is a complete reversal of the way in which firms were managed a decade or so earlier is lost in time. What is not lost is that the ever more pressing need to squeeze returns to shareholders devastated the lives of workers, who became a cost rather than an asset.

This is also a salutary lesson for economists who sometimes still deny culpability for their discipline's impact on their fellow citizens. Ideas matter. You had better stress test them before allowing them to filter into related fields, and if you still believe in them, then take responsibility for the results. Hayek led to Freidman, which led to shareholder value, which led to wage stagnation. Period. Put that in the textbooks and explain.

The entire modern corpus of management theory stands on the perverse definition of economic liberty imported from economics. The notion of agency is fundamental to it. Because there are no social relations everything is conceived of in the context of a contract. Agency theory is a simple extension and explication of the relationship between managers and shareholders. In it, managers are seen as nothing but agents of shareholders, and since the latter are deemed owners of the property known as the corporation, it is only right that managers act in the shareholder's interests. Or that's the story. There are no agents working on behalf of anyone else, particularly workers, who, don't forget, are conceived of in libertarian literature as liberated agents in their own right. They need no agents. How odd, then, that shareholders do. Perhaps they don't have the mental fortitude that workers do. Or is it because they are thought of as property owners and there is a subsequent need to explain what happens when they allow someone else to dictate what happens to that property. Workers don't have property in this world. They are a cost of production. The hyper-simplicity of this relationship is a strong echo of the world conceived by Freidman. There are no complex cooperative interdependencies. Just, in the words of one theory of the firm, a nexus of contracts with the shareholder holding all the ultimate rights. This is a libertarian dream. It is also far distant from reality.

For one thing we might reasonably ask whether shareholders do, in fact, own a corporation. There are some who would dispute this notion. They make sense. A corporation is a ward of the state. It is established under law as an entity prior to receiving any funding. The sequence of steps in creating a firm assume a corporation exists in order to receive funds. In return for receiving those funds it creates for itself an obligation to the funders. It does not sell itself into bondage to them. Shareholders own certain financial rights. They do not own the actual corporation which continues to persist without them. Indeed, this concept of a corporation being an individual-in-law is exactly the source of a great deal of legal history in the United States beginning as far back as the early 1800s and culminating in the infamous Citizen's United decision in which the Supreme Court undermined democracy by entitling corporations to pour cash into elections and buy subsequent legislation. The Court was being particularly narrow in the Citizen's decision, but it was firmly within precedent. In law, corporations are individuals. They cannot be owned, and they have rights. Here we have in one compact example the extent of the infestation of our values by the oddball concept of liberty undergirding free market economics. It gets everywhere. Like a pandemic. Our institutions are turned inside out in order to preserve the error and contradictions that a return to equaliberty would resolve.

The plague unleashed by shareholder value inevitably resulted in most of the great harms done by modern corporations. Managers administering the complex organization of economic activity continuously replicated the error by making decisions based on shareholder whims. What became known as core competencies were the source of outsourcing activities. The desire for higher returns on equity drove the turn away from domestic to foreign production. Globalization grew in response to the same impulse. Worker retirement and health benefits, things that ought never have been within the purview of private management, were re-cast as a cost to be cut. The work relationship itself was redefined wherever possible to get rid of pension and other benefit obligations. The worker-as-cost philosophy inherent in our modern economy has reduced millions to a precarious lifestyle. All as a result of the Freidman injunction being taken seriously and worked up into elaborate sub-theories.

Yes, ideas matter. And it is little wonder that millions of our fellow citizens might look a little skeptically at the so-called benefits of the Great Enrichment. It is one thing to have a super television set with capabilities unheard of 20 years ago, it is another not to be able to pay the rent. There is no greatness in the Great Enrichment if it ends in an ethical desert.

So dominant did the singularity of economic liberty became and so in conflict with the reality that it created that it became necessary for the democratic domain to be subordinated to the economic. How else was it going to be possible to maintain the illusion that economic liberty was in the interests of everyone? Growing inequality suggested otherwise. The contradictions within helter-skelter potpourri of ideas collected under the heading of economic liberty or just plain "liberalism" and their increasingly anti-social consequences needed shoring up. The problem is, as Rosanvallon points out, that as it spread it tentacles into fields further away from its Hayekian origin liberalism lost its coherence. It morphed into a culture. Rosanvallon put it this way:

> "The proliferation and occasionally contradictory character of this literature, all called 'liberal' is an irritant only if one begins by thinking that it is a matter of understanding liberalism as a *doctrine*, that is a coherent if differentiated body of judgements and analyses. For it is clear that there is no doctrinal unity to liberalism. But if it is not a doctrine, *liberalism is a culture*."

And cultures are difficult to root out. Not only this, but, they infest our institutions. They co-opt institutions to do their bidding.

Once inequality is culturally acceptable it is possible to ignore it as a benign fact of life. It can be dismissed as inconsequential. An irritant, nothing more. Our elite can barrel along acquiring an ever-larger share of the pie of fortune because their flanks is protected by a wall of ideas built on the economic conception of liberty. If the hollowing out of the middle class is called for in order to press along with the liberal project, then so be it. If people object, then the state itself must be subordinated to the project. The justification for the very existence of the state becomes shoring up the market to protect economic liberty.

Wendy Brown is concise in her articulation of the result of this capture of our culture:

"The market is the organizing and regulative principle of the state and society, along three different lines: (a) The state openly responds to needs of the market, whether through monetary and fiscal policy, immigration policy, the treatment of criminals, or the structure of public education. ... (b) The state itself is enfolded and animated by market rationality: that is, not simply profitability but a generalized calculation of cost and benefit becomes the measure of all state practices. ... (c) Putting (a) and (b) together, the health and growth of the economy is *the* basis of state legitimacy" (emphasis in the original).

With a culture so enraptured by market reasoning and with economic liberty, it has been a simple task to ensure the majority of the fruits of the Great Enrichment flow to a small self-regarding and self-promoting elite. Our society has been thrown out of balance. It was once, possibly, a defensible argument to suggest that the elite may capture a disproportionate piece of the pie of fortune, because the constituents of the elite are constantly changing. There is always opportunity for newcomers to barge in and the incompetent to fall out. In other words, the constant churn within the elite prevents inequality from creating a permanent ruling class. Inequality is simply a recognition of the marginal productivity of those at the top, it is not the product of exclusion. In the light of recent research this is no longer a tenable position. The elite are rapidly occluding opportunity. The stairway up is more than offset by many more trapdoors down. The economy is more exclusive than inclusive. To the greater benefit of the elite, which is settling into permanency.

Okun was being generous in his arguments. He compared the one-person-one vote of politics to the one-person-many-votes of the marketplace. He saw benefits in both sides. He did not anticipate the total dominance of our culture by a conception of economic liberty that has its roots in a political argument to set the bourgeois free. He did not anticipate our capitulation to the economic machinery of the corporation misconceived as an agent of shareholders. He did not foresee the great tilt towards inequality that would follow, necessarily, from the breaking apart of equaliberty and the ideological pursuit of economic liberty as our sole form of freedom. Because in an arena where some people have many more votes they inevitably win.

It is, ultimately, the successful conquering of our culture that has allowed inequality to arise unchecked. All our best efforts, and all the good intentions of the current wave of thinkers pushing back against inequality, have to overcome the inertia of that deeply imbedded culture. A culture that bends our institutions to do the bidding of those with many votes. It is not enough, then, to change economics. Although that is a start. Piketty was nowhere near the first to sound the alarm, but his call to arms resonated well because of the context within which it was sounded. Economic inequality is rampant, and the elite has, as Scheidel would surely have warned us, turned economic inequality into social and political inequality too. It is not enough for Philippon to suggest, as he does at the very start of his recent book, that the two big questions in economics are growth and inequality. By making this argument he is trying to wrest the discipline away from the likes of Lucas, a disciple of Hayek and who famously scoffed at the value of investigating inequality. Yes, Solow, the father of modern growth theory applauds Piketty, but the heirs of Hayek still protect their heritage ferociously. They, to this day, pretend that the Great Enrichment was the product of the isolation of economic liberty from its equaliberty forbearer. They still dominate our culture and our values.

To overcome that culture, we need more than well designed programs to redistribute prosperity. They are easy to design, and we are getting well-armed with them. We need to recognize that inequality, because of the severance of market justice from social justice, or rather, the displacement of the latter by the former, extends now into the political realm as much as into the economic realm. We must fuse the two together. We must deny that economic liberty exists by itself. We must recognize that modern economies, being built on the foundation of the division of labor, are the constructs of economic solidarity. Cooperation is a more powerful force in such economies than competition. Call it the art of balance, call it equaliberty, or call it democratic equality, whatever we call it, we must reject the notion of economic liberty as a stand-alone and dominant idea. It has done enough damage. It has produced our current inequality. It has to go.

References

Anderson, Elizabeth S. (1999) "What Is the Point of Equality?" *Ethics* 109 (January): 287-337.

Balibar, Etienne (2014) *Equaliberty: Political Essays*. Durham: Duke University Press.

Brown, Wendy (2005) "Neoliberalism and the End of Liberal Democracy", *Edgework: Critical Essays on Knowledge and Politics*. Princeton, N.J.: Princeton University Press.

Clark, J.B. (1899) *The Distribution of Wealth: A Theory of Wages, Interest, and Profit*. New York: Macmillan.

Coase, R.H. (1937) "The Nature of the Firm." *Economica* (November).

Friedman, Milton (1970) "The Social Responsibility of Business is to Increase its Profits." *The New York Times Magazine* (September 13).

Frankfurt, Harry (1987) "Equality as a Moral Ideal." *Ethics* 98 (October): 21-43.

Galbraith, John Kenneth (1967) *The New Industrial State*. Princeton N.J.: Princeton University Press.

Hayek, Friedrich von A. (2001[1944]) *The Road to Serfdom*. London: Routledge.

Jensen, Michael C. and Meckling William H. (1976) "The Theory of the Firm: managerial Behavior, Agency Costs, and Ownership Structure." *Journal of Financial Economics*, 3, 305-360.

McCloskey, Deirdre N. (2016) *Bourgeois Values: How Ideas, Not Capital or Institutions, Enriched the World*. Chicago: Chicago University Press.

Okun, Arthur M. (1974) *Equality and Efficiency: The Big Tradeoff*. Washington, D.C.: The Brookings Institution.

Philippon, Thomas (2019) *The Great Reversal: How America Gave Up on Free Markets*. Cambridge Massachusetts: The Belknap Press of Harvard University Press.

Piketty, Thomas (2014) *Capital in the Twenty-First Century, Cambridge Massachusetts.* Cambridge Massachusetts: The Belknap Press of Harvard University Press.

Polanyi, Karl (1944) *The Great Transformation: The Political and Economic Origins of Our Time.* New York: Farrar & Rinehart.

Prahalad C.K. and Hamel, Gary (1990) "The Core Competencies of the Corporation." *Harvard Business Review,* Vol 68, No. 3, 79-91.

Robbins, Lionel (1932) *Essay of the Nature and Significance of Economic Science.* London: MacMillan.

Rosanvallon, Pierre (2006) *Democracy Past and Future.* New York: Columbia University Press.

Rosanvallon, Pierre (2013) *The Society of Equals.* Cambridge, MA: Harvard University Press.

Scheidel, Walter (2017) *The Great Leveler: Violence and the History of Inequality from the Stone Age to the Twenty-First Century.* Princeton N.J.: Princeton University Press.

Shonfield, Andrew (1969) *Modern Capitalism: The Changing Balance of Private and Public Power.* New York: Oxford University Press.

Solow, Robert (2017) "Thomas Piketty Is Right." In Boushey et al, (Eds) *After Piketty: The Agenda for Economics and Inequality.* Cambridge Massachusetts: Harvard University Press.

Stout, Lynn A. (2013) "The Shareholder Value Myth." *Cornell Law Faculty Publications.* Paper 771.

Streeck, Wolfgang (2014) *Buying Time: The Delayed Crisis of Democratic Capitalism.* London: Verso Books.

Thompson, E.P. (1993) "The Moral Economy Reviewed." In *Customs in Common.* New York: The Free Press.

Winkler, Adam (2018) *We the Corporations: How American Businesses Won Their Civil Rights.* New York, W.W. Norton.

Chapter 11

Climbing to 10^{11}: globalization, digitization, shareholder capitalism and the summits of contemporary wealth

David A. Westbrook[1]

I. Introduction: summits of wealth

If we examine any society, we find elites, hierarchies, and so inequality of one sort or another. This may be necessarily true: perhaps relative social positions cannot be understood in, much less actually reduced to, the ultimately quantitative terms of equality. Or so I might argue, but that would be another essay. For now, the simple historical and anthropological observation of the ubiquity of inequality suffices. The mere fact of inequality is to be expected, in itself hardly an outrage, at least insofar as social life itself is not an outrage (pace, Sartre). The question is what kind of inequality?

---

[1] Louis A. Del Cotto Professor, University at Buffalo School of Law, State University of New York. My thanks to Jim Gardner, John Henry Schlegel, and Amy Deen Westbrook for their help working out and through this essay. Jyla Serfino provided research assistance, which is much appreciated. The weaknesses, as ever, are mine.

The fact of inequality is hardly brute – there must be as many forms of hierarchy as there are kinds of birds in the jungle or fish on the reef. Inequality is really very interesting, as a human matter. And, for those inclined to activism, prior to the practice of any sort of situated political economy, it behooves us to undertake a bit of critical analysis, to ask what sort of inequality do we observe in this time and place? To what degree are people unequal (and what does "degree" mean, here)? What differentiates the higher from the lower, and what legitimates or otherwise maintains such differences? In other words, what is the structure of *this* society, and so the meaning of its inequalities?

While we may find many sorts of inequality in the United States and elsewhere, this essay is about the specific form of inequality exemplified by Jeff Bezos[2] or Bill Gates,[3] that is, the Himalayan summits of contemporary wealth, mostly in the United States.[4]

I would like to suggest that such wealth results from the confluence of three historical developments.

---

[2] Jeff Bezos is the Founder and CEO of Amazon, and the world's richest person. Isabel Togoh, "Jeff Bezos 'Trillionaire' Is Trending on Twitter. Here's Why", *Forbes* (May 14, 2020), (noting that Amazon's online shopping, streaming, and delivery services have been one of the "winners" of the COVID-19 pandemic, boosting Bezos' net worth to over $140 billion in May 2020).

[3] Bill Gates is the founder of Microsoft Corp., and the world's second-richest person. CNN Editorial Research, "Bill Gates Fast Facts", CNN (May 6, 2020), https://www.cnn.com/2013/05/07/us/bill-gates-fast-facts/index.html (noting that he was ranked as the world's richest person from 1995-2007).

[4] For a more general discussion of the gap between the poor and the super-rich in the United States, and the role of technology, see David Rotman, "Technology and Inequality", *MIT Technology Review* (Oct. 21, 2014), (discussing, among other things, economist Thomas Piketty's book about the increasing wealth of the super-rich, *Capitalism in the Twenty-First Century*).

First, the social processes referred to under the rubric of "globalization" have created vast markets. A dominant position in such markets leads not only to great wealth, but also to the elimination of peers. Since there are few such markets, relatively significant wealth is possessed by very few people. There is only one Jeff Bezos, one Bill Gates.

Second, digital markets powerfully tend toward monopolization,[5] of both their products and the narrative of the future. Those fortunate enough to be the monopolists profit accordingly, both directly, by doing business, but especially by investor interest.

Third, the actors in such digital markets are generally corporations, which are in turn largely owned by their founders.[6] As a result, a few individuals have acquired almost unbounded wealth, at least as wealth is conventionally measured, nominal US dollars. Conversely, entire economic sectors (like "food" or "data") are at least nominally under the dominance of such individuals. Political economy has been individualized, at least formally, to an astounding extent.

---

[5] Joseph E. Stiglitz, "America Has a Monopoly Problem – and It's Huge", *The Nation* (Oct. 23, 2017), https://www.thenation.com/article/archive/america-has-a-monopoly-problem-and-its-huge/ (arguing that the dominance of large corporations has enriched a small percentage of the country). Mark Jamison, "Applying Antitrust in Digital Markets: Foundations and Approaches", AEI Economics Working Paper 2019-18 (November 2019), https://www.aei.org/wp-content/uploads/2019/11/Jamison-Digital-Markets-WP.pdf.

[6] Rolfe Winkler & Maureen Farrell, "In 'Founder Friendly' Era, Star Tech Entrepreneurs Grab Power, Huge Pay", *The Wall Street Journal* (May 28, 2018), https://www.wsj.com/articles/in-founder-friendly-era-star-tech-entrepreneurs-grab-power-huge-pay-1527539114.

A normative political discussion of this state of affairs is beyond the bounds of this essay.

So where to start? A listing of the ten richest Americans[7] at the end of 2019 is illustrative:

Rank	The ten richest Americans		Net worth
10	Jim Walton	Heir to the fortune of Walmart	$51.6 billion
9	Steve Ballmer	Chief Executive Officer of Microsoft from 2000–2014	$51.7 billion
8	Michael Bloomberg	Majority owner and co-founder of Bloomberg L.P (software company)	$53.4 billion
7	Sergey Brin	Co-founder of Google President of Alphabet Inc., Google's parent company, until 2019	$53.5 billion
6	Larry Page	Co-founder of Google President of Alphabet Inc., Google's parent company, until 2019	$55.5 billion
5	Larry Ellison	Co-founder, executive chairman, etc., of Oracle Corporation	$65 billion
4	Mark Zuckerberg	Co-founder, chief executive officer, and controlling shareholder of Facebook	$69.6 billion

[7] Louisa Kroll & Kerry A. Dolan, "The Forbes 400: The Definitive Ranking of the Wealthiest Americans", *Forbes* (Oct. 2, 2019), www.forbes.com/forbes-400/#210c76247e2f.

3	Warren Buffett	CEO of Berkshire Hathaway	$80.8 billion
2	Bill Gates	Co-founder of Microsoft	$106 billion
1	Jeff Bezos	Founder, CEO, and president of Amazon	$114 billion

Seven of the ten fortunes are derived from purely digital enterprises (six, if one argues that Bloomberg is also media/information/content, albeit delivered digitally). Amazon sells physical things, and brokers the sale for other sellers, collecting data all the while.[8] Amazon is also a collector and purveyor of personal information, and a seller of cloud services – virtual as opposed to tangible activities.[9] Walmart is a highly digitized global network for the distribution of things, and a provider of some services.[10] In short, nine of the ten fortunes can fairly be said to be derived from "tech".

A listing of the wealthiest American women (four Walmart fortunes) tells much the same story, but mostly indirectly, through inheritance or, in one case, divorce settlement.[11] A recent worldwide listing has eight

---

[8] Leo Kelion, "Why Amazon Knows So Much About You", BBC NEWS https://www.bbc.co.uk/news/extra/CLQYZENMBI/amazon-data (last visited May 28, 2020).

[9] "What We Do", Amazon.com (last visited May 28, 2020) (describing Amazon's product sales, web services, video, music, tablets, TV, smart home devices, and Kindle e-readers and books).

[10] For example. Walmart offers financial services. Mark Kolakowski, "Walmart's Money Centers and Other Financial Services", *The Balance* (June 25, 2019), https://www.thebalance.com/walmart-moneycenters-1287260. Many Walmarts also offer auto maintenance and repair services. Auto Care Centers, Walmart.com, https://www.walmart.com/cp/auto-services/1087266 (last visited May 26, 2020).

[11] Taylor Borden, "The 15 Richest Women in America Right Now, Ranked", *Business Insider* (Apr. 7, 2020)

Americans, with Bezos and Gates retaining the top two spots.[12] The additions are France's Bernard Arnault (Chairman and CEO of LVMH Moët Hennessy – Louis Vuitton, purveyor of luxury brands to the planet)[13] and Spain's reclusive Amancio Ortego (founder of Zara and controller of many companies).[14]

Just as interesting is who and what is not on the list. There are no women on the list of the wealthiest persons in the United States or the world. There are no non-white men. None of the fortunes are derived from industrial manufacturing. None of the fortunes are derived from extractive industries like oil. None of the fortunes are derived from celebrity. Many of the richest people unsurprisingly hold executive positions, but the list does not really reflect corporate America's audaciously generous executive compensation packages, which are available in a wide range of industries. Only one of the richest Americans is a capitalist in the pure sense of financier, Warren Buffet. What was once confidently called "late capitalism" seems to have taken a turn.

There are no rulers on the list, although this invites argument over the nature of "wealth" and the distinctions between purely monetary assessments of nominal wealth (the market capitalization of shares

[12] Hillary Hoffower, "These Are the 15 Richest People in the World Right Now", *Business Insider*, (Apr. 7, 2020).
[13] Bernard Arnault, LVMH, https://www.lvmh.com/group/about-lvmh/governance/executive-committee/bernard-arnault/ (last visited May 26, 2020).
[14] Katie Warren & Melissa Wiley, "Meet Amancio Ortega", *Business Insider* (Oct. 29, 2019), https://www.businessinsider.com/zara-founder-amancio-ortegas-life-and-houses.

owned is hardly cash, at least not at such scale), and power or at least agency, a matter to which I will return. One may quibble in other ways. There are other lists.

A great deal of money is controlled by few people in China and Japan. Stock market shifts will move rankings. Institutions of various sorts control even more wealth. (BlackRock, for example, has trillions under management.)[15] One could go on, of course, but such things said, the general point stands: the digitization of U.S., and much of global, commerce, has created astonishing levels of personal wealth, and consequently, inequality. "The five richest men in the US are worth a mind-boggling combined $435.4 billion, according to the Forbes 400 ranking of 2019's richest Americans. And all but one of them made their fortunes in the tech industry."[16]

Although the novel coronavirus has immiserated much of the global economy, it has made these rich quite a bit richer. As discussed below, one of the salient aspects of digital technology is the tendency to make distance, geography, less important. In this pandemic, a time of social distancing, tech companies and so their founders have done very well. Bezos is worth some $36 billion

---

[15] John Coumarianos & Leslie P. Norton, "BlackRock Passes a Milestone, With $7 Trillion in Assets Under Management", *Barrons* (Jan. 15, 2020), https://www.barrons.com/articles/blackrock-earnings-assets-under-management-7-trillion-51579116426. That number dipped with the advent of the COVID-19 pandemic. Dawn Lim, "BlackRock's Profit, Assets Under Management Fall", *The Wall Street Journal* (Apr. 16, 2020), https://www.wsj.com/articles/blackrocks-first-quarter-profit-fell-23-11587033254.
[16] Katie Warren, "The 5 Richest Men in the US Have a Staggering Combined Wealth of $435.4 Billion. That's More than 2% of America's GDP", *Business Insider* (Oct. 2, 2019).

more than he was at the start of the year,[17] and he is not alone. Reports estimated that the five richest Americans (Bezos, Bill Gates, Mark Zuckerberg, Warren Buffett and Larry Ellison, combined, saw their fortunes increase by $75.5 billion.[18]

Here's another way to think about this concentration of wealth. Median household income in the US, before the pandemic, was roughly $63,000, or 6.3 x 10^4 (10 to the 4th power)[19] (Median net worth was also less than $100,000.[20] Pre-pandemic, Jeff Bezos was worth 1.14 x 10^{11} (10 to the 11th power). His wealth has increased by about a third since the pandemic, but not yet by an order of magnitude. A difference of seven orders of magnitude is hard to think through, but it is the difference between someone who has a net worth of $5 and someone with a net worth $99,000,000.

How did such concentrations of wealth come about? How is it even possible?

---

[17] Supra n. 1.

[18] Megan Henney, "US Billionaires Got $434 Billion Richer Since Coronavirus Pandemic Began", Foxbusiness (May 22, 2020), https://www.foxbusiness.com/money/american-billionaires-richer-since-coronavirus-pandemic-began.

[19] U.S. Census Bureau, Real Median Household Income in the United States, retrieved from FRED, Federal Reserve Bank of St. Louis; https://fred.stlouisfed.org/series/MEHOINUSA672N, May 26, 2020 (estimating the real median household income at $63,179 in 2018 dollars). U.S. Median Family Income is higher, at $78,646, but my point remains the same. U.S. Census Bureau, Median Family Income in the United States, retrieved from FRED, Federal Reserve Bank of St. Louis; https://fred.stlouisfed.org/series/MEFAINUSA646N, May 26, 2020.

[20] The median net worth of the average U.S. household was estimated at $97,300 in January 2020. Dayana Yochim, "What's Your Net Worth, and How Do You Compare to Others?" Marketwatch (Jan. 23, 2020), https://www.marketwatch.com/story/whats-your-net-worth-and-how-do-you-compare-to-others-2018-09-24.

II. Globalization

Suppose we understand markets in fairly simple-minded fashion, as social contexts in which folks buy, sell, and invest. Markets have often been understood individualistically – *homo economicus* is not a friendly guy – and orthodox economics even proposed "methodological individualism" to be a cardinal intellectual virtue. But the social simply must be stressed at the present juncture. As digital enterprises make inescapably clear, markets are constructed through mutually intelligible communication. "The market" is not a place that exists *ex ante*, to which self-interested rational actors go to buy and sell. Instead, markets are socially constructed "spaces," which can be real or virtual, in which economic communication and even law (most obviously contract and property) happen, and "where" actors must conform if they are to participate.

To tell a story by now familiar: once upon a time, there were many markets, more or less geographically distinct, for much the same thing, say wine, to echo Adam Smith. Traders might connect different markets, but transportation was slow, expensive, and often dangerous. And, to echo Smith again, actors could be expected to seek market power, rents.[21] But the extent of their wealth was limited by the extent of the market in which they operated.[22]

---

[21] Adam Smith, *Wealth Of Nations* p. 232 (Penguin Classics Ed. 1974) ("People of the same trade seldom meet together, even for merriment and diversion, but the conversation ends in a conspiracy against the public, or in some contrivance to raise prices.").

[22] Adam Smith, *Wealth Of Nations* p. 109 (Penguin Classics Ed. 1974) ("in those trifling manufactures which are destined to supply the small wants

In the fullness of time, the implementation of new technologies and the set of processes collectively referred to as globalization lowered the cost of transport and other barriers to trade, notably tariffs. Distance became much less significant. After the digital revolution, prices and other information, as well as digital goods writ large, could be transferred instantaneously, and at almost no cost. There are many ways to complicate this "just so story,"[23] of course, but many geographically distinct markets merged, that is, the social contexts in which trade was conducted became much larger, both geographically and in terms of the number of people involved. While globalization may make an individual's world feel bigger and more diverse, for markets, globalization mostly has meant consolidation and simplification, and, due to the instant transfer of information, virtual locality. The social contexts in which folks bought and sold became national, regional, even global. Airport shopping is much the same worldwide. LVMH sells globally branded cognac and watches and purses and suchlike from Rio di Janeiro to Hong Kong,[24] and for a little while, Bernard Arnault was the second richest person on earth.[25] Dominating enormous markets, unsurprisingly, results in great wealth.

---

of but a small number of people, the whole number of workmen must necessarily be small").

[23] Rudyard Kipling originally published his book of *Just So Stories* in 1902, and the term is now popularly used to denote a story that claims to explain the origin of something.

[24] The LVMH Group has approximately 5000 stores worldwide. Liam O'Connell, "Total Number of Stores of the LVMH Group Worldwide from 2008-2019", *Statistica* (Feb. 24, 2020), https://www.statista.com/statistics/245854/total-number-of-stores-of-the-lvmh group worldwide/.

[25] Luisa Kroll, "France's Bernard Arnault Is Now World's Second-Richest Person", *Forbes* (Jul. 18, 2019).

Such wealth often concentrates – global markets tend to be "winner take all". There is no second Arnault. One could imagine luxury goods being produced in different societies, by different companies, whose owners would presumably prosper – but would not be among the wealthiest people on earth. That was, in fact, largely the state of affairs in living memory. But such goods would, by hypothesis, not be globally branded. Prestige would be understood within specific social contexts. Other social contexts, presumably, would have other objects of envy.

Indeed, LVMH itself is a collection of what had been independent firms, mostly French. Today, however, LVMH's brands are neither independent nor are they understood in particularly French terms.[26] Thus, just as globalization implies fewer, larger, markets, it also implies fewer dominant positions, and by extension fewer, but vastly wealthier, rich people, than one would expect from a collection of relatively discrete markets, each dominated by its own magnates. While globalization lowered costs and generated a great deal of wealth through the consolidation of thitherto discrete markets, the same dynamics have increased inequality.

III. Digitization

Any number of markets have been globalized, creating inequalities along the lines suggested above. If we look at

---

[26] In addition to Louis Vuitton, Moët & Chandon, and Hennessy, LVMH also owns Dom Pérignon, Givenchy, Sephora, Fendi, Bulgari, and Christian Dior, and in 2019 agreed to buy Tiffany & Co. Dominic-Madori Davis, "LVMH Is the Top Luxury Conglomerate in the World", *Business Insider* (Feb. 4, 2020), https://www.businessinsider.com/lvmh-brands-iconic-luxury-goods-bernard-arnault-2019-10.

the US and global lists of wealthy individuals, however, we see that almost all of the great fortunes come from control of tech companies. Control will be discussed in the next section, but what makes tech companies so valuable?

In short, technology markets also tend to be "winner take all", that is, they tend toward a monopolistic structure. For example, Facebook has 2.6 billion monthly active users.[27] The earth's population is estimated to be 7.8 billion, so a third of the world is on Facebook every month.[28] (The digital divide is evidently silting up.) Microsoft continues to own the desktop, and Google (Alphabet) owns search. Globally, if not exactly 100%.

Such companies presumably display the ordinary incentives to avoid competition noted by Adam Smith, but more interestingly, tech markets tend toward monopoly for reasons intrinsic to tech itself. The engineering, and hence economics, of deploying computer software is simply different from the production and sale of material objects in the physical world, for example, cars. Little of this was obvious a generation or so ago, and it is hardly clear yet,[29] but for the purpose of discussing this particular form of inequality, a brief sketch of some of the peculiar aspects of digital enterprises suffices.

---

[27] J. Clement, "Number of Facebook Users Worldwide 2008-2020", *Statistica* (Apr. 30, 2020),
https://www.statista.com/statistics/264810/number-of-monthly-active-facebook-users-worldwide/.
[28] Current World Population, https://www.worldometers.info/world-population/ (last visited May 26, 2020).
[29] Much of what follows in the meantime has acquired its own literature, which will not be reviewed here.

A story. When I was a youth in a public high school in the '80s, it was said with great assurance that computers were the wave of the future (which was true) and that therefore everyone would have to learn to program (which really was not true). Not until studying mathematics in college did I understand that some people were *very good* at programing. Once their program was written, it would be difficult to improve on it, maybe impossible, and rarely worth the effort. The program was done, and somebody who needed it could simply copy it.

Not just computers but things from toasters to televisions contain innumerable programs, and nobody thinks to (or could, in most circumstances) rewrite them. We all use copies. So, the number of computer programmers is a tiny fraction of the number of computer users.[30] Even computer programmers use copies almost all of the time. Programmers have been kept in demand by the need to tailor software to particular settings and users, and by opportunities to digitize new things, and things that had not been digitized before (cars are a good example). Presumably this last source of demand will dwindle as the initial work is completed and improvements are incremental, and programming itself is made more efficient through the use of meta-languages, machine learning, and the like.

The fact that programs (here including data) are almost infinitely scalable at virtually zero cost has profound

---

[30] There were estimated to be $4.2 million software engineers in the United States in 2019. How Many Software Developers Are in the US and the World, DAXX (Feb. 9, 2020).

implications for digital economies.[31] While traditional enterprises often exhibited some economies of scale, making it a good idea to grow (think General Motors), once the cost of scale converges upon zero, the enterprise can be both global yet physically quite small (think how few people Alphabet employs vis-à-vis its market capitalization).[32] In order to grow, digital enterprises do not need many more facilities, and certainly not many more employees, unless one counts baristas in the neighborhood. Digital enterprises grow simply by adding more users, sales.

A digital enterprise has exceptional potential for profits. Unlike a public good (such as clean air), a digital good such as a program is excludable, at least in a society with a working intellectual property regime. That is the function of the license, which creates the opportunity to charge a fee, and hence the contractual charade familiar to anybody who has done anything on a computer. At the same time, a digital good is non-rivalrous, meaning it

---

[31] Jonathan P. Allen, "Technology And Inequality: Concentrated Wealth In A Digital World" pp. 37-39 (2017), available at https://www.technologyandinequality.com/wp-content/uploads/2017/06/techineq-sample.pdf (discussing the scalability of information technology and wealth concentration).

[32] In 2019, Alphabet was estimated to have 103,549 employees. Seth Fiegerman, "Google's Parent Company Now Has More than 100,000 Employees", CNN (Apr. 29, 2019) https://www.cnn.com/2019/04/29/tech/alphabet-q1-earnings/index.html (noting a recent surge of employment of 20,000 employees had contributed to its crossing the 100,000 threshold). Facebook had about a third as many employees as Alphabet. *Id.* In January 2020, Alphabet became the fourth U.S. company to reach a $1 trillion market value. Amrith Ramkumar, "Alphabet Becomes Fourth U.S. Company to Reach $1 Trillion Market Value", *The Wall Street Journal* (Jan. 16, 2020), https://www.wsj.com/articles/alphabet-becomes-fourth-u-s-company-to-ever-reach-1-trillion-market-value-1157920 8802 (Alphabet joined Apple, Amazon, and Microsoft in that exclusive club).

can be used by more than one person at once, and is not consumed by its use. Microsoft sells the same intellectual property over and over and over. More simply put, when digits are for sale, there need be little overhead, no need to replace the product sold (though incremental improvements are good manners), and the owners may profit accordingly.

Why are users so important? Not only are virtual businesses much more easily scalable than physical ones, large virtual businesses are relatively more valuable than smaller ones, i.e., twice as big is more than twice as valuable. From the user side, this is due to so called network efficiencies.[33] The classic explanation of network efficiency begins with an old-school child's "phone", two tin cans joined by a string, or the first telegraph transmission, for that matter. The communication "network" is not worth very much, because only two people can use it, at least at a time. But as one adds users to the network, so that one can call the fire department or get a pizza, or eventually deliver legal documents and trade stock, the network becomes more and more valuable. Phone systems have long been considered natural monopolies, and regulated as such. But various other businesses that are less obviously networks –

---

[33] *See* Robert Pitofsky, Chairman of the Federal Trade Commission, "Antitrust Analysis in High-Tech Industries: a 19th Century Disciple Addresses 21st Century Problems", 4 *Texas Review of Law and Politics* p. 129 (1999). Chairman Pitofsky defines network efficiencies as occurring when "the value of a product or service is positively correlated with the number of individuals who use the product or service". *Id* at p. 132. He goes on to note "On the one hand, such networks are efficient and occasionally inevitable; on the other hand, they increase the likelihood that one firm, by achieving a critical mass, will dominate a market or retain market power for an extended period of time." *Id.* at p. 133.

notably "the social network" – exhibit network efficiencies.

If the process of adoption continues, and as demonstrated by Zoom[34] and Facebook[35] during the COVID-19 pandemic, the network is likely to become indispensable. At some point, the idea of network efficiencies merges into the idea of brand. Both the network and the brand are understood, relied upon, and may become synonymous for one another. We "google" things we want to know. Hardware (network) and software (culture) mesh.

From the sell side, a bigger network enterprise is not only therefore better, it is also a higher quality business. Scale increases the amount and quality of data that can be harvested from users, analyzed and used to target sales, sold to advertisers, and the like, in what Shoshana Zuboff has aptly called surveillance capitalism.[36] Especially by using learning systems (AI), the more a firm knows, the better it knows, and the bigger a player it is in the market for information, which in a sense all markets are, just some more obviously than others. It is illustrative that the richest individual on Wall Street is Bloomberg.

---

[34] Rupert Neate, "Zoom Booms as Demand for Video-Conferencing Tech Grows", the *Guardian* (Mar. 31, 2020), (noting that founder Eric Yuan's net worth had already increased by more than $4 billion since the coronavirus crisis started).

[35] Elizabeth Dwoskin, "As Facebook's Profit Doubles, CEO Mark Zuckerberg Sounds Off on Reopening the Economy Too Soon", the *Washington Post* (Apr. 29, 2020).

[36] Shoshana Zuboff, *The Age of Surveillance Capitalism: The Fight for a Human Future at the New Frontier of Power* (2019).

Understandably, tech industry participants speak incessantly about innovation, about what's next. And, sometimes, innovation happens, and new markets emerge. Innovation can make so much money, however, in part because of the importance of history, a truth somewhat obscured by all the "creative destruction,"[37] "move fast and break things,"[38] and "innovate or die"[39] rhetoric. Steve Jobs has in fact died. Neither Jeff Bezos nor Bill Gates nor Larry Ellison are young. Even Sergei Brin and Larry Page have given up day-to-day management of Alphabet. But their companies remain dominant, decades on. All of these companies innovated, surely, but once they established dominance in their markets, each company consolidated its position, and having done so, is difficult to unseat. To quip, innovation may create a potential market, but it is history that makes the money.

A host of concepts, familiar to most of this audience, suggest the importance of past behavior in economic activity generally, and for computer users (everyone) more specifically. Path dependence, for example, suggests that once a given structure is adopted, it cannot be changed without considerable costs, and therefore won't be, unless a substantially better structure emerges,

---

[37] The term "creative destruction" is most often associated with Joseph Schumpeter. Joseph Schumpeter, *Capitalism, Socialism and Democracy* (1942). More recently, the term has been associated with Steve Jobs. Zephrin Lasker, "Steve Jobs: Create. Disrupt. Destroy", *Forbes* (Jan. 14, 2011).
[38] Chris Benner & Kung Feng, "Elon Musk Reflects Silicon Valley's 'Move Fast and Break Things' Culture", *San Francisco Chronicle* (May 15, 2020).
[39] Adi Ignatius, "Innovation on the Fly", *Harvard Business Review* (Dec. 2014), https://hbr.org/2014/12/innovation-on-the-fly (noting that although the origin of the phrase is disputed, it is frequently associated with Peter Drucker).

and resources are available.[40] Contemporary institutions of all sorts struggle with their "legacy" computer systems and software, and are to greater or lesser extent a prisoner of their "installed base."[41] Who has the money and the freedom to suspend operations and start completely over? Users, too, become habituated. Why retrain, unless one absolutely must?[42] As the network and the culture mesh, dominant positions become institutionalized, even required. The Microsoft enterprise software on which I'm writing this is cluttered, ugly, and often mystifying, but what are the odds that a major university decides to adopt some new enterprise software, developed by some kid in his Harvard dorm room? Bill Gates, who dropped out of Harvard himself, will remain rich. But if the kid develops a way to "monetize loneliness," in a world where almost everyone has a smartphone, we might have something like Facebook.[43]

These aspects of digital enterprises have clear strategic consequences for technology start-ups. New businesses

---

[40] For an early discussion of path dependence in the technology context, see Stan Liebowitz & Stephen E. Margolis, "Policy and Path Dependence: From QWERTY to Windows 95", 33 *Regulation* 3 (1995), available at https://www.cato.org/sites/cato.org/files/serials/files/regulation/1995/7/v18n3-4.pdf.

[41] For a discussion of how legacy technologies persist even when new systems are clearly superior, see Willy C. Shih, "Breaking the Death Grip of Legacy Technologies", *Harvard Business Review* (May, 28, 2015), https://hbr.org/2015/05/breaking-the-death-grip-of-legacy-technologies.

[42] Relative success may begin to become something of a problem for digital enterprises. Users may sensibly ask "Why do I need to invest time, money and attention in another smart phone, or new office software, etc.? What I have works fine and I have other things to do."

[43] *See* Jill Lepore, "The History of Loneliness", *The New Yorker* (Apr. 6, 2020), https://www.newyorker.com/magazine/2020/04/06/the-history-of-loneliness.

regularly enter new(ish) markets and try to reap "first mover advantages."[44] They attempt to achieve scale at any cost, often using copious venture capitalist money. Making money is not the point; acquiring users is. Sometimes, building a multimillion, even billion, dollar business without actual revenue leads to hilarious and bizarre (at least from an old-school business perspective) tales of fortunes evidently squandered, as in the case of WeWork and Uber.[45] But sometimes it works: the new business thrives, eliminates all significant competition, and reaps monopoly rents. Like Facebook. The point of this business model is not to create a good firm making solid products, wine or cars or what have you, in a competitive marketplace. The point is to define and utterly dominate a marketplace. Monopoly, and hence inequality, is the purpose of the enterprise.[46]

Elites, certainly including the wealthiest people in a society, are authoritative by definition. More broadly still,

---

[44] For an early, clear explanation of the first-mover advantage, see Marvin B. Lieberman & David B. Montgomery, "First-Mover Advantages", 9 *Strategic Management Journal* 41 (1988), *available at* https://uol.de/f/2/dept/wire/fachgebiete/entrepreneur/download/Artikel_ Internetoekonomie/Lieberman_First_Mover. pdf. *See, also,* Rajshree Agarwal & Michael Gort, "First-Mover Advantage and the Speed of Competitive Entry", 1887-1986, 44 *Journal of Law and Economics*. 161, 162-165 (2001) (providing an historical overview).

[45] For a discussion of the some of the ways in which the drive to capitalize on first-mover advantage and grow at any cost may result in adverse results for companies and their investors, see Amy Deen Westbrook, "We['re] Working on Corporate Governance: Stakeholder Vulnerability in Unicorn Companies", 23 *University of Pennsylvania Journal of Business Law* [ ] (forthcoming 2021).

[46] Of course, this does not always work. The Softbank Vision Fund was known for flooding its chosen startups with cash, enabling them to dominate the consumer space and become monopolies. Its strategy backfired very publicly in 2019 with WeWork and Uber. Linette Lopez, "Softbank Is Getting Exactly What It Deserves, and It's Thanks to Something Way Bigger Than WeWork", *Business Insider* (Nov. 10, 2019).

the social is inescapably somewhat coercive by nature –
which is what it means to speak of civilization and its
discontents.   Again, markets are social contexts, and
economic life is nothing if not social. It is therefore
unsurprising that markets are also coercive, in all sorts of
ways. Simple, practical examples: universities, like other
large businesses(!), must have enterprise software. Law
firms have IT departments. Most everyone must have a
cell phone – at least insofar as one wishes to participate
in the economy at all. (It would be easy enough to give all
sorts of more complicated examples involving language,
law, and other culturally received understandings, but
there is no need.) The coercion of markets is often briefly
acknowledged under the rubric of "competition," but the
markets at issue here are not competitive. Few actors
have any hope of "competing" with an entity many
orders of magnitude more valuable. Instead of
competition, at issue is the necessity and possibility of
participation in the contexts such entities create. In order
to participate economically (and this is, after all, our
access to the supply chain for life's necessities),
institutions and individuals pay monopoly rents to the
Amazons, Googles, and Apples of the world, thereby
creating magnates. Even churches need a Facebook
account.

Knowing that this business model can work, and that an
investor just might acquire wealth beyond spending,
venture capitalists recently have been willing to fund any
number of ideas that do not immediately seem to be so
scalable, do not seem to fit the paradigm. Consider

Airbnb[47] or DoorDash.[48] Long shots at a substantial stake in, if not the next Google, at least the next PayPal,[49] seem fairly reasonable chances to take. And, despite all the loose talk of dominance and monopoly rents in this essay, antitrust (competition) law hardly obstructs the dominant players in digital markets.[50] So, raising capital, sometimes substantial amounts, has not been a problem for tech start-ups. And in those cases when market dominance is achieved, investors, including institutional investors, have kept valuations high. Given the centrality of endowed institutions to contemporary life, tech market dominance has been woven into the portfolios, and so the fabric, of our society. Again, this is our elite – it is not just about the money.

In this light, the libertarian ideologies that suffuse microeconomics, computer science, and Silicon Valley are bizarre. The computer may be the greatest instrument for imposing economic structures, concentrating wealth, and generating inequality ever, or at least since craftsmen in Toledo started making swords for conquistadors. This particular blindness is, however, familiar, history rhyming again. The turn of the last century, the era of

---

[47] *See* Rebecca Aydin, "How 3 Guys Turned Renting Air Mattresses in Their Apartment into a $31 Billion Company, Airbnb", *Business Insider* (Sept. 20, 2019), (providing a basic history of the company).

[48] *See* Biz Carson, "DoorDash Is Now Worth $12.6 Billion after New $600 Million Investment", *Forbes* (May 23, 2019), (discussing some of the background of the company).

[49] Brian O'Connell, "History of PayPal: Timeline and Facts", *The Street* (Jan. 2, 2020), https://www.thestreet.com/technology/history-of-paypal-15062744 (discussing the company's explosive growth).

[50] *See* Diana L. Moss, President, American Antitrust Institute, "Breaking Up Is Hard to Do: The Implications of Restructuring and Regulating Digital Technology Markets," 19-OCT *Antitrust Source* 1 (Oct. 2019) (providing an overview of recent proposals to breakup or restructure the large U.S. digital technologies).

the Robber Barons,[51] was also the era of the *Lochner* Supreme Court majority,[52] with their belief in the transcendent freedom of contract. Today we speak of blockchain and self-executing digital contracts, as if we could somehow, finally, escape the social. Naïveté, perhaps dangerous, but more than a little pathos, too.

IV. Shareholder capitalism

To be careful: the fact that global digital enterprises may be enormously lucrative need not necessarily imply that *individuals* are so very rich. There are other global enterprises which have not generated anything like the personal wealth of the tech companies. As noted, with the exception of Warren Buffett, there are no financiers on the list, nor oilmen, nor celebrities, nor other sorts of rich folk. In January 2020, BlackRock had over $7 trillion in assets under management,[53] and its principles and executives are certainly wealthy, but not like Jeff Bezos or Bill Gates or Mark Zuckerberg, nor even Jim Walton, just

---

[51] For a discussion of the Robber Barons and inequality in the current markets, see Amy Deen Westbrook & David A. Westbrook, "Unicorns, Guardians, and the Concentration of the U.S. Equity Markets", 96 *Nebraska Law Review* 693-700 (2018).

[52] *Lochner v. New York*, a case about bakers' work hours decided by the U.S. Supreme Court in 1905, famously held that the Due Process Clause of the Fourteenth Amendment protects the individual right to freedom of contract of both the employer and the employee. Lochner v. N.Y., 198 U.S. 45 (1905).

[53] John Coumarianos & Leslie P. Norton, "BlackRock Passes a Milestone, with $7 Trillion in Assets Under Management", BARRONS (Jan. 15, 2020) https://www.barrons.com/articles/blackrock-earnings-assets-under-management-7-trillion-51579116426. However, that total subsequently fell during the Covid 19 pandemic. Dawn Lim, "BlackRock's Profit, Assets Under Management Fall", *The Wall Street Journal* (Apr. 16, 2020), https://www.wsj.com/articles/blackrocks-first-quarter-profit-fell-23-11587033254.

one of the heirs of Walmart founder Sam Walton. At his death in 2019, Jack Bogle, founder and CEO of the Vanguard Group, was worth some 80 million.[54] Chump change, and a point of pride for Bogle. This, despite the fact that Vanguard largely invented index funds, and on January 31, 2020 had approximately $6.2 trillion in assets under management.[55] Why do tech companies concentrate wealth to such an astonishing degree?

All of the men on the list of the ten wealthiest Americans have substantial ownership interests in, in most cases, outright control of, a publicly traded firm that dominates a market.[56] As noted, in nine of the ten cases, the firm may be fairly characterized as a "tech" company, with Warren Buffett's Berkshire Hathaway being the exception. All of these men founded or cofounded the company, with three exceptions: Jim Walton, who inherited his Walmart stock; Steve Balmer, who was a longtime CEO of Microsoft and who thereby acquired a founder-like stake in the firm; and again Warren Buffett, who long ago acquired the shirt manufacturer Berkshire Hathaway and transformed it into a conglomerate. In sum, the 8,000-meter peaks of American wealth are generally climbed, in this stage of the nation's history, by

---

[54] Edward Wyatt, "John C. Bogle, Founder of Financial Giant Vanguard, Is Dead at 89", *The New York Times* (Jan. 16, 2019), https://www.nytimes.com/2019/01/16/obituaries/john-bogle-vanguard-dead.html (citing a Forbes estimate from the year before).
[55] Fast Facts about Vanguard, Vanguard, https://about.vanguard.com/who-we-are/fast-facts/ (last visited May 28, 2020).
[56] The rise of so-called unicorns is fascinating, and raises many questions. At least at present, however, being considered one of the very richest individuals requires ownership of a substantial stake in a publicly traded company. *See generally* Amy Deen Westbrook & David A. Westbrook, "Unicorns, Guardians, and the Concentration of the U.S. Equity Markets", 96 *Nebraska Law Review* 688 (2018).

founding a tech company, and retaining a great deal of ownership in the form of shares.

The proposition that Jeff Bezos is the wealthiest man in the world is not a simple fact, but an accounting based upon legal, institutional, social and economic assumptions, some widely believed, most tacit and by no means obvious. Amazon's shares, securities, are bought and sold in highly regulated markets, for dollars, which establishes a price per share, a rational number (as I type, $2411.27). What could be simpler? But this number comprises so much: centuries of corporation law, which in turn rests on deep understandings of the law of property, contract, and master and servant (now euphemistically called agency); almost a century of securities law, which presumes many of the same understandings, but also "information" and administrative law and lore; the arcane practices of the securities industry ("Wall Street") and the increasingly important storage of institutional capital there; macroeconomic policy and the associated ancient practices of banking and so money supply; to say nothing of investor sentiment about Amazon's future, and the future generally, all of which will somehow inform the return on investment. Indeed, why shares are valuable to individuals at all is almost as mysterious as why dollars are valuable.[57] Ignoring all of that so we can get on with crowning the richest man in the world, the price/share is multiplied by the number of shares in question, an integer, and we produce another, much larger, rational

---

[57] See Amy Deen Westbrook & David A/ Westbrook, "Snapchat's Gift: Equity Culture in High-Tech Firms", 46 Florida State University Law Review 861 (2019).

number, which we round off for convenience, producing, in this case, \$114,000,000,000.[58] Simple, no?

It must be admitted that the scale of this number is not due solely to the confluence of globalization, digitization, and Amazon's capital structure. Through the 21st century, the advanced economies have seen slow growth and great liquidity, much of it provided by central banks attempting to rescue financial systems and, that more or less done, stimulate real economy growth. The New York Stock Exchange has been the recipient of much of this cash; share prices have increased accordingly. But there is more than a rising tide, which lifts all boats, at work here. Tech stock has done well relative to other stock; founders of tech companies have done well relative to the owners of other sorts of business.

It must also be admitted that these estimations of wealth are both derivative and in some sense nominal. Market capitalization is an accounting technique. Shares are not dollars, and even dollars are not wealth itself, but represent wealth. Expressing wealth in dollars makes it somewhat more comprehensible – or amazing, if the number is large enough – to those of us who use dollars daily. It would be difficult if not impossible, however, for Bezos to sell his stake in Amazon, turning his nominal dollars into "real" ones, without depressing the price of Amazon stock. Wealth, here, is a matter of the estimation of the stock market. A certain community has assigned a certain value to a certain set of legal instruments owned by a man, thereby anointing him "wealthiest".

---

[58] Whether or not the list-maker bothered to figure out what Bezos' non-share assets and liabilities are seems irrelevant.

Apart from the title, however, it is difficult to know what this wealth means to its nominal owner as he moves through the world. Shares are a form of fiat money for some purposes, notably the acquisition of companies and the compensation of executives, so Amazon could use stock as it moved from selling books to brokering online trading to advertising to cloud services to selling just about everything else. Not that Amazon needs to use stock for such things. The company has so much cash that it bought Whole Foods for $13.4 billion in cash, "in a bid for total retail domination."[59] So one thing a powerful shareholder can do is cause the company to make business decisions, which, if successful, will make the shareholder yet wealthier, at least on paper.

Even within the corporation, however, shareholders are constrained by corporate law, and law generally. Indeed, it is corporate law that gives the shareholder power over the enterprise, and that is presumably coveted, at least in the abstract, by investors whose demand sets the stock's price. Bezos does not hold a majority of Amazon's voting shares, though he clearly is in *de facto* control.[60] Several other members of the list have clear voting control, i.e., can unilaterally replace the board and thereby senior management. Even in such cases, legal processes must be followed within the corporation, and the corporation itself is regulated in many ways, deregulation

---

[59] Beth Kowitt, "How Amazon Is Using Whole Foods in a Bid for Total Retail Domination", *Fortune* (May 21, 2018), https://fortune.com/longform/amazon-groceries-fortune-500/.

[60] Bezos' ability to control the company was notable when the COVID-19 pandemic erupted in the United States. Karen Weise, "Bezos Takes Back the Wheel at Amazon", *The New York Times* (Apr. 22, 2020), https://www.nytimes.com/2020/04/22/technology/bezos-amazon-coronavirus.html.

notwithstanding. It is tempting to say that shareholders, even majority shareholders, are not kings.

Surely shareholders are not kings outside the corporation. While they can buy things, shareholders have little power to discover, make, coerce, or legislate, for starters. They are subject to the same laws as most other folks, at least most of the time and no doubt more comfortably. In corporation law classes, we teach that the one real power of the shareholder is the vote for the board of directors.[61] The law is a little more complicated than that, but the statement is true enough to mean that wealth defined by shareholding is wealth rather narrowly understood. The legal vehicle, the share, just does not capture the range of possibility implied by "wealth." Even astronomically wealthy shareholders have little power to change things outside of the business of their firms, as any number of foundations have discovered (Gates,[62] Ford[63] and Rockefeller[64] spring to mind).

For his part, Jeff Bezos paid the largest divorce settlement in history; unlike King Henry VIII he did not have his wife beheaded. If wealth is understood as the capacity to have one's way with their world – or perhaps,

---

[61] *Alan Palmiter, Frank Partnoy, & Elizabeth Pollman, Business Organizations; A Contemporary Approach* 72 (3d ed. 2019) (explaining that voting for the board of directors is one of shareholders' fundamental rights).

[62] *See* Peter Kotecki, "Bill and Melinda Gates Were Just Named the Most Generous Philanthropists in America – Here Are Their Biggest Projects", *Business Insider* (Aug. 20, 2018) (discussing the Gates' generosity).

[63] *See* Larissa MacFarquhar, "What Money Can Buy", *The New Yorker* (Dec. 28, 2015), https://www.newyorker.com/magazine/2016/01/04/what-money-can-buy-profiles-larissa-macfarquhar (discussing the foundation's efforts to conquer inequality).

[64] *See* William H. Schneider, "The Difficult Art of Giving", 497 *Nature* 311 (May 16, 2013), https://www.nature.com/articles/497311a.pdf?proof=true (reflecting on the impact of the foundation on its centenary).

to ignore the world's demands – then Henry VIII and lots of other people have been, or are now, wealthier than the men currently listed as "wealthiest." It might be said that this comparison of divorce proceedings confuses wealth with power, and it does, but the two are difficult to keep distinct. One cannot talk about wealth, represented by dollars or shares or other form of property, without reference to law, and hence to power.

Conversely, however, kings are literally anointed, "made" and constrained by the laws of the monarchy, albeit often proved by God and my right arm. Kings "claim" their kingship, take a legal position, and are obeyed only insofar as they are collectively believed, either to be legitimate, or to command force, which may practically come to the same thing. Power, even of an illegitimate but at least for now successful regime, entails social authority, usually expressed as law, the same sort of social authority that makes dollars, or shares, acceptable, and is embedded in our notions of wealth.

So, to conclude this essay where it began: what does this hierarchy, the billions of dollars ascribed to the nation's wealthiest men, mean for its society? What do those of us who accept, willingly or not, this particular inequality as the way of their world, think?

Conclusion

In recent history, a number of corporations have emerged with a technology or occasionally a collection of brands that creates a new market that can be globally scaled. Within that market, at least, the companies have utterly dominated, and have been immensely profitable for some substantial amount of time. It could happen again. From the perspective of an investor, the lesson is clear. Early stage investors attempt to identify such companies as they emerge, often long before they are profitable, and buy equity. If the company is successful, demand will increase. Once the company is sufficiently highly valued, the portfolio requirements of institutional investors will increase demand yet further. In many cases, the founders of the company retain substantial equity. Increasing demand for whatever equity is available for sale will increase the wealth of the founders, making some of them at least nominally the wealthiest people on the planet. But, from an investor perspective, why be jealous? Surely being an early stage investor in Facebook is reward enough, even if that kid is much richer still? Even some middle-class guy with a 401(k) portfolio run by Vanguard benefits from Facebook's wealth.

From any other perspective that I can think of, analytical or normative, things are much less clear, and much more could be said. I will confine myself to two observations.

First, as a society we pay relatively little attention to the specific sort of wealth discussed here, and do not seem very disturbed when we do. Perhaps the historically recent conjunction of globalization, the peculiar economics of digital enterprises, and corporation law are a bit much to think. True, Bernie Sanders railed against inequality in his recent Presidential campaign,[65] but in a

---

[65] Bernie Sanders on Economic Inequality, feelthebern.com, https://feelthebern.org/bernie-sanders-on-economic-inequality/ (last visited May 28, 2020).

general "soak the rich" sort of way that cuts against the grain of the American love of capitalism. Moreover, this wealth is in some senses rather nominal, in part a function of accounting, and so difficult to perceive. Nominal or not, billions of dollars are hard to comprehend, even for people who spend time worrying about financial matters. At least one can see Versailles or one of the Pyramids, but 10^{11}? Michael Bloomberg spent almost a billion dollars on his unsuccessful bid to become (a democratically elected!) President, which sounds like a lot, but that was less than 2% of his wealth.[66]

On occasion, the vast personal wealth generated by digital industries is acknowledged, but generally justified as the price to be paid for technological progress. Perhaps – the argument that shareholder capitalism is the mother of progress is an old one.[67] Many people believe in progress, at least in the abstract, though I have yet to hear a theory of technology or history that makes sense for the present situation. And for some, entrepreneurs like Elon Musk (not on the list, at least not yet) are heroes.[68] At any rate, it is hard to see somebody like Bill Gates, who has lately adopted an almost Mr. Rogers

---

[66] Shane Goldmacher, "Michael Bloomberg Spent More Than $900 Million on His Failed Presidential Run", *The New York Times* (Mar. 20, 2020), https://www.nytimes.com/2020/03/20/us/politics/bloomberg-campaign-900-million.html.

[67] *See* David A. Westbrook, *Between Citizen And State: An Introduction To The Corporation* 31-37 (discussing veneration of the corporate form, including Nicholas Murray Butler's description of it as the greatest single discovery of modern times).

[68] Ashlee Vance, "Elon Musk Is the Hero America Deserves", *Bloomberg Businessweek* (May 22, 2020), https://www.bloomberg.com/news/features/2020-05-22/elon-musk-speaks-frankly-on-coronavirus-spacex-and-rage-tweets (discussing many of the controversies surrounding Musk, including his pandemic denialism).

persona, as a villain. And while a more equitable economy might be nice, we do have smart phones and facts at our fingertips, and that's something.

Second, the companies at issue dominate their markets, and are in turn dominated by their founders. Amazon is struggling for the domination of retail, that is, food, clothing, household items – the supply chain for most households.[69] Perhaps it will not achieve complete domination.   Perhaps a duopoly with Walmart will emerge.   Google is not the only search engine, but is so dominant that YouTube's earnings are not material for the purposes of securities disclosure.[70] Bloomberg is hardly the only provider of information to the public writ large, but it (and so he) is the key provider of information to the financial markets (and so capitalism?). Writing in the midst of the COVID-19 pandemic, which has exposed the fragility of our supply chains, and especially the vulnerabilities of overly concentrated markets, it is hard to believe that anyone would intentionally assign economic sectors like "food supply" or "financial information" to a single or even two or three sources, much less to individuals. But, through the accident of history (progress!), that is pretty much our situation. We

---

[69] *See* Lauren Thomas, "74% of Consumers Go to Amazon When They're Ready to Buy Something. That Should Be Keeping Retailers Up at Night", CNBC (Mar. 20, 2019),
https://www.cnbc.com/2019/03/19/heres-why-retailers-should-be-scared-of-amazon-dominating-e-commerce.html (explaining that by the end of the year, Amazon was expected to account for 52.4% of the e-commerce market in the United States).
[70] Daisuke Wakabayashi, "YouTube Is a Big Business. Just How Big Is Anyone's Guess", *The New York Times* (Jul. 24, 2019),
https://www.nytimes.com/2019/07/24/technology/youtube-financial-disclosure-google.html (citing estimates that YouTube generates $16-25 billion in annual revenue but noting that it is "lumped in" with Google which generated $137 in revenue in 2018).

have, to an astonishing degree, decided that political economy, at least the political economy of technology, is a matter not for more or less democratic governance, not for bureaucratic regulation, and not for civil society with competitive markets. Instead, we seem content with the idea that technology markets are the domain of individual monopolists, whom we are pleased to honor for their successes. It is a strange view of politics, and conversely, of citizenship.

Appendices

The 10 Wealthiest Women in America[71]

Rank			Net worth
10	Nancy Walton Laurie	Heiress to Walmart fortune	$7.1 billion
9	Blair Parry-Okeden	Heiress to Cox Enterprises (Global conglomerate media company)	$7.6 billion
8	Anne Walton-Kroenke	Heir to Walmart fortune	$7.9 billion
7	Christy Walton	Married into Walton family by marrying John Walton, son of Walmart's founder	$8.9 billion
6	Abigail Johnson	Heiress, CEO, etc. Fidelity Investments	$10.8 billion
5	Laurene Powell Jobs	Heiress of Steve Jobs (Apple)	$16.4 billion

[71] Taylor Borden, "The 15 Richest Women In America Right Now, Ranked", *Business Insider*, (Apr. 7, 2020), www.businessinsider.com/richest-women-us-america-billionaires-ranking-walton-koch-bezos-mars.

4	Jacqueline Mars	Heiress of Mars Inc. (manufacturer of pet food and other food products) Owns a third of the Snickers and M&M's confectionery empire	$24.7 billion
3	MacKenzie Bezos	Divorce with Jeff Bezos resulted in largest settlement in history owns 4% of Amazon company and is the company's second largest shareholder	$36 billion
2	Julia Koch	Heiress Koch Industries (chemical manufacturing company)	$38.2 billion
1	Alice Walton	Inherited fortune through her father/founder of Walmart, Sam Walton	54.4 billion

The Ten Wealthiest People Worldwide[72]

Rank	Name	Country		Net worth
10	Rob Walton	USA	Heir to Walmart fortune (Rob is the eldest son of Sam Walton, the co-founder)	$54.1 billion
9	Alice Walton	USA	Heir to Walmart fortune (daughter of Sam Walton, the co-founder)	$54.4 billion

[72] Hillary Hoffower, "These Are the 15 Richest People in the World Right Now", *Business Insider*, (Apr. 7, 2020), www.businessinsider.com/richest-people-in-the-world-wealthiest-billionaires#1-jeff-bezos-15.

8	Jim Walton	USA	Heir to the fortune of Walmart	$54.6 billion
7	Mark Zuckerberg	USA	Internet entrepreneur and philanthropist Co-founder, chief executive officer, and controlling shareholder of Facebook Co-founder and a board member of a sail spacecraft project called Breakthrough Starshot	$54.7 billion
6	Amancio Ortega	Spain	Founded Zara (clothing company)	$55.1 billion
5	Larry Ellison	USA	Business magnate, philanthropist, and investor Co-founder, executive chairman, and chief technology officer of Oracle Corporation (Computer software company)	$59 billion
4	Warren Buffett	USA	Investor and philanthropist CEO of Berkshire Hathaway (multinational conglomerate company that has subsidiaries in GEICO, Dairy Queen, Duracell and more)	$67.5 billion
3	Bernard Arnault	France	Chairman and Chief Executive of LVMH (luxury goods company)	$76 billion
2	Bill Gates	USA	Software developer, investor, and philanthropist Co-founder of Microsoft	$98 billion
1	Jeff Bezos	USA	Industrialist, media proprietor, and investor Founder, CEO, and president of Amazon	$113 billion

Chapter 12

Poverty and income inequality: a complex relationship

Victor A. Beker

"There is, perhaps, no better test of the progress of the nation than that which shows what proportion are in poverty" (Bowley, 1923, p. 214).

Introduction

For a long time, poverty has not been an important concern for mainstream economists. In fact, it is a relatively new area in orthodox economic analysis. Economics of Poverty was only identified by JEL as a distinct field of research in 1969.

This was because it was assumed that poverty reduction is just an automatic by-product of economic growth. So, the emphasis was placed on growth enhancement rather than on poverty alleviation.

Piketty's best-seller book has brought distributional issues to the fore of economic debate. This is perhaps its main contribution. Piketty centers his analysis on inequality, which, under capitalism, goes hand in hand with economic growth, according to his analysis. In my critical review of the book (Beker, 2014) I asked whether reduction of inequality or reduction of poverty should be our main concern, warning that the relationship between inequality and poverty is a rather complex one.

Of course, this does not happen if poverty is measured in relative terms. As I point out in section 4.2, a relative poverty measure is essentially a measure of inequality. In such a case, poverty and inequality move in parallel.

As Milanovic (2016b) points out, "it is precisely the growth in the middle, fueled by the resurgent Asia, and the quasi-stagnation of incomes around the 80-90th percentile of the global income distribution where Western middle classes are, that have attracted most attention." The middle class in the developed world has been the big loser of a process in which it has been squeezed by the twin forces of globalization and technological innovation. This is the source of so much middle-class discontent in advanced economies reflected in events such as Brexit, the election of Donald Trump and protests in France.

In this paper I refer to poverty as absolute poverty, which I think is the concept that better let us analyze the situation in the low-income countries where most of the world's population lives. Relative poverty becomes an urgent concern only once absolute poverty is no longer a first order problem. Contrary to an extended belief, there is no necessary positive correlation between income inequality and (absolute) poverty. Moreover, there are examples that show that inequality may rise and simultaneously poverty may decline and vice versa. For example, one case is when a society becomes absolutely equalitarian because everybody is poor; another one, when a society changes toward a more inegalitarian one where, however, everybody is better off than before.

It is worthwhile remembering that the first of the United Nations' "Millennium Development Goals" set by the world's leaders in September 2000 had to do with poverty. The target was to halve the incidence of poverty between 1990 and 2015. The proportion of people living on less than $1.25 a day globally fell from 36 per cent in 1990 to 15 per cent in 2011 (UN, 11). However, the poorest and most vulnerable people are still being left behind (ibid, 8).

As a matter of fact, multiple issues are involved in the relationship between economic growth, income inequality and poverty. Let us have a look at some of them.

First, does economic growth increase or decrease income inequality? Second, does poverty increase or decrease with economic growth?

Third, does growing inequality mean increasing poverty? Or increasing inequality is compatible with decreasing poverty?

In what follows I present a survey of the literature on these matters which illustrates that the relationship between inequality and poverty is a rather complex one and that empirical results are, in some cases, contradictory. There is still a vast field open for research in this area.

Section 1 is devoted to the relationship between growth and inequality; Section 2 has to do with the relationship between economic growth and poverty; Section 3 deals with the relationship between inequality and poverty; Section 4 is devoted to the geography of poverty; Section 5 analyzes several issues connected with anti-poverty policies. Section 6 concludes. An Addendum with some preliminary reflections on the effects of the COVID-19 pandemic on inequality and poverty is included.

1. Growth and inequality

1.1. The effect of growth on inequality

Whether growth leads to increased inequality or not is an old question in economics.

The Kuznets curve hypothesis proposed by Simon Kuznets (1955 and 1963) holds that as incomes grow in the early stages of development, income distribution would at first worsen and then improve as a wider segment of the population participates in the rising national income. In fact, Kuznets found an inverted U-shaped relation between income inequality and GNP per head. At a first stage incomes would become more unequal while at a second stage growth would reduce inequality after some crucial level was reached.

The initial studies on the Kuznets curve hypothesis used cross-sectional data and compared poor countries to rich countries in order to test hypotheses about income distribution and growth. Several investigations have found some support for the Kuznets hypothesis (e.g. Oswang, 1994; Ali, 1998; Milanovic, 1994; as well as Fishlow, 1995). However, further work on the Kuznets curve has found the relationship weak, as it is dependent on the precise functional form adopted (e.g. Anand and Kanbur, 1993; Deininger and Squire, 1998).

> "Histories of individual countries show that in some countries income distribution has worsened over time (e.g. Brazil) and in others it has improved (e.g. Indonesia in the 1970s). In fact we can observe countries in each of the four possible quadrants representing combinations of growth and changes in income distribution" (Stewart, 2000).

So, empirical evidence has been inconclusive with respect to the relationship between economic growth and income distribution.

In this context, Piketty published his best seller providing an impressive amount of data which shows that under capitalism wealth and income inequality increases with economic growth. He argues that to the extent that the rate of capital accumulation (r) is higher than the rate of growth of the economy (g), inequality expands; In particular, Piketty (2014, 32) argues that the rapid increase observed in income inequality in the United

States, which started in the 1980s, largely reflects an unprecedented explosion of very elevated incomes from labor. Although this phenomenon is seen mainly in the United States and to a lesser degree in Britain, the trend in other wealthy countries is in the same direction. Inequality has much to do with the advent of "supermanagers" who obtain extremely high, historically unprecedented compensation packages for their labor, he concludes.[1]

Varoufakis (2014, 28) argues that a very simple argument leads to Piketty's conclusions without being necessary to resort to the so called "laws" the French author uses in his now famous book: "It is, demonstrably, a simple matter to prove that when the rich have a higher propensity to save than the average person, the chances are that their share of wealth will be rising. As long as they save more than the poor and receive total income (wage income plus returns to their wealth) well over and above the average citizen's income, the rich will find themselves on a perpetual escalator that guarantees them a constantly increasing share of aggregate wealth. And even if they enjoy less than half of aggregate income, it is still possible to show that their wealth share will be rising as long as their marginal propensity to save is considerably greater than that of the poorer citizens."

Some time ago, Frank and Cook (1995) described capitalism as a winner-take-all society where there is a commanding financial advantage for those at the top but

---

[1] For a critical review of Piketty's book see Beker (2014) and other articles in the same volume.

nothing like it for those, however good, who are further down in the hierarchy.

This means that not only wealth and income distribution follow a power law – as is well known since Pareto's times – but also that wealth and income growth rates are distributed according to a power law. Once a firm – or an individual – gets some advantage over its competitors the process becomes reinforcing producing the so called Matthew effect according to which the rich get richer and the poor get poorer. Once the playing field is slightly tilted positive feedbacks tip the system in favor of the initially benefitted.

Grave inequalities in the distribution of income are the straightforward result. Winner-take-all markets dramatically widen the gap between rich and poor by concentrating all rewards among just a small handful of winners.

1.2. Inequality and technical change

Aghion et al. (1999) postulated three candidate explanations for the increasing inequality in developed countries namely, trade liberalization, skill-biased technical change, and organizational change.

Aghion et al. (1999) argue that trade between high-skill and low-skill economies should cause, in the former, an increase in the demand for domestic skill-intensive commodities at the expense of the demand for domestic unskilled intensive commodities. In the poor country where abundant unskilled labor is cheap the trade boom drives up the demand for unskilled labor and drives down the demand for skilled labor. Thus, earnings inequality increases in the rich economies but declines in the poor ones. However, empirical studies have shown that these effects seem to be rather small.

Technical change has been pointed out as another possible responsible for growing inequality. If technological change is to generate an increase in wage inequality, it must be because technological change is biased toward certain skills or specializations.

Skill-biased technical change induces a shift in labor demand towards skilled labor within all industries. Empirical studies for the US and the UK corroborate that most of the increase in the non- manual share in total employment was due to within industry shifts. Therefore, technical change and not trade liberalization seems to be the main responsible for increasing inequality in developed countries.

Finally, Aghion et al. (1999) identify organizational change as another likely source of inequality. The productivity gap between individuals with different skill levels increases when changes in the organization take place. It happens because organizational change itself is skill-biased.

Aghion et al. (1999) conclude that technological change is the most important factor to explain increasing inequality, since both trade liberalization and organizational change only affect earnings inequality insofar as they are associated with technical change.

Technical progress is by itself a crucial source of inequality whenever itis not neutral, that is, if it affects differently the productivity of the various types of labor.

Milanovic (2016a) introduces the concept of "Kuznets waves": inequality rises, falls and then rises again, perhaps endlessly. According to this author, Kuznets waves are driven mostly by a technological revolution. In the case of the present Kuznets cycle, it is mainly driven by the transfer of labor from more homogenous manufacturing into skill-heterogeneous services (and thus producing a decline in the ability of workers to organize) together with globalization. These two forces together are responsible for the hollowing out of the middle classes in the west and the consequently rise in inequality. According to Milanovic, since the 1980s developed countries are on the first part of a second Kuznets cycle. This implies that inequality is only a transitory phenomenon: in a certain future the second part of the Kuznets wave will come on and the present inequality trend will be offset, counteracted, canceled and reversed. In this way he rejects the idea of the existence of a permanent increasing inequality trend. Time will tell. Anyway, he admits that in the short run inequality will not come down.

1.3 Inequality and economic policy

Piketty (2014, 27) admits that "the resurgence of inequality after 1980 is due largely to the political shifts of the past several decades, especially in regard to taxation and finance." But this implies that the main determinant of the ups and downs of inequality has been the changing correlation of forces between capital and labor and not the "laws" which the French author would have discovered. This changing balance of forces has resulted in different policies over time from the welfare state of the post-war period to neoliberal deregulation of the 1980s. Until the appearance of Piketty's book, the resurgence of inequality after 1980 has been mainly considered the direct effect of Reagan-Thatcher economic policies that, among other things, eroded union power. Piketty admits that the inequality r>g is a contingent historical proposition, which is true in some periods and political contexts and not in others. The crucial issue to elucidate is whether inequality is just the result of an intrinsic trend in capitalist development or is the consequence of policies like the ones which consisted of deregulation, weakening of the labor unions and the like. Piketty himself seems to choose a middle-of-the road explanation. He recognizes that there are "powerful mechanisms pushing alternately toward convergence and divergence" as far as wealth distribution is concerned. However, he predicts that "certain worrisome forces of divergence" will prevail in the future; but his forecast is based precisely on the behavior of the United States and Europe after 1980. He maintains that "the return of high capital/income ratios over the past few decades can be explained in large part by the return to a regime of relatively slow growth" (Piketty, 2014, 33). This kept the rate of return on capital significantly above the growth rate. But weren't the low rate of growth and the high rate of return on capital just the results of Reaganite and Thatcherite policies? If so, the inequality r>g is just the outcome of those policies and may be reversed by a change of policies.

2. Growth and poverty

2.1. The causes of poverty

For the economically active population there are two basic causes of poverty, whatever precise definition one uses for it:

1. Unemployment.[2]
2. Income that cannot meet the basic needs level.

Poor people are those who do not earn an income at all or those who earn an income which is insufficient to satisfy their basic needs.

So, any research on the causes of poverty should be focused on the causes of unemployment and of low remunerations.[3] Any policy aimed at fighting poverty should be oriented towards the elimination of unemployment and low payment. For instance, in 2012, 10.8% of the workforce in the European Union was unemployed and an estimated 9.5% was affected by in-work poverty, summing up a total of more than 32 million people, (European Anti-Poverty Network, 2013).

Of course, it may be discussed how to appropriately measure poverty. Sen (2006) showed why the usual indicators are not satisfactory remarking that "there is a long way to go still to make adequate social sense of

---

[2] In those countries where there is an unemployment subsidy the contribution of unemployment to poverty depends on the amount of that subsidy.
[3] On the subject see the contribution by Bhaduri et al (2015).

economic measures" (Ibid, 46). I come back on this issue in section 4.2.

2.2. *Some arithmetic on inequality, poverty and growth*

Kanbur (2005) points out some mechanical properties in the relationship between poverty, growth and inequality. "First, holding inequality constant, an increase in per capita income (in other words, growth) reduces poverty. Second, holding per capita income constant, an increase in inequality increases poverty" (Kanbur, 2005, 224). This means that, although growth is positively correlated with poverty reduction, if growth is accompanied by increased inequality, then the net effect on poverty is no longer clear.

Kanbur (2005, 228) goes on with some awkward questions. For instance, if the total number of the poor goes up but, because of population growth, the percentage of the poor in the total population goes down; has poverty gone up or down? Even worse, the incidence of poverty falls each time a poor person dies because of poverty. Another case: let us suppose that poverty declines because the poor who are engaged in activities that are favored by growth are better off, but those engaged in activities that are not favored are worse off than before. Shall we consider this outcome as an improvement? This is an issue of great ethical and political significance.

Poverty persistence might indicate one of two things; either the determinants of poverty reduction are not known, or they are known but the policies to fight them are not being put in place or a combination of the two (Kanbur, 2010).

2.3. Growth and poverty

The relationship between growth and poverty is subject to some controversy.

The importance of economic growth as a basis for lessening poverty cannot be overstated. Table 1 shows how small differences in growth rates may generate, in the long run, quite different outcomes.

Table 1

Years later	Country A 1% growth	Country B 5% growth	Country C 10% growth
0	$1.000	$1.000	$1.000
10	$1.105	$1.629	$2.594
20	$1.220	$2.650	$6.727
30	$1.348	$4.322	$17.449
40	$1.489	$7.040	$45.259
50	$1.645	$11.467	$117.391

Let us have a look at the effect of different rates of growth on the standard of living of three hypothetical countries (A, B, and C) that start with a per capita income of \$1,000. 50 years later, the country C that has been growing at an annual 10 percent gets a per capita income 70 times higher than the country that has only grown by 1% and 10 times higher than of the country B which has grown at an annual rate of 5%.

This means, among other things, that, in the long run, the poor in a country with a higher rate of growth may attain a better standard of living than the middle class of a country with lower rate of growth. Of course, this happens if income distribution remains constant over time.

However, if income distribution became less equal with growth, poverty might not be declining or even worsen.

The depth and persistence of poverty has created serious doubts about the ability of economic growth to reduce poverty by itself. Poverty however we define it has gone down in some parts of the world but gone up in others over the past half century.

2.4. Empirical studies on the relationship between growth and poverty

Empirical studies have found that a lesser level of development and a higher level of inequality reduce the growth elasticity of poverty (Bourguignon, 2003, 16). This means that countries with a very low level of development and very concentrated income distributions have very low probabilities of leaving the poverty trap. The mineral-rich economies are a typical case; they are usually very underdeveloped and have very concentrated income distributions.

Salvatore and Campano (2012) created a data base of income distributions by quintiles with multiple years for most countries. The results show that the 25 year period from 1980 to 2005 has been beneficial to the poorest populations in both the developed and the developing countries. Moreover, the income gap between the developed and developing countries has been closing. Much of this can be accounted for by the rapid growth rates in China and India. However, the authors conclude that if the present growth rates prevail it would take developing country people hundreds of years to close the income gap with the developed country people.

Ravallion (1995) uses a sample of 16 developing countries in the decade of 1980s and finds that a 3% rate of growth in consumption per capita can be expected to result in a 6–10% rate of reduction in the proportion living on less than $1 per day.

On the other hand, while the Gini coefficient decreased from 0.4414 to 0.4081 in developed countries, in the developing countries it increased from 0.5219 to 0.5414 (Salvatore and Campano, 2012, 10). This outcome seems to endorse the idea that, for less developed countries, economic growth goes hand in hand with increasing inequality.

However, as it was pointed out before, even with growing inequality poverty may be declining. Therefore, let us have a look to the relationship between inequality and poverty.

3. Inequality and poverty

3.1. *Inequality and poverty: empirical studies*

In the literature on income distribution, the terms inequality and poverty are often used as if they were interchangeable. An increase in inequality is interpreted as an increase in poverty and vice versa. For instance Dagdeviren et al.(2000, 5) refer to poverty-reducing policies and then they state: "the 'High Performing' Asian countries, prior to the financial crisis of the late 1990s, combined rapid growth of per capita income with relatively stable and low inequality," concluding that "the experience of the 'high performers' suggested, at the least, that there might be policy measures to foster the benign combination of high growth and rapid poverty reduction," as though lower inequality would unequivocally mean lower poverty. And it is just one example among many.

However, as it is easy to realize, a decrease in poverty is not necessarily accompanied by a decrease in inequality;[4] it may in fact be accompanied by an increase in it. China experienced a sharp reduction in poverty together with a significant increase in inequality. Conversely, an increase in poverty may be accompanied by a decrease in

---

[4] Unless inequality is part of the definition of poverty. We shall discuss this issue later in section 4.2.

inequality overall. Finally, there may be widespread poverty in a society and yet very little economic inequality.

Ravallion (1995) finds that there is no sign that growth has been associated with a clear tendency for inequality within developing countries to either increase or decrease.

De Janvry and Sadoulet (1999) analyze poverty and income inequality data for 12 Latin American countries between 1970 and 1994; they find that income growth reduces urban and rural poverty but not inequality. They also find that there is an asymmetry in the impact of growth on poverty and inequality, with recessions having stronger effects on both poverty and inequality than equivalent increases in income. De Janvry and Sadoulet (ibid, 9) find that urban poverty is anti-cyclical, falling with income growth and rising in recession. However, they also find that growth is only effective in reducing urban poverty when inequality is not too high. Thus countries with high levels of inequality cannot rely on growth to reduce poverty. This result coincides with Bourguignon's, which has been mentioned above. Although it cannot be said that growth is unequalizing, neither can reliance be placed on growth to reduce inequality.

De Janvry and Sadoulet's results coincide with those in Bruno et al. (1996) who found the effect of growth on inequality to be indeterminate. However, they point out that lower initial inequality raises the likelihood that growth will reduce poverty.

Quah (2002) analyzes the cases of China and India, which carry within them a third of the world's population. He concludes that aggregate economic growth might well come about only with increases in inequality. In spite of this he argues that growth is unambiguously beneficial for the poor. He underlines that only under inconceivably high increases in inequality would economic growth not benefit the poor.

Besley and Burgess (2003, 11) find a positive and significant association between inequality and the level of poverty within a country. However, as Honohan (2004) points out, this association is almost tautological: if the mean income is held constant the more of the national income is taken by the rich the less is available for the rest and more people are likely to be poor.

Kraay (2006) decomposes poverty changes into three elements: a) growth in average incomes; b) the sensitivity of poverty to growth; and c) changes in the distribution of income. In a large cross-country sample, he finds that growth in average incomes accounts for some 70 percent of the variation in (headcount) poverty changes in the short run, and over 95 percent in the medium to long run. So, he concludes that growth is the key instrument for poverty reduction.

López and Servén (2006) use a large cross-country database including both industrial and developing countries and spanning almost 40 years to test the null hypothesis that the size distribution of per capita income can be described by a lognormal density. The empirical tests are supportive of the lognormal approximation to the distribution of per capita income. Lognormality of the distribution of income allows the authors to derive some qualitative and quantitative implications for the relative roles of growth and inequality in poverty reduction under alternative initial conditions, using a variety of poverty measures.

The authors highlight four main points:

I. inequality hampers poverty reduction, both because of its negative impact on the growth elasticity of poverty and because of its negative impact on the inequality elasticity of poverty;

II. for a given poverty line, the impact of growth on poverty is stronger in richer than in poorer countries, and hence the latter will find it harder than the former to achieve fast poverty reduction;

III. the share of the variance of poverty changes attributable to growth should be generally lower in richer and more unequal countries; this means that in poorer and more equal countries growth should be expected to be the main driver of poverty reduction, while inequality changes tend to play a more prominent role in richer and/or more unequal countries; and

IV. given the initial levels of development and inequality, the relative poverty-reduction effectiveness of growth and inequality changes depends on the poverty line – the higher the poverty line, the bigger the role of growth and the smaller the role of distributional change (ibid, 2).

The inequality elasticity falls as inequality rises, for a given value of average income relative to the poverty line. However, the relationship is highly nonlinear, and at very low levels of development its sign is reversed. The more equal and the poorer the economy the more effective growth will be relative to redistribution in attacking poverty. As the economy becomes richer and more unequal, distributional change plays a relatively larger role in poverty changes. At very low levels of development the poverty-reducing effects of growth outweigh the poverty-raising effects of a worsening distribution of income. So, the authors pose that when poverty reduction is the overriding policy objective, poorer and relatively equal countries may be willing to tolerate modest increases in income inequality in exchange for faster growth -more so than richer and highly unequal countries.

Housseima and ben Rejeb (2012) use panel data from 52 developing countries over the period 1990-2005, to determine the main sources of poverty reduction and show the interdependence between poverty, inequality and growth. They find that an increase of 1 percentage point in per capita GDP causes a reduction of poverty rate of 0.40 percentage points. On the other hand, they find that increased levels of inequality increase the proportion of poor in the population. Estimation results show that an increase of 1 percentage point in the Gini coefficient causes an increase of the poverty rate of 3.26 percentage points. Therefore, increasing inequality may hamper economic growth's role in reducing poverty.

However, Alvaredo and Gasparini (2013, find a weak relationship between poverty and inequality. The correlation coefficient between the headcount ($2 line) and the Gini coefficient is only 0.17.

3.2. The poverty trap

It has been argued that there exists a poverty trap which explains why people (and countries) that start poor remain poor. A set of self–reinforcing mechanisms determine that poverty begets poverty. An early example of this kind of literature is Nelson (1956) who developed a growth model with low saving and investment rates at low income levels. So, low levels of income generate low saving and investment rates, trapping countries in poverty. The same scheme may be applied to individuals.

Kraay and McKenzie (2014) reject this point of view arguing that even the initially poorest 10 percent of countries has grown at a rate similar to the historical growth rate of the United States over the last 50 years. However, this argument does not contradict the idea of a poverty trap if those that initially were the poorest remain the poorest 50 years later. The issue at stake is whether the income growth rate of the poor exceeds the growth rate of the non-poor. Using data on poverty measures over time for 90 developing countries Ravallion (2012) finds that although their overall poverty rate has been falling since at least 1980 the proportionate rate of decline has not been higher in the poorest countries. The author finds that the initial level of poverty has a negative effect on growth rates and that a high poverty rate also weakens the effect of growth on reducing poverty. According to Ravallion both effects explain the lack of poverty convergence. Countries starting out with a high incidence of poverty do not have a higher proportionate rate of poverty reduction, which would allow poverty convergence.

In her analysis of anti-poverty policies in USA, Sawhill (1988) examines the period between 1967 and 1985 and concludes that the rise in unemployment is one of the main explanatory variables of their failure; she adds that the chance of being poor in US is greatly increased if one is black, lives in a female-headed family or is a child under 18. Children who are born in a poor family go on to spend a long time living in poverty.

In her analysis of the role of segregation, Ananat (2011) finds that segregation creates places where black poverty and inequality are higher while white poverty and inequality are lower, compared to places that are less segregated.

Husmann (2016) reminds that marginality is a root cause of poverty; marginality refers to a position of individuals or groups at the margins of social, political, economic, ecological, and biophysical systems. She uses this concept to create a marginality map of Ethiopia by overlaying seven indicators capturing different aspects of marginality. Marginality hotspots are identified.

Sawhill's, Ananat's and Hussmann's studies suggest that poverty may be path dependent: people belonging to particular social groups and/or living in specific neighborhoods have a higher probability of being poor.

4. The geography of poverty

4.1. Where are the poor?

The main source of statistical information for poverty analysis at a large international scale is the World Bank's PovcalNet,[5] a compilation of distributive data built up from national household surveys, generally fed by national statistical offices. However, this database does not include the developed countries. In fact, the use of a low international poverty line has the unintended effect of limiting poverty statistics to developing countries.[6]

According to PovcalNet, in 2011, 2.1 billion people – 36 per cent of the developing world's population – lived with less than \$2 a day in 2011 purchasing power parity. In absolute numbers, income poverty was concentrated in India and China. Around 740 million people in India lived with less than \$2 a day, representing 60% of its total population. The number in China was 250 million, which was 19% of this country's population. Both countries are home of 46% of the poor in the world. The following three countries – Bangladesh, Indonesia and Pakistan – represent 14%. So, income poverty is highly concentrated from a geographical point of view. The other geographical area which greatly contributes to poverty numbers is the Sub-Saharan region with 617 million which represented 70% of its total population. Altogether, these areas summed up 89% of the developing world's income poverty.

---

[5] http://iresearch.worldbank.org/PovcalNet/.
[6] Some of the problems that involve the use of an international poverty line are detailed in Deaton (2010).

Gentilini and Sumner (2012) compute global poverty using the national poverty lines officially set in each country instead of using international poverty standards; they include developing as well as developed countries. They find that 22.5 per cent of the world's population, or some 1.5 billion people, live in "poverty" as locally defined. 30% of this total belongs to South Asia, 17% to East Asia and 24% to Sub-Saharan Africa. This shows that the geographical distribution of poverty is not substantially affected by the way of measuring it. However, they find that 11% of the world's poor live in high-income countries – United States and some European countries. Moreover, 3 countries – Brazil, Mexico and United States – contribute with 139 million to the 1.5 billion total. Each of them has more poor population than Pakistan or Indonesia.

Therefore, when analyzed with a national poverty lines lens, poverty is less geographically concentrated.

The use of national poverty lines provides for some countries a substantially lower aggregate than the $2 a day line. This indicates that for some countries those living with such a budget are not considered poor. A notable case is India. Out of the 740 million people who in 2011 lived with less than $2 a day, the national poverty line only considered poor 355 million.

The discrepancies between poverty measured by an international *vis a vis* a national poverty line emerge primarily from the fact that what is considered poor is socially determined and therefore varies across time and space. What we consider poor now is not the same as what was considered poor 200 years ago. The same applies between countries of different levels of development.

For example, the countries in the European Union consider poor those with incomes below 60 percent of the median. So, the definition of poverty is tied up to income evolution. The absolute incomes of low-end households may increase but if the household incomes at the median increase in the same proportion the poverty rate will remain the same. Probably many of the people labeled as poor in Europe will not be considered as such in India or Pakistan.

We have here two issues at stake. First, international versus national poverty lines. Second, the national poverty line may be an absolute value – $2 a day for some countries and $1 for others – or it may be defined in relative terms as it is the case of the EU.

This leads us to the discussion between absolute and relative measures of poverty.

4.2. Relative and absolute measures of poverty

People who do not have their basic necessities that they need to lead a reasonable life – the food, the shelter, the clothing – are considered to be poor. However, what a reasonable life is varies across countries and over time.

Once it is recognized that needs are socially determined, a poverty line can be established for a given country at a given time. It will measure the amount of money needed to buy the basket of commodities necessary to satisfy the socially determined basic needs in that country at that time. This may be an absolute value or a relative one. For example, the poverty line may be estimated in $2 a day or it could be set at some percentage of the country's mean income. This leads us to the postponed discussion on how to measure poverty.

Some authors argue that poverty should necessarily be measured in relative terms. For instance, MacEwan (2007, 10) claims that "there are no poor unless there are also rich". In an egalitarian society poverty has no meaning at all, he adds. So, poverty refers to a certain layer in the social structure. The lack of goods and services does not mean poverty if all members of society are in the same situation. Following this reasoning he argues that

> "in two societies where the absolute income of the bottom segment (say the bottom quintile) is the same, poverty will be greater in the society where income distribution is more unequal because in that society the bottom segment will be further from the norm and thus more lacking in that society's socially determined needs" (ibid, 11).

The way of reflecting this difference is by using relative measures of poverty.

This has a direct impact on the policies to deal with poverty. If poverty is measured in relative terms there is no way of reducing it without changing the income distribution. If income increases across all quintiles at the same rate poverty will remain unchanged. On the contrary, if income decreases for all quintiles but at a smaller rate for the lowest one, poverty measured in relative terms will decline. A relative poverty measure is essentially a measure of inequality within the bottom half of the income distribution.

On the other hand, if poverty is measured in absolute terms it might be reduced just with economic growth.

Therefore, the way poverty is measured is not an innocent issue. It is directly linked to the policies recommended to reduce it. Those who argue in favor of a relative measure are in favor of income redistribution. Those who back an absolute measure advocate in favor of economic growth.

The relative one is a measure of subjective poverty. People may feel better off if their income decreases but their neighbors' incomes decrease in a higher proportion. In the same way, they may feel worse off if their income increase at a slower speed than the rest of society.

The absolute measure assumes that poverty has to do with the amount of commodities available to an individual – or a family – to satisfy the basic needs disregarding what happens to the rest of the people.

The relative measure mixes up poverty with equality. But they are two different concepts. One has to do with the lack of means to satisfy one's needs, whatever defined. The other refers to the way income or wealth is distributed within society. Relative poor are people whose income or wealth is less than the average one of the rest of society, independently of the quantity of goods they can consume with that level of income or wealth.

The policies to deal with poverty may or may not be the same to reduce inequality. There are some authors – from Kuznets to Quah to Basu – who have argued that there is a trade-off between fighting poverty and reducing inequality. China seems to be a clear example of this.

Therefore, in evaluating policies against poverty it seems advisable to measure it in absolute terms and reserve relative poverty to inequality analysis together with other instruments as the Gini coefficient, the Lorenz curve or the Theil-index.

5. Some policy issues concerning poverty and inequality

Martin Feldstein (1999) argues that policy should address poverty, not inequality. He points out that changes that increase the incomes of high-income individuals without decreasing the incomes of others clearly satisfy the Pareto principle. However, it may be argued that although the poor are not worse off in absolute terms they are in relative ones; this may make them feel poorer as if they had lost part of their income. A policy change which improves the situation of the upper one percent of the population without changing the situation of the rest is undoubtedly a Paretian improvement. However, this more efficient alternative will be rejected in many societies in the name of equity. The Pareto improvement concept implicitly assumes that absolute and not relative situations are relevant. However, it is society and not economists who should decide what weight should be given to efficiency and what weight to equity: it is typically a value judgment. It will depend on the idea of equity that in that society prevails (Beker, 2005, 17).

Basu (2005) introduced the concept of poverty-minimizing inequality as the amount of inequality that society should tolerate to minimize poverty. He remarks that a society of perfect equality would be crushingly poor (Basu, 2005, 1367). Therefore, instead of attempting perfect equality he suggests to take as welfare criteria a normative simple rule: maximizing the per capita income of the poorest 20 per cent of the population. He calls this the "quintile income" of a country.

Basu warns that the quintile measure should not be confused with a poverty measure of a society. It is a practical objective for policy design purposes. It can be generalized by giving weights to the incomes of people at different levels of poverty with the poorest people getting the highest weights and then looking at the weighted per capita income of society (Basu, 2005, 8).

Klasen (2003, 65) argues that pro-poor growth should at a minimum involve disproportionate growth of the incomes of the poor; the income growth rate of the poor must exceed the growth rate of the non-poor.

The much used elasticity of the poverty rate with respect to the mean growth rate (the so-called poverty elasticity of growth) does not consider information about the distribution of incomes among the poor. Indeed, a high poverty elasticity of growth might often just mean that many poor who were close to the poverty line were lifted above it rather than high income growth among the severely poor, who should be of particular concern (ibid, 64/65).

Governments should ideally be able to focus on policies that have the largest marginal effect on pro-poor growth. Some policies have a large effect on growth, but may not be particularly pro-poor; others do not have such a large effect on growth, but are extremely pro-poor. The best policies are obviously those that have a large effect on both, but not enough is known about which policies fall into what category (ibid, 84).

Klasen underlines that, according to experience, successful reform was particularly likely in countries that faced severe economic crises with few economic options. These countries built up a consensus for change prior to reforms, had substantial indigenous technical capacity at their disposal, and used aid and technical advice to sustain the reforms. Donors were able to assist successful reformers, although donor aid sometimes also delayed reforms or reduced the ownership of reforms through excessive conditionalities (ibid, 85).

Promoting pro-poor growth in countries with high inequality and where the poor are politically and economically marginalized is likely to be difficult. As a result, success in implementing pro-poor policies depend greatly on creating and strengthening pro-poor coalitions, which can involve parts of governments, nongovernmental organizations, donors, and civil society (ibid, 85). In this respect Kanbur points out that if a set of instruments harms the interests of the dominant coalition, it will not be implemented, even if it is known to be a determinant of poverty reduction (Kanbur, 2010).

Given the importance of unemployment as a determinant of poverty, one should pay attention to the effect of economic policies on the level of employment. For example, the adjustment policies inspired in the Washington Consensus have implied a vast destruction of jobs where they were applied.[7]

6. Conclusions

For a long time, poverty has not been an important concern for mainstream economists. The reason for this was that it was assumed that poverty reduction is just an automatic by-product of economic growth.

The first of the United Nations' "Millennium Development Goals" set by the world's leaders in September 2000 was to halve the incidence of poverty between 1990 and 2015. The goal has been achieved. The proportion of people living on less than $1.25 a day globally fell from 36 per cent in 1990 to 15 per cent in 2011. However, the poorest and most vulnerable people are still being left behind.

---

[7] See Beker (2012, 14) for the Argentine case.

The paper addresses some of the multiple issues involved in the relationship between economic growth, income inequality and poverty.

The main conclusions arrived at are the following.

- First of all, although empirical evidence is not conclusive there are strong signs that there is a positive association between economic growth and rising inequality. If so, the gap between rich and poor widens as the economy grows. China seems to be a clear example of this.

- Second, skill-biased technological change is an important factor to explain increasing inequality.

- Third, economic growth reduces poverty if income distribution remains constant or improves over time. However, if income distribution becomes less equal with growth, poverty might not be declining or even worsen.

- Fourth, poverty seems to be path dependent: people belonging to particular social groups and/or living in specific neighborhoods have a higher probability of being poor.

- Fifth, the initial level of poverty has a negative effect on growth rates and a high poverty rate also weakens the effect of growth on reducing poverty. Countries with a very low level of development and very concentrated income distributions have very low probabilities of leaving the poverty trap without income redistribution. In poor but more equal countries growth should be expected to be the main driver of poverty reduction, while inequality changes tend to play a more prominent role in richer and/or very unequal countries.

- Sixth, using the national poverty lines officially set in each country, 22.5 per cent of the world's population or some 1.5 billion people, live in 'poverty' as locally defined. 30% of this total belongs to South Asia, 17% to East Asia, 24% to Sub-Saharan Africa and 11% to high-income countries.

- Seventh, governments should focus on policies that have the largest marginal effect on pro-poor growth. This implies to choose policies which warrant that the income growth rate of the poor exceeds the growth rate of the non-poor.

- Last but not the least, some authors have argued that there is a trade-off between fighting poverty and reducing inequality. China seems to be a clear example of this. If so, it is society who should decide what weight should be given to poverty and what weight to equity: it is typically a value judgment. It is society who should decide how much more poverty is tolerable in order to reduce inequality or how much more inequality is acceptable when reducing poverty.

In sum, the relationship between inequality and poverty is not a simple one; policies addressed to fight inequality have to take into consideration their side effects on poverty and vice versa. There is still a vast field open for research on this subject.

Addendum: inequality and poverty after the coronavirus (AC)

The article above has dealt with the Before Coronavirus (BC) era. This addendum has to do with the After Coronavirus (AC) era.

Perhaps it is too early to draw general conclusions about the main consequences the COVID-19 pandemic may have on income inequality and poverty. However, there are some clues of what they may be.

Historically, epidemics led to a decrease in population, an increase in mean income, higher wages (because of labor scarcity) and thus lower inequality. This time it is quite different.

The pandemic has shown the vulnerabilities and fragility of the present socio-economic system based on human labor. This time it was the coronavirus pandemic, tomorrow it may be another yet unknown global virus pandemic.

For this reason, large scale substitution of machines, robots, and other digital technologies for labor in the production process will accelerate. Machines and robots do not get sick or stay home when there is a pandemic. Dependence on human labor will be reduced as far as possible. Technological unemployment will significantly increase. On the other end, some reduced number of highly skilled workers will see their wages increased due to the high demand for their skills. Longstanding inequalities will exacerbate.

The intensified use of capital and technology instead of human labor will have far-reaching consequences for developing countries. Low-wage countries will lose their main competitive advantage. This will make it even more difficult for them to provide jobs for their population; higher unemployment and lower wages for unskilled labor will be likely outcomes. Probably, inequality and poverty will rise together.

The BC era world economy will not be restored. On the contrary, saving labor existing trends will deepen.

Providing income for large numbers of unemployed will become an urgent need. The time for a universal basic income may have come. It should be implemented together with a highly progressive income tax to make sure that those people who do not need it refund that money to the state.

References

Aghion, P., Caroli, E. and Garcia-Peñalosa, C. (1999) "Inequality and Economic Growth: The Perspective of the New Growth Theories." *Journal of Economic Literature*. Vol. 37, Nº4, 1615-1660.

Ahuja, V., Bidani, B., Ferreira, F. and Walton, M. (1997), "Everyone's Miracle?: Revisiting Poverty and Inequality in EastAsia". The World Bank Washington, DC.

Ali, A. A. G. (1998) "Dealing with poverty and income distribution issues in developing countries: Cross-regional experiences." *Journal of African* Economies Vol.7, N°2 (AERC Supplement), 77-115.

Alvaredo and Gasparini (2013). "Recent Trends in Inequality and Poverty in Developing Countries." CEDLAS Working Paper N° 151. www.cedlas.econo.unlp.edu.ar/wp/wp-content/uploads/doc_cedlas151.pdf

Ananat, E.O. (2011). "The Wrong Side(s) of the Tracks: The Causal Effects of Racial Segregation on Urban Poverty and Inequality." *American Economic Journal: Applied Economics.* Vol. 3, No. 2, 34-66. April.

Anand, S. and Kanbur R (1993a) "Inequality and Development: A Critique." *Journal of Development Economics.* Vol.41, N° 1, June, 19-43.

Banerjee, A. and Duflo, E. (2011) *Poor Economics: A Radical Rethinking of the Way to Fight Global Poverty.* Public Affairs. New York.

Barro, R. J. and Sala-i-Martin, X. (1995) *Economic Growth.* MIT Press, Cambridge, Mass.

Basu, K. (2005) "Globalization, Poverty, and Inequality: What is the Relationship? What Can Be Done?" *World Development.* Vol. 34, No. 8, 1361–1373.

Beker, V.A. (2014) "Piketty: inequality, poverty and managerial capitalism." *real-world economics review*, issue N° 69.

Besley, T. and Burgess, R. (2003a). *Journal of Economic Perspectives.* Vol. 17, N° 3. Summer, 3-22.

Besley, T. and Burgess, R. (2003b). "Halving Global Porverty". http://www.lse.ac.uk/economics/people/facultyPersonalPages/facultyFiles/RobinBurgess/HalvingGlobalPoverty0303.pdf

Besley, T. and Ghatak, M. (2004). "Public Goods and Economic Development." URL: http://personal.lse.ac.uk/GHATAK/public.pdf. Reprinted in *Understanding Poverty*, by Banerjee, A. V., Benabou, R., and Mookherjee, D. (Eds.). Oxford University Press. Oxford.

Bourguignon, F. (2003) "The growth elasticity of poverty reduction: Explaining heterogeneity across countries and time periods." In Eicher, T. S. and S. J. Turnovsky (Eds.), *Inequality and Growth: Theory and Policy Implications*. MIT Press. Cambridge, Mass., 3-26.

Bowley, A.M. (1923) *The Nature and Purpose of the Measurement of Social Phenomena*. P.S. King. London.

Bruno, M., Ravallion, M. and Squire L. (1996) "Equity and Growth in Developing Countries.Old and New Perspectives on the Policy Issues." Policy Research Working Paper. The World Bank.

Dagdeviren, H., van der Hoeven, R. and Weeks,J. (2000) "Redistribution Matters: Growth for Poverty Reduction." URL: https://www.soas.ac.uk/economics/research/workingpapers/file 28875.pdf

Datt, G. and Ravallion, M. (1998) "Why Have Some Indian States Done Better than Others at Reducing Rural Poverty?" *Economica*, vol. 65, 17-38.

Deaton, A. (2010) "Price Indexes, Inequality and the Measurement of World Poverty." *American Economic Review*. Vol. 100, N° 1, 5-34. March.

Deininger, K. and Squire, L. (1998) "New ways of looking at old issues: Inequality and growth." *Journal of Development Economics*. Vol. 57, N° 2, 259-287.

De Janvry, A. and Sadoulet, E. (1999) "Growth, Poverty, and Inequality in Latin America: A Causal Analysis, 1970-94." Conference on Social Protection and Poverty. Inter-American Development Bank. URL: http://citeseerx.ist.psu.edu/viewdoc/download?doi=10.1.1.200.20 41&rep=rep1&type=pdf.

Dijkstra, G. (2013) "The new aid paradigm: A case of policy incoherence." UN/DESA Working Paper No. 128.

Duclos, J.I., Araar, A. and Giles, J. "Chronic and Transient Poverty: Measurement and Estimation, with Evidence from China." IZA Discussion Paper No. 2078. URL: http://ftp.iza.org/dp2078.pdf

European Anti-Poverty Network (2013) "Working and Poor." EAPN Position Paper on In-Work Poverty.

Feldstein, M. (1999) "Reducing poverty, not inequality." *The Public Interest*. Number 137, Fall.

Fishlow, A. (1995) "Inequality, poverty and growth: Where do we stand?" Annual World Bank Conference on Development Economics. Washington DC, World Bank.

Foxley, A. (2004) "Successes and Failures in Poverty Eradication: Chile." Scaling Up Poverty Reduction: A Global Learning Process and Conference. Shanghai, May 25-27.

Frank, R. H. and Cook, P. J. (1995).*The Winner-Take-All Society*. The Free Press. New York.

Gentilini, U. and Sumner, A. (2012) "What Do National Poverty Lines Tell Us About Global Poverty?" IDS Working Paper, Nº. 392. URL: https://www.ids.ac.uk/files/dmfile/Wp392.pdf

Ghatak, M. (2015) "Theories of Poverty Traps and Anti-Poverty Policies." *World Bank Economic Review*. Vol. 29, suppl. 1, S77-S105.

Ghosh, J. (2010) "Poverty reduction in China and India: Policy implications of recent trends."
https://www.un.org/esa/desa/papers/2010/wp92_2010.pdf

Honohan, P. (2004) "Inequality and Poverty." *Journal of Economic Perspectives*. Vol. 18, Nº 2. Spring. 271-276.

Housseima, G. and ben Rejeb, J. (2012) "Poverty, Growth and Inequality in Developing Countries." *International Journal of Economic and Financial Issues*. Vol.2, Nº 4, 470-479.

Hu A., Hu L. and Chang Z., (2003) "China's economic growth and poverty reduction." URL:
https://www.imf.org/external/np/apd/seminars/2003/newdelhi/angang.pdf

Husmann, C. (2016) "Marginality as a Root Cause of Poverty: Identifying Marginality Hotspots in Ethiopia." *World Development*. Vol. 78, 420-435. February.

Jalan, J. and Ravallion, M. (1998) "Determinants of Transient and Chronic Poverty: Evidence from Rural China." Policy Research Working Paper. World Bank. Washington DC.

Kaldor, N. (1957) "A model of economic growth." *Economic Journal* 67, 591-624.

Kanbur, R.M. (2005) "Growth, Inequality and Poverty: Some Hard Questions." *Journal of International Affairs.* Vol. 58, No. 2, pp. 223–232.

Kanbur, R.M. (2010) "What Determines Poverty Reduction?" Foreword to *What Works for the Poorest?* Edited by Hulme, D., Lawson, D., Matin, I. and Moore, K. Practical Action Publishing.

Klasen, S. (2004) "In search of the Holy Grail: how to achieve pro-poor growth?" In *Toward Pro-poor Policies: Aid, Institutions, and Globalization,* edited by Tungodden, B., Stern, N., and Kolstad, I., World Bank / Oxford Univ. Press, Washington, Oxford, 63-94.

Komives, K. and Dijkstra, G. (2011) "The Legacy of the Poverty Reduction Strategy Processes in Latin America: Introduction and Overview." *European Journal of Development Research.* Vol. 23,181–190.

Kraay, A. (2006): "When is Growth Pro-Poor? Evidence from a Panel of Countries", *Journal of Development Economics.*Vol. 80, Issue 1, June, 198-227.

Kraay, A., and McKenzie, D. (2014) "Do Poverty Traps Exist? Assessing the Evidence." *Journal of Economic Perspectives.* Vol. 28, Nº3, 127-48.

Kuznets, S. (1955) "Economic Growth and Income Inequality" *American Economic Review,* Vol. XLV, Nº 1. March, 1-28.

Kuznets, S. (1963) "Quantitative Aspects of the Economic Growth of Nations." *Economic Development & Cultural Change.* Vol. 11, Nº 2, 1–92.

Lin, J.Y. (1992) "Rural Reforms and Agricultural Growth in China." *American Economic Review.*Vol. 82, No.1, March, 34-51.

López, J.H. and Servén, L. (2006) "A Normal Relationship? Poverty, Growth, and Inequality." World Bank Policy Research Working Paper 3814. URL: http://documents.worldbank.org/curated/en/620771468150322825/pdf/wps3814.pdf

MacEwan, A. (2007) "The Meaning of Poverty Questions of Distribution and Power." Political Economy Research Institute. University of Massachusets Amherst . Working Paper N° 148.

Milanovic, B. (1998) "Explaining the increase in inequality during the transition." World Bank Working Paper 1935. Washington DC, World Bank.

Milanovic, B. (2016a) "Why the Global 1% and the Asian Middle Class Have Gained the Most from Globalization." *Harvard Business Review.*

Milanovic, B. (2016b) *Global inequality: A new approach for the age of globalization.* Harvard University Press.

Montalvo, J.G. and Ravallion, M. (2009) "The Pattern of Growth and Poverty Reduction in China." World Bank Policy Research Working Paper 5069, World Bank.

Ogun, T.P. (2010) "Infrastructure and Poverty Reduction. Implications for Urban Development in Nigeria." UNU-WIDER Working Paper No. 2010/43.

Oswang T. (1994) "Economic development and income inequality: A nonparametric investigation of Kuznets U-curve hypothesis." *Journal of Quantitative Economics.* Vol.10, 139–153.

Piketty, T. (2014) *Capital in the Twenty-First Century.* Cambridge: Harvard University Press.

Quah, D. (2002). *One Third of the World's Growth and Inequality.*: http://eprints.lse.ac.uk/2019/1/One_Third_of_the_World's_Growth_and_Inequality.pdf

Ravallion, M. (1995) "Growth and poverty: Evidence for developing countries in the 1980s." *Economics Letters*, Elsevier, vol. 48(3-4), 411-417, June.

Ravallion, M. and Datt, G. (1996) "How Important to India's Poor Is the Sectoral Composition of Economic Growth?" *World Bank Economic Review*. Vol. 10, N° 1, 1-25.

Ravallion, M. (2012) "Why Don't We See Poverty Convergence?" *American Economic Review*. Vol. 102, N° 1, 504-23. February.

Salvatore, D. and Campano, F. (2012) "Globalization, Growth and Poverty." *Global Economy Journal*, 2012, vol. 12, issue 4, 1-15.

Sawhill, I.V. (1988) "Poverty in the U.S.: Why is it so Persistent?" *Journal of Economic Literature*. Vol. 26, No. 3, 1073-1119.

Sen, A. (2006) "Conceptualizing and Measuring Poverty." In Kanbur, R. M. and Grusky, D. V. (Eds.) *Poverty and Inequality*. Stanford University Press, Stanford, California, 30-46.

Stewart, F. (2000) "Income Distribution and Development." QEH Working Paper Number 37. U.N. The Millennium Development Goals Report 2015.

UN-Habitat, (2011) "Infrastructure for Economic Development and Poverty Reduction." http://www.uncsd2012.org/content/documents/UN-HabitatReport.pdf

Varoufakis, Y. (2014) "Egalitarianism's latest foe." *real-world economics review*, issue N° 69.

Chapter 13

The inequalities that could not happen: what the Cold War did to economics

Erik S. Reinert

This chapter attempts to flag the profound changes that underwent *economic practice* and *economic theory* during the Cold War – from 1947 to 1991 – as being at the roots of the present Inequality Crisis. Two aspects are raised. As regards the worsening inequality *between* nations it is argued that a key distinction between economic activities – at the core of the 1947 Marshall Plan – was increasingly marginalized as the tools of neo-classical economics carried the profession towards higher levels of abstraction.

As regards the worsening inequality *within* nations it is argued that a) the system of wage- setting changed from a virtual ratchet wheel effect, making wages practically irreversible without a devaluation, to a system of "internal devaluations" (whether or not recognized by that name) and b) the distinction between *financial capital* and *production capital* – which had been there since the Bible and the Quran via Medieval church fathers and persisted in Continental European economics from Marx to Schumpeter – gradually disappeared, leading to the present financialization of economic life.

During the Cold War we find that a very successful *economic practice* – starting with the 1947 Marshall Plan – dominated *economic policy* up until and including the theoretical foundation for the Maastricht Treaty and the European Single Market: Paulo Cecchini's 1988 book *The European Challenge 1992. The Benefits of a Single Market.*[1]

This period from the 1947 Marshall Plan to the Cecchini report 41 years later represents an important continuity. The insights from the Marshall Plan about the importance of manufacturing industry were built into the original foundations of the European Union, and – in that same spirit – Cecchini argued in 1988 that almost all of the benefits from the Single Market would be the result of the *increasing returns to scale* mostly found in the manufacturing sector. However, the practice of the European Union after Maastricht slowly changed to represent almost the opposite of Cecchini's vision.

Simultaneously – but completely separately from what happened in *economic policy* – at the start of the Cold War Paul Samuelson brought David Ricardo's trade theory into the core of economics with two articles in *The Economic Journal* in 1948 and 1949.[2] This theory – as did Ricardo's trade theory from 1817 – left out the contrast

---

[1] Aldershot, Wildwood House, 1988.
[2] Samuelson, Paul A. "International Trade and the Equalisation of Factor Prices", *Economic Journal*, June 1948, Vol 58., pp. 163-184, and "International Factor-Price Equalisation once again", *Economic Journal*, June 1949, Vol. 59, pp. 181-197.

between manufacturing (increasing returns and imperfect competition) on the one hand, and agriculture and other resource-based industries (diminishing returns and generally perfect competition) on the other.[3] As did David Ricardo's 1817 version, this theory defended what was in effect the essence of colonialism: manufacturing *does not* matter, i.e. the opposite of the Marshall Plan.

We can trace the 1947 ideas of the Marshall Plan paradigm in EU policy all through the 1980s, including the gradual integration of Spain while saving its manufacturing industry. But after the 1991-92 Maastricht meetings virtually all traces of George Marshall's and Paulo Cecchini's ideas are gone.[4] Economics became a profession which to a large extent came to profess that "free markets" automatically would create a world of economic harmony, a type of theory that Lionel Robbins had called a *Harmonielehre*.

In 1997 the Ricardo/Samuelson theorem saw its final ideological victory when WTO Director-General, Renato

---

[3] However, in the 10th edition of his famous textbook *Economics* (New York, McGraw-Hill, 1976) Paul Samuelson – with some qualifications – confirms the validity of the infant industry/infant economy argument for protectionism (pp. 701-703). However, his discussion is not tied to the critical increasing/diminishing returns argument lastly proved in the United States by Frank Graham's 1923 article "Some Aspects of Protection Further Considered", *Quarterly Journal of Economics* 37: 199-227.

[4] I analyze this problem in an EU publication: Reinert, Erik, "European Integration, Innovations and Uneven Economic Growth: Challenges and Problems of EU 2005", in Compañó, R, C. Pascu, A. Bianchi, J-C. Burgelman, S. Barrios, M. Ulbrich, I. Maghiros (eds.), *The Future of the Information Society in Europe: Contributions to the debate*, Seville, Spain, European Commission, JRC, Institute for Prospective Technological Studies (IPTS), 2006, pp. 124-152. Also published in The Other Canon Foundation and Tallinn University of Technology Working Papers in Technology Governance and Economic Dynamics, No 5, 2006. http://technologygovernance.eu/eng/the_core_faculty/working_papers/

Ruggiero, declared that we should unleash *"the borderless economy's potential to equalize relations among countries and regions"*.[5] This illusion – that trade under all circumstances would tend to even out economic differences among nations – is the main mechanism that since then has created an increasing inequality crisis between nations.

At the same time – as mentioned above – the qualitative separation between *financial capital* and *production capital* came to an end, best illustrated by contrasting the policies of the Federal Reserve under Marriner Eccles (1934-1948) and the European Central Bank under Mario Draghi (2011-2019). While Eccles – in a Keynesian fashion – created purchasing power, Draghi spread Bernanke's "helicopter money" with a perfect aim at financial capital, creating asset price inflation, artificially bloated stock prices, and an income distribution rapidly skewing in favor of the 99 %.[6]

For those of us who remember it – as does this author living in a NATO member country bordering the Soviet Union – the Cold War represented a constant threat. However, the theoretical foundations that came to front the theories behind the cold war ideological extremes were exceedingly abstract and too simplistic to be practical guides to human societies. The defense of the "market economy" was essentially built on tautologies

---

[5] Ruggiero, Renato, Speech in Berlin October 23, 1997 (italics mine).
[6] This is discussed in detail in Reinert, Erik "Financial Crises and Countermovements. Comparing the times and attitudes of Marriner Eccles (1930s) and Mario Draghi (2010s)", in Dimitri Papadimitriou (ed.), *Contributions of Economic Theory, Policy, Development and Finance. Essays in Honor of Jan A. Kregel*, London, Routledge, 2014, pp. 319-344.

where the conclusions to a large extent were built into the assumptions: it is not surprising that a system where all inputs are assumed to be qualitatively identical – as in Ricardo's trade theory – leads to harmonious outcomes. "Equality in, equality out." But, for political reasons these theories were highly in demand. We in the West really wanted to believe in the superiority of our system, regardless of the fanciful assumptions that accompanied the proofs of this superiority. And the economics profession delivered.[7]

The implicit conclusion when the Cold War was over in 1989 appears to have been that because communism had proven to be wrong, neoliberalism – the other political extreme – could be assumed to be perfect. The policies emanating from this belief – sometimes referred to as *triumphalism* – have since the times of Thatcher and Reagan been an important source of economic inequality. Since markets were assumed to be perfect, it became too easy to blame the poor – peoples or nations – for their poverty.

What was forgotten with the neoliberalist triumphalism after the Cold War, however, was the one important thing communism and capitalism had in common. How and why this happened – why David Ricardo's 1817 theory suddenly during the Cold War reached a level of

---

[7] I have previously written about this methodological problem in "Full Circle: Economics from Scholasticism through Innovation and back into Mathematical Scholasticism". Reflections around a 1769 price essay: "Why is it that Economics so Far has Gained so Few Advantages from Physics and Mathematics?" in *Journal of Economic Studies*, Vol. 27, No. 4/5, 2000, pp. 364-376.

popularity never before thought possible – is explained in the next section of this paper.

Figure 1 The one thing Capitalism and Communism had in common but neoliberalism forgot. The cult of manufacturing industry was a key common element between communism and capitalism during the Cold War, and the core element of the Marshall Plan. Here represented with the theorist behind this strategy, German economist Friedrich List (1789-1846) (in stamps by capitalist West Germany to the left and communist East Germany to the right). List's work entered the communist sphere through his Russian translator, Sergei Witte (1849-1915), Minister of Finance under the two last tsars.

1. Paul Samuelson and the Cold War rebirth of David Ricardo (1817)

In complete contradiction to the ruling *practice* of the Marshall Plan at the time, Paul Samuelson started building what was to become Cold War economic *theory* with two articles in *The Economic Journal* in 1948 and 1949. Communism advanced under the utopian slogan "from each according to his ability, to each according to his needs". With his renewed interpretation of David Ricardo, Paul Samuelson produced a counter-utopia:

under the standard assumptions of neo-classical economics free trade would produce a tendency towards factor-price equalization: the prices of labor and capital would tend to equalize across the planet. This became the *noble lie* of the neo-classical economics and of neoliberalism as the West faced the evils of communism.

Today's economists would naturally tend to believe that Cold War Economics – the theories that stood victorious after the 1989 Fall of the Berlin Wall – is part of a tradition that has ruled in economic science since David Ricardo's 1817 book. However, recent n-gram technology has made it possible to illustrate how David Ricardo and his theory of "comparative advantage" were virtually neglected until the Cold War.

Figure 2 The frequency of "David Ricardo" (in English) during the first 100 years after the 1817 publication of his main work, Principles of Economics, compared to that of two other, then much more famous, English economists.

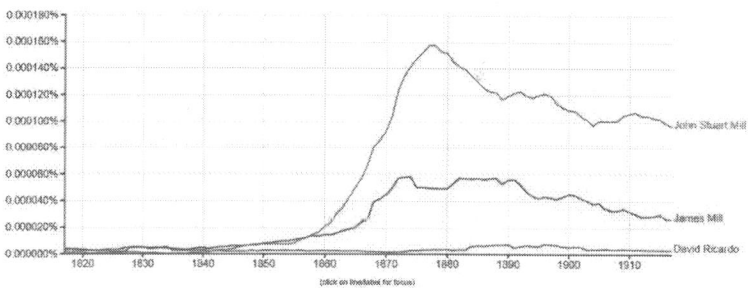

Figure 3 Frequency of the term "comparative advantage" (in English) from 1817 until today. As is clearly shown the term was very little used for the first 100 years of existence, but the use of the term started with the birth of the planned economy and exploded with the start of the Cold War in the late 1940s.

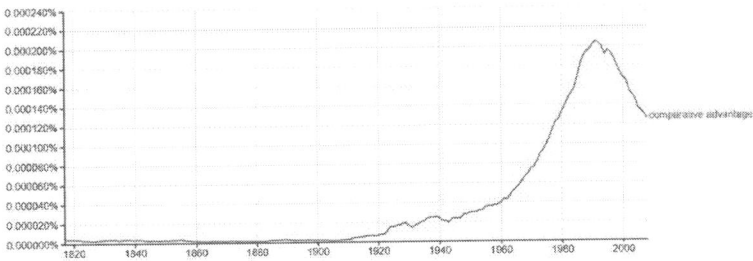

The n-grams above show how Cold War economics brought David Ricardo out of the shadows. Compared to other English economists and economic philosophers – father and son James and John Stuart Mill – David Ricardo had indeed been much less important during the first 100 years after his 1817 theory.

On the theoretical level, the Cold War (1947-1989) was fought between two *cosmo*political theories. Neither in neo-classical/neo-liberal theory nor in communism was the nation state a unit of analysis. In both *theories* the nation-state was not seen as having a place. Neo-classical economics is built on methodological individualism – the state assumed away – and also in Marxism the state was supposed to wither away as obsolete after a brief "dictatorship of the proletariat". In practice, of course, it was not the state but the rights of individuals that withered away under communism.

An important goal of science must be objectivity. Friedrich Nietzsche described objectivity as attempting to gain as many perspectives as possible on a matter:

"There is only a perspective 'seeing', only a perspective 'knowing'; and the more affects we allow to speak about one thing, the more eyes, different eyes, we can use to observe one thing, the more complete will our 'concept' of this thing, our 'objectivity', be."[8]

In this way – by seeing the world from as many angles as possible – one can potentially understand the interplay between economic contexts and economic policies: how formulas for economic development will vary in different contexts. A condition for scientific objectivity, then, is the ability to observe diversity.

With Cold War neo-classical economics, however, came a theory a) void of context, and b) with only one angle from which to see international trade. With the politics of neoliberalism arriving with Thatcher and Reagan came two myths – not only of creating free trade as the historical normality, as did Samuelson – but as part and parcel of the same problem came the myth of *laissez faire*. All seriously studying the subject have come up with the same conclusion as an American business

---

[8] Nietzsche, Friedrich, *Genealogy of Morals, third Essay*, New York, Oxford University Press, 1999 [1887].

historian did: "King Laissez Faire was not only dead; the hallowed report of his reign had all been a mistake".[9]

As economics Nobel Laureate James Buchanan wrote: "Any generalized prediction in social science implies at its basis a theoretical model that embodies elements of *an equality assumption*. If individuals differ, one from the other, in all attributes, social science becomes impossible."[10] Faced with this trade-off between "science" and "diversity", neo-classical economics chose a supposedly "scientific" path, by in effect making all human beings (perfect information) and all economic activities (perfect competition) qualitatively alike. The basic metaphor of economics became equilibrium, taken from the physics profession of the 1880s.

A great intellectual mystery of the 20th century is how, on the one hand, standardized mass production and the concomitant growing importance of increasing returns to scale under imperfect competition came to dominate economic life in the rich industrialized countries. On the other hand, sometime in the 1930s increasing returns to scale – the very basis for standardized mass production – was thrown out of economic theory because it was not compatible with equilibrium.[11] The logical thing had been to throw out equilibrium because it was not compatible

---

[9] Lively, Robert, "The American System: A Review Article", in Business History Review, Volume 29, Issue 1, March 1955, pp 81–96.
[10] Buchanan, James, *What Should Economists Do?*, Indianapolis, Liberty Press, 1979, p. 231. Italics added.
[11] For a discussion see Reinert, Erik, *How Rich Countries Got Rich... and Why Poor Countries Stay Poor*, London, Constable, 2007. New edition, New York, publicaffairs, 2019.

with the most prevalent of all economic "laws" at the time, increasing returns.

Some philosophers came to see diversity as a goal in itself. Johann Gottlob Fichte (1762-1814) was one of them. When most Germans felt that the subdivision of Germany into a large number of small states – after the 1648 Peace of Westphalia there had been about 400 of them – Fichte argued that the diversity of the many states was an advantage.

The European Union has forced a one-size-fits-all policy on its member states, while at the same time locking many of them into the straightjacket of a common currency. "Fichte sought to establish that there were no inherent limits on the extent to which a world of multiple states would come to approximate his humanitarian ideal, despite remaining a world of states".[12] With an asymmetrical economic integration tearing the union apart, Fichte's is a perspective which is probably worth re-considering in Europe, and also at the global level.

2. The 1848 moment and the balance of countervailing powers

1848 produced both Marx and Engels' *Communist Manifesto* and English liberalist John Stuart Mill's *Principles of Political Economy*. The same year also gave us an early work in the tradition of the German Historical School, Bruno Hildebrand's *Economics of the Present and the Future (Die National-Oekonomie der Gegenwart und*

---

[12] Isaac Nakhimovsky in the introduction to Fichte, *Addresses to the German Nation*, Indianapolis, IN, Hackett Publishing, 2013. p. xvi.

Zukunft). Bruno Hildebrand (1812–1878) was an early representative of the German historical school of economics. All three books gave support to strategies of industrialization. As opposed to David Ricardo, the great liberalist Mill was a strong supporter of "infant industry protection" for countries that were not yet industrialized, and Hildebrand strongly criticized the theories of Ricardo. One of his criticisms was that Ricardo's theories were *cosmopolitical,* they did not consider the fact that different nations might be facing very different contexts. At the time it was obvious that just as medicines prescribed for a person should be tailored to the condition of the patient, economic policies should be tailored to the context of a nation. In this period in the United States, *snake oil* was the name given to fake cure-all medicines. The same criticism could be made against Ricardian theory at the time, as well as against today's neoliberalist theories.

We shall come back to this problem when we discuss the issue of the *level of abstraction* in economic theory, and the possible rent-seeking that may occur if this abstraction is too high. Manchester Liberalism – the 18th century version of today's neo-liberalism – was not really a brainchild of David Ricardo (1772–1823), but rather of Richard Cobden (1804–1865). An n-gram comparing the two authors shows Cobden passing Ricardo in mentions already in the early 1840s, and by the 1880s Cobden has about six times as many mentions as Ricardo. It is only 100 years later – in the late 1940s – that Ricardo again passes the number of mentions that Cobden has.

The hatred towards the state that we later saw during the Cold War was already there in Manchester Liberalism. John Bright (1811-1889) – Richard Cobden's partner in the free trade movement – was convinced that "Most of our evils arise from legislative interference".[13] Here we find ourselves at the start of the school also represented by Ronald Reagan, when he pronounced in 1986 that "The nine most terrifying words in the English language are: I'm from the government and I'm here to help." In times of the Corona virus these statements come across as particularly misplaced.

The Manchester School contrast sharply with what was to be become, in Bright's lifetime, a very different approach in Germany. In 1872 German economists, among them Hildebrand, founded the *Verein für Socialpolitik*. This association, with their annual meetings, would bring forth the theories and practical policies for what became the European Welfare State. By 1932, when the *Verein* ceased functioning, 188 volumes of proceedings – organized according to annual themes – had been published.

The reason for organizing the *Verein für Socialpolitik* was a much discussed problem which at the time was called *Die Soziale Frage* (*The Social Question*). This was an *inequality crisis* similar to our own. In the first founding meeting of the Verein, in the Fall of 1872, Gustav Schmoller (1838-1917) expressed the worries of the time in the following way:

---

[13] C. A. Vince, *John Bright,* [1898] Kessinger Publishing, 2005, p. 35.

We believe the healthiest and most normal society can be expressed by a ladder containing rungs between different existences, depicting easy access from one step to another. Today's society threatens more and more to look like a ladder which grows fast at the top and at the bottom, but where the middle steps increasingly fall out, and where there is solid hold only at the very top and at the very bottom" (Verein für Socialpolitik 1873:5).

Over the next 60 years the *Verein* was to build the institutional design of generalized European welfare, and the prescription was copied in many other countries. The starting point in the *Verein's* discussions was practical problems at hand, and whether the private sector or the public sector would be the best agent to solve a specific problem was part of a pragmatic discussion. In the United Kingdom the 1942 Beveridge Report played a similar role of creating a holistic view of the social agenda.

Today both Schmoller's ladder metaphor and William Beveridge's "five giants" – want, squalor, ignorance, disease and idleness – ring a bell of recognition, more than ever since World War II. New is particularly that the United States – for so long the land of opportunity – seems to suffer from the same European-type problems from which the country had seemed free except during the 1930s.

The two cosmopolitical ideologies that came to fight the Cold War – communism and neoliberalism – were already taking shape during the latter part of the 19th century. However, English economic theory at the time – represented by Cambridge economists Alfred Marshall,

John Neville Keynes (John Maynard Keynes' father) and Herbert Somerton Foxwell[14] – were far more experienced-based and pragmatic than English theories had with David Ricardo. y. They were all free from what Schumpeter called "the Ricardian vice", building extremely abstract theories and drawing policy applications from these, leaving out key complexities of real life. These English economists were closer to the German tradition.[15] The Ricardian vice was, however, to come back with a vengeance during the Cold War. As we shall see later, in section 4, with it came what I have dubbed the "Krugmanian vice": having models that better describe how the real world works, but refusing to recommend them in practical policies.

Gustav Schmoller – already mentioned above as the founder of the *Verein für Sozialpolitik* – clearly saw that both political extremes were unfit for practical purposes. In his 1897 inaugural speech as *Rektor* of the University of Berlin, Schmoller expressed the hope that the world had seen the end of the two ideological extremes, Manchester Liberalism (today's neoliberalism) and communism. His characterization of both these ideologies was harsh:

> "...the naïve optimism of "laissez-faire" and the childish and frivolous appeal to revolution, the naïve hope that the tyranny

---

[14] Herbert Foxwell, in his 110 page introduction to a book by Anton Menger, delivered the fiercest attack ever on the economics of David Ricardo. Foxwell, Herbert S., "Introduction" to Anton Menger, *The Right to the Whole Produce of Labour*, London: Macmillan, 1899.
[15] Unfortunately neo-classical economics came to be more based on Alfred Marshall's appendices in his 1890 *Principles of Economics* than on his texts in the same book and elsewhere, i.e. the necessary qualifications for these abstractions in the appendices were left out.

of the proletariat would lead to world happiness, increasingly showed their real nature, they were *twins of an ahistorical rationalism"*[16] (Schmoller 1897, my translation, italics added).

In practice, the ideological extremes of "the irrational twins" opened up for a wide spectrum of possible economic policies. In Western Europe Germany's *soziale Marktwirtschaft* (social market economy)[17] and Sweden's *Middle Way*[18] were successful models navigating the broad spectrum of opportunities between the "irrational twins".

The 20th century Swedish model of capitalism expresses John Kenneth Galbraith's balance of countervailing powers in successful capitalism: big business, big government, and big labor.[19] Swedish economists Gunnar Myrdal (1898-1987) – who had produced a theory where vicious and virtuous circles were dominating forces – and pragmatic economist Johan Åkerman (1896-1992) also provided the theoretical background for the Swedish model. That country's industrial policy after WW II is didactically interesting because for a very long period it

---

[16] Schmoller, Gustav, *Wechselnde Theorien und feststehende Wahrheiten im Gebiete der Staats- und Socialwissenschaften und die heutige deutsche Volkswirthschaftslehre: Rede bei Antritt des Rectorats gehalten in der Aula der Königlichen Friedrich-Wilhelms-Universität am 15. October 1897*, Berlin, W. Büxenstein, 1897. Italics added.

[17] Economist Alfred Müller-Armack used the term in a 1947 book, also defining it as a Third Way, but it became popular later.

[18] Childs, Marquis William, *Sweden; the middle way*, New Haven, Yale University Press, 1936.

[19] John Kenneth Galbraith, *The New Industrial State*, Boston, Houghton Mifflin, 1967.

was dominated by just three individuals, industrialist Marcus Wallenberg (1899-1982), also the main shareholder of Stockholms Enskilda Bank, Schumpeterian economist Erik Dahmén (1916-2005) who worked for the bank for several decades, and Labour Party politician Gunnar Sträng (1906-1992). Sträng held ministerial posts in the Swedish government from 1947 to 1976, the last 21 years as Minister of Finance.

Industrialist Wallenberg and his economic advisor Dahmén[20] - who had been working on "development blocks"[21] – had lunch in the bank every Wednesday. Wallenberg and Sträng were also in close contact, seemingly also unofficially, to discuss economic policy. The result is what economists of the French regulation School refer to as "the Fordist wage regime".[22] The fruits of innovations and productivity growth were divided between capital and labor: roughly would 4 per cent productivity increase give 4 per cent wage increase. Theever-increasing real wages made labor increasingly more expensive in relationship to capital while increasing demand was assured. This provided a very strong incentive for industrial mechanization, and in inflationary periods – like in the 1970s – there is no doubt that the combination of ever-increasing wages, sometimes combined with negative cost of capital for the industrialists, helped mechanization. Wages developed in

---

[20] This story was told by Erik Dahmén at the 1991 Schumpeter conference in Stockholm.

[21] Similar to what François Perroux called "growth poles" and what Michael Porter later came to call "clusters".

[22] Boyer, Robert, "Development and régulation theory", in Reinert, Erik, Jayati Ghosh and Rainer Kattel, *Handbook of Alternative Theories of Economic Development,* Cheltenham, Edward Elgar, 2016, pp. 352-385.

the industrial export sector, then spread to the whole economy, also e.g. to barbers – who had small possibilities for productivity improvement – and to the public sector as well.

Strangely enough this wage policy resulted in high real growth also in Italy, although here the union-driven wage policy appeared to be irresponsible.[23] During the 1970s and 1980s, I ran a small industrial company in Northern Italy. With a certain unwillingness I have come to think that the communist threat – in spite of what it did to economic theory – actually served the purpose of increasing the capital-labor ratio in industry and services and thus creating labor-saving innovations, not only in manufacturing but also exemplified by containers and self-service supermarkets. History would prove David Ricardo wrong when he assumed that the natural wage level would be subsistence![24]

In the US the existence of free land at the Western frontier had kept wages up,[25] and later in the 19th century, the "muckraking" started by American journalists and the theories of Thorstein Veblen kept any attempt of

---

[23] The details are explained in my chapter "Financial Crises and Countermovements. Comparing the times and attitudes of Marriner Eccles (1930s) and Mario Draghi (2010s)", cited above.

[24] When David Ricardo, in the third edition of his Principles (1821), added a new chapter "On Machinery", he assumed that the sole effect of machinery would be to bring down prices. In Reinert (1994) I have discussed the different ways that technological change may spread in the economy, this mechanism – which I call the "classical" mechanism – being one ("Catching-up from way behind - A Third World perspective on First World history" in Fagerberg, Jan, Bart Verspagen and Nick von Tunzelmann (eds.) *The Dynamics of Technology, Trade, and Growth*, Aldershot, Edward Elgar, 1994, pp. 168-197.

[25] Sombart, Werner, *Why is there no socialism in the United States?*, White Plains, NY, M.E.Sharpe, [1905] 1976.

creating feudal-like traditions and institutions – such as in the Europe the immigrants had left – at bay. In Europe, however, wages historically had lagged. But with industrialization came political pressures from the left that lifted wages.

Sometimes these came at the cost of inflation, but they always tended to increase the relative price of labor compared to the cost of capital. Wages came to be locked as in a *ratchet wheel*, movements upwards were possible, movements backwards were not.

The adjustment to the ratchet wheel system came in the form of devaluations: countries with "irresponsible" wage policies were forced to devalue. These devaluations made the wage level responsible again, and they would also automatically devalue the national debt (which tended to be in the national currency). In my view this combination of wage pressures combined with devaluations must be seen as a key mechanism producing the golden years of Western capitalism. In Europe neoliberalism carried with it the end of these mechanisms: first of all with "austerity" came the idea of "internal devaluation" (whether or not called by that name): where nominal wages were often cut, and secondly the Euro made the after all well-functioning adjustment mechanism of devaluations come to an end. While "old-fashioned" devaluations devalued capital and wages alike, internal devaluations directly reduce wages as a percentage of GDP, thus benefitting the capital sector at the cost of labor.

With the exchange rate flexibility gone for the Euro countries, the only mechanism to adjust economic mismatches between countries ended up being moving people: Greeks and Italians had to migrate, creating political tensions in the European Union between the "responsible North" and the "irresponsible South". Few, if anyone, now care to look into the political background for this "irresponsibility": Both in Italy and in Greece the inflation-creating mechanisms were at the time – probably correctly – seen as the only political option in order to save democracy from communist parties with a very strong popular support.

3. The simple dichotomy that separates rich from poor countries

In 1613 Italian economist Antonio Serra produced a theory presenting two dichotomies, between the *real economy* and the *financial economy*, and between activities subject to *diminishing returns* to scale – where one factor of production is limited by an act of nature (agriculture, mining, and fisheries) – and *increasing returns* to scale, where there are no limits to how costs can fall as the volume of production increases. The dichotomy between *the real economy* and *money by itself (mammon)* had been there since biblical times, but the distinction between increasing and diminishing returns is new with Antonio Serra.[26]

---

[26] See Serra, Antonio, *A Short Treatise on the Wealth and Poverty of Nations [1613]*, edited and with a foreword by Sophus A. Reinert, London, Anthem, 2011 & Patalano, Rosario and Sophus A Reinert (eds), *Antonio Serra and the Economics of Good Government*, Basingstoke, Palgrave Macmillan, 2016.

This is the first theoretical observation as to why – as former World Bank Chief Economist Justin Yifu Lin put it very succinctly – "Except for a few oil-exporting countries, no countries have ever gotten rich without industrialization first".[27]

In my view, the mechanism suggested by Serra is still the main reason for the income gap between rich and poor countries. In 19th century English economics one side of the argument was strongly present: the dismal science created by Reverend Malthus in 1798 was based on diminishing returns, and fifty years later John Stuart Mill was acutely aware of its consequences. Four decades later than Mill, Alfred Marshall, the founder of neo-classical economics – came up with a plan that would have pleased classical development economists:

"One simple plan would be the levying of a tax by the community on their own incomes, or on the production of those goods which obey the Law of Diminishing Returns, and devoting the tax to a bounty on the production of those goods with regard to which the Law of Increasing Returns acts sharply."[28]

Here Marshall describes what all presently wealthy countries have done, mostly through the protection of increasing returns activities through tariffs, ever since England in the 1400s started to tax the export of raw wool, while at the same time subsidizing the local

[27] Lin, Justin Yifu, *New Structural Economics: A Framework for Rethinking Development and Policy*, Washington DC, World Bank Publications, 2012, p. 350.
[28] Marshall, Alfred, *Principles of Economics*, London, Macmillan, 1890, p. 452.

production of woollen cloth. Although the tools differed, this was the essence of import-substitution industrialization that took some non-Western countries out of economic colonialism. It was also the core of the Marshall Plan, a plan which in its essence addressed the intimate relationship between *economic structure, possible population density,* and GDP per capita.

In early 1947, worries grew in Washington that an impoverished Germany – where manufacturing industry had been forbidden in the allied zones under the Morgenthau Plan – would fall an easy prey to the Soviet Union.[29] US President Truman therefore sent former president Herbert Hoover on a fact-finding mission to Germany. One powerful sentence in Hoover's report of March 18 zeroed in on the basic problem:

"There is the illusion that the New Germany left after the annexations can be reduced to a 'pastoral state' [i.e. a country without industry]. It cannot be done unless we exterminate or move 25,000,000 out of it."[30]

Hoover understood that the population density of a country is determined by its economic structure. Industrialization makes it possible to dramatically increase the population-carrying capacity of a nation. "Exterminate" was a very strong word to use after the

---

[29] I have described the mechanisms behind this in Reinert, Erik, "Increasing Poverty in a Globalised World: Marshall Plans and Morgenthau Plans as Mechanisms of Polarisation of World Incomes" in Chang, Ha-Joon (ed.), *Rethinking Economic Development*, London, Anthem, 2003, pp. 453–478.
[30] Quoted in Baade, Fritz, "Gruß und Dank an Herbert Hoover", *Weltwirtschaftliches Archiv*, 74(1), 1–6, 1955.

horrors of the Second World War, and everyone understood that there was no place where 25 million Germans could be sent. Re-industrialization was the only option.

The lesson from the Marshall Plan is that only extreme danger, in this case a communist takeover of Germany, will convince the West temporarily to give up what has been called "free-trade imperialism". As the memory of the Marshall Plan faded, this wisdom disappeared with the economics of the Cold War, giving birth to the kind of Ricardian / Samuelsonian free trade neo-colonialist ideology that still dominates.

4. Levels of abstraction and assumption-based rent-seeking

In neo-classical economics, rent-seeking – the practice of manipulating public policy as a strategy for increasing profits – is a serious sin. But, if the world actually functions as outlined in the section above, what if national wealth is actually a kind of rent produced by dynamic imperfect competition which is not available in all economic activities? The fact that the most efficient farmers in the world – in the US and EU – normally need heavy subsidies and/or protection is a sign confirming this. Nations engaged in agriculture alone become – in this perspective – the only rent-free societies.

History has abundantly shown that the above statement of Justin Yifu Lin is correct. If neo-classical mainstream economics *pretends* that this distinction between increasing and diminishing returns activities does not exist – if the theory is placed at such a high level of abstraction that there is no room for this distinction – then, I would argue, this high level of abstraction is a tool for massive rent-seeking by the industrialized countries, a type of rent-seeking that is a major source of the present global inequality crisis. In other words, high levels of abstraction are *per se* sources of assumption-based rent-seeking. Assuming away differences increases the level of abstraction of our understanding.

In some sports – like boxing and wrestling – the existence of weight categories opens up for games that are perceived as much fairer than if no categories existed. The outcome of a match between a feather-weight boxer and a heavy-weight one is fairly predictable. So, if we imagine that all weight categories would be eliminated from boxing and wrestling, most sportsmen – those in the lower weight categories – would not be able to participate in their sport any longer. A degree of fairness is provided by establishing different categories. One could say that if boxing eliminated weight categories – if all boxers, regardless of their weight, were seen as being "alike" – this would create a "winner takes it all" for the heaviest of them. The elimination of qualitative differences would be a source of rent-seeking for heavyweight boxers, as it is for heavy-weight industrial nations towards poor countries.

The essence of colonialism was the prohibition of manufacturing activities in these areas. This becomes clear when now long forgotten economic bestsellers are studied.[31] Joshua Gee's 1720 book *The Trade and Navigation of Great Britain Considered* is just one example of this. Gee's book became immensely popular, appearing in at least 20 editions before 1780, in English in London, Glasgow and Dublin, in French translations published in London, Amsterdam and Geneva, and further translations into Dutch, Spanish, and German.[32]

One factor leading both to the geographical spread of Gee's book, and to its later oblivion is probably that Gee not only was very straightforward when he described English interest in protecting their manufacturing industry, he was also unusually honest about the intention of colonialism being the opposite, to hinder manufacturing there:

> "That all Negroes shall be prohibited from weaving or spinning or combing of Wool, or manufacturing hats, ...Indeed, if they set up manufactures, and the Government afterwards shall be under a Necessity of stopping their progress, we must not expect that it will be done with the same ease that now it may."

---

[31] Reinert, Erik S. & Fernanda Reinert, "33 Economic Bestsellers published before 1750", in *The European Journal of the History of Economic Thought*, Vol. 25 (6), 1206–1263, 2018.

[32] Gee, Joshua, *The trade and navigation of Great-Britain considered: shewing that the surest way for a nation to increase in riches, is to prevent the importation of such foreign commodities as may be rais'd at home. That this Kingdom is capable of raising within itself, and its colonies, materials for employing all our poor in those manufactures, which we now import from such of our neighbours who refuse the admission of ours. Some account of the commodities each country we trade with take from us, and what we take from them; with observations on the Balance.* London, Sam. Buckley, 1729.

Since the Irish at the time were subject to the same kind of policies, it must have been clear to them that the statement above is not as racist as it appears at first sight. In 1779 John Hely-Hutchinson, then Provost of Trinity College, Dublin, anonymously published *Commercial Restraints of Ireland considered in a series of letters addressed to a Noble Lord.*[33] The English authorities thought Hely-Hutchinson's book protesting against the prohibition to export woolen manufactures from Ireland so insidious that the book became the last book in the United Kingdom to be publicly burned by the hangman.

Many economists have returned to Antonio Serra's and Alfred Marshall's discussion of increasing and diminishing returns. All come to the same conclusion, a conclusion which does not enter into the sphere of economic policy. In a 1981 article, Paul Krugman again – once – raises the issue.[34] He reaches the same conclusion as Antonio Serra and Alfred Marshall, the country producing under increasing returns benefits, noting "that in addition to exporting capital, the industrial region might, in the second stage of growth, begin importing labor" – Krugman specifically mentions that this was noted both by Hobson and Lenin.[35]

The interesting question here is *why* these insights are kept away from the policy level. Above I have referred to this as the "Krugmanian Vice": economic theorists

---

[33] Dublin, William Hallhead, 1779. For the reproduction of a second edition (Dublin, M. H. Gill & Son, 1882), see
http://www.gutenberg.org/files/38841/38841-h/38841-h.htm
[34] "Trade, accumulation, and uneven development", in *Journal of Development Economics* (8), 1981, pp. 149-161.
[35] English economist John Hobson inspired Lenin's theory of imperialism.

produce many kinds of models, but those models that would favor poor countries are not employed in practical policies. This is not how a scientific community is supposed to work: if this had been seen from another planet – free from political noise – it is as if a political racket sorts out the theories that will be employed by the OECD and the Washington Institutions – inevitably those in favor of a Samuelsonian neo-colonialism – and those that will be discarded. Apart from the ideological contributions from a myriad of "think-tanks",[36] I am suggesting this is the outcome of Veblenian "vested interests" coming together, rather than "conspiracies". The result of this, however, is in line with Herbert Hoover's theory above: massive migrations from poor non-industrial countries to North America and Northern Europe. If North Americans and Europeans want to diminish immigration – and let most people live in the country where they were born, which most prefer – they will have to reinvent the logic of Herbert Hoover.[37]

The assumption that "all economic activities are alike" creates a blind eye to the fact that all industrialized countries de-facto collect rents based on this assumption. Allowing models separating increasing returns activities from diminishing returns activities would clearly add an element of fairness to world trade.

---

[36] A recent article by Quinn Slobodian addresses the role of think-tanks in this process
 https://www.theguardian.com/commentisfree/2019/nov/11/democracy-defenders-economic-freedom-neoliberalis m
[37] See https://oecd-development-matters.org/2018/10/19/africa-time-to-rediscover-the-economics-of-population-density -and-development/.

Although not expressed in terms of rent-seeking – a recent term – 19th century US economists understood that David Ricardo's trade theory was working against them at the moment, but would be working in their favor if they managed to create the same economic conditions England had.

Joseph Dorfman, the historian of US economic thought, expresses this 19th century position of the United States particularly well, partly using quotes from List and partly using his own words as follows:

"...free trade is the ideal, and United States will proclaim the true cosmopolitan principles when the time is ripe. This will be when the United States has a hundred million people and the seas are covered with her ships; when American industry attains the greatest perfection, and New York is the greatest commercial emporium and Philadelphia the greatest manufacturing city in the world; and when no earthly power can longer resist the American Stars, then our children's children will proclaim freedom of trade throughout the world, by land and sea."[38]

In this prophetic statement, the English strategy for growth was recreated. The United States indeed had the courage to follow the strategy that England had followed, and not the one she preached at the moment. As a result of this, in the end the United States surpassed the old master, England. This required what John Stuart Mill in 1848 would call "infant industry protection", a level of

---

[38] Dorfman, Joseph, *The Economic Mind in the American Civilization*, Vol 2., London, Harrap, 1947, p. 581.

protection that for most of the 19th century would be the main income for the US Federal Government.

Figure 4 Customs duties as share of the US Federal Budget 1796 to the present.

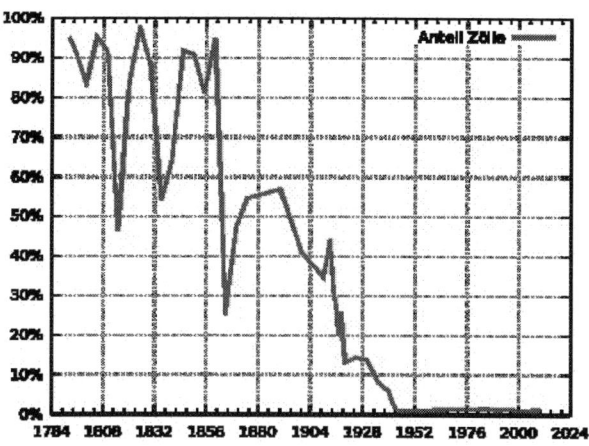

5. The collapse of the balance of countervailing powers and of the ratchet wheel effect

During the triumphalism following the 1989 fall of the Berlin Wall, and the political reign of the Washington Institutions, these previously mentioned "middle ways" were in practice outlawed. In his review of Thomas Piketty's *Capital in the Twenty-First Century*, James Galbraith – in my view correctly – criticized the author for not seeing the role of minimum wages and labor unions in the rising inequalities within nations.[39]

---

[39] Galbraith, James, "*Kapital* for the 21st Century", in *Dissent Magazine*, spring 2014.

In this section we shall look at the effect of an economic crisis under two crisis scenarios, the 1930s and the 2000s. If the ratchet wheel mechanism – the irreversibility of wages – were functioning, we would expect an economic crisis to show up as shrinking sales, higher unemployment, and obviously falling profits.

This is the result arrived at by German economist Wilhelm Krelle[40] in the figure below. During the crisis in the 1930s in the United States, Krelle's data shows us that the percentage of GDP going to labor *increased,* meaning that capital income decreased more than labor income during the crisis. This would be the case if – in spite of high unemployment – the workers who kept their jobs tended to keep their wages. With the ratchet wheel of trade unionism intact, profits – rather than wage level – would be the factor suffering first during a recession.

The dramatic losers in the 1930s, however, were the farmers who had no market power or unions to protect them. Comparing the above figure of recent data with the record of the crisis in the 1930s it would seem that the loss of union power has – in later decades – put workers in the same position that farmers used to be in in the 1930s.

---

[40] Krelle, Wilhelm, *Verteilungstheorie.* Tübingen, Mohr, 1962.

Figure 5 United States. Percentage of Pre-Tax income by Sector 1909–1951
- Top: share of total US income from interests, dividends, and rents.
- Middle: share of total US income from the self-employed (mostly farmers).
- Bottom: Share of total US income from salaries and wages.

Total 100%. All incomes pre-tax. Social transfers have been added salaries and wages. Profits retained in companies are not included.

Source: Krelle, page 12.

The graph of what happened in the 1930s – which has a certain logic to it – contrasts sharply with what happened during the crisis in the early 2000s. The figure below shows the share of labor in the output of the non-farm business sector in the United States from 1947 to 2016.

The recessions clearly mark the start of sometimes precipitous falls in the share of labor. This appears to show an entirely new ball game, where the ratchet wheel effect appears to be gone.

In the 1930s the ratchet wheel effect was no product of the market, but of political decisions. If we look at Secretary of Labor Robert Reich's failed attempts to raise minimum wages in the 1990s during the Clinton administration, it was clear that the vast majority of US economists at the time wanted "the market" to set wages. Cold War economics had brought back the social Darwinism of the American past[41] and – this time around – in a sense proves that David Ricardo was right when he predicted that the "natural" wage level would be subsistence.

Comparing the philosophy behind the careful and gradual economic integration of Spain, Portugal and Greece into the EU in the 1980s on the one hand, and the 1 May 2004 integration eastwards on the other, we can observe a qualitative quantum leap towards the worse. The 2004 integration destroyed most of what was left of the ratchet wheel effect in the European labor markets.

These negative consequences of the 2004 enlargement of the European Union were predictable, as my Estonian colleague Rainer Kattel and I argued already from 2004.[42] A free trade shock had, since the fall of the Berlin Wall

---

[41] Hofstadter, Richard, *Social Darwinism in American Thought, 1860–1915*, Philadelphia, University of Pennsylvania Press, 1944.

[42] Reinert, Erik S. and Rainer Kattel, "The Qualitative Shift in European Integration: Towards Permanent Wage Pressures and a 'Latin-Americanization' of Europe?" *Praxis Working Papers* No. 17, Praxis Foundation, Estonia, 2004. Downloadable at: https://ideas.repec.org/p/pra/mprapa/47909.html & by the same authors "European Eastern Enlargement as Europe's Attempted Economic Suicide." *The Other Canon Foundation and Tallinn University of Technology Working Papers in Technology Governance and Economic Dynamics* No. 14, 2007.

and the subsequent disintegration of the COMECON trade pact, led to a massive de-industrialization of the former communist countries. On May 1, 2004, these same countries became subject to a new free trade shock with the European Union. In a situation where "losers" in Germany were sweeping the streets of Frankfurt for € 10 an hour while the most successful workers in Estonia were mounting cell phones at € 1 an hour, a minimum sense of economic gravity would predict that this would put enormous pressures on wages in Western Europe.

Figure 6 Labor's share of output in the non-farm business sector, in the first quarter 1947 through third quarter 2016

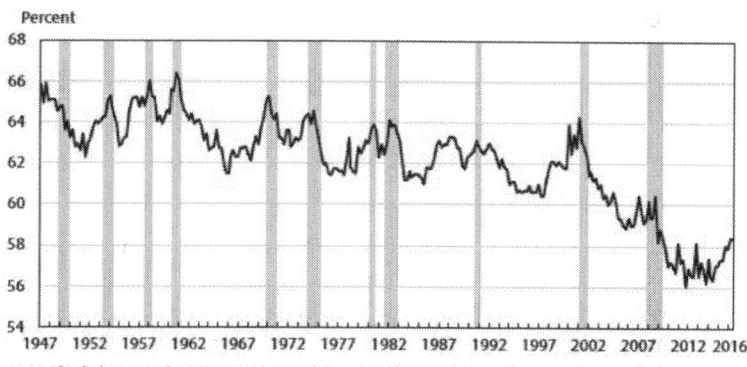

Note: Shaded areas indicate recessions, as determined by the National Bureau of Economic Research.
Source: U.S. Bureau of Labor Statistics.

That English construction workers – and others – lost around 30 per cent of their real wages due to labor migration from the East was one reason for Brexit. In Norway we could observe an interesting case of technological retrogression[43] with the arrival of cheap labor in the construction industry. Building sites with less than 5-6 floors discontinued the use of lifts: it was cheaper to have Polish workers carry the cement up ladders than to install lifts. This migration of Polish workers to the West had curious effects in other Eastern European countries. Asking, on a visit to Western Ukraine, about the situation there, one response was that the only good news was that construction workers in Western Ukraine now got well-paying jobs in Poland. About a year later, on a visit to Moldova, I was told that the good news there was that many Moldovan workers found well-paying jobs in the Ukraine. Here we can observe an interesting version of what Hollis Chenery and the World Bank once promoted as the "trickle-down effect" in development economics. In this case wealth did not trickle down, instead a reduction of real wages in the wealthy countries trickles down – via migration to lift the wages in poor countries in what clearly is not a positive-sum game.

6. Beggar-thy-neighbor in a novel fashion: imposing overvalued exchange rates as an economic policy

The term beggar-thy-neighbor refers to policies that a country enacts to favor its own economy in ways that, in turn, actually worsen the economic problems of other countries. The impact of such policies may make "a beggar" out of neighboring countries.

One typical example would be devaluations in countries that are not really under heavy pressure in order to

---

[43] Endresen, Sylvi, *Technological Retrogression*, London, Anthem, forthcoming 2021.

increase their "competitiveness". Sweden had several devaluations starting in the late 1970s that would – at least according to neighboring Finland at the time – fit the term beggar-thy-neighbor, particularly because the two countries were competing internationally in many of the same industries, such as paper.

The European Union brought with it a new form of beggar-thy-neighbor policies – which in my definition also fits the term rent-seeking – by creating a system that overvalues the exchange-rates of other countries. The effect is similar to the examples above, with the difference that in this case the strong country – instead of devaluing its own currency – manages to increase the value of other nations' currencies.

We saw the first sign of this during the German reunification, the *Wiedervereinigung*. At the time of the 1990 monetary unification of East and West Germany, the value of the currency of the two countries – both called Mark – had drifted apart. At the time the market exchange rate was as low as 4,3 Ostmark to one Westmark, and the black market rates were much higher in favor of the Westmark. In spite of this many items, such as savings, were converted at the rate of 2 Ostmark to 1 Westmark. This favored the savings of the East Germans. However, running wages were converted at an exchange rate of 1 to 1. This of course gave an initial burst of increased purchasing power in the East, but – in spite of probably being the most high-tech of the Soviet Block – and in spite of some large industrial relocations eastward, the technologically inferior East German industry could not survive the cost shock. In spite of

Germany doing all the right things in terms of building infrastructure, production – and with it, people – moved to the West. It might be argued that keeping wages high in East Germany would prevent migration to West Germany. In effect this policy might have slowed migration a bit, but definitely making migration much stronger in the medium term than it would have been using a more realistic exchange rate. The destructive long-term effects of an over-valued currency were soon obvious, but still the same mistake was systematically repeated in the EU.

At the end of section 2 I explained how – as a result of political pressures – countries in Southern Europe had developed high inflation economies. When this kind of inflationary pressures becomes part of the system it is virtually impossible to stop it overnight. Part of this story is also that the Euro originally was intended only for the strong currencies of the European Union, such as the German Mark and the Dutch Guilder. It is said that German chancellor Helmuth Kohl – who was also in power during the *Wiedervereinigung* exchange rate policy with East Germany – when travelling back from a meeting in Maastricht, decided also to do the countries in the poorer periphery in Europa "a favor" by including them in the Euro. As with the East German wages, the initial reaction was positive. The high-inflation countries benefitted short-term from low interest rates, but as the underlying inflationary pressures continued, the countries in what to the European Union later became "the irresponsible South" saw their manufacturing industries losing out due to the wage drift that could not be stopped instantly. The basic mechanism had been the same as the one that came to destroy much of the industry in former East Germany: German rent-seeking improving its own "competitiveness" by creating mechanisms overvaluing the currencies of other nations.

In a second round of events, the Southern EU periphery saw debts, and the costs of servicing those debts, growing fast. This situation recalls a term describing the situation of Germany in the 1920s and 1930s: Greece and Italy are being forced into *Zinsknechtschaft*, or "debt serfdom". Having unlearned Keynes' "paradox of saving", the European Union now forces budget savings in Italy than can only further the shrinking of the economy.[44] The disastrous consequences of the Covid 19 in Italy can be partly explained by the brutal savings forced on Italy under neoliberalism. The governments of Berlusconi and Monti cut the health budgets by 25 Billion Euro between 2010 and 2015, while other governments cut another 15 Billion between 2015 and 2019.[45] The German health budget per capita is now almost the double of that of Italy.

7. Separating the real economy from the financial economy

---

[44] Kregel, Jan, "Growth and the Single Currency", 2018, pp. 55-73 in the following
http://documenti.camera.it/leg18/resoconti/commissioni/stenografici/pdf/14c14/audiz2/audizione/2018/09/25/leg.18.stencomm.data20180925.U1.com14c14.audiz2.audizione.0003.pdf (in English)
[45] See my article https://www.lafionda.org/2020/05/19/litalia-e-il-coronavirus/

Journalists coming home from abroad with reports based on their conversations with local taxi drivers is an old joke. A couple of years ago, on a job for the EU research center (JRC) in Seville, I had a very interesting talk on the way from the Seville airport to the hotel. On a very general question from me, the driver – who did not know I was an economist – started to paint a broad picture of what was going on in the Spanish economy: "You see", he said, "The European Central Bank under Mario Draghi is printing a lot of money, and this money is invested in assets like apartments" [he did not use the term "asset-price inflation", but that was really what he referred to]. "This makes it impossible for normal people like myself to afford buying an apartment. In addition to that", he said, "while the rent of an apartment goes up with the price of apartments, real wages for people like myself are shrinking. So we are in a double squeeze". Austerity for the poor and helicopter money accurately aimed at the rich have been the 21st century approach to solving economic crises.

A key element in Western culture has been the prevention of hoarding. In other words, making sure money was circulating, not idle. The biblical term for idle money is *mammon*. We find a clear expression of this principle in the Bible (Mathew 25; 14-30), where servants are given money (*talents*), and, later, the servant who has simply buried the money – instead of putting it in circulation – is severely punished. Below we shall see how 14th century monetary theorist Nicolas Oresme testifies to the importance of keeping money in circulation in order for the real economy – and the very process of life – to keep going. We also find this issue raised by Martin Luther (1483-1546), whose measure of good and bad was "does it serve life?". Luther lived in a time where a lot of money was buried in the ground instead of being in circulation.[46] In the US tradition we find this focus on *the process of life* in John Dewey, and in economics with Thorstein Veblen and Clarence Ayres.[47]

Continental European economics has always continued this in a sense Biblical separation of the *financial economy* from the *real economy*. We find this from Marx (in volume 3 of Das Kapital) on the left of the political axis to the conservative Schumpeter on the right. Figure 7 below renders Schumpeter's idea of separating the *money* (Rechenpfennige/accounting units) from what you can buy for money in the *real economy* (Güterwelt, the world of goods and services).

Figure 7 Separating the Real Economy in a Schumpeterian fashion, Güterwelt = the world of goods (and services), Rechenpfennige = accounting units. The EU solution to the financial crisis has been to create more

---

[46] See Rössner, Philipp Robinson, "Burying Money. The Monetary Origins of Luther's Reformation", *The Other Canon Foundation and Tallinn University of Technology Working Papers in Technology Governance and Economic Dynamics*, No. 54, 2013.
[47] Both of these great pioneers [John Dewey and Thorstein Veblen] recognized this process as (in Veblen's words) "'the life process' of mankind, a process that runs in unbroken continuity through the activities of all societies and has the same meaning for all, so that a good charitable bequest, or a good peace treaty, or a good system of regulation of the flights of airplanes, is good in exactly the same sense that a cave man's striking stone was good: good in the sense of bringing home the bacon" in Ayres, Clemence E, *Toward a reasonable Society. The Values of Industrial Civilization,* Austin, University of Texas Press, 1961, p. 29.

"accounting units", inflating the size of the financial sector, but – through austerity – preventing these newly created accounting units from reaching the real economy in the form of increased demand for goods and services. In this way the financial economy goes from working in symbiosis with the real economy into being a parasite decreasing the size of the real economy.

The Circular Flow of Economics

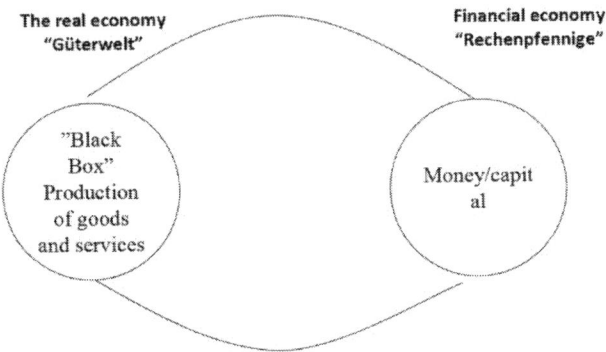

In good times the financial economy serves as scaffolding for the real economy, as a bridge in time as Keynes put it. If allowed to grow in ways that do not positively impact the real economy – by making money on money without going through production in the real economy – the financial sector will become like a parasite which grows at the expense of the real economy.[48] Since the times of Hammurabi, 1.500 BC, societies which survived have

---

[48] Hudson, Michael, *Killing the Host: How Financial Parasites and Debt Bondage Destroy the Global Economy*, New York, Perseus Books Group, 2015.

managed to cancel unpayable debt.[49] Bankruptcy, like bookkeeping, was a necessary invention in the early centuries of capitalism. At the moment the combination of printing new money, which are assets in the financial sector but liabilities in the real economy,[50] coupled with austerity in the real economy appears to be producing the situation Lenin looked forward to: the last stage of capitalism will be when financial capital takes the reign. Presumably because the real economy will collapse under the weight of debt and underconsumption.

With a single-minded focus on preventing inflation – at all costs – Mario Draghi was elected head of the European Central Bank for an eight-year period, from 2011 to 2019. Interestingly enough, Mario Draghi himself had issued a written warning against monetary power coming into the hands of the wrong people in a process resembling rent-seeking:

> "The currency...is one of those precious institutions which may become malignant if used to the advantage of organized groups".[51]

---

[49] See my article "Mechanisms of Financial Crises in Growth and Collapse: Hammurabi, Schumpeter, Perez, and Minsky", in *Jornal Ekonomi Malaysia*, No. 46 (1) (2012), pp. 85-100, and *The Other Canon Foundation and Tallinn University of Technology Working Papers in Technology Governance and Economic Dynamics*, No 39, 2012.

[50] This is one of the basic principles of double entry bookkeeping, a system which macroeconomists rarely study.

[51] Draghi writes this in reference to economist and first President of Italy, Luigi Einaudi: "La moneta, nella sua visione (i.e. Einaudi's), è una di quelle istituzioni preziose che possono però divenire perniciose se usate a vantaggio di gruppi organizzati", Draghi, Mario 'Prefazione', in Gigliobianco, Alfredo, *Luigi Einaudi: Libertà economica e coesione sociale*, Collana Historica della Banca d'Italia, Bari, Laterza, 2011, p. vii.

This is an exact description of what happened to the Euro in the hands of Mario Draghi: the currency is used to the advantage of the financial sector – *of high finance* – in the disfavor of the real economy. German fear of inflation and that country's obvious short-term benefits from the present frozen exchange rates increase the power of the financial sector. What is now taking place is financial hoarding on a large scale, huge amounts of money are essentially out of circulation in the real economy. It is time to go back and read Nicolas Oresme and Martin Luther on the subject of hoarding.

In practice Draghi's Quantitative Easing ends up being the opposite of Keynesianism – creating money instead of creating jobs – and it is surprising that this ideological turnaround has not created more political discussions than it has. To the extent that the problem at hand is one of too low inflation, this could have been solved by increasing wages in a systematic way, e.g. parallelly inside the European Union. This would have been a Keynesian version of Ben Bernanke's "helicopter money" because it would have been distributed widely, and as purchasing power rather than as *mammon*.

Quantitative Easing is part of the new logic of Supply Side economics, and at odds with pre-Cold War understandings of the relationship between capital and production. Supply-side economics brought back what Schumpeter had labelled "the pedestrian view that it is capital per se which propels the capitalist engine".[52] This theory justified tax cuts for the rich – the 1 per cent – as

---

[52] Schumpeter, Joseph, *History of Economic Analysis,* New York, Oxford University Press, 1954, p. 468.

an engine of growth, whereas what actually happened was that the concurrent destruction of demand among the rest (the 99 per cent) killed off investment and led the rich to seek revenue in what was often financial speculation: instead of making money from the production of goods and services, increasingly money was being made in schemes that never left the financial sector.

The same type of propaganda that during the Reagan years gave us "trickle-down economics", over the last ten years or so has been re-incarnated in the term "job creator". Meaning that anyone with funds – be they productively employed or unproductive *mammon* – has come to be seen as a *job creator*.

But, *cui bono?* – who benefits from the present crises? The answers are very clear: The major beneficiary of the crisis is the financial sector, which is growing far too big also according to IMF.[53] When the financial sector is allowed to print money, they in effect print debt. What is on the asset side of the balance sheets of the banks is on the liability side of the balance sheets of the real economy. When bankruptcies – as the one that obviously should have happened in Greece – are no longer permitted, the financial sector becomes a parasite shrinking the size of the real economy: wages and consumption.

In the real economy, the only short-term beneficiary is Germany and to some degree Holland, which get to keep

---

[53] http://www.ft.com/cms/s/0/4b70ee3a-f88c-11e4-8e16-00144feab7de.html

their manufacturing sector. On the other hand, this advantage is shrinking as the purchasing power in the rest of the EU – important customers for Germany and Holland – is shrinking. Henry Ford's idea that one's customers should be given more purchasing power is another casualty of Cold War economics. The whole concept of austerity has become a tool for financial hoarding, rather than for creating markets for production capitalists.

Since financial capital was criticized by the wrong people in the 1930s, a deeper discussion of the separation between financial capital and production capital raises some uncomfortable issues. In these times of the Corona virus, perhaps we should have monetary theorist Nicholas Oresme (1320-1382) have the last word as regards the conflict between hoarding and human well-being. His worry is that money – in those days gold and silver – would be withdrawn from circulation:

> "And therefore so much of them ought not to be allowed to be applied to other uses that there should not be enough left for money. It was this consideration that led Theodoric, king of Italy [493-526[54]], to order the gold and silver deposited according to pagan custom in the tombs, to be removed and used for coining for the public profit, saying: *'It was a crime to leave hidden among the dead and useless, what would keep the living alive'*."[55]

---

[54] Years added by this author.
[55] Oresme, Nicolas, *De Moneta*, 1356.

Chapter 14

I LOVE YOU – investing for intergenerational wellbeing

Girol Karacaoglu

In *The Faith of a Heretic* (1961), Chapter X on Morality, German philosopher Walter Kaufman proposes four cardinal virtues as a foundation for answering the following questions: How are we to live? By what standards should we judge ourselves? For what virtues should we strive?

His four cardinal virtues are: "humbition" (a made-up word referring to a fusion of humility and ambition), love, courage, and honesty.

It is the second one of these (*love*) that is the centre of our interest, as it relates to public policy. Kaufman gives the word a very specific meaning. As Wes Cecil, the producer and narrator of the series *Forgotten Thinkers*, interprets it, "I love you" for Kaufman means: I want you to live the life that you want to live. I will be as happy as you, if you do; and as unhappy as you, if you don't.

How would we design, govern, implement, and evaluate public policy, if it were based on our love for future generations, true to the meaning that Kaufman gives to: "I love you"?

We have no idea what future generations will value and how they will want to live. Nor do we wish to prescribe how they should choose to live – so long as, that is, they do not prevent others from living the lives they value. We want to prepare and look after the "wellbeing garden" (the broader ecosystems) that will provide them with the opportunities and capabilities to *survive* and *thrive* – i.e. flourish in safety. As Walter Benjamin expressed it, "We want to liberate the future from its deformation in the present" (Wellmon 2020).

Wellbeing and justice

Wellbeing is about the ability of individuals and communities to live the lives they value – now and in the future (i.e. it is about their human rights). It would be extremely unjust to prevent the enjoyment of valued lives. Preventing such injustice across generations would be the primary focus of a public policy that has intergenerational wellbeing as its objective.

There is a rich variety of possible lives, conditioned by personal circumstances, including capabilities, opportunities, and preferences, as well as cultures, religions, political arrangements, geographical surroundings, and so on. Nevertheless, there is considerable evidence to suggest a set of common contributors to wellbeing across humanity (Figure 1 – OECD 2020, p. 21).

Figure 1 OECD Well-being Framework

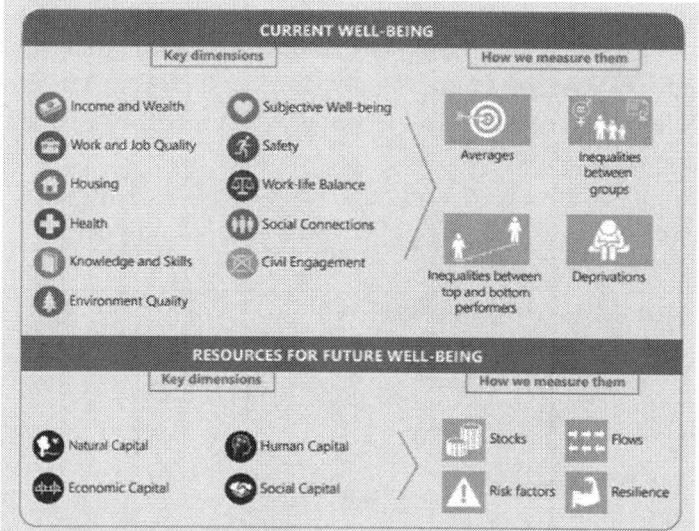

These common contributors to current wellbeing, listed in the upper left-hand side of the Figure, can be classified under the categories, *material conditions* (income and wealth, work and job quality, housing) and *quality of life* (health, knowledge and skills, environment quality, subjective well-being, safety, work-life balance, social connections, civic engagement).

At the bottom-left of the Figure are a set of capital stocks that represent the sources of future wellbeing: natural capital, economic capital, human capital, social capital. Brief descriptions of these can be found in New Zealand Treasury (2019).

In the context of intergenerational wellbeing, if we do wish to liberate the future from its deformation in the present, we need to achieve two outcomes through public policy. First, preserve the resources for future wellbeing. Second, decouple the opportunities and capabilities (i.e. substantive freedoms) (Sen 1999, 2009) of future generations from the specific circumstances into which they are born.

Figure 2 Intergenerational Wealth Distribution

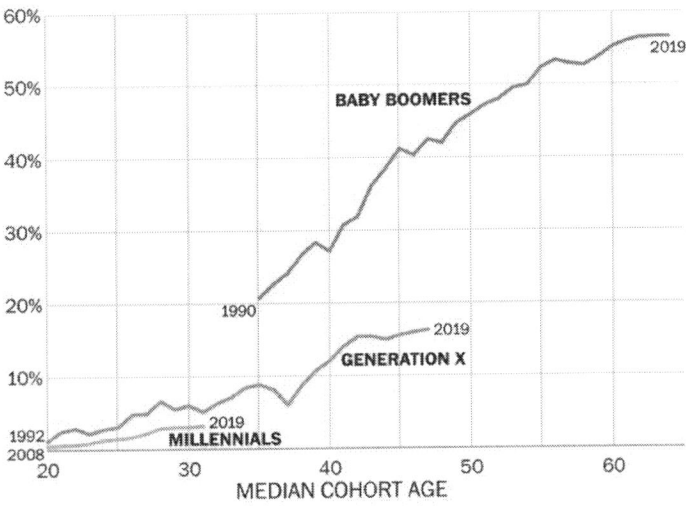

Intergenerational wealth

Share of national wealth owned by each generation, by median cohort age

Source: Federal Reserve Distributional Accounts

THE WASHINGTON POST

Chart adapted from Gray Kimbrough

The growing disparity across generations, in their access to material sources of wellbeing such as income and wealth (including housing), has been well documented (Ingraham 2019, Wolf 2018). Figure 2 provides an example referring to the growing disparity of wealth across generations in the USA (Ingraham 2019).

As Ingraham explains, "baby boomers – those born between 1946 and 1964 – collectively owned 21 percent of the nation's wealth by the time their generation hit a median age of 35 in 1990. Generation X (born from 1965 to 1980) came of age during the era of wage stagnation and growing inequality ushered in by the 1970s and '80s.

When the typical Gen Xer reached 35 in 2008, his or her share of the nation's wealth was just 9 percent, less than half that of boomers at a comparable point in life. Millennials haven't hit the 35 mark yet – that won't happen until about 2023 – but their financial situation is relatively dire. They own just 3.2 percent of the nation's wealth. To catch up to Gen Xers, they'd need to triple their wealth in just four years. To reach boomers, their net worth would need a sevenfold jump."

In terms of sources of future wellbeing, there are emerging concerns on a much wider front than simply material sources: "Looking forward, there is no room for complacency. As storm clouds gather on the horizon, mainly from environmental and social challenges, all OECD countries need to take action if they are to maintain today's well-being for future generations.

> "Nearly two-thirds of people in OECD countries are exposed to dangerous levels of air pollution. ... Reductions in greenhouse gas emissions (GHG) in the OECD are far from sufficient to meet climate policy goals

and, in almost half of OECD countries, more species are at risk of extinction. Household debt in almost two-thirds of the OECD exceeds annual household disposable income and has deepened in a third of member states since 2010.

"While trust in government has improved by 3 percentage points on average since 2010, less than half of the population across OECD countries trust their institutions, and only 1 in 3 people feel they have a say in what the government does. Women hold just one-third of all seats in OECD parliaments, and hence, inclusive decision-making remains a distant goal.

"Overall, recent advances in well-being have not been matched by improvements in the resources needed to sustain well-being over time. From financial insecurity in households, through to climate change, biodiversity loss and threats to how democratic institutions perform their functions, we need to look beyond maximising well-being today. Ensuring continued prosperity for people and the planet will require bold and strategic investments in the resources that underpin well-being in the longer run" (OECD 2020, p. 17).

On the second outcome, about decoupling the opportunities and capabilities (i.e. substantive freedoms) of future generations from the specific circumstances into which they are born, the distinction that is often made between equity and equality (McCloskey, 2014) may not be that useful in an intergenerational context. Today's outcomes determine tomorrow's opportunities: "Inequality of outcome among today's generation is the source of the unfair advantage received by the next generation. If we are concerned about equality of opportunity tomorrow, we need to be concerned about inequality of outcome today" (Atkinson, 2015, p.12). The less wealth you start with the less you are likely to accumulate in the rest of your life (Ingraham 2019).

As Rajan (2020) puts it, "Inequality is a real problem today, but it is the inequality of opportunity, of access to capabilities, of place, not just of incomes and wealth. Higher spending and thus taxes may be necessary, not to punish the rich but to help the left- behind find new opportunity. This requires fresh policies not discredited old ones."

A radically different approach to public policy

Our public policy platform is the concept of "love" that we introduced at the beginning. The objective of public policy is to make it possible for individuals and communities to live the kinds of lives they value, in the present and into the future – without compromising others' rights to do the same. This is what individual and community wellbeing is all about.

We agree with Layard and O'Donnell (2015). After quoting Thomas Jefferson ("The care of human life and happiness [...] is the only legitimate object of good government"), they go on to write, "What should be the goal of public policy? We agree with Thomas Jefferson. What matters is the quality of life, as people themselves experience it. And the best judge of each person's life is that same person. Is she happy with her life; is she satisfied? In a democracy that should be the criterion for good policy" (*ibid.*, p. 77).

There are multiple layers of public policy. Our focus is on the design and implementation of public policy at a *system* level – as it relates to the "large world" (as Kay and King 2020 refer to it). We explore and provide an answer to the questions: how do we create the (natural, social, and economic) environment (*opportunities*) where the pursuit of valued lives is possible; and then, support the acquisition of the *capabilities* that enable the pursuit of these valued lives.

In this setting, there are six critical justifications underpinning our call for a radically different approach to public policy. First, wellbeing is *multi-dimensional*. Second, wellbeing is *intergenerational*. Third, both the various dimensions and sources of wellbeing are strongly *interdependent*. Fourth, individual lives are lived in *social settings*. Fifth, the "large world" in which our social life is imbedded is *radically (or fundamentally) uncertain* (Kay and King 2020). Sixth, both individual and social lives are dominated by *adaptive complexity and reflexivity* (Arthur 2014, Soros 2003).

Multi-dimensionality and Interdependence

There is a very rich literature on both the meaning and sources of wellbeing (Adler and Fleurbaey 2016). Although there is considerable debate on these matters, everyone agrees that the sources of wellbeing are diverse (Figure 1), interconnected, and complex (Figure 3) (Reid 2019).

Figure 3 Diverse and Interconnected Sources of Human Wellbeing

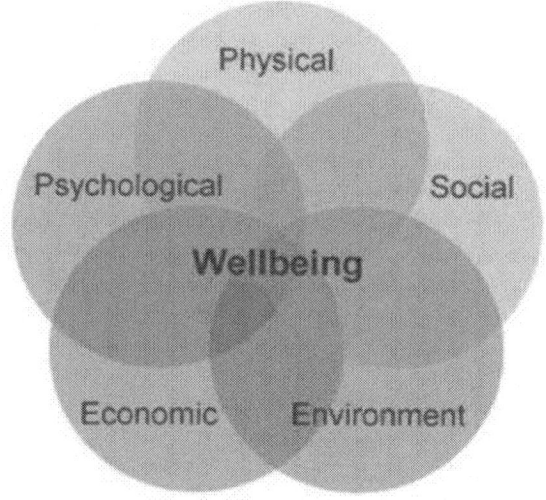

Wellbeing is a state of mind that reflects a set of complex relationships between material, relational, and subjective domains. This interplay must be understood as firmly located in society and shaped by social, economic, political, cultural, and psychological processes (Gough *et al.* 2007, McGregor 2007, White 2010).

Improving wellbeing requires as much focus on the processes followed as they do on the outcomes being sought; indeed desired outcomes cannot be achieved on an enduring basis unless the processes followed are genuinely inclusive.

Social context

The list of domains of wellbeing in Figure 1 relates to individual wellbeing. Needless to say, individual lives are lived in social settings. There are strong interdependencies between individual and community wellbeing.

Societies, communities, and individuals have a very strong sense of the way they wish to live their lives. Kay and King (2020) refer to these as "reference narratives". The major systemic risk that public policy needs to concern itself with is the threat to these narratives. If we can give individuals and communities an assurance that their preferred way of living will be protected, that provides a platform for exploration, creativity, and human flourishing.

In addition, as Helliwell (2019) reports, social sources of well-being, especially those delivered in person, are of even greater importance for subjective wellbeing (one of the domains of individual wellbeing listed in Figure 1) than previously thought. In recent *World Happiness Reports* (Helliwell *et al* 2019), six factors have been found to explain three-quarters of the differences in average life evaluations among countries and over time: GDP per capita; healthy life expectancy; and an additional four that can be conceptualised as "social factors" (having someone to count on in times of trouble; a sense of freedom to make life choices; generosity; and trustworthy environment, as proxied by the absence of corruption in business and government).

In short, if our purpose is to improve human lives, as people wish to live their lives, then we need to place a lot of emphasis on the health and wellbeing of the communities in which those lives are lived.

Radical uncertainty

We are trying to improve lives in a world dominated by *radical uncertainty* (Kay and King 2020; King 2016, Chapter 4) and *adaptive complexity* (Arthur 2014). In this type of world, which is the real world we are living in, there are no buttons to push to generate well-defined outcomes. By way of example, which button would you push to "solve" a mental health problem?

Under *radical (or fundamental) uncertainty*, with the set of possible states of the world and/or their probabilities unknown, optimisation at a public policy level (in the "large world") becomes impossible. We simply do not know what the future will look like, although we may have a broad idea of the types of catastrophes our natural environment, society, and economy may be exposed to.

Adaptive complexity

Under *adaptive complexity*, particularly in a social context, actions and outcomes cannot be separated – there is "reflexivity": there are no external (exogenous) social or economic facts that are independent of our actions. Individuals' actions and interactions with others influence the social and economic outcomes that emerge, which in turn lead to reactions, and on it goes (Soros, 2003).

One of the main teachings of complexity economics is that creative ideas are primarily generated bottom up, not top down – through interactions and cross-fertilisations of ideas promulgated by human contacts via various means. A critical role for the policy maker is that of supporting and connecting. Creativity remains the source of innovation, technological progress, and prosperity under all frameworks – how we encourage and support it is the point of difference. Think of a landscaper instead of an architect – the focus is on creating the right ecosystems for people, communities, and ideas to flourish.

The primary consequences of these justifications, for the approach to public policy that we are advocating, are as follows. The *multi-dimensional* aspect of wellbeing affects both the framing and the assessment of public policy. The focus on *intergenerational* wellbeing has a major influence on how the policy approach is governed and implementation is funded. *Interdependence* affects the prioritisation of both public policies and supporting investments. *Radical uncertainty* shifts the focus of public policy from searching for "optimal solutions" to investing towards building resilience. *Complexity, reflexivity,* and the emphasis on *social settings* all affect the implementation of public policy, and the nature of effective policy interventions, with a critical focus on inclusivity.

Wellbeing garden

The framing of a wellbeing-focused public policy is grounded in the following concepts and principles.

First, wellbeing is associated with the capabilities and opportunities of individuals and communities to live the lives they value. Second, we respect the rights of individuals and communities to choose how they wish to live. Third, valued lives are diverse, and are history, time, culture dependent. Fourth, lives are lived in social settings. Fifth, we want everyone to live the lives they value – provided they respect others' rights to do the same. Sixth, everyone includes future generations.

Figure 4 conceptualises the primary purpose of a wellbeing-focused public policy as the enlargement of the "wellbeing garden" in which social life takes place, now and into the future. The key dimensions ("corners") of the perimeter of that garden are: environmental quality, potential economic growth (i.e. material sources of wellbeing), social cohesion, personal freedoms and political voice, and equity. These are the key dimensions of the social and individual "reference narratives". They are the systemic outcomes that public policy needs to deliver.

Figure 4 Wellbeing Garden

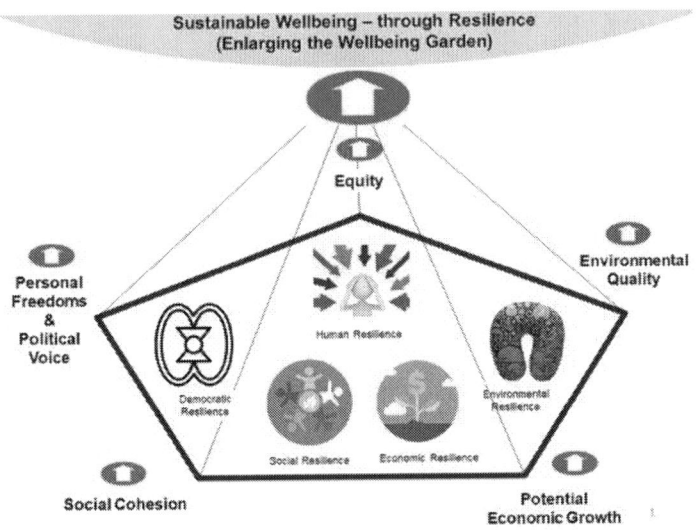

These outcomes provide the environment (natural, social, political, and economic environment) which makes the pursuit of valued lives possible (i.e. the *opportunities*). The key focus of the strategy would be to invest towards building systemic resilience to potential threats to the key dimensions of the way we wish to live – to our "reference narratives". The components of systemic resilience that sit in the middle of Figure 4 provide individuals and communities with the *capabilities* to pursue their valued lives. They represent the foundations of sustainable collective wellbeing – and they are strongly interdependent.

Resilience as a platform for sustained prosperity

In a world of fundamental uncertainty, the pursuit of the policy objective of intergenerational wellbeing requires investments in building resilience to systemic risks to our preferred way of living – to our reference narratives. Thus achieving *systemic resilience* emerges as a critical output of public policy. Resilience provides the critical bridge to the sustainability of wellbeing across generations.

The garden of Figure 4 can be enlarged through appropriate (in terms of quantum, quality, and composition) investments. In summary, investing in *Social resilience* delivers social cohesion. *Human resilience* provides a major platform for equity. *Democratic resilience* underpins the protection of individual freedom and political voice. *Economic and financial resilience* enhances potential economic growth. *Environmental resilience* helps sustain environmental quality.

Resilience can be usefully defined as the ability to prepare and plan for, absorb, recover from, and more successfully adapt to adverse events (National Research Council, 2012).

In an intergenerational context, systemic resilience has three distinct but complementary attributes – one is shock-absorbing (*surviving*) capacity (following, e.g., earthquakes; financial-system or social disruptions); a second is *adaptability* following shocks; a third is creativity and inventiveness, or *thriving* (which are critical ingredients of adaptability) – underpinned by individual freedoms and social cohesion. A system may show resilience to major systemic shocks not necessarily by returning exactly to its previous state following a shock, but instead by finding different ways to carry out essential functions; that is, by adapting.

Haldane (2018), partly based on the work of Broadberry and Wallis (2017), provides a very powerful and persuasive example of the interface between resilience, institutions, public policy, and wellbeing over a long period of time covering hundreds of years. The underlying narrative is summarised in Figures 5 and 6.

Under this revised narrative, the sustained growth in human prosperity since the Industrial Revolution turns out to be not exclusively an economic growth story underpinned by innovation and productivity growth – the standard narrative, but also a resilience story. Growth spurts were ever present for at least a thousand years. Deliberately created social institutions (including schooling, health services, social welfare) that protected humanity from the potential negative effects of contractionary periods owing to war, disease, economic catastrophes, and others, over the period since the Industrial Revolution, made a huge difference.

Figure 5 Real GDP per head since 1000 AD

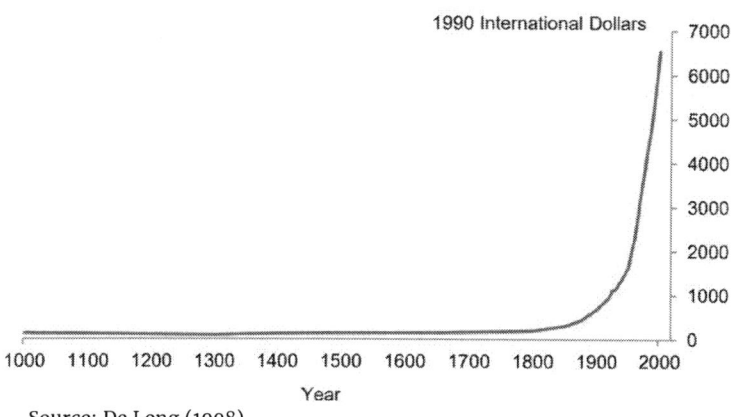

Source: De Long (1998).

Figure 6 Real GDP per head since 1000 AD

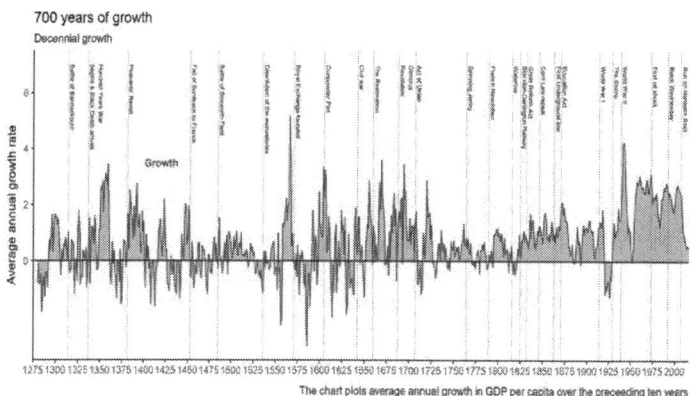

Sources: Broadberry and Wallis (2017) and Bank calculations.

One key insight of Mazzucato's work (2013, 2015) is the role of the public sector as the initial (pioneering) investor and ecosystem creator in providing a platform

447

for systemic resilience. This provides the fertile and profitable ground for the private sector, NGOs and others to invest it – and to flourish. As Mazzucato points out, most of the radical, revolutionary innovations that have fuelled the dynamics of capitalism – from railroads to the Internet, to modern-day nanotechnology and pharmaceuticals – trace the most courageous, early and capital-intensive 'entrepreneurial' investments back to the State.

Governing for intergenerational wellbeing

In a world dominated by radical (or fundamental) uncertainty and adaptive complexity, a public policy that aspires to deliver sustainable (across generations) wellbeing as its primary *outcome*, needs to be supported by governance arrangements that can deliver five critical *outputs*: a long-term focus in policy making; inclusive decision-making mechanisms that aggregate the wisdom, expertise, and experiences of all stakeholders; institutions that enable and encourage (and indeed mandate) an integrated environmental, social, and economic approach to public policy; a suitable supporting funding infrastructure; and adaptive time consistency (i.e. ongoing alignment of public policy with collective wellbeing, as the preferences of society evolve over time).

Long-term focus in policy making

Assuming there is political will, the governance steps to be followed are clear – and are each being implemented somewhere in the world (OECD, 2019). They are very much aligned with the steps advocated by Wallace (2019)

– see also Boston (2017 a, b), Boston *et al* (2019), Warren (2019).

We need a clear separation of the short-term (three-four year) management role of Government, from the long-term stewardship role of Parliament. Parliament specifies intergenerational wellbeing as the core objective of public policy. It also sets the long- term (environmental, social, and economic) objectives (and associated targets) aligned with shared and sustainable wellbeing.

Parliament does so under advice from an independent office for wellbeing (IOW) – directly accountable to Parliament. A multi-party Parliamentary Governance Group (PGG) acts as the governance group for the IOW. IOW's advice is informed by input from a *What Works Wellbeing* network of NGOs, local and regional government representatives, academics, and so on, working collaboratively to generate policy informing information based on engagements with communities, other sources of data, and research – very much based on the UK model (Hey 2019).

A dedicated investment manager for each long-term outcome (say, child poverty), and reporting to the IOW, plays the public sector stewardship role. Cost-Benefit Analyses, using wellbeing as the currency, provides the main analytical tool for the interactions between these investment managers and the IOW. [See Adler and Fleurbaey 2016, Fujiwara and Dolan (2016), Frijter *et al.* (2019), Jara and Schokkaert (2016).]

Parliament also legislates that the government will set short-term targets, as part of its annual Budget each year, towards achieving the long-term targets it sets, and will provide a report on how it is progressing against those targets.

Finally, Parliament ensures, through appropriate collaborations with local Councils, that regional and local voices are reflected in setting wellbeing objectives and priorities. Where it is deemed appropriate by the IOW that the delivery of a certain long-term outcome requires substantive community ownership and participation in the achievement of that outcome, a community-based manager and budget holder (typically part of local / regional government), accountable to the IOW, is established.

Funding

There is a critical nexus between finance and sustained development, which provides not only a critical bridge between long-term development and finance, but also a distinctive role for public policy. Innovation-supporting investment needs a long-term commitment, supported by "patient finance", as well as an appetite for risk-taking in the face of "radical uncertainty". This is especially the case when we are referring to transformative ecosystem investments, such as those supporting "green growth", nanotechnology, biotechnology, and so on. These are the circumstances when the state needs to lead (and has historically done so); only then does the private sector (including venture capital) follow (Mazzucato and Wray 2015; Mazzucato and Perez 2014; Mazzucato and Semienuk 2018).

The State's share of long-term investments in ecosystems will be eventually funded through taxes or levies (Pay as You Go – PAYGO) or "Social Insurance" (i.e. public saving in various forms to fund future needs and contingencies) – Save as You Go (SAYGO). If the real return on capital is higher than the real growth rate of the economy, which it typically is, funding long-term investment expenditures via SAYGO is intergenerationally more efficient and equitable than doing so via PAYGO (Piketty 2018). This should be complemented by a gradual and well-managed switch from a progressive income to a progressive consumption tax, aimed to encourage long-term saving and investing (Metcalf 1973).

Integrated approach to sustainability

Unless an integrated environmental, social, and economic policy framework is adopted, taking into account the critical interdependencies between the associated ecosystems, a public policy that is focused on intergenerational wellbeing cannot achieve its objective. Human lives are lived in social settings, and society is embedded in a natural environment.

Figure 7 attempts to capture two main ideas. First, the interactions between various types of capital in generating sustained wellbeing. As Costanza *et al.* (2017), where we have borrowed this figure from, emphasise, it is the complex interactions between these various forms of capital assets that affect human wellbeing. Built capital and human capital are embedded in society, which is in turn embedded in the rest of nature.

Second, "sustainability" refers to the sustainability of human wellbeing, not necessarily to the sustainability (or preservation) of any particular form of natural capital. We should allow for the possibility of substitutability of various types of natural and other forms of capital in generating human wellbeing.

Figure 7 Sustainable human wellbeing

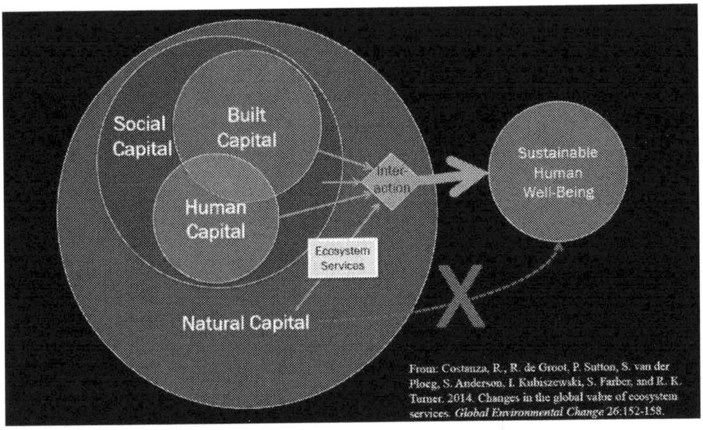
Social Capital
Built Capital
Human Capital
Inter-action
Ecosystem Services
Natural Capital
Sustainable Human Well-Being
X
From: Costanza, R., R. de Groot, P. Sutton, S. van der Ploeg, S. Anderson, I. Kubiszewski, S. Farber, and R. K. Turner. 2014. Changes in the global value of ecosystem services. Global Environmental Change 26:152-158.

Adaptive time consistency

"Time consistent policies are not policies that are never changed, but policies where any changes required by new circumstances are consistent with maintaining the original purposes of the policy. They are important for the socially desirable performance of the private and public sectors. This is because they provide stability that enables individuals and the state to plan for the future" (Evans *et al.* 2013, p. ii).

Democratic institutions are critical in helping us resolve tensions through public reasoning and deliberation (see Bertram and Terry 2013; Sen 2009; Walzer 1983). It is the democratic process, in the form of representative democracy, supported by appropriate institutions, that provides the forces that push towards an alignment of collective action (implemented through the government as our agent) with evolving private and communal interests (i.e., government action is endogenous). This ensures time consistency.

Inclusive processes as a requirement for sustainable wellbeing

One of the critical outputs that wellbeing-focused governance arrangements need to deliver is *inclusive* decision-making mechanisms that aggregate the wisdom, expertise, and experiences of all stakeholders to inform the end-to-end policy approach. "Policies aimed to improve people's quality of life need to include their experiences, aspirations, and priorities" (Reid 2019, p. 44). This provides the crucial link between the *participatory* and *capabilities* approaches to public policy.
The foundations of such a policy would include (Scott, 1998): a recognition of the limits of what we are likely to know about a complex and functioning order; a recognition that individuals and communities will respond and adapt to whatever changes are put in place; the contributions to resilience of social, natural, regional diversity; the indispensable role of practical knowledge,

informal processes and improvisation in the face of unpredictability; an appreciation of the complementary roles of "the centre" and the local/regional communities; and, in that very context, the advantage that "the centre" has in seeing the big picture, identifying trends early, and intervening in a timely fashion in epidemics.

This type of policy framework embraces localism, encouragement of experimentation at local level, small steps in implementation, reversibility and fast failures, and planning on surprises. It is built around the benefits of decentralisation and emergence. Collective wellbeing is pursued not by searching for investment levers that will enhance well-defined social outcomes, but rather by making it easier for people to pursue the varied lives they value, with no pre-defined desired social outcomes.

Rajan (2019) describes localism as, "the process of decentralising power to the local level so that people feel more empowered in their communities. The community, rather than the nation, will become a possible vehicle for ethnic cohesiveness and cultural continuity" (p. 285). The underlying principle is that of *subsidiarity* – "powers should stay at the most decentralised level consistent with their effective use" (p. 285).

Localism is not a panacea for well-balanced collective decisions (Olson 1965), but it is an integral part of a well-designed and governed, integrated and inclusive process.

Assessment: how do we know if policy is effective

Where intergenerational wellbeing is the objective of public policy, there needs to be an assessment specifically targeted at evaluating whether public policy is creating the platform for sustainable intergenerational wellbeing. Good public policies, in this specific context, are those that expand or enlarge the "wellbeing garden".

Figure 8, which uses New Zealand data simply because we happen to live here, should be seen as illustrative only, since the underlying data is pretty weak. That is why we have deliberately provided only two representations of the frontier, based roughly on data for the periods 2005 and 2018. Treating 2005 as the base (index no = 100), we have simply represented the 2018 data as a deviation (a ratio in this case) of the same (or corresponding) measure from that base.

- The *Equity* dimension of the wellbeing frontier conceptually represents widespread access to all forms of wealth. We have used the data presented in one of the reports to the Tax Working Group (IRD and NZ Treasury 2018) on wealth inequality – using a wealth Gini coefficient as a measure.
- The *Environmental Quality* measure is from Wendling *et al.* (2018) based on their *Environmental Performance Index*. The index covers 24 performance indicators across 10 "issue categories" covering environmental health and ecosystem vitality. New Zealand's ranking went from 1 to 17 between 2006 and 2018 – and its performance index went from 88.0 to 76.0 (although the authors warn that, because of changes in index-

construction methodology, these two numbers are not strictly comparable).

- The *Economy* represents the potential growth rate of the economy – and is sourced from the OECD Databases OECD Data; OECD Statistics).
- The *Society* dimension represents *social cohesion* and is proxied by survey-based "generalised trust" data, obtained from Ortiz-Ospina and Roser (2016)
- The *Freedom* measure is based on the *The Human Freedom Index* constructed by Vásquez and Porčnik (2019).

Figure 8 Evolution of the New Zealand Wellbeing Garden

	Equity	Environment	Economy	Society	Freedom
2005	100	100	100	100	100
2018	96	86	96	110	99

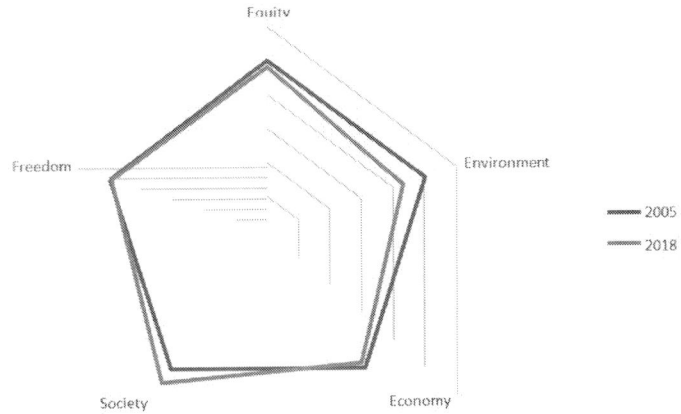

Broadly speaking, based on the evidence and data presented in this section, we can conclude that there are stresses building on New Zealand's wellbeing frontier. These stresses are centred on the natural environment and equity. If these stresses are not addressed, they have the potential to create pressure on social cohesion and potential economic growth as well. From a public policy perspective, these are the main sources of concern about the strength of the platform for intergenerationally sustainable wellbeing.

If required for policy analysis and prioritisation, the total "size" of the wellbeing garden can be calculated by multiplying the measures of each the five domains: WG = Eq x En x Ec x So x Fr. "Viable" policy interventions can then be prioritised by ranking their impact on the ratio of the change in the size of the frontier to the cost of the intervention (some sort of benefit/cost analysis). We would do this in comparing only "viable" policy interventions – i.e. those that extend or leave unchanged each of the five dimensions of the wellbeing frontier.

Prioritisation: what would we prioritise and why

Martin and Pindyck (2015) pose the following question: faced with numerous potential catastrophes, with uncertainties surrounding occurrences and timings, which should society attempt to avert? Of course, we can also ask the question in a positive way: faced with numerous investment opportunities at a system level, which should society prioritise?

In answering this question, we need to keep in mind the policy objective of improving wellbeing on a sustainable basis across generations. In this context, the priorities identified and discussed below have been influenced by two important pieces of information.

First are the stresses, on the wellbeing frontier, that were identified above. In the case of New Zealand, they happen to centre on the natural environment and equity; other countries will have their own circumstances. If these are not attended to with some degree of urgency, they will also start putting pressure on the other key dimensions of the wellbeing frontier, such as social cohesion. On the flip side, if they are dealt with adequately, and in the right manner, they will have positive benefits for the other dimensions of wellbeing, such as potential economic growth.

The second important influence on the policy priorities advocated below are the inter-dependencies between the various dimensions of systemic resilience that sit in the middle of Figure 4. Such interdependencies are at the centre of our modelling work (see Karacaoglu *et al.*, 2019). They help us prioritise potential policy interventions aimed at expanding the wellbeing garden.

Given where we are right now in New Zealand, we suggest that the top two priorities of a public policy that has intergenerational wellbeing as its primary objective, should be: a universal and comprehensive "leave no one behind" strategy, complemented by environment-friendly investments that build resilience to systemic risks to the natural environment while also creating sustained, high quality, employment.

Giving top priority to a "leave no one behind" strategy would make a positive contribution to all five dimensions of systemic resilience that sit in the middle of Figure 4. Broadening the availability of opportunities and capabilities helps reduce inequity and increase social cohesion. Through that channel, it increases potential economic growth, as well as increasing social and economic resilience. It also directly reduces environmental degradation and increases environmental resilience because poverty is one of the biggest enemies of the natural environment.

A "leave no one behind" strategy makes everyone a stakeholder in society. It does so by giving everyone access to education, healthcare, and housing; by giving everyone who is capable of working, an employment opportunity; by making sure that everyone has a minimum level of adequate income; by looking after those who cannot look after themselves; by making sure that everyone has a voice in matters that affect them. This ensures that every citizen is "invested" in their country. Every citizen would then be intensely interested in how the country is feeling and do their best for the wellbeing of the country at large – because when the country is doing well, everyone does well.

"Many current social problems are rooted in our neglect of the democratic process. The solution isn't to dribble out enough crumbs to keep people at home, distracted, and otherwise pacified. Rather, we need to rejuvenate democratic politics, boost civic involvement, and seek collective solutions. Only with a mobilized, politically active society can we build the institutions we need for shared prosperity in the future, while protecting the most disadvantaged among us" (Acemoglu, 2019).

A "leave no one behind strategy" needs to be concurrently focused on reducing suffering, while increasing opportunities and capabilities to pursue valued lives. For the current adult population, this needs to be delivered through training and employment opportunities as the top priority, and conditional cash support if the employment option is not available. Care also involves, in-kind support as required *viz* health and housing. For the young generation, the most effective and enduring way of showing care is to invest in them – in their education, health, and housing.

Access to assets also provides a source of opportunities and capabilities for the young. In this vein, Smith (2018) argues for asset-based assistance for high-risk children. Having identified children who are at high risk of future poverty ("wards of the state"), we would provide them with a reasonably generous cash endowment at the age of 18, so that they have the foundation for a positive start to their adult lives. What purposes this asset can be used for (such as education and skilling) would be strictly prescribed.

Poverty-reducing (or opportunity increasing) measures provide examples of policy interventions that have multiple benefits. These are the ideal types of interventions when we are dealing with multi-dimensional and mutually dependent environmental, social, and economic systems.

Breunig and Majeed (2016) provide empirical evidence in support of their policy advice to, "reduce inequality by attacking poverty rather than by redistributing income," on the basis that this has a wider positive impact on wellbeing through its positive impact on potential economic growth, the quality of institutions, and social cohesion.

A "give and care" system (to paraphrase Banajee and Duflo's (2019) "Cash and Care" proposal) needs to be based on a strong partnership between central government, local and regional government, and communities. This is where the "localism" discussion and the governance proposals developed earlier also become critically important. There needs to be a lot of investment in building capability in communities (through major local and regional government involvement).

Poverty reduction positively influences wellbeing through several, mutually- reinforcing, channels. It is good for the environment because poor people do not have the choices to consume environment-friendly products. It is also good for social cohesion because poverty is a source of all kinds of social tensions. Through these impacts, it then creates a series of second-round positive influences on wellbeing (including social and environmental resilience).

The complementary "clean environment" strategies would be implemented through a combination of taxes, regulations, and subsidies (including research and development subsidies) to encourage the switch of both production and consumption towards cleaner technology and products.

This can be achieved with the help of policies that simultaneously support the switch of production towards the use of "clean" technology (through a combination of subsidies and taxes), while concurrently (through R&D support and related measures) encouraging investment in (and thereby increased supply of) human capital in the form of skilled labour and scientists who can work with "clean" technology (Acemoglu *et al.*, 2012).

The specific sets or combinations of investments that will achieve the desired outcomes, and the distinctive role of public policy (including public investments) in creating the required ecosystems to support these investments, will be determined by a cooperative process between the various stakeholders. This process needs to involve, in a spirit of genuine partnership, central and local governments, the scientific community, the private and public business sectors, NGOs, and representatives of various disciplines, ethnicities, and genders. Harnessing the collective imagination and wisdom of all these stakeholders, in prioritising the long-term investments as well as agreeing on a division of labour between them is a critical role for governance.

The underlying narrative supporting this strategy package, including the inclusive processes to be followed, needs to be extremely well communicated and widely accepted if there is to be any chance of it being tried – let alone tried for long enough to work. What we are talking about is a massive transformative change in the way we govern. It will require a commitment across several generations. This will not be achieved unless we have a shared narrative. The reasoning and evidence supporting various facets of this narrative are extremely well developed in Acemoglu and Robinson (2019), Banerjee and Duflo (2011; 2019), and Rajan (2019).

Reason for hope – *circular wellbeing*

Let us end where we started. How are we to live? By what standards should we judge ourselves? For what virtues should we strive?

So far we addressed these questions through the lens of public policy. But what about individual behaviour? Public policy cannot achieve its objectives unless human behaviour is aligned with these objectives. For example, if we each live lives that damage the natural environment, we cannot maintain or enhance *environmental quality*. If we each refuse to live in harmony with those from other backgrounds and cultures, we cannot achieve *social cohesion* in aggregate, and so on.

So, what kind of individual behaviour and actions would be fully aligned with expanding the aggregate (collective) wellbeing garden?

Look after yourself – invest in yourself – in your own health, education and so on. Be fair in dealing with others. Minimise your activities that harm the natural environment. Work hard. Build networks and social connections. Do not hurt others. Enjoy your freedom – and passionately protect the freedoms of everyone else.

There is good news. *The Science of Wellbeing* suggests that, if we do live our lives on the basis of these principles, we will also achieve individual wellbeing – through enhanced resilience (Santos, 2020).

We have here the recipe for *circular wellbeing*. Pursue a life that is fully aligned with expanding the social wellbeing garden, and you will have achieved personal wellbeing. Everybody, including unborn generations, wins.

References

Acemoglu, Daron (2019) "Why a Universal Basic Income is a Bad Idea." *Project Syndicate*; 7 June 2019.

Acemoglu, Daron; Aghion, Philippe; Bursztyn, Leonardo; and Hemous, David (2012) "The Environment and Directed Technical Change". *The American Economic Review*. Vol 102, pp. 131–166.

Acemoglu, Daron and Robinson, James A. (2019) *The Narrow Corridor – States, Societies, and the Fate of Liberty*. Penguin Press.

Adler, Matthew D and Fleurbaey, Marc (2016), eds. *The Oxford Handbook of Well- being and Public Policy*. Oxford: Oxford University Press.

Arthur, W. Brian (2014) *Complexity and the Economy*. Oxford: Oxford University Press.

Atkinson, Anthony B. (2015) *Inequality*. Cambridge: Harvard University Press.

Banerjee, Abhijit V. and Duflo, Esther (2011) *Poor Economics*. London: Penguin Books.

Banerjee, Abhijit V. and Duflo, Esther (2019). *Good Economics for Hard Times*. London: Penguin Books.

Beinhocker, Eric (2016) "How the Profound Changes in Economics Make Left versus Right Debates Irrelevant." *Evonomics*. 26 May.

Benjamin, Walter (1996) *Walter Benjamin, Selected Writings Volume 1, 1913-1926* (Belknap Press of Harvard University Press, Cambridge, MA: 1996).Translated by Rodney Livingstone.

Bertram, Geoff and Terry, Simon (2013) *Green Border Control: Issues at the Environment/Economy Border*. Prepared for Royal Forest and Bird Protection Society of New Zealand Inc. Simon Terry Associates.

Boston, Jonathan (2017 a) *Safeguarding the Future – Governing in an Uncertain World*. BWB Texts.

Boston, Jonathan (2017 b) *Governing for the Future – Designing Democratic Institutions for a Better Tomorrow*. Emerald.

Boston, Jonathan; Bagnall, David; and Barry, Anna (2019) *Foresight, Insight and Oversight: Enhancing Long-Term Governance through Better Parliamentary Practices*. Institute for Governance and Policy Studies.

Breunig, Robert and Majeed, Omer (2016) "Inequality or Poverty: Which is Bad for Growth?" *Centre for Applied Macroeconomic Analysis Working Paper* 43/2016, Canberra, Australian Capital Territory.

Broadberry, Stephen and Wallis, John (2017). "Growing, Shrinking, and Long Run Economic Performance: Historical Perspectives on Economic Development". *Technical Report*. National Bureau of Economic Research.

Cecil, Wes (several) *Forgotten Thinkers Series*. YouTube. https://www.wescecil.com/forgotten-thinkers

Costanza, Robert; de Groot, Rudolf; Braat, Leon; Kubiszewski, Ida; Fioramonti, Lorenzo; Sutton, Paul C.; Farber, Steve; Grasso, Monica (2017) "Twenty years of ecosystem services: How far have we come and how far do we still need to go?" *Ecosystem Services*, 28, 1–16.

Evans, Lewis; Quigley, Neil (2013) "Intergenerational Contracts and Time Consistency: Implications for Policy Settings and Governance in the Social Welfare System", *New Zealand Treasury Working Paper* (13/25). December.

Frijters, Paul; Clark, Andrew E.; Krekel, Christian; Layard, Richard (2019) "A Happy Choice: Wellbeing as the Goal of Government," *CEP Discussion Paper*, No 1658 (October).

Fujiwara, Daniel and Dolan, Paul (2016) "Happiness Based Public Policy." In: M. Adler and M. Fleurbaey (eds.) *The Oxford Handbook of Well-being and Public Policy.* Oxford: Oxford University Press; pp. 286-320.

Gough, Ian; McGregor, J. Allister; Camfield, Laura (2007) "Theorising Wellbeing in International Development". In I. Gough and J. A. McGregor (eds.), *Wellbeing in Developing Countries: from Theory to Research* (pp. 3 - 44). Cambridge: Cambridge University Press.

Haldane, Andrew G. (2018) "Ideas and Institutions – A Growth Story. *Bank of England Speech.* The Guild Society. University of Oxford.

Helliwell, John H. (2019) "Measuring and Using Happiness to Support Public Policies," *NBER Working Paper Series*, December 2019.

Helliwell, John H.; Layard, Richard; Sachs, Jeffrey D.; De Neve, Jan-Emmanuel (2019). *World Happiness Report.* United Nations Sustainable Development Solutions Network.

Hey, Nancy (2019) "Building the Evidence Base and Civil Service Capacity". Presentation at the OECD international workshop on *Putting Well-being Metrics into Policy Action* (2-4 October 2019), Paris.

Ingraham, Christopher (2019) "The Staggering Millennial Wealth Deficit, in One Chart," *The Washington Post.* 12/3/2019.

IRD and NZ Treasury (2018) *Distributional Analysis – Background Paper for Session 5 of the Tax Working Group.* Tax Working Group.

Jara, H. Xavier and Schokkaert, Erik (2016) "Putting Subjective Well-being to Use for Ex-ante Policy Evaluation," *Euromod Working Paper Series*, EM 9/16, December.

Karacaoglu, Girol; King, Anita; Krawczyk, Jacek B (2019) *Intergenerational Wellbeing and Public Policy – an integrated environmental, social, and economic framework.* Springer.

Kaufman, Walter (1961) *The Faith of a Heretic.* Princeton University Press.

Kay, John and King, Mervyn (2020) *Radical Uncertainty – Decision-Making Beyond the Numbers.* W. W. Norton.

King, Mervyn (2016) *The End of Alchemy: Money, Banking, and the Future of the Global Economy.* New York: W. W. Norton & Company.

Layard, Richard and O'Donnell, Gus (2015) "How to make policy when happiness is the goal". In: *World Happiness Report*; edited by John F Helliwell, Richard Layard, and Jeffrey D Sachs; pp. 76–87; Sustainable Development Solutions Network, New York.

Martin, Ian W. R. and Pindyck, Robert S. (2015) "Averting catastrophes: The strange economics of Scylla and Charybdis". *The American Economic Review*, 105, 2947–2985.

Mazzucato, Mariana (2013) *The Entrepreneurial State: Debunking Public vs. Private Myths in Risk and Innovation.* Anthem Press.

Mazzucato, Mariana (2015) "The Green Entrepreneurial State". *SPRU Working Paper Series.*

Mazzucato, Mariana (2016) "From Market Fixing to Market-creating: A New Framework for Innovation Policy". *Industry and Innovation*, Vol 23, pp 140–156.

Mazzucato, Mariana and Perez, Carlota (2014) "Innovation as Growth Policy: The Challenge for Europe." *SPRU Working Paper Series.* No 13.

Mazzucato, Mariana and Semieniuk, Gregor (2018) "Financing Renewable Energy: Who is Financing What and Why it Matters." *Technological Forecasting and Social Change.* 127, 8–22.

Mazzucato, Mariana and Wray, L. Randall (2015) "Financing the Capital Development of the Economy: A Keynes-Schumpeter-Minsky Synthesis." *Levy Economics Institute Working Paper*, No 837.

McCloskey, Deidre Nansen (2014) *Exordium*. University of Illinois at Chicago.

McGregor, J. Allister (2007) "Researching Human Wellbeing: From Concepts to Methodology" (Working Paper 20). Retrieved from University of Bath website: http://www.bath.ac.uk/soc-pol/welldev/research/workingpaperpdf/wed20.pdf

Metcalf, Gilbert E (1973). *Consumption Taxation*. Urban Institute.

National Research Council (2012) *Disaster Resilience: A National Imperative*. Washington, DC: The National Academies Press.

New Zealand Treasury (2019) at https://www.treasury.govt.nz/publications "The Start of a Conversation on the Value of New Zealand's Human Capital"; "The Start of a Conversation on the Value of New Zealand's Natural Capital"; "The Start of a Conversation on the Value of New Zealand's Social Capital"; "The Start of a Conversation on the Value of New Zealand's Financial/Physical Capital".

OECD (2019) *Putting Well-being Metrics into Policy Action*. OECD international workshop (2-4 October 2019).

OECD (2020) *How's Life 2020: Measuring Well-being.*Paris.

Olson, Mancur (1965). *The Logic of Collective Action. Public Goods and the Theory of Groups*. Cambridge, M.A.: Harvard University Press.

Ortiz-Ospina, Esteban and Roser, Max (2016) "Trust." *Our World in Data*. University of Oxford.

Ostrom, Elinor (2009) "Beyond Markets and States: Polycentric Governance of Complex Economic Systems." Nobel Prize Lecture. Stockholm.

Piketty, Thomas (2017) *Capital in the 21st Century*. Harvard University Press.

Rajan, Raghuram (2019) *The Third Pillar – the Revival of Community in a Polarised World*. William Collins.

Rajan, Raghuram (2020) "Thomas Piketty's 'Capital and Ideology': scholarship without solutions," *Financial Times*, March.

Reid, Chelsey (2019) *Complexity in Wellbeing and the 'Leave No-One Behind' Agenda –Studies in Aotearoa New Zealand*. Masters' of Development Studies Thesis. School of Geography, Environment and Earth Sciences. Victoria University of Wellington, New Zealand.

Rockström, Johan; Steffen, Will; Noone, Kevin; Persson, Åsa; Chapin III, F. Stuart; Lambin, Eric; Lenton, Timothy M.; Scheffer, Marten; Folke, Carl; Schellnhuber, Hans Joachim; Nykvist, Björn; de Wit, Cynthia A.; Hughes, Terry; van der Leeuw, Sander; Rodhe, Henning; Sörlin, Sverker; Snyder, Peter K.; Costanza, Robert; Svedin, Uno; Falkenmark, Malin; Karlberg, Louise; Corell, Robert W.; Fabry, Victoria J.; Hansen, James; Walker, Brian; Liverman, Diana; Richardson, Katherine; Crutzen, Paul; and Foley, Jonathan (2009) "Planetary Boundaries: Exploring the Safe Operating Space for Humanity". *Ecology and Society* 14(2): 32. [online] URL: http://www.ecologyandsociety.org/vol14/iss2/art32/

Santos, Laurie (2020) *The Science of Wellbeing*. Yale Lectures. https://www.coursera.org/learn/the-science-of-well-being

Scott, James C. (1998) *Seeing like a state: How certain schemes to improve the human condition have failed*. New Haven: Yale University Press.

Sen, Amartya K. (1999) *Development as Freedom*. New York: Oxford University Press.

Sen, Amartya K. (2009) *The Idea of Justice*. Cambridge: Belknap.

Smith, Conal (2018) "Tackling Poverty NZ – the nature of poverty in New Zealand and ways to address it." *Policy Quarterly*, Victoria University of Wellington; Vol. 14(1), February

Soros, George (2003) *The Alchemy of Finance*. New Jersey: Wiley.

Vásquez, Ian and Porčnik, Tanja (2019) *The Human Freedom Index 2019 – A Global Measurement of Personal, Civil, and Economic Freedom*. CATO Institute.

Wallace, Jennifer (2019) "What can Scotland, Wales, and Northern Ireland tell us about the role of legislation in promoting societal wellbeing?" Presentation at the OECD international workshop on *Putting Well-being Metrics into Policy Action* (2–4 October 2019), Paris.

Walzer, Michael (1983) *Spheres of Justice: A Defense of Pluralism and Equality*. New York: Basic Book.

Warren, Ken (2019) "Designing a new Collective Operating and Funding Model in the New Zealand Public Sector." **DRAFT** *New Zealand Treasury Working Paper*, December.

Wellmon, Chad (2020) "The Scholar's Vocation." *Aeon Newsletter.* 8 April.

Wendling, Zachary A.; Emerson, John W.; Esty, Daniel C.; Levy, Marc A.; de Sherbinin, Alex, *et al.* (2018) *2018 Environmental Performance Index*. New Haven, CT: Yale Center for Environmental Law & Policy. https://epi.yale.edu/

White, Sarah C. (2010) "Analysing wellbeing: a framework for development practice". *Development in Practice*, 20(2), 158–172. doi:10.1080/09614520903564199

Wolf, Martin (2018) "The Focus on Intergenerational Inequity is a Delusion." *Financial Times.* 18 May.

Chapter 15

Inequality in development: the 2030 Agenda, SDG 10 and the role of redistribution[1]

Holger Apel[2]

Relevance of inequality for development

With the adoption of the Sustainable Development Goals (SDGs) by the United Nations General Assembly in 2015, the issue of inequality was prominently anchored in an international development agenda for the first time. The inclusion of SDG 10 – reducing inequality within and between countries – was not based on a broad agreement among the member states but highly contested (Fukuda-Parr, 2019). The goal was only included as a stand-alone goal against considerable resistance (ibid.). This contestation is also reflected in a relatively weak SDG 10. For example, there is not a single indicator that explicitly refers to inequality. Furthermore, SDG 10 is characterized by an imprecise language and a missing road map to

[1] I would like to thank Heiner Salomon for helpful comments and discussions on earlier drafts.
[2] This paper was written by the author as part of his own research, and does not necessarily represent the views of his employer.

achieve the goal (Anderso, 2016; Saiz and Donald, 2017). However, references to inequality can be found in at least 13 of the 17 SDGs (Freistein and Mahlert, 2016). Inequality can thus be considered one of the central themes of the Agenda 2030. It echoes that "the persistence of high, and often rising, income inequality in many developing countries is a growing concern for policymakers and the public" (IMF, 2015:57).

This concern is justified. The reduction of inequality – in its many dimensions[3] – is related to positive changes for societies. According to a World Bank study, SDG 1 – the elimination of extreme poverty – is highly unlikely to be accomplished without a simultaneous reduction of income inequality (Lakner et al., 2019). Inequality is also a major barrier to the implementation of the 2030 Agenda as a whole (UNDESA, 2019). For example lowering inequality between population groups (horizontal inequality) reduces the probability of conflicts (Stewart, 2008). Moreover, reducing income inequality correlates positively with a number of socio-economic indicators that are fundamental for sustainable development (Wilkinson and Pickett, 2007).

This contribution makes the case for redistribution as an indispensable strategy for sustainable development. In the following pages two main arguments will be put forward. First, redistribution as an explicit strategy to reduce inequality is largely absent in international cooperation but fundamental for the implementation of

---

[3] Inequality is multi-dimensional and goes beyond the income dimension. However, for the sake of clarity inequality is referred to in the singular throughout the remainder of this paper.

the 2030 Agenda. Second, new approaches to redistribution need to be developed and should consider challenges posed by global trends such as the climate crisis and technological change.

Inequality is a broad concept. It can be analysed in terms of inequality of outcome (measured in income or wealth), or in terms of inequality of opportunity (access to services such as education and health or employment). Vertical inequality means that all observations are ranked from poorest to richest individual or household (or lowest to highest access). Horizontal inequality looks at differences in terms of outcome or opportunities between population groups (ethnicity, gender etc.). Changes in inequality can be measured in absolute or relative terms, before and after redistribution. To measure inequality a variety of indicators with different properties such as the Gini coefficient, Palma ratio or Theil index can be applied. Furthermore, a variety of databases exist which report different levels (and sometimes trends) of inequality because of assumptions made when calculating the indicators or extrapolating gaps in data points. To complicate the matter further, it can be distinguished between within-country and between-country inequality. While the former looks at inequality within countries using the above-mentioned concepts, the latter looks at inequality between countries by comparing the per capita income. The focus of this chapter is mostly on within-country inequality. This by no means suggests that between-country inequality is of less or no importance.

Inequality has increased worldwide. "Countries where inequality has grown are home to more than two thirds (71 per cent) of the world population" (UNDESA, 2020:3). It is outside of the scope of this article to discuss trends and measurements of inequality in detail. There is a plethora of research published which analyses, causes, drivers and trends of inequality (Alvaredo et al., 2019; OECD, 2015; UNDESA, 2020; UNDP, 2013a). Often the concept of inequality is criticized for not providing a clear cut-off line, from when onwards inequality should be considered unsustainable. The acceptable level of inequality depends on the country-context and can vary considerably. It is indeed difficult to pinpoint the exact level of "acceptable" inequality. Some research suggests that inequality already has a detrimental effect in many countries. One working paper by the International Monetary Fund (IMF) finds that a relatively low Gini coefficient of 0.27 already has negative effects on economic development (Grigoli and Robles, 2017). Reducing inequality does not aim to make everyone the same, it implies to reduce inequality to levels which enable societies to prosper and develop sustainably.

Absence of redistribution in international cooperation

The relevance of inequality and the importance to reduce it is increasingly recognized by many actors in and outside of international cooperation (Dabla-Norris et al., 2015; World Bank, 2016). Another example of changing attitudes towards inequality and redistribution is an article by the Editorial Board of the Financial Times which calls for a turnover of the policies of the last 40 years. "Radical reforms – reversing the prevailing policy direction of the last four decades – will need to be put on the table. Governments will have to accept a more active role in the economy. They must see public services as investments rather than liabilities [...]. Redistribution will again be on the agenda [...]. Policies until recently considered eccentric, such as basic income and wealth taxes, will have to be in the mix" (*Financial Times*, 2020).

The inclusion of a stand-alone goal on reducing inequality between and within countries is yet another example of what the *Financial Times* Editorial board calls "reversing the prevailing policy direction" (ibid.). However, such a new and explicit focus on reducing inequality comes along with a major conceptual change for international cooperation because for the first time it shifts the attention of international cooperation to a relative indicator. Absolute indicators exist for a reason. This article does not intend to dismiss absolute indicators altogether, but it criticizes the reliance on them and points out the importance of a relative concept such as inequality.

Inequality is by definition a relative concept. Inequality measures the distribution of income, wealth or access to basic services across the whole population – including the ones with the highest income or the best access to services. The society is viewed as a whole, which is a big difference when compared to a narrower focus of most other concepts widely applied in international cooperation such as extreme poverty. Extreme poverty restricts the analysis, as it is limited to a target group smaller than the whole population. A limited focus, at the same time, obscures potential solutions to reduce inequality (Fischer, 2018). Reducing inequality, however, is a prerequisite for the elimination of extreme poverty and the implementation of the 2030 Agenda.

The Inequality Crisis can be understood in two ways: As the crisis of high and increasing inequalities but also as the crisis of a lack of tools to address the issue. Analyses of causes and drivers and research on how to improve statistics on inequality have increased throughout the last couple of years (Atkinson, 2015; OECD, 2015; Ostry, Berg and Tsangarides, 2014; Piketty, 2014; UNDP, 2013b; Wilkinson and Pickett, 2009). This has led to a more nuanced understanding of the negative effects of high and rising inequality (Dabla-Norris et al., 2015; World Bank, 2016). It has also been increasingly recognized that inequality is not a necessary by-product of economic growth or development. Long-prevailing beliefs such as the trickle-down effect or the Kuznets Curve are increasingly disputed and the idea that income and wealth generated through economic growth automatically reduce inequality has been disregarded (Dabla-Norris et al., 2015; IMF, 2017). The continuous concentration of income and wealth at the top and stagnating real wages or the declining labor share of income (ILO, 2019) show that exactly the opposite has happened in many countries. This growing research and reflection on inequality has contributed to a more nuanced understanding about trends, causes and effects. However, this knowledge has hardly been translated into new strategies and concepts that are necessary to reduce inequalities.

Figure 1 Low-income developing countries, growth, poverty and inequality, 1996-2013

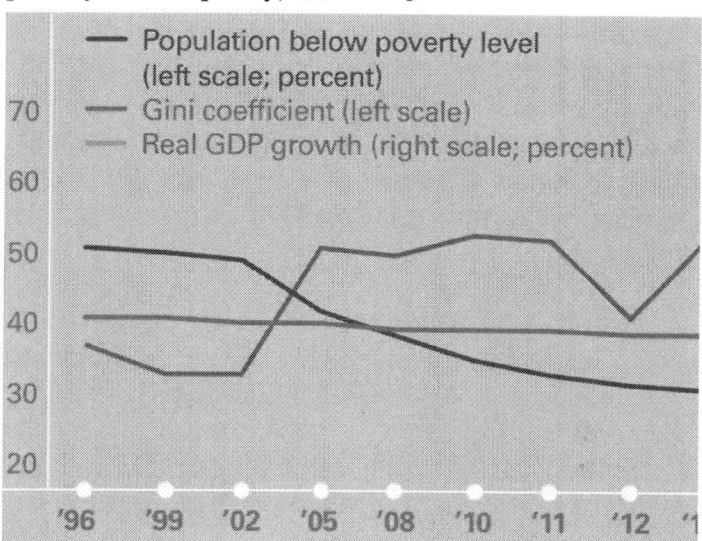

Source: (IMF, 2017:12).

Even though the major share of the varying degree of inequality in the global north and the global south can be explained by the varying degrees of redistribution between countries, redistribution has never been part of the toolbox of international cooperation. The 2019 UNDP Human Development Report finds that in selected "developed countries, taxes and transfers led to a 17-point reduction in the Gini coefficient, when comparing pre-tax and post-tax incomes. But in developing countries the reduction was just 4 points" (UNDP, 2019:15). This gap shows that redistribution is in general a feasible option for the global south which should be strategically explored to achieve sustainable development. "[I]t may be difficult to significantly improve income distribution in the short-term. However, this should not be allowed to discourage immediate efforts in this direction: distributional equity is a permanent goal against which to judge the effects of short-term measures" (UNDESA, 2007:36). However, there is no automatism: Development or economic growth does not automatically reduce inequalities. The reduction of inequalities needs to be strategically implemented.

But what does this mean for international cooperation? First, inequality is not inevitable. Second, redistribution is possible without detrimental effects on growth. Third, there is scope for more redistribution which remains largely untapped (Hoy, 2016). The scope for redistribution is highly context-dependent and countries face challenges such as high informal sector, low tax to GDP ratios and lack of political will – just to name a few. However, this does not necessarily imply that international cooperation should not be incorporating inequality reducing analyses, strategies and tools in its portfolios. Failure to strategically explore potential for increasing distributive policies would be a foregone chance for sustainable development. Or to use the words of the United Nations Global Sustainable Development Report: "The entire 2030 Agenda is threatened by rising inequalities in income and wealth" (UNDESA, 2019:16).

Figure 2: Redistributive direct taxes and transfers explain nearly all the difference in disposable income inequality between advanced and emerging economies

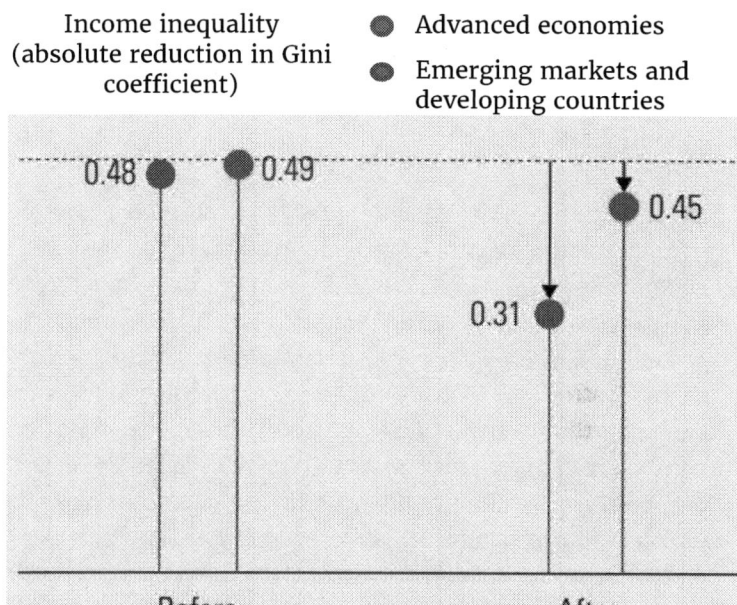

Income inequality (absolute reduction in Gini coefficient)

● Advanced economies

● Emerging markets and developing countries

Inequality, shared prosperity and SDG 10

Current levels and trends of inequality are highly detrimental to sustainable development. The question that immediately comes up is whether international cooperation has adjusted to the new challenge of reducing inequality. As indicated above, the concept of inequality is very broad, and it can be analyzed from many different angles. In the following paragraphs I am arguing that it is highly important to understand and measure inequality in its full meaning and to use a relative indicator which explicitly includes the top end of the income distribution. Through a brief comparison of the World Bank *shared prosperity* goal and the target 10.1 of the 2030 Agenda, I conclude that the understanding of inequality of relevant institutions in international cooperation is not suitable to tackle the structural causes of high inequality.

In 2013 the World Bank adopted two new goals as an overall guidance for its work and strategies. The first one, *ending poverty*, aims to reduce the number of people living in extreme poverty worldwide to below 3 percent. The second one, *shared prosperity*, aims to increase the income of the bottom 40 percent of the income distribution in each country. The two new goals are put at the center of the World Bank's work as they "provide a new context for policy assessment. They provide a framework in which to evaluate policies and their potential contribution to poverty reduction and inclusive growth" (World Bank, 2014:2).

The World Bank's shared prosperity goal is an example of how a (mis)interpretation of inequality can lead to an understanding that addresses the symptoms without tackling the structural problem. The World Bank does not claim the *shared prosperity* goal to be an indicator for inequality. The institution states that shared prosperity is "not a measure of poverty, inequality or social welfare [...]. Shared prosperity is probably best thought of as a measure of change in a particular notion of social welfare, which is sensitive only to the bottom (two-fifths) of the distribution" (Ferreira, Galasso and Negre, 2018:4). However, a background paper which was drafted by the World Bank for an Expert Group Meeting which discussed the development of the indicator framework for the Sustainable Development Goals (SDGs) maintains that the "the shared prosperity measure implicitly places emphasis on changes in inequality in society" (World Bank, 2015:3). In other instances the connection is made more openly, the sub-headline "Taking on Inequality" of the Poverty and Shared Prosperity 2016 (World Bank, 2016) is one example.

However, even if the income of the bottom 40 percent of a population increases, it does by no means imply that inequality is reduced as the income of top of the income distribution is not considered. Even if the shared prosperity premium which is defined as the "difference in the growth rate in the average incomes among the poorest 40%, and the growth rate in the overall average income" (Ferreira et al., 2018:7), shows a positive development, inequality is not necessarily reduced. It is not difficult to imagine a context where the income of the top end of the income distribution is increasing at similar (absolute or relative) rate. This can lead to a risky situation where the indicators show positive development, while the gap between the bottom and top end of the income distribution is actually increasing. Furthermore, since the *shared prosperity* goal relies on a relative comparison (as most inequality indicators do) one can also imagine scenarios in which relative inequality is stagnating or decreasing, while inequality measured in absolute terms is increasing. Some research suggests that it is the absolute difference that counts. "Perceptions of inequality may be likely related to increasingly obvious absolute differences in income, not only to the perhaps less apparent relative differences" (Niño-Zarazúa, Roope and Tarp, 2017:680). Hence, an improvement as measured by shared prosperity indicator or shared prosperity premium does not necessarily lead to a sustainable reduction of inequality.

The formulation of the SDG's target 10.1 has a great resemblance to the shared prosperity goal of the World Bank. Target 10.1 states "By 2030, progressively achieve and sustain income growth of the bottom 40 per cent of the population at a rate higher than the national average" (UNGA, 2015:21). Despite many critical voices and raised concerns regarding the inappropriate formulation of this target, it was nevertheless adopted. "Measuring the income of the poorest 40% against national growth means the SDG target lacks the [...] comparison with the rich. It supports the shared-prosperity goal's implication that the wealth of the people at the top is unimportant – all that matters is a measurable improvement for people at the bottom" (Cobham, Schlogl and Sumner, 2015). The discussion whether the *shared prosperity* goal is ambitious enough to make a meaningful contribution to reducing inequality has been going on for the last five years. A think piece written by the German Executive Director of the World Bank critically analyses whether the World Bank has taken the right measures to contribute to reducing inequality (Zattler, 2020). The author suggests that the shared prosperity might not be the measure to ensure a sustainable reduction of inequalities by pointing out that the World Bank "must ask whether the way it currently measures the shared prosperity goal appropriately reflects the key challenges developing countries are facing" (Zattler, 2020:7).

The (mis)interpretation of inequality by the World Bank and the vague formulation of target 10.1 acknowledge the challenge of rising inequality. However, the understanding of inequality put forward by the World Bank and SDG 10 does not call for "reversing the prevailing policy direction" like the *Financial Times* (2020) does. Inequality cannot be fully understood when the income and wealth of the top end of the income distribution is disregarded. *The Inequality Crisis* is only partially understood and addressed by the World Bank's *shared prosperity* goals and SDG 10 of the 2030 Agenda. A meaningful reduction of inequality requires an understanding of inequality which also includes the development of new strategies and policies which have so far not been part of the policy discussion.

Technological and climate change require new forms of redistribution

The negative effects of high and rising inequality are not always directly visible. However, on two occasions throughout the last two years the negative ramifications have become apparent. First, inequality reduces social cohesion (Wilkinson and Pickett, 2009) as was shown by the popular uprisings in 2019 in many countries of the world. While inequality is not the sole cause of the uprisings, it is considered a major contributing factor, particularly in Ecuador, Chile, France and Lebanon (BBC News, 2019; Goodman, 2019). Second, less than a year later, the pandemic caused by the spread of the Covid-19 virus highlights how a pandemic can have a very different impact on different income and ethnic groups (Fisher and Bubola, 2020; Jones, 2020; Oliver, 2020). In the case of the United Kingdom, preliminary academic analysis confirms the observation that the Covid-19 crisis has a different impact across ethnic groups (Platt and Warwick, 2020) and income groups (Adams-Prassl et al., 2020).

These examples show that high and rising inequality has direct consequences. Additionally, it shows how analyses guided by an inequality framework can reveal new and important differences in outcomes. It is well known that averages of socio-economic indicators obscure the highly heterogenous outcomes (Ravallion, 2016:351). Those become visible when the indicators are decomposed based on income groups or the distribution of income and access to services is analyzed across the whole population. A very strong example is the stark variation of life expectancy across income groups (Wilkinson, 2020).

Furthermore, these examples support the need to actively reduce inequality through redistribution. There are other trends which will have a major impact on the ability of governments to implement distributive systems. First, the fast pace-change caused by technological disruptions. Often it is argued that technological change will create as many new jobs as it will make redundant (ILO, 2018). However, a substantial change coming along with technological disruption and automation is the concentration of productive resources and gains. Among the many drivers of inequality, one stands out in many analyses. The so-called "skill premium" implies that the benefits of digitalization and computation are mostly reaped by people with higher education (UNDESA, 2020).

As it is the case with economic growth, the technological dividend will not benefit everyone to the same extent. Institutions must make innovative technologies accessible to everyone. Technological change is also likely to increase productivity. Gains in productivity and real wages used to go hand in hand. However, in OECD countries some three or four decades ago (depending on the country) one can witness the decoupling of productivity and wages. "[T]hese developments have resulted in the decoupling of growth in low and median wages from growth in productivity" (OECD, 2018:52). Again "[p]ublic policies and institutions are important determinants of the link between productivity and wages" (ibid.).

The second global trend which will have a strong impact on distributive systems is the climate crisis. While "the top 10% of world population, are responsible for about 34% of [...] carbon emissions" (Hubacek et al., 2017), its ramifications have contributed to the widening of global economic inequality already (Diffenbaugh and Burke 2019). At the same time, the ones who contribute the least in terms of CO_2 emissions are the ones who suffer the most as "[p]oorer countries and poorer people will be hit earliest and hardest" (UNDP, 2019:175) and have fewer resources to cope and recover (UNDESA, 2020). Also, when it comes to climate – similarly to the Covid-19 pandemic – the crisis reveals and intensifies underlying inequalities. Hence, reducing inequalities and fighting climate change have to be thought of together. Climate-related policies need to incorporate a distributive angle and vice versa.

The challenges for increasing inequalities related to technological and climate change outlined above further strengthen the argument to develop strategies for a stronger focus on redistribution. Traditional policy frameworks only provide a partial answer. The rapidly unfolding technological development requires policy makers to adjust and develop new approaches to taxation and ways to reduce the impact of climate change. A policy framework based on inequalities brings about advantages. It provides the analytical lens and suggests indicators to measure its success. An integrated response to these challenges entails applying an inequality approach to climate, social and economic goals. Policies should be measured against its most likely impact they will have on inequality.

Conclusion

The absence of redistribution from international cooperation severely hampers its chances to contribute to sustainable development. Economic growth and poverty do not tell the whole story of successful and sustainable development. Inequality makes a significant contribution to the international cooperation because it adds a very important dimension to the debate: the relative dimension. It is very much possible to have increasing inequality in times of a growing economy poverty reduction while.

Attention should also be given to the absolute gap between the bottom and top end of the income distribution. This absolute gap is likely to contribute to the negative impact inequality has. Even if the bottom is relatively better off and their income is growing, but the distance between the bottom and the top is growing simultaneously, sustainable development can be hampered. Hence, in order to reduce inequality sustainably it is not enough to aim for "shared prosperity" as suggested by the World Bank or to increase the income of the bottom 40 percent of the population as suggested by SDG 10. To sustainably reduce inequality, redistribution should be part of developing strategies to close the gap that has been growing so immensely.

Redistribution is on average significantly higher in the global north than in the south. This shows that a higher degree of redistribution does not automatically stifle economic growth and hinder development. The stark difference shows that it is viable to strategically develop and employ distributive policies as strategy for development. However, tools and strategies for redistribution in the 21st century need to take into consideration technological and climate change. As many countries show, policies to reduce inequalities can be designed and implemented. Besides, systems of redistribution need to adapt constantly to changing circumstances. For example, the effectiveness of redistribution in most OECD countries was reduced and inequality increased. "Over the past three decades, income inequality has risen in most OECD countries, reaching in some cases historical highs" (OECD, 2015:20).

Due to several factors – for example government capacity, political economy, lobbying, narrow tax base and high informal sectors, it is not possible for all countries to simply implement distributive systems. However, because of the urgency to reduce inequalities, the discussion about suitable models of redistribution for the 21st century should be strategically strengthened. Additionally, the awareness regarding the negative impact of inequalities is growing and along with it the motivation to act upon. The international cooperation should strategically develop distributive strategies to contribute to sustainable development. Reducing inequality allow to develop a comprehensive policy framework which contributes to sustainable development. It is necessary to strategically develop and increase the applicability of such a framework for different country contexts to achieve the 2030 Agenda.

References

Adams-Prassl, Abi, Teodora Boneva, Marta Golin, and Christopher Rauh (2020) *Inequality in the Impact of the Coronavirus Shock: New Survey Evidence for the UK*. Cambridge Working Papers in Economics No. 2023.

Alvaredo, Facundo, Lucas Chancel, Thomas Piketty, Emmanuel Saez, and Gabriel Zucman (2019) *World Inequality Report 2018*. Paris: World Inequality Lab.

Anderson, Edward (2016) "Equality as a Global Goal." *Ethics & International Affairs* 30(2):189–200.

Atkinson, Anthony (2015) *Inequality: What Can Be Done*. Cambridge: Harvard University Press.

BBC News (2019) "Do Today's Global Protests Have Anything in Common?" *BBC*. Retrieved May 31, 2020 (https://www.bbc.com/news/world-50123743).

Cobham, Alex, Lukas Schlogl, and Andy Sumner (2015) "Top Incomes Drive Inequality – So Why Does the Inequality Target Ignore Them?" *The Guardian.* Retrieved May 31, 2020

Dabla-Norris, Era, Kalpana Kochhar, Nujin Suphaphiphat, Frantisek Ricka, and Evridiki Tsounta (2015) *Causes and Consequences of Income Inequality: A Global Perspective.* IMF Staff Discussion Note SDN/15/13. Washington, DC: International Monetary Fund.

Diffenbaugh, Noah, and Marshall Burke (2019) "Global Warming Has Increased Global Economic Inequality." *Proceedings of the National Academy of Sciences* 116(20):9808–13.

Ferreira, Francisco, Emanuela Galasso, and Mario Negre (2018) *Shared Prosperity: Concepts, Data, and Some Policy Examples.* IZA Discussion Paper Series No. 11571.

Financial Times (2020) "Virus Lays Bare the Frailty of the Social Contract." *Financial Times.* Retrieved April 13, 2020 (https://www.ft.com/content/7eff769a-74dd-11ea-95fe-fcd274e920ca).

Fischer, Andrew (2018) *Poverty as Ideology: Rescuing Social Justice from Global Development Agendas.* London: Zed Books.

Fisher, Max, and Emma Bubola. 2020. "As Coronavirus Deepens Inequality, Inequality Worsens Its Spread." *The New York Times.* Retrieved May 31, 2020

Freistein, Katja, and Bettina Mahlert (2016) "The Potential for Tackling Inequality in the Sustainable Development Goals." *Third World Quarterly* 37(12):2139–55.

Fukuda-Parr, Sakiko (2019) "Keeping Out Extreme Inequality from the SDG Agenda – The Politics of Indicators." *Global Policy* 10(S1):61–69.

Goodman, Peter. 2019. "Inequality Fuels Rage of 'Yellow Vests' in Equality-Obsessed France." *The New York Times.* Retrieved May 31, 2020. (https://www.nytimes.com/2019/04/15/business/yellow-vests-movement-inequality.html).

Grigoli, Francesco, and Adrian Robles (2017) *Inequality Overhang*. IMF Working Paper WP/17/76.

Hoy, Chris (2016) *Gasoline, Guns, and Giveaways: Is There New Capacity for Redistribution to End Three Quarters of Global Poverty?* Center for Global Development Working Paper No. 433.

Hubacek, Klaus, Giovanni Baiocchi, Kuishuang Feng, Raúl Muñoz Castillo, Laixiang Sun, and Jinjun Xue (2017) "Global Carbon Inequality." *Energy, Ecology and Environment* 2(6):361–69.

ILO (2018) *The Economics of Artificial Intelligence: Implicationsfor the Future of Work*. Future of Work Research Paper Series No. 5.

ILO (2019) *The Global Labour Income Share and Distribution*. Geneva: ILO Department of Statistics.

IMF (2015) *Inequality and Fiscal Policy*. Washington, DC: International Monetary Fund.

IMF (2017) *IMF Annual Report 2017: Promoting Inclusive Growth*. Washington DC: International Monetary Fund.

Jones, Owen (2020) "We're About to Learn a Terrible Lesson from Coronavirus: Inequality Kills." *The Guardian*. Retrieved May 31, 2020. (https://www.theguardian.com/commentisfree/2020/mar/14/coronavirus-outbreak-inequality-austerity-pandemic).

Lakner, Christoph, Daniel Gerszon Mahler, Mario Negre, Espen Beer Prydz, Ikechukwu Dialoke, Onyi Akachukwu Joseph, and Edeh Friday Ogbu (2019) *How Much Does Reducing Inequality Matter for Global Poverty ?* Policy Research Working Paper No. 8869.

Niño-Zarazúa, Miguel, Laurence Roope, and Finn Tarp (2017) "Global Inequality: Relatively Lower, Absolutely Higher." *Review of Income and Wealth* 63(4):661–84.

OECD (2015) *In It Together: Why Less Inequality Benefits All*. Paris: OECD Publishing. OECD. 2018. *OECD Economic Outlook, Vol. 2018 Issue 2*. Paris: OECD Publishing.

Oliver, Laura (2020) "Coronavirus: A Pandemic in the Age of Inequality." *World Economic Forum*. Retrieved May 31, 2020 (https://www.weforum.org/agenda/2020/03/coronavirus-pandemic-inequality-among- workers/).

Ostry, Jonathan, Andrew Berg, and Charalambos G. Tsangarides (2014) *Redistribution, Inequality, and Growth*. IMF Staff Discussion Note SDN/14/02. Washington, DC: International Monetary Fund.

Piketty, Thomas (2014) *Capital in the Twenty-First Century*. Cambridge: Belknap Press.

Platt, Lucinda, and Ross Warwick (2020) *Are Some Ethnic Groups More Vulnerable to COVID-19 than Others?* London: The Institute for Fiscal Studies.

Ravallion, Martin (2016) *The Economics of Poverty: History, Measurement, and Policy*. New York: Oxford University Press.

Saiz, Ignacio, and Kate Donald (2017) "Tackling Inequality through the Sustainable Development Goals: Human Rights in Practice." *International Journal of Human Rights*.

Stewart, Frances (2008) *Horizontal Inequalities and Conflict*. Edited by F. Stewart. London: Palgrave Macmillan.

UNDESA (2007) *The United Nations Development Agenda - Development for All*. New York: United Nations Department of Economic and Social Affairs.

UNDESA (2019) *Global Sustainable Development Report: The Future Is Now - Science for Achieving Sustainable Development*. New York: United Nations Department of Economic and Social Affairs.

UNDESA (2020) *World Social Report 2020: Inequality in a Rapidly Changing World*. New York: United Nations Department of Economic and Social Affairs.

UNDP (2013a) *Humanity Divided: Confronting Inequality in Developing Countries*. New York: United Nations Development Programme.

UNDP (2013b) *The Rise of the South: Human Progress in a Diverse World*. New York: United Nations Development Programme.

UNDP (2019) *Beyond Income, Beyond Averages, Beyond Today: Inequalities in Human Development in the 21st Century.* New York: United Nations Development Programme.

UNGA (2015) *Transforming Our World: The 2030 Agenda for Sustainable Development.* New York: United Nations General Assembly.

Wilkinson, Richard (2020) "The Impact of Income Inequality on Life Expectancy." In *Locating Health: Sociological and Historical Explorations*, edited by S. Platt, H. Thomas, S. Scott, and G. Williams. New York: Routledge.

Wilkinson, Richard, and Kate Pickett (2007) "The Problems of Relative Deprivation: Why Some Societies Do Better Than Others." *Social Science & Medicine* 65(9):1965–78.

Wilkinson, Richard, and Kate Pickett (2009) *The Spirit Level: Why Equal Societies Almost Always Do Better.* New York: Bloomsbury Press.

World Bank (2014) *A Measured Approach to Ending Poverty and Boosting Shared Prosperity: Concepts, Data, and the Twin Goals.* Washington, DC: World Bank.

World Bank (2015) *Shared Prosperity: A Technical Note on Measuring and Monitoring Growth with Equity (Expert Group Meeting on the Indicator Framework, 25-26 February 2015).* ESA/STAT/441/2/58A/5.

World Bank (2016) *Poverty and Shared Prosperity Report: Taking on Inequality.* Washington DC: The World Bank.

Zattler, Jürgen (2020) *Rising Inequality: What Are the Implications for Policymaking at the World Bank?* New York: Friedrich Ebert Stiftung.

Chapter 16

Inequality and the case for UBI funded by sovereign money

Geoff Crocker[1]

Introduction

The current economic system is generating increasing inter-personal inequality in income and wealth. This is well documented by several observers, including others in this collection of essays, such as James Galbraith, and not least Thomas Piketty in his two books and on-line database (Piketty, 2014; 2020). I therefore don't intend to rehearse the data analysis of inequality in this brief paper, but to take it as a working assumption. My aim rather is to locate causes of inequality, and to consider whether universal basic income (UBI) can claim to alleviate inequality (for background see Crocker, 2020). The main focus for evidence is the UK, but the issues generalise.

---

[1] Geoff is a partner in "The Economics of Basic Income" research project, IPR, University of Bath and "Basic Income Conversation" as well as editor of "The Case for Basic Income" ; and author of "Basic Income and Sovereign Money – the alternative to economic crisis and austerity policy".

Contexts of inequality

For our purposes, income inequality arises:

1. between those employed and unemployed
2. within employment
3. between those unemployed.

Causal variables for income inequality can be proposed, researched, analysed, and potentially mitigated. Wealth inequality is a more random outcome, arising from huge financial success within a lifetime, or resulting from inter-generational inheritance of extremely concentrated wealth holding through aristocratic or meritocratic social classes. Prior to the coronavirus crisis, unemployment was remarkably low in many developed economies, but low wage rates were pervasive, leading to in-work poverty. Employment no longer guarantees income sufficiency. Huge and growing inequality has become endemic between CEOs and other top earners, compared to low wage earners.

Various causes of this rise in inequality have been suggested (see other essays in this collection). The main *political* explanation is that capitalism is essentially exploitative of labour. The power balance has seen a huge shift in favour of capital, and a reduction in labour bargaining power. The specific cause of the power shift is not clear, but a progressive step in the historic stage of capitalism is assumed. According to this diagnostic, the remedy is therefore political, focusing on a return to trade union bargaining power, job guarantees, and high redistributive taxation on top incomes and wealth.

The *technology* explanation (see Crocker, 2012) is that productivity has inevitably reduced the wage share of output. Wage becomes insufficient for personal economic well-being, leading to poverty. Aggregate demand becomes deficient in the macroeconomy, raising household borrowing, thereby leading to crisis. As earned income declines relative to output, so unearned income necessarily rises. This takes four main forms of pensions, dividends, welfare benefits and household debt. The increase in the share of unearned income further drives inequality, since between these sources of unearned income, pensions and dividends are privileged with secure growth, whilst welfare benefits are constrained by austerity, and low-income households bear unsustainable debt, serviced at the punitive interest rates of payday lenders. If the technology explanation for inequality is correct, then apart from resisting technology, which supposes a view on the philosophy of technology that it is subject to human agency, the remedy has to be other than high-wage full employment.

Put another way, if the cause and result of inequality can be adequately countered by high-wage full employment, then well and good. The worry is that technology has hugely weakened both employment and wage as a tool to ensure inclusive economic well-being. Political and technology explanations for inequality are, however, not necessarily incompatible. If technology does reduce labour demand, then labour bargaining power is thereby weakened. In paradigmatic terms, Marx in his 1847 *Poverty of Philosophy* observed that technology can thus drive the political power structure; writing "the hand-mill gives you society with the feudal lord; the steam-mill society with the industrial capitalist". Data definitively shows a huge secular reduction in working hours throughout the 20th century. If the tide of technological automation is at least partly irresistible, then no amount of labour bargaining power can mitigate its effects on reducing the labour share of output. We, therefore, *have to ask* whether income, rather than employment wage, is the more appropriate corrective to inequality, and whether UBI can fulfil this role. This can be approached in terms of a series of logical steps.

1. A long term steady state reduction in earned income against consumer expenditure

There is an undeniable inexorable long-term trend for labour income to decline as part of consumer expenditure. For example, Exhibit 1:

Exhibit 1 UK Labour Income and Consumer Expenditure 1948-2016

Source: UK ONS (note that ONS define "Labour income"=wages + self-employed income) with thanks to David Matthewson and other staff at ONS for valuable help in defining and interpreting UK income data streams.

In the UK, from 1948 to 1995, labour income was sufficient to meet consumer expenditure, but from 1995 onwards, labour income became insufficient to fund consumer expenditure, which is now increasingly funded by a growing proportion of unearned income.

2. Inference to best explanation prefers the technology hypothesis

Since there is a long term trend of labour income decline as a proportion of consumer expenditure, and this trend persists throughout the period through various regimes of changing trade union power, then a more continuous causal explanation is needed. Whilst there is significant dispute in economics and political economy about the *role* of technology, technology remains the preferred hypothesis as the underlying fundamental influence, i) since it is clear from *a priori* arithmetic that higher productivity will reduce the wage content of output, and ii) because technological innovation has continued unabated throughout the whole period. It is possible however, as a secondary phenomenon, that the rate of reduction in the labour income share was retarded in periods of high labour bargaining power. In the UK case, the argument would specifically be that the labour share reduced at a higher rate from 1980 with the advent of the Thatcher government, which legislated reduced trade union power. Also possible is the hypothesis that "globalisation" (or at least the many factors we associate with this term) has reduced UK labour income per unit of output in the period since 1995. The pattern may vary between countries but the trend remains significant.

These alternative hypotheses are being tested in a research project *The Economics of Basic Income* at the Institute for Policy Research at the University of Bath UK.[2] As noted earlier, one feature of the labour market is that it is bifurcated between senior executives, highly skilled professionals, and more functional roles, sometimes disparagingly referred to as "bullshit jobs". It is not that senior executives have greater representative bargaining power, but that they are equipped with skill sets valued in relation to technology. This observation therefore reinforces technology as the preferred explanatory factor of inequality in employment. As much of the material on a "fourth industrial revolution" and "industry 4.0" claims, this is an advantage which may not last long for skilled professionals, as more of their role is threatened by sophisticated automation and the application of artificial intelligence. We therefore see that unearned income is increasing within consumer expenditure, and in analysing the components of unearned income, we now find that there are changes in the component shares of unearned income which are also driving inequality

3. Changes in the component shares of unearned income are further driving inequality

The composition of unearned income has changed significantly over the last 20 years in the UK. Private

---

[2] See, IPR, University of Bath "The Economics of Basic Income" www.bath.ac.uk/projects/the-economics-of-basic-income/.

pensions and consumer credit have accounted for relatively stable shares of unearned income as Exhibit 2 indicates.

Exhibit 2 UK component shares of unearned income 1997–2016

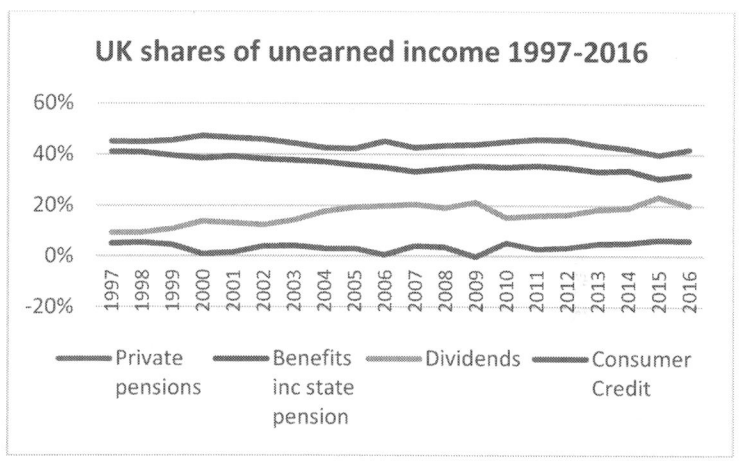

Source ONS

The notable changes have been that:

- Welfare benefits including state pension have reduced from 41% of unearned income to 32%.
- Dividend income has increased from 9% to 20% of unearned income.

Wages and benefits have been relatively displaced by dividend income in the UK economy, perhaps partly due to self-employed earnings being redefined as dividend. This has fuelled inequality as higher income shareholders and pensioners benefit at the expense of lower income wage earners and benefit recipients.

The general point is that unearned income is increasingly "necessary" in the macroeconomy, but unearned income itself is driving inequality through shifts in its components. As a form of unearned income, Universal Basic Income (UBI) therefore needs to be defined to achieve greater income equality.

4. Basic income is the preferred form of unearned income

The worrying component of unearned income is annual new household debt. This rose to £166bn in the UK 2004. Its unsustainability against the same low wages which had required it, led to the 2007 economic crisis. Numerous subsequent contributions in political economy argue that household debt feeds inequality, not least because much of it is advanced to low income households at premium interest rates, (e.g. Montgomery 2019).

Since unearned income is demonstrably *necessary* in contemporary high technology economies, then the preferred variant of this unearned income is a basic income paid unconditionally and universally to all citizens (UBI). This is because:

1. UBI avoids the demeaning intrusion of means-tested welfare benefits.
2. UBI, therefore, has the lowest administrative cost of any welfare system.

3. UBI is effective since it has an automatic 100% take up rate, compared to current welfare benefits, especially those targeted to elderly people which have low take up rates.

4. Most importantly, UBI avoids the unemployment and poverty traps of current welfare benefits which are withdrawn when a recipient takes work, whereas a basic income is retained, thus removing any disincentive to work.

Clearly, the question then arises as to *how* a substantial level of UBI can be funded. There are many different funding proposals, but the most attractive is a sovereign money system.

5. The technology hypothesis requires unearned income and sovereign money

Many advocates for UBI (e.g. Torry, 2013) propose schemes which are revenue neutral and therefore funded by increased taxation and/or reduction in other areas of government expenditure, including reducing or eliminating current welfare benefits. Marginal socio-economic change results from such conservative funding schemes, encountering the objection that UBI is either too small to be meaningful, or too high to be affordable. Other proposals to fund UBI from wealth taxes or pollution taxes encounter operational difficulty. For example in taxing the many forms of wealth, or in relying on pollution taxes which are designed to achieve better environmental outcomes and so become self-cancelling. A more radical funding concept is needed to achieve a substantial UBI to reduce inequality.

At present, government expenditure and money creation are funded by the sale of interest-bearing government bonds. This accumulates mountains of national debt, equal to or greater than annual GDP in many economies, and therefore in reality, unrepayable. However, the interest cost of this debt is substantial, amounting to £39bn annually in the UK. This seigniorage is paid from general taxation to privileged bodies in the financial sector and is therefore likely to increase inequality.

A thought experiment shows how basic income is necessary in high technology economies. In a totally automated economy with neither labour nor wage, output would be distributed by annual government vouchers, destroyed and renewed each year. In this paradigm, 100% of GDP becomes basic income, funded 100% by sovereign money. The vouchers represent both basic income and the sovereign money which funds it. Whilst we have not and may not ever reach this extreme of automation, nevertheless there are strong elements of this effect in our contemporary high-tech economies. A nuanced hypothesis is therefore that high-tech economies require some degree of UBI funded by sovereign money. As such, UBI would be necessarily funded by debt-free sovereign money. Since sovereign money is not interest bearing, it removes the inequality in the seigniorage of money creation by the sale of government bonds, which is currently set to rise by a further £645bn in the UK economy to fund response measures to the coronavirus epidemic. There is no reason why this funding cannot be by debt-free sovereign money.

6. How UBI reduces inequality

In a simple sense, one might think UBI *must* gradually increase equality in a society of unequal incomes, since it is a payment of the same amount made to all individuals. However, this depends on how great the UBI payment is, and how it is funded. If it is funded to be revenue neutral by increasing top level taxation, then it will reduce inequality, though less so than the same funding applied as a targeted welfare benefit transfer payment. If on the other hand it is funded exclusively by reducing welfare benefits, then inequality will almost certainly increase. Indeed, some versions of a UBI scheme have been shown to increase child poverty, so that very careful UBI scheme design is needed to ensure the preferred balance of winners and losers compared to current income outcomes. If UBI is funded by debt-free sovereign money, then income inequality will reduce, although probably only marginally.

What debt-free sovereign money would enable is the reversal of austerity cuts to the value of full potential output GDP, the latter constraint ensuring a non-inflationary outcome. This would more definitely reduce inequality by the restoration of welfare spending cuts, whether these are re-instated as means-tested benefits, or preferably, as UBI. Clearly, this requires a huge paradigm shift away from current financial orthodoxy, which insists that government budgets should balance, that government expenditure must be accounted as revenue or debt, that money is real and cannot be created or destroyed, and that government financial balances determine economic affordability. Modern Monetary

Theory (MMT) is one way to think differently about the potential (see Fullbrook and Morgan, 2020). MMT insists that sovereign states can create money (e.g. Ehnts, 2017). Exact propositions differ between:

1. MMT advocates who invoke sovereign money to fund Job Guarantee, Green New Deal, and US Medicare for All proposals (e.g. Kelton 2020). In this interpretation, sovereign money remains balanced in double-entry accounting as interest-bearing debt. The proposal is that the debt is manageable because it is itself balanced by surpluses in the other two financial sectors of the economy according to the "Godley identity" (see Godley and Lavoie, 2012, however see Teixeira, 2012).
2. Sovereign money advocates, who propose shifting *all* money creation from commercial banks to the state central bank, to avoid excessive lending creating economic crisis, and to return seigniorage to the state (e.g. Huber, 2017)
3. UBI advocates who argue for sovereign money to fund UBI and a reversal of austerity cuts (Crocker, 2020). In this definition, sovereign money is simply issued without any associated sale of government bonds, assumption of debt, or payment of interest.

Recall that in our previous thought experiment, a totally automated economy operating with 100% GDP as basic income, has the option to implement total equality by allocating all individuals the same annual income. This is where the prefix "basic" has meaning and force. The practical question then remains as to how to design a basic income scheme such that everyone has a reasonable standard of living enabled by natural resources, the deployed technology, and the inherited infrastructure, whilst leaving scope for extra personal initiative and skill to generate more individual income.

UBI has been piloted, though never thoroughly implemented at macroeconomic level as a truly universal unconditional scheme. Various pilot projects in Brazil, Iran, Namibia, India and Finland have been extensively reviewed (Torry, 2019). The Finnish pilot project found little effect in the labour market, but reported a general increase in well-being associated with the guarantee of a secure income. The problem with microeconomic pilot schemes is that they tend to report a positive response to secure income, which is hardly unexpected. Community response depends on what alternative welfare benefit schemes are already in place in any specific country. Hence Nordic communities with high current welfare provision are less interested in UBI than Eastern European communities where current welfare provision may be negligible. Since pilot projects can only test temporary basic income with limited coverage, they can never report on the macroeconomic effects on aggregate demand which are a main driver of the case for UBI. Pilots take several years and delay the macroeconomic UBI which is more urgently needed – the current pandemic only serves to underscore this.

Conclusion

UBI is proposed as a human right, a fundamental *equality*. As Guy Standing (2010) has argued, we all have certain "birthrights", including to the benefits of commonly inherited infrastructure and technology. Current levels of inequality in income and wealth fail to recognise and respect fundamental human worth and dignity. Today's economic system is delivering inequality, poverty, even in-work poverty, low pay, pervasive debt, austerity, ecological damage, and crisis. This is in the *richest* countries in the world in a system that likewise harms even as it "develops" the rest of the world (see for example Wade's essay in this collection). The system needs a radical re-think and re-engineering. UBI and sovereign money are key to this re-definition.

Detailed UBI scheme design must then ensure that inequality is reduced by its implementation, since this is not necessarily so. Sovereign money makes a meaningful level of UBI affordable, and also enables the restoration of austerity cuts, the latter possibly proving more effective than UBI alone in reducing inequality. Sovereign money and UBI in combination are mutually reinforcing and more than additive in their effect, invoking Aristotle writing in his "Metaphysics" that "the whole is greater than the sum of the parts".

References

Crocker, Geoff (2020) *Basic Income and Sovereign Money – the alternative to economic crisis and austerity policy.* Basingstoke: Palgrave Pivot.

Crocker, Geoff (2012) *A Managerial Philosophy of Technology.* Basingstoke: Palgrave Macmillan.

Ehnts, Dirk (2017) *Modern Monetary Theory and European Macroeconomics.* Routledge.

Fullbrook, Edward and Morgan, Jamie (eds.) (2020) *Modern Monetary Theory and Its Critics.* Bristol: World Economics Association Books.

Godley, Wynne and Lavoie, Marc (2012) *Monetary Economics.* Basingstoke: Palgrave Macmillan.

Huber, Joseph (2017) *Sovereign Money.* Basingstoke: Palgrave Macmillan.

Kelton, Stephanie (2020) *The Deficit Myth: Modern Monetary Theory and the Birth of the People's Economy.* New York: John Murray; Public Affairs.

Montgomery, J. (2019) *Should we abolish household debts?* Cambridge: Polity.

Piketty, Thomas (2014) *Capital in the Twenty-First Century.* Cambridge: Harvard University Press.

Piketty, Thomas (2020) *Capital and Ideology.* Cambridge: Harvard University Press.

Standing, Guy (2014) *The Precariat: The New Dangerous Class.* London: Bloomsbury Academic.

Teixeira, Lucas (2012) "Deficits and Debts in the US economy: a critique of Godley's Imbalances Approach to Macroeconomics." www.centrosraffa.org/public/4ce234ef-405d-4a0e-aabb-f1ed94ba7c60.pdf

Torry, Malcolm (2013) *Money for Everyone: Why We Need a Citizen's Income.* Bristol: Policy Press.

Torry, Malcolm (ed.) (2019) *The Palgrave International Handbook of Basic Income.* Basingstoke: Palgrave Macmillan.

Chapter 17

Inequality and morbid symptoms of a financialised system

Ann Pettifor[1]

Introduction

Today as the world endures the crisis of a global pandemic, "an old order is ending in convulsions". So writes Rebecca Spang, historian of the French revolution in *The Atlantic* (Spang, 2020). In the 1790s, money, debt and the non-payment of taxes by France's rentiers, played a critical role in revolutionizing France. Today purveyors of money and debt – creditors, investors and speculators – both avoid taxes and prey on a global economy radically weakened by the Great Financial Crisis and the policy response to the events of 2007-9. As a result, and unsurprisingly, the international economic system is both unprepared for, and prone to increasingly frequent "convulsions". COVID19 is but the latest, and will cause long-lasting economic damage. Above all, and according to Case and Deaton, COVID19 is expected to

[1] Director, Policy Research in Macroeconomics (PRIME), www.primeeconomics.org, @AnnPettifor.

widen the US's "already vast inequalities in health and income".[2]

The "pillars" of the global economic system are fabricated on shaky, "liberal" foundations (see Pettifor, 2006, 2017a). It is an international system specifically designed to expand markets for creditors and investors; and to protect, above all others, the interests of private creditors. The most important foundations of the system are capital mobility, the marketisation of interest rates and exchange rates. The system is largely maintained by the world's hegemon – the United States – which uses its role as issuer of the world's reserve currency to protect the interests of private finance, in particular Wall Street. US monetary power is backed in turn by military power, used to maintain control over access to, or the denial of access to markets worldwide.

A central tenet of the system is that wherever possible, the policy autonomy of governments (whether democratic or not) must be constrained and subordinated to governance by those active in capital, goods and labour markets. The global system – its regulations and laws – are thus largely governed by *private authority.*

Obscene levels of inequality are but one of the *outcomes* of the current global economic order or architecture. Addressing inequality is, therefore, not just about individual policy focus, it is about international system change.

---

[2] Anne Case, Angus Deaton, Jun 15, 2020, Project Syndicate. *United States of Despair.*

Inequality is not the only outcome of the system. Other worldwide outcomes include: immense, and unaccountable corporate power; high levels of costly private and public debt; sky high levels of rent (wealth) extraction by the owners of both financial and physical assets; weak or non-existent public health infrastructure; low levels of investment; high levels of fraud, illiteracy, homelessness. Capital mobility facilitates drug dealing which in turn leads to escalating levels of addiction and mental illness. Globalised transport systems – aeroplanes and international travel - act as passports and vectors of disease and pandemics. These expose systemic problems for the many who have functioned as global reserves of low-paid, insecure, non-unionised and unskilled workers.

In the United States these outcomes are worsened by a costly, exclusive private healthcare system, lavish levels of public spending on the military; and a privatised prison-industrial complex, accompanied by extensive surveillance and policing. With the constitution and democracy corrupted by corporate power, elites mimic their French predecessors. Like Norman noblemen, they appear largely unaware of the social and political stresses unleashed by the privatised economic system. While the rentier class have made extraordinary capital gains, many US workers in employment can only function by drawing on high levels of debt. In the bottom half of US income distribution, Americans have experienced essentially no income growth since the late 1970s after accounting for taxes, inflation, and cash benefits from the government. [3] Those that are unemployed and without healthcare, suffer what Case and Deaton dub "deaths of despair" (Case and Deaton, 2020). Their work reveals that:

> "[I]n the past two decades, deaths of despair from suicide, drug overdose, and alcoholism have risen dramatically, and now claim hundreds of thousands of American lives each year – and they're still rising."

Between just March 18 and April 10, 2020, over 22 million people lost their jobs in the USA as the unemployment rate surged toward 15 percent. Over the same three weeks, American billionaire wealth increased by $282 billion. This was an almost 10 percent *gain*, according to a US Institute for Policy Studies (IPS) report *Billionaire Bonanza* (Collins et al, 2020).[4] Market capitalizations may have become erratic, perhaps there will be losses to

---

[3] Matthew C. Klein and Michael Pettis, 2020, p. 177. *Trade Wars are Class Wars.*

[4] For example, in the case of Jeff Bezos: "The stock market crash initially left Bezos" net worth deeply damaged, down to a meager $105 billion on "Black Thursday" March 12, the stock market's lowest point. Bezos' wealth has been trending upward ever since, with no company better positioned to profit from the pandemic than Amazon. The closure of hundreds of thousands of small businesses is giving Amazon the opportunity to increase its market share, strengthen its place in the supply chain, and gain more pricing power over consumers. Despite Amazon's e-commerce dominance, Bezos has been unable to protect his workforce from Covid 19: workers in ten different Amazon warehouses tested positive for the disease in late March. Instead, in early April, Bezos announced a donation of $100 million of his $140 billion in wealth to Feeding America (Collins et al., 2020: 11).

some, but the wealthy face a different world than the many. As the IPS report also states:

> "Billionaire wealth... tends to rebound from market meltdowns. In the immediate aftermath of the global economic crisis of 2008, the *Forbes* 400 saw their combined wealth decline $300 billion from $1.57 trillion in 2008 to $1.27 trillion in 2009. Within 30 months of the September 2008 crash, most of these fortunes recovered. By 2012, billionaire wealth had reached $1.7 trillion, exceeding pre-2008 levels. Between 2010 and 2020, the combined wealth of the U.S. billionaire class surged by a staggering 80.6 percent, from $1.631 trillion to $2.947 trillion in 2020 dollars" (Collins et al 2020: 10).

If we are to address "billionaire bonanzas" and reverse inequality and other morbid outcomes of the current system, then we must begin by transforming the international system which generates such inequality. Fundamental to such a transformation will be the removal of private authority over the globalised financial architecture and the restoration *of public* authority over financial regulation and economic policy (Pettifor, 2017a).[5]

---

[5] There are many other associated issues and policies, including a Green New Deal (see Pettifor, 2019).

Inequality and the Global South

The rise of extreme levels of inequality within domestic economies is mirrored in the inequality that exists between the world's richest and poorest economies. The injustice of the inequality of power – not just over the international economy, but over domestic economies – was starkly exposed by the Coronavirus crisis. A shortage of US dollars worldwide, led the Federal Reserve and the IMF to lend dollars to certain governments, but denied this largesse to others. The Fed's "swap lines" covered fourteen central banks, but excluded Turkey, South Africa, Nigeria and Indonesia, despite their need for dollar finance to pay for vital imports, including oil; and despite the challenges posed to their health systems by a global pandemic.

The failure of the international financial system to provide quantities of the world's reserve currency to low income countries at a critical period, does not bode well for those countries most exposed to forthcoming shocks, including climate breakdown (for issues and alternatives see Pettifor, 2019).

To add to the stresses imposed by coronavirus, emerging and frontier markets experienced the sharpest portfolio flow reversal on record, according to the International Monetary Fund's recent *Global Financial Stability report* (IMF, 2020). Low-income countries faced a "perfect storm" and "big reversals", for example, on portfolio flows, see figure below (IMF, 2020: 13):

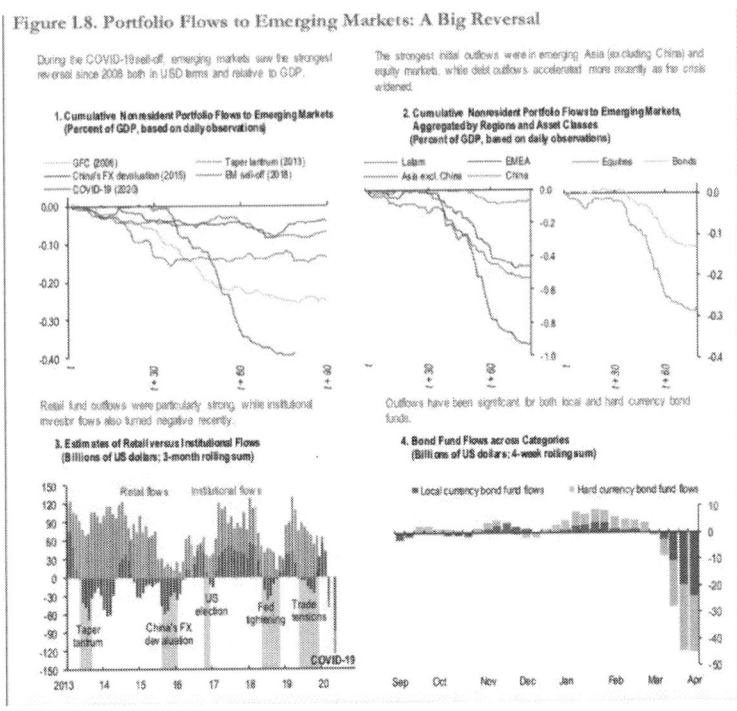

Figure 1.8. Portfolio Flows to Emerging Markets: A Big Reversal

During the COVID-19 sell-off, emerging markets saw the strongest reversal since 2008 both in USD terms and relative to GDP.

The strongest initial outflows were in emerging Asia (excluding China) and equity markets, while debt outflows accelerated more recently as the crisis widened.

One hundred billion dollars of capital stampeded out of emerging markets over the last few weeks of March and early April, 2020. These outflows, sparked by fickle and volatile investors and creditors, crushed the currencies of low-income countries, while simultaneously inflating the dollar's value. Because the US dollar alone is recognised by international markets for the payment of vital imports, including oil, the cost of dollar-denominated imports rose. This in turn led to trade and capital account imbalances, which then prompted the ghouls of the global economy – western-based rating agencies – to downgrade countries that were victims of capital flight. Downgrades in turn raised borrowing costs and tightened credit availability at a time when global markets for poor country commodity exports were already weak, and prices falling, cutting their income. Simultaneously weakened currencies raised the cost of purchasing vital equipment and pharmaceuticals from abroad.

As they faced the challenges of a pandemic, impoverished countries were effectively sacrificed on the cross of the US dollar and the international order.

Capital flight on the whim of investors, coupled with the subsequent strengthening of the US dollar, are not accidental nor inevitable consequences of the pandemic. The virus, after all, portends greater economic failure in the United States than in many emerging markets. Nor can it be explained directly by sudden changes in the economic circumstances of the countries trampled down by investors' rush for the exit. Instead, it is a consequence of the international system's *design* – an architecture purposed to accommodate the whims, no matter how irrational, of investors, and to protect the interests of creditors.

What has to be done?

Taking action to transform the current highly unbalanced system requires, in the first place, a fuller understanding of how and why the international financial architecture was constructed.

Ken-Hou Lin and Donald Tomaskovic-Devey argue in their important paper "Financialization and U.S. Income Inequality, 1970–2008" (Lin and Tomaskovic-Devey,

2013) that the rise in inequality is undoubtedly the consequence of the deliberate financialisation of the global economy in the late 1960s and early 1970s.

Financialisation has permitted the almost effortless making of extraordinary capital gains by those that derive income from the possession of financial assets that generate interest, or from scarce assets or assets made artificially scarce (like patents and intellectual property). Rental income from land, property, minerals or financial investments, are the best-known forms of rentier capitalism. And as Guy Standing has argued:

> "[T]hey include the income lenders gain from... capital gains on investments; 'above normal' company profits (when a firm has a dominant position); income from subsidies; and income of financial intermediaries derived from third-party transactions" (Standing, 2017).

Tackling rentierism and its consequences by restoring public authority over the system at the level of the domestic economy, is the internationally coordinated policy action required.

Conclusion

As I explained in a 2012 article for *Real-World Economics Review*, on the causes and consequences of President Donald Trump, the collapse of the Bretton Woods system in 1971 represents a decisive episode in the process of financial globalisation, and with it the corresponding weakening of regulatory democracy. The OECD recognises that:

> "[T]he easing of capital controls, and the international branching of business firms or establishment of their finance companies, made domestic regulations easier to circumvent by conducting financial transactions outside national boundaries" (Pettifor, 2017b).

Up until the early 1970s, financial systems in most western economies were governed by the regulation of market forces, enacted within the policy-making boundaries of democratic nation states. These constraints included: interest rate controls; securities market regulations; quantitative investment restrictions on financial institutions; line-of-business regulations and regulations on ownership linkages among financial institutions; restrictions on entry of foreign financial institutions; and controls on international capital movements and foreign exchange transactions. The reason for constraint is based on common sense. The nature of money-creation as a largely effortless *social* construct or technology, requires social, or society-wide regulation of the public good that is the monetary system in order to prevent the capture of this public good by a small elite. As John Maynard Keynes understood better than many of his peers:

> "Interest today rewards no genuine sacrifice, any more than does the rent of land. The owner of capital can obtain interest because

capital is scarce, just as the owner of land can obtain rent because land is scarce. But whilst there may be intrinsic reasons for the scarcity of land, there are no intrinsic reasons for the scarcity of capital..." (Keynes, 1936).

From the perspective of Keynes, the consequences of markets governed effectively by rentiers were entirely predictable: rising and even obscene levels of inequality, political instability and recurring financial crises. Such inequality and financial instability is particularly problematic as societies struggle to meet threats posed by present and future climate and health shocks.

We need a different international financial system, one governed by public authority, if inequality and its harms are to be addressed. To paraphrase Karl Marx: political economists have only interpreted the world, in various ways. The point, however, is to *change* the current global financial architecture. An understanding of the systemic and international causes of inequality enables us to claim this moment of crisis as a revolution. To do so, is to claim it for human action, as Rebecca Spang argues.

References

Case, A. and Deaton, A. (2020) *Deaths of Despair and the Future of Capitalism*. Princeton: Princeton University Press.

Collins, C. Ocampo, O. and Paslaski, S. (2020) *Billionaire Bonanza 2020: Wealth, Windfalls, Tumbling Taxes, and Pandemic Profiteers*. Washington DC: Institute for Policy Studies.

IMF (2020) *Global Financial Stability Report*. Washington DC: IMF

Keynes, J.M. (1936) *The General Theory of Employment, Interest and Money.* London: Macmillan

Lin, K.H. and Tomaskovic-Devey, D. (2013) "Financialization and U.S. Income Inequality, 1970–2008." *American Journal of Sociology* 118(5): 1284-1329.

Marx, K. (1842) "On the theft of woods." Article series in *Reinische Zeitung*, available:
https://www.marxists.org/archive/marx/works/download/Marx_Rheinishe_Zeitung.pdf

Pettifor, A. (2006) *The Coming First World Debt Crisis.* Basingstoke: Palgrave Macmillan.

Pettifor, A. (2017a) *The Production of Money: How to break the power of bankers.* London: Verso.

Pettifor, A. (2017b) "The Causes and Consequences of Donald Trump." *Real-World Economics Review* 78: 44-53.

Pettifor, A. (2019) *The Case for the Green New Deal.* London: Verso.

Spang, R. (2020) "The revolution is underway already." *The Atlantic*, April 5th.

Standing, G. (2017) *The Corruption of Capitalism: Why Rentiers Thrive and Work Does Not Pay.* London: Biteback Publishing.

Chapter 18

Why COVID-19 is the great unequalizer: the pandemic's impact is being experienced disproportionately by minorities and the poor

Marshall Auerback

In the daily TV press conferences that New York Governor Andrew Cuomo conducted throughout the spring, he referred to COVID-19 as "the great equalizer." In the sense that anybody can be infected by the virus, the governor is right. Yet after several months, the data shows clearly the impact is unequally landing on the shoulders of people of color and all but the wealthiest. The health impacts and absence of economic measures to protect them are so extreme that Cuomo's statements are more than hollow – they are cruel cover-ups.

If anything, COVID-19 has been little more than a novelty for the 1 percent and a dystopian nightmare for the rest of us. The U.S. now has the highest number of cases in the world. Nearly 2.1 million people have been infected by the disease and more than 115,000 people have died, according to data from Johns Hopkins University. Had we experienced a repeat economic crash more along the lines of what happened in 2008, that might have forced a true reckoning and consequent reform in our system. Instead, we have a pandemic that is facilitating public looting under the cover of a collective surgical mask as it is entrenching pre-existing inequities. A toxic mix of racial, financial, and geographic disadvantage is literally proving to be a death sentence.

In the first instance, workers of color, particularly black Americans, who have long been overrepresented in the lowest-paying service and domestic occupations, are again being hit with a double whammy. Their jobs and income have evaporated with the shutdown, and they have long had minimal household savings relative to Caucasians to act as a buffer against unexpected layoffs or lost wages.

As *Time* reporter Abby Vesoulis writes, many low-income jobs – meat processing, agricultural work, nannies, and store clerks – "can't be done remotely" (to say nothing of the digital divide that also divides on income grounds), "and the majority of low-income jobs don't offer paid sick days." People with these jobs are also "disproportionately more likely to be uninsured or underinsured for medical care," even though the government has agreed to cover COVID-19 related health coverage.

That brings to the fore another significant "unequalizer". Low-income communities and workers of color are experiencing substantially higher rates of mortality.

Consider a few regional examples, cited in MedPage Today:

> "In Louisiana, African Americans accounted for 70% of COVID-19 deaths, while comprising 33% of the population. In Michigan, they accounted for 14% of the population and 40% of deaths, and in Chicago, 56% of deaths and 30% of the population. In New York, black people are twice as likely as white people to die from the coronavirus."

Likewise, CDC researchers have also found that "80% of Georgia residents hospitalized with COVID-19 are black," Blavity reports. In the Native American communities, "the added burdens of chronic disease and persistent underfunding of American Indian health systems have put the nation's indigenous population at higher risk of poor outcomes from the disease", according to the American Medical Association (AMA). "Latinos make up 60% of the population in the 10 Illinois ZIP codes with the fastest growing number of new COVID-19 cases," according to the Chicago *Sun-Times*.

No one should have to choose between going broke and becoming infected with and spreading a fatal virus. But that is a literal life consequence for working people in a system that goes on lockdown to flatten the curve. That binary choice in itself is a product of decades of fiscal austerity in which social safety nets and health care systems were gradually eviscerated in the interests of privatizing everything in sight.

The privatized mode that we have largely embraced in the United States is clearly a bad one, but it is showing no signs of stopping, even during a pandemic. Still today, an alliance of private hospitals, health insurance companies, and large pharmaceutical companies have formed a campaign group – the Partnership for America's Health Care Future Action (PAHCF) – to counter growing political support for single-payer health insurance. Even as one state government after another has declared a public state of emergency (and corresponding lockdowns), the PAHCF has persisted in its principal lobbying activity, all the while also wrangling massive bailouts from the government to cope with the ill effects of the very market-driven system they have spent decades championing but which has failed to defend us during this pandemic.

We classify our health care workers as "essential," but they are poorly paid and treated as disposable. Our health care system features a chronic shortage of N95 surgical masks, or nurses wearing garbage bags, given a lack of sufficient protective gear, let alone the average worker, who is tasked with sustaining what's left of our functioning economy in food processing plants or grocery delivery services. Essentially, these workers have been faced with the choice of literally risking their lives to sustain their incomes and livelihoods or joining the ranks of the unemployed. This has become a more acute problem as the first wave of the coronavirus is now passing through communities that were not as badly exposed in the early spring, leading businesses in many states, such as Arizona and Oregon, to close again, citing increased COVID-19 exposures and the consequent inability to generate profits due to increased restrictions.

Common patterns of domestic working-class life compound the risk of spread: fewer square feet for family members to share at home, fewer options for public transport. It is much easier, by contrast, to sustain self-isolation comfortably in a spacious suburban home, let alone a palatial spread in the Hamptons or Malibu. The risks of transmission are further mitigated because the jobs of the affluent are often facilitated by sophisticated internet connectivity that precludes the need to engage in lengthy commutes on public transportation. Even though low-income Americans have made gains in tech adoption, the digital divide very much largely remains a function of income disparity.

Income disparity also has significant healthcare implications in relation to the elderly. It has become increasingly evident that COVID-19 has been particularly lethal for older adults with underlying health conditions that can spread more easily through congregated facilities such as nursing homes. In many instances the spread of the disease is a product of these nursing homes paying so poorly that many workers have to split their time between several facilities, thereby exacerbating the contagion's spread. This is part of decades-old, nationwide problem of a deliberate and corrupt lack of adequate public health inspection/enforcement to prevent the proliferation of appalling conditions in a large number of elderly care facilities, other than for the wealthy. Far from representing optimal conditions for our senior citizens, many of these facilities are more accurately described as privately run profit centers that operate as storage facilities for the elderly, irrespective of infirmity.

In the meantime, home confinement has not created any inhibition in terms of getting on board the government gravy train. Government support programs are often being directed via private banking networks, which invariably means preferential treatment to those with strong pre-existing banking relationships. That makes a mockery of the Small Business Administrations' proviso that the loans will be granted on a first-come, first-served basis.

The April unemployment figures showed the largest one-month blow to the American labor market on record. Even though there was some bounce-back recorded in May, in truth the reduction in May's unemployment rate, (which fell to 13.3 percent from 14.7 percent in April), was more apparent than real. The Bureau of Labor Statistics (BLS) reported that the payroll survey response "was about 15 percentage points lower than in months prior to the pandemic", and further acknowledged that the unprecedented government relief programs distorted the underlying employment classifications: "If the workers who were recorded as employed but absent from work due to 'other reasons' (over and above the number absent for other reasons in a typical May) had been classified as unemployed on temporary layoff, the overall unemployment rate would have been about 3 percentage points higher than reported (on a not seasonally adjusted basis)." That would suggest an underlying unemployment rate more than 16 percent, indicating ongoing deterioration in the job market, despite the stimulus programs undertaken so far. Broader measures, such as the labor underutilization measure (U6) fell by 1.6 points to 21.2 per cent, in part, because of a fall in the number in the part-time works and labor participation rates.

All of which suggests that there are significant structural headwinds going forward. Business travel is not coming back any time soon. People are getting accustomed to telecommuting via Zoom and Skype. That is a fundamental blow to airlines, airport vendors, hotels, restaurants, and convention centers, all of which have the additional challenge of covering costs while capacity is limited on public health grounds. As the economist James Galbraith has argued, "Faced with radical uncertainty, US consumers *will* save more and spend less. Even if the government replaces their lost incomes for a time, people know that stimulus is short term. What they do not know is when the next job offer – or layoff – will come along." Federal Reserve Chairman Jerome Powell has also warned of "significant uncertainty" from the pandemic as well as acknowledging that the pandemic downturn could widen prevailing inequalities.

Nationalizing payroll, as the Norwegians and Danes have largely done, would have been a far more efficient way of ensuring direct relief from those most adversely affected by the economic shutdown, as well as mitigating the adverse long-term economic impacts. Our government already has pre-existing tax and employment data and distribution networks in place to avoid the cumbersome application processes that characterize business support programs (all of which seem to run out of money within weeks of implementation) or avoiding the problems of those who have tried to file for unemployment insurance, but haven't been able to thanks to crashing websites and overwhelmed phone lines. And it would deliver much more bang for the economic buck: Economist Pavlina Tcherneva estimates that "If the government paid 100% of total labor compensation for 3 months, it would be spending $2.85 trillion."

That certainly would have provided far more comprehensive and equitable relief than the trillions of dollars already extended by the Treasury and Federal Reserve programs, which instead have ensured that the rich are getting richer: "[T]he American billionaire class's total wealth [has] increased about 10% – or $282 billion more than it was at the beginning of March," writes Kristin Toussaint for Fast Company. By contrast, in addition to the rising unemployment levels, "one in three [American workers have] lost half or more of their income due to COVID-19," according to RIWI Corporation, a Canadian-based data aggregator. Even more concerning is that Chinese citizens, now ahead of the rest of the world on the reopening front, report more significant income losses – up to 45% – a possible harbinger of what lies in store for the rest of us as and when western economies begin to reopen.

Nor are the elites going to let the pandemic interfere with their leisure when current government restrictions are alleviated. According to the *Times* of London, "the super-rich are snapping up the citizenship of countries in different parts of the world to ensure they will always have a virus-free, sunny haven to escape to on holiday or if there is another lockdown." Caribbean communities, long reliant on mass tourism, will now likely offer additional incentives, as The Bahamas and Grand Cayman already do, to ensure that they become tax friendly domiciles in order to offset the resultant losses they are now experiencing. Passports and citizenship offer a new way to do this.

Speaking of passports, "immunity passports" are likely to become another major dividing line going forward. While coronavirus infections were initially viewed as something akin to a scarlet letter, if these infections ultimately confer a form of immunity from recurrence or spread of the virus, they may well become badges of honor. Governments might seek to legislate against preferential hiring preferences because of race, age, or gender, but it is harder to make that case where pandemic prevention becomes paramount. Immunity could well alleviate the challenges where physical and social distancing is virtually impossible (whether that be factory work, farms, hospitals, etc.). But "immunity passports", if implemented widely, would likely be rife with corruption. Imagine a black market developing in fake "immunity passports" or plasma.

These issues all relate to the short and medium term. However, there are also long-term impacts. Economists use the term "hysteresis" for when an event in the economy persists well into the future, even after the original factors that led to that event are ultimately removed. Even under a best-case scenario – for instance, assuming the adoption of a successful regimen of testing and contact tracing (as in South Korea), or a vaccine (there is hope that one of those being developed may establish scientifically peer-reviewed efficacy by June) – the damage sustained by the economic lockdown will still persist well into the future. Many small businesses will never reopen. Those that do survive will be loath to invest and expand, given the possibility of recurrent waves and additional lockdowns in response. Not only will work or health care remain prone to massive inequality in terms of access and quality, but in another cruel twist of fate wrought by this pandemic, tourism and leisure activities too may well be viewed increasingly as luxuries restricted to the rich and well-to-do.

COVID-19's impact may have been underestimated when it first emerged from China. Likewise, the long-term disproportionality of its effects on the poor remains similarly underappreciated and therefore will likely be insufficiently addressed for the foreseeable future. Calling this coronavirus a great equalizer is an obscenity. What is even worse is that we appear to be letting another crisis go to waste in terms of effecting fundamental change that would help the many, as opposed to perpetuating the position of our privileged elites.

Made in the USA
Middletown, DE
28 October 2020